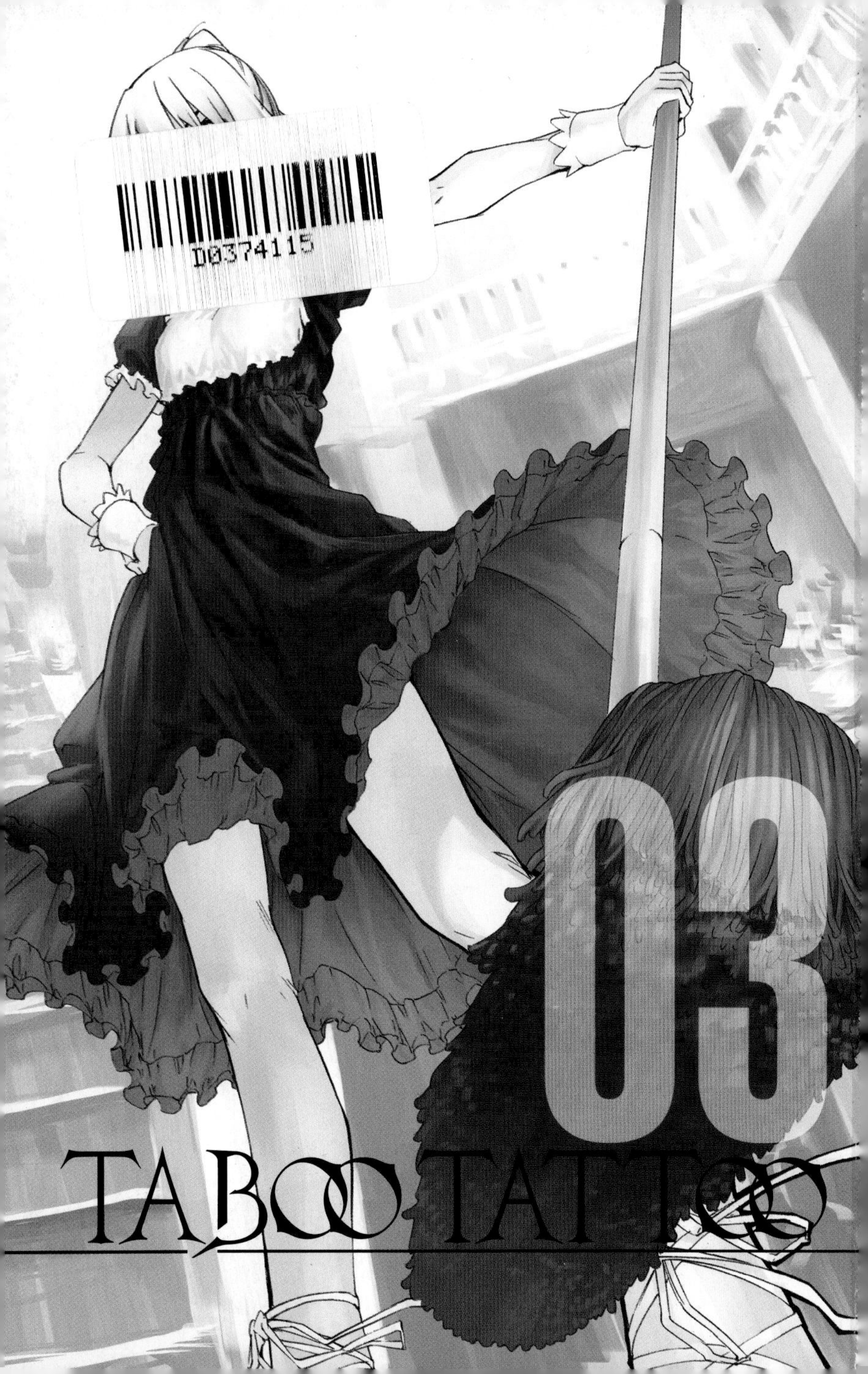
03
TABOO TATTOO

TABOO TATTOO 03

CONTENTS

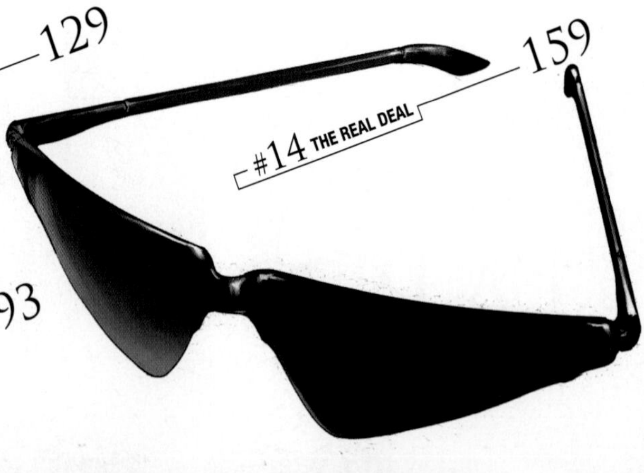

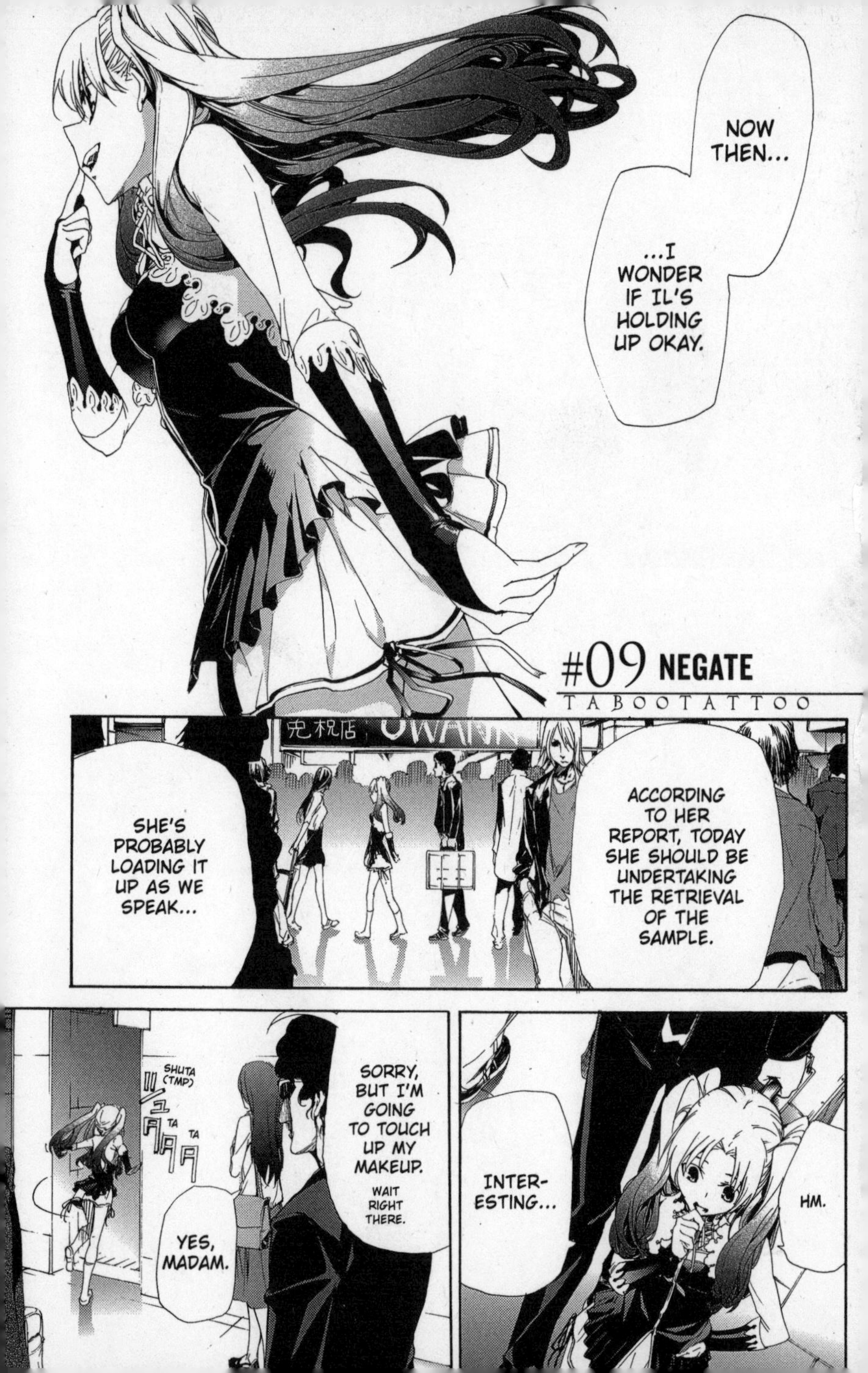
NOW THEN...
...I WONDER IF IL'S HOLDING UP OKAY.
#09 NEGATE
TABOOTATTOO
ACCORDING TO HER REPORT, TODAY SHE SHOULD BE UNDERTAKING THE RETRIEVAL OF THE SAMPLE.
SHE'S PROBABLY LOADING IT UP AS WE SPEAK...
HM.
INTER-ESTING...
SORRY, BUT I'M GOING TO TOUCH UP MY MAKEUP.
WAIT RIGHT THERE.
YES, MADAM.
SHUTA (TMP)
TA
TA

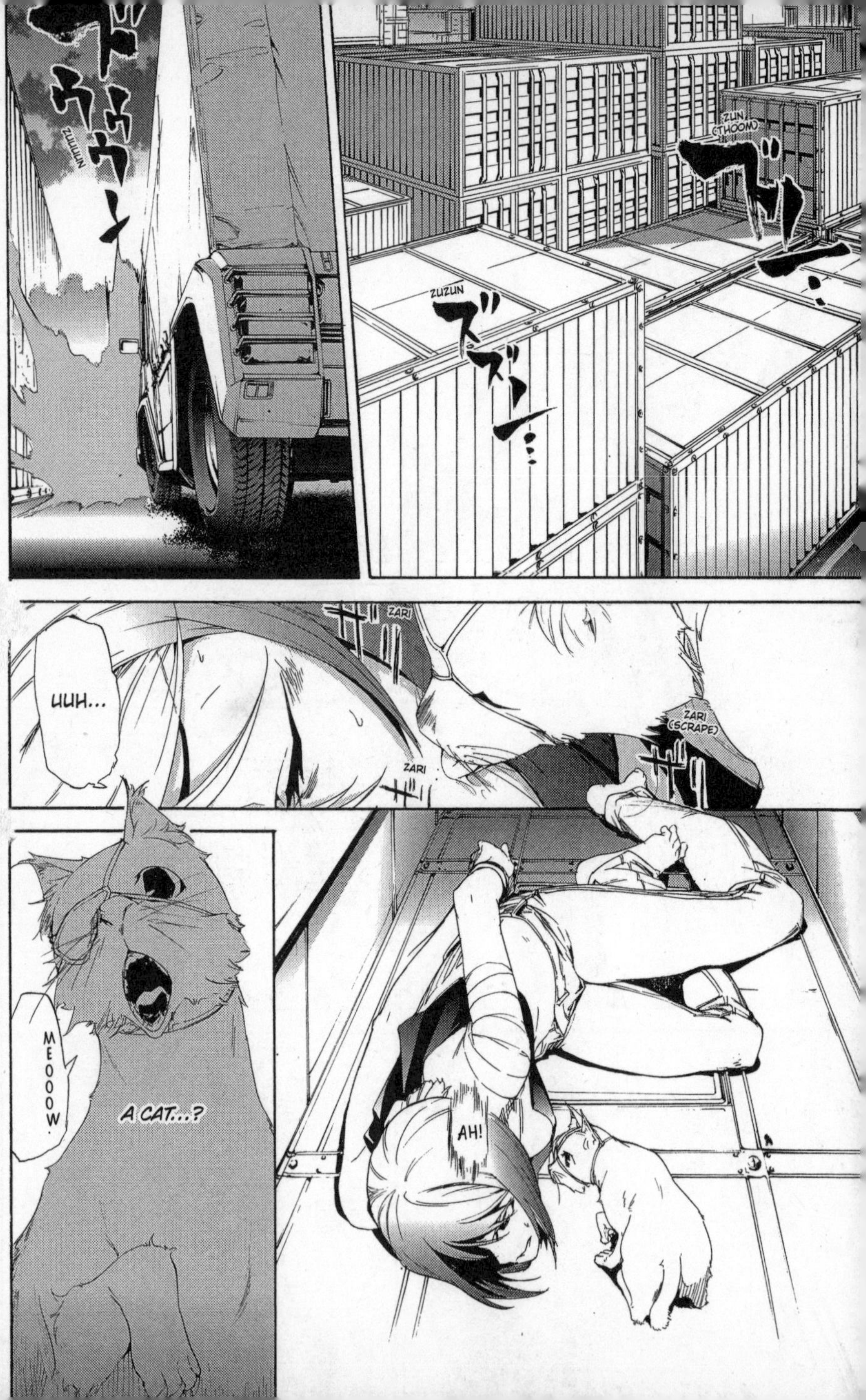

ZUN (THOOM)
ZUZUN
ZUUUN
ZARI
ZARI (SCRAPE)
ZARI
UUH...
AH!
MEOOOOW.
A CAT...?

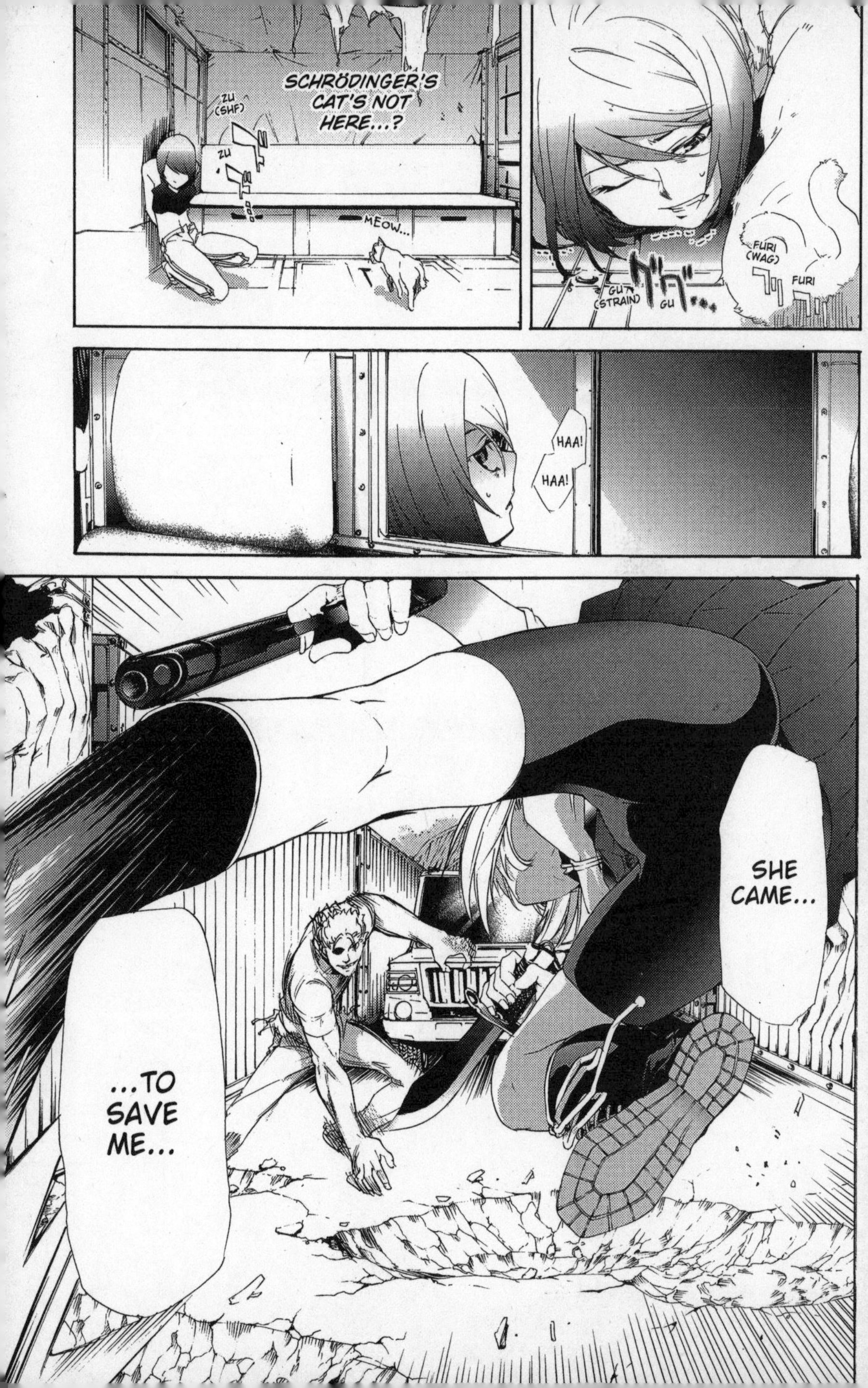
FURI (WAG)
FURI
GU (STRAIN)
GU
SCHRÖDINGER'S CAT'S NOT HERE...?
ZU (SHF)
ZU
MEOW...
HAA!
HAA!
SHE CAME...
...TO SAVE ME...

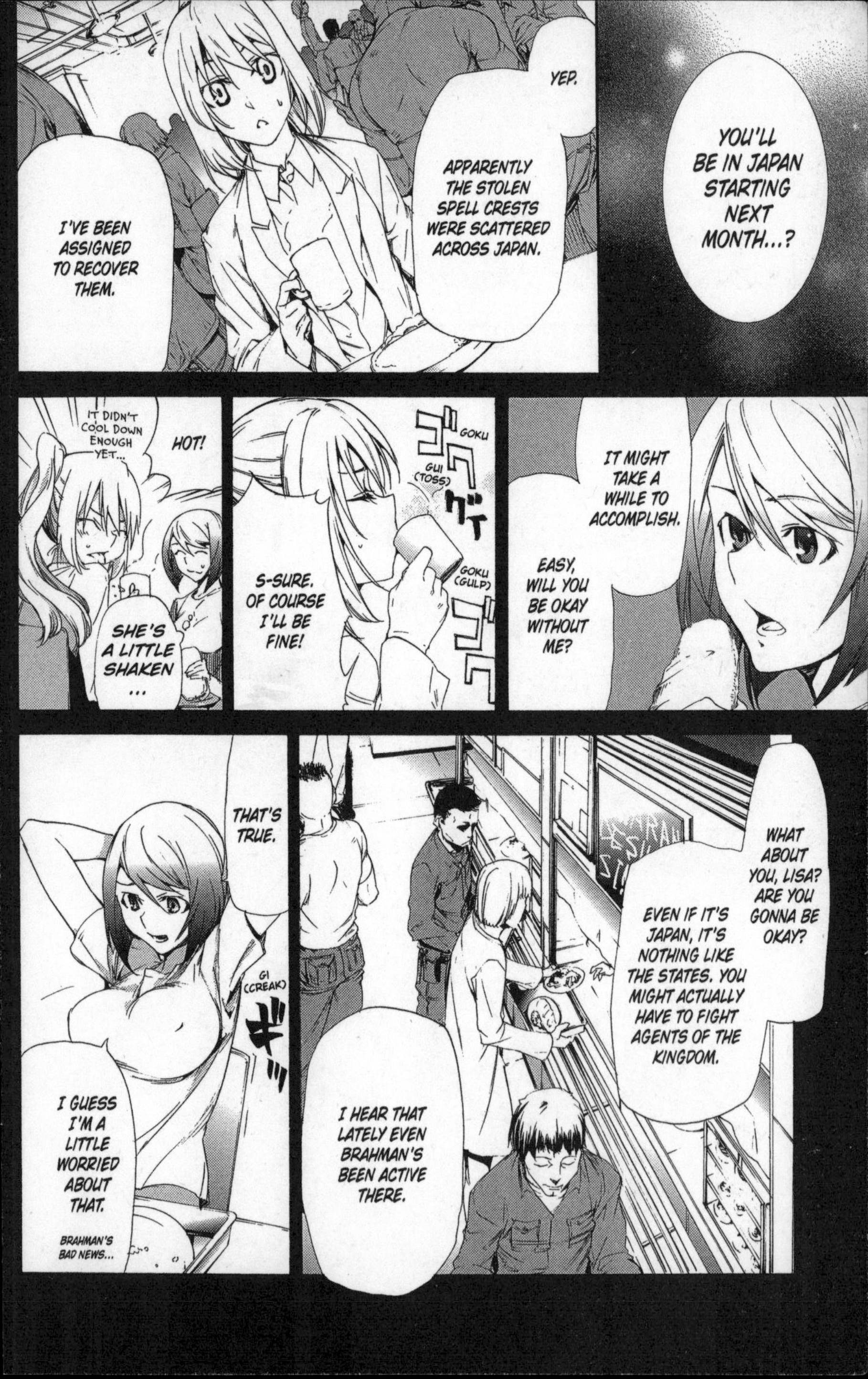
YOU'LL BE IN JAPAN STARTING NEXT MONTH...?
YEP.
APPARENTLY THE STOLEN SPELL CRESTS WERE SCATTERED ACROSS JAPAN.
I'VE BEEN ASSIGNED TO RECOVER THEM.
IT MIGHT TAKE A WHILE TO ACCOMPLISH.
EASY, WILL YOU BE OKAY WITHOUT ME?
ゴク
GOKU
グイ
GUI (TOSS)
S-SURE. OF COURSE I'LL BE FINE!
ゴク
GOKU (GULP)
HOT!
IT DIDN'T COOL DOWN ENOUGH YET...
SHE'S A LITTLE SHAKEN...
WHAT ABOUT YOU, LISA? ARE YOU GONNA BE OKAY?
EVEN IF IT'S JAPAN, IT'S NOTHING LIKE THE STATES. YOU MIGHT ACTUALLY HAVE TO FIGHT AGENTS OF THE KINGDOM.
I HEAR THAT LATELY EVEN BRAHMAN'S BEEN ACTIVE THERE.
THAT'S TRUE.
ギッ
GI (CREAK)
I GUESS I'M A LITTLE WORRIED ABOUT THAT.
BRAHMAN'S BAD NEWS...

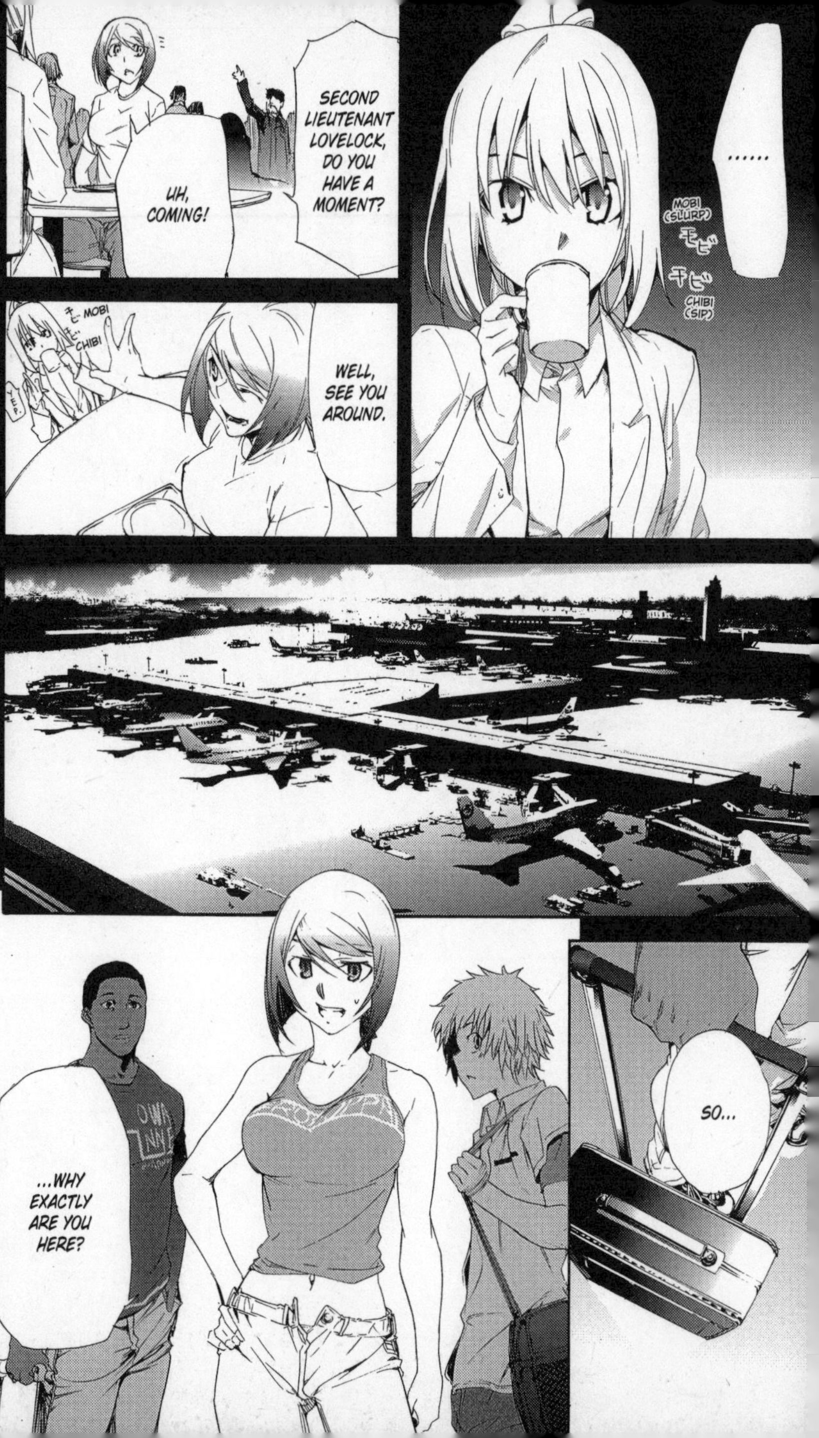
......
MOBI (SLURP)
モビ
チビ
CHIBI (SIP)
SECOND LIEUTENANT LOVELOCK, DO YOU HAVE A MOMENT?
UH, COMING!
モビ MOBI
チビ CHIBI
WELL, SEE YOU AROUND.
YEP.
SO...
...WHY EXACTLY ARE YOU HERE?

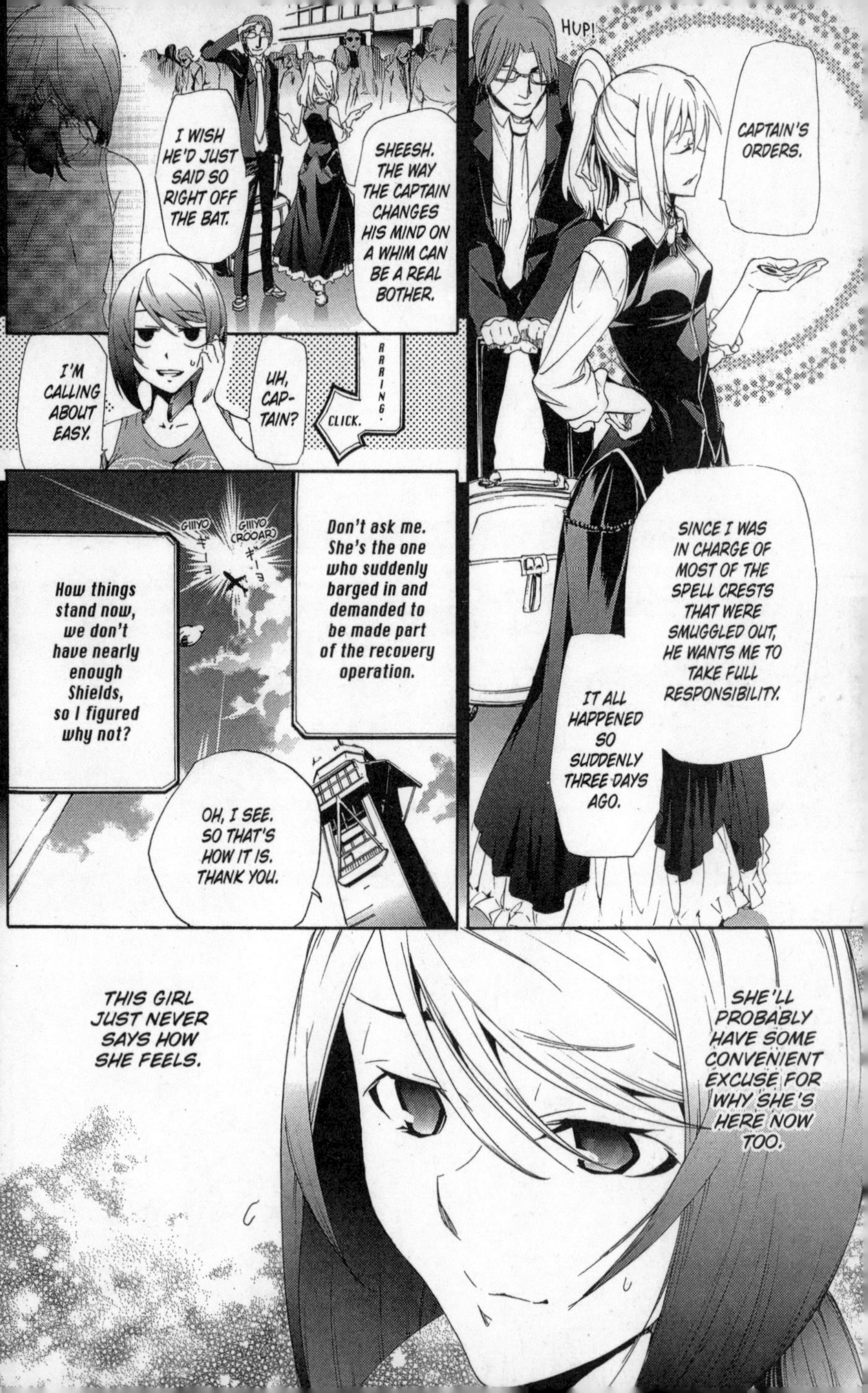
HUP!
CAPTAIN'S ORDERS.
SINCE I WAS IN CHARGE OF MOST OF THE SPELL CRESTS THAT WERE SMUGGLED OUT, HE WANTS ME TO TAKE FULL RESPONSIBILITY.
IT ALL HAPPENED SO SUDDENLY THREE DAYS AGO.
SHEESH. THE WAY THE CAPTAIN CHANGES HIS MIND ON A WHIM CAN BE A REAL BOTHER.
I WISH HE'D JUST SAID SO RIGHT OFF THE BAT.
RRRING.
CLICK.
UH, CAP-TAIN?
I'M CALLING ABOUT EASY.
Don't ask me. She's the one who suddenly barged in and demanded to be made part of the recovery operation.
GIIIYO (ROOAR)
GIIIYO
How things stand now, we don't have nearly enough Shields, so I figured why not?
OH, I SEE. SO THAT'S HOW IT IS. THANK YOU.
SHE'LL PROBABLY HAVE SOME CONVENIENT EXCUSE FOR WHY SHE'S HERE NOW TOO.
THIS GIRL JUST NEVER SAYS HOW SHE FEELS.

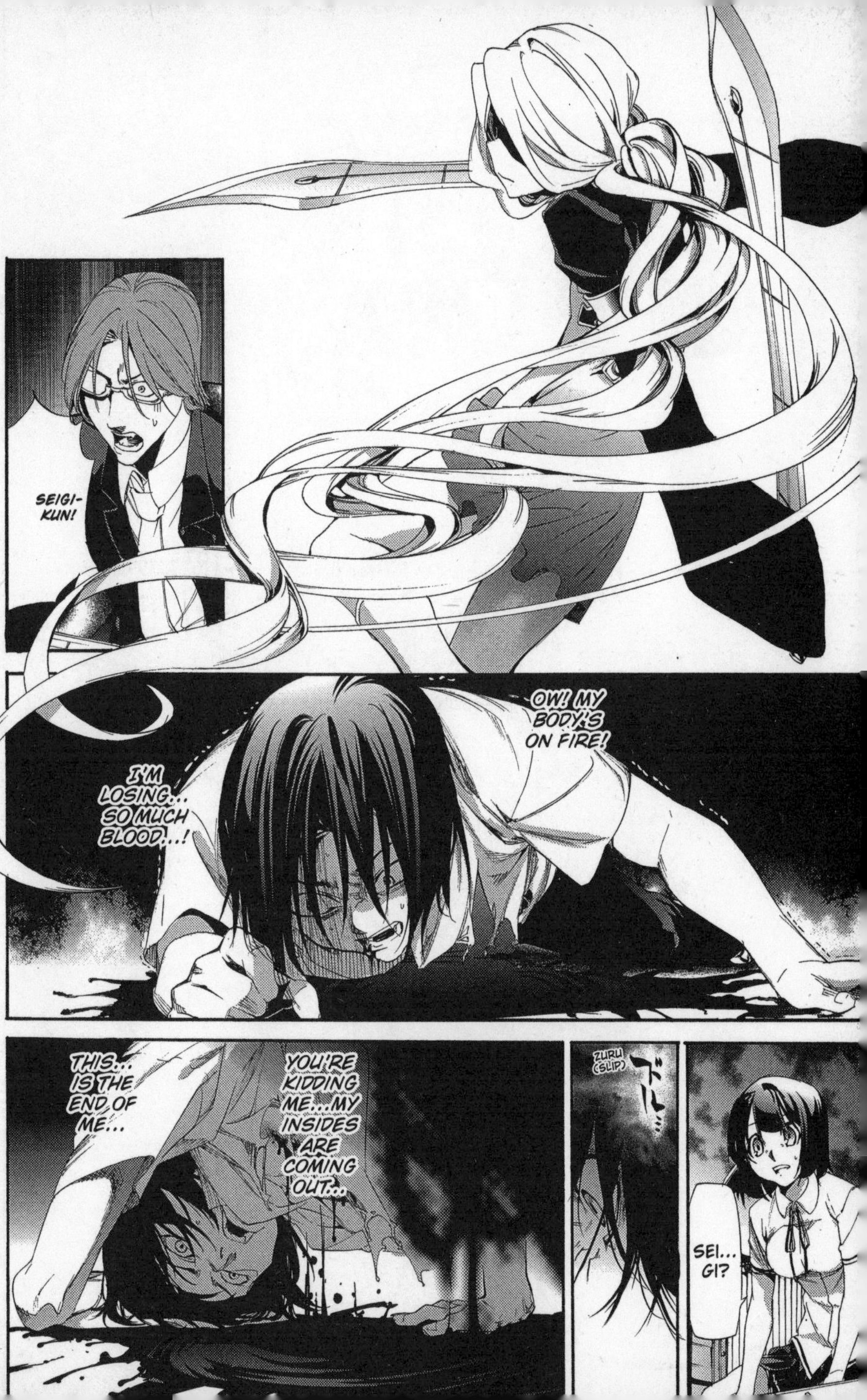
SEIGI-KUN!
OW! MY BODY'S ON FIRE!
I'M LOSING... SO MUCH BLOOD...!
SEI... GI?
ZURU (SLIP)
YOU'RE KIDDING ME... MY INSIDES ARE COMING OUT...
THIS... IS THE END OF ME...

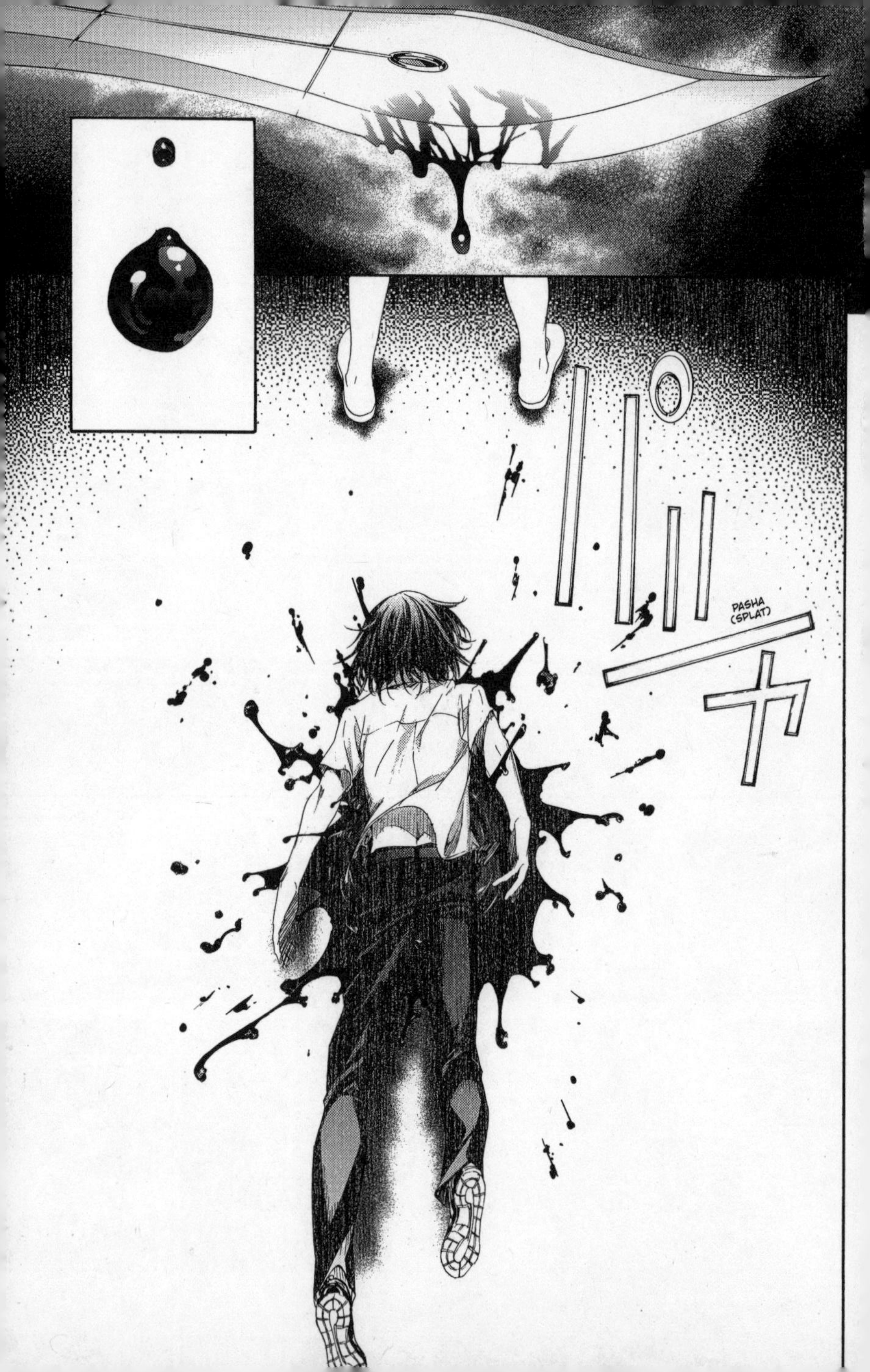
パシャ
PASHA
(SPLAT)

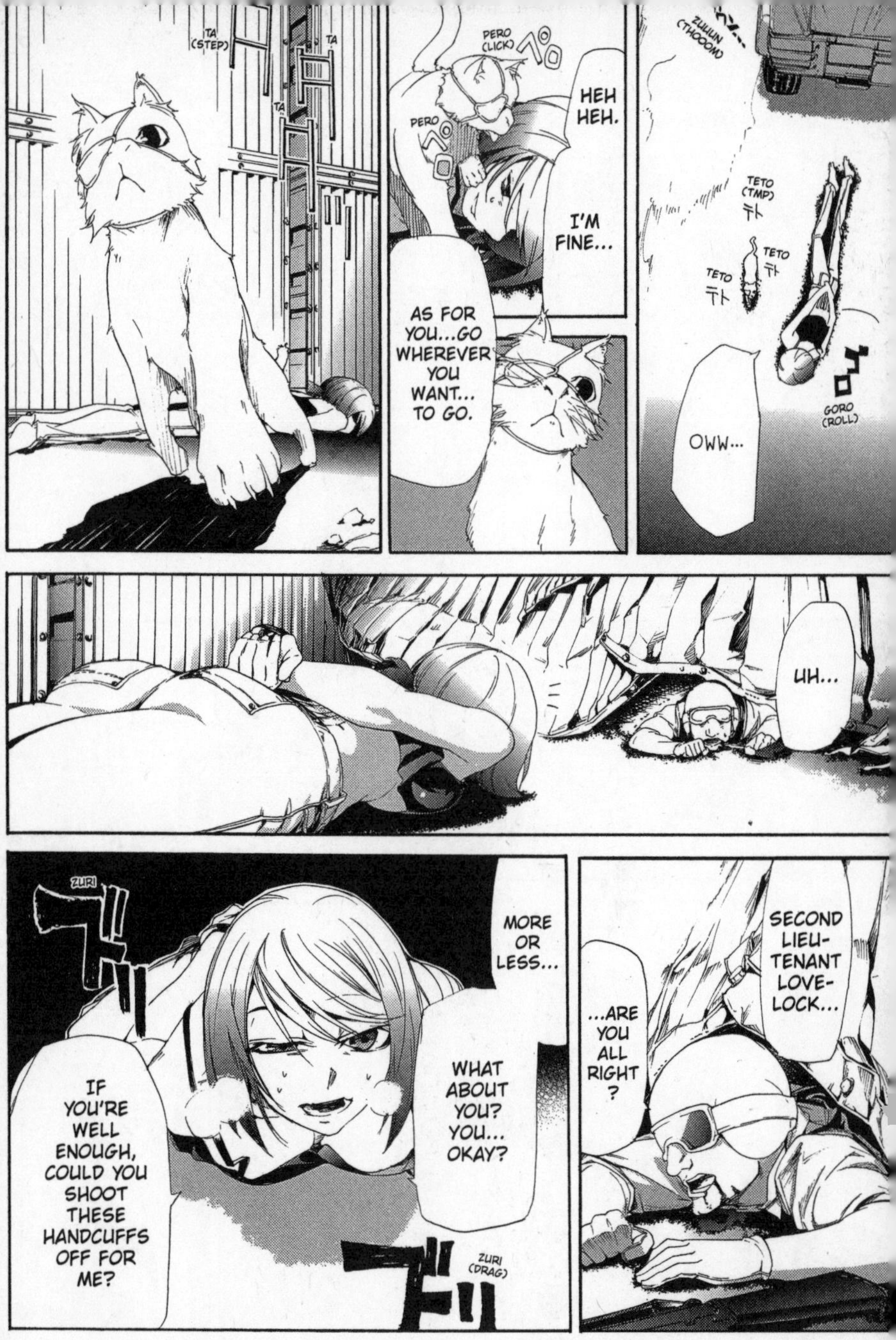
ZUUUN (THOOOM)
TETO (TMP)
TETO
TETO
GORO (ROLL)
OWW...
PERO (LICK)
PERO
HEH HEH.
I'M FINE...
AS FOR YOU...GO WHEREVER YOU WANT... TO GO.
TA (STEP)
TA
TA
UH...
SECOND LIEU-TENANT LOVE-LOCK...
...ARE YOU ALL RIGHT?
MORE OR LESS...
WHAT ABOUT YOU? YOU... OKAY?
ZURI
IF YOU'RE WELL ENOUGH, COULD YOU SHOOT THESE HANDCUFFS OFF FOR ME?
ZURI (DRAG)

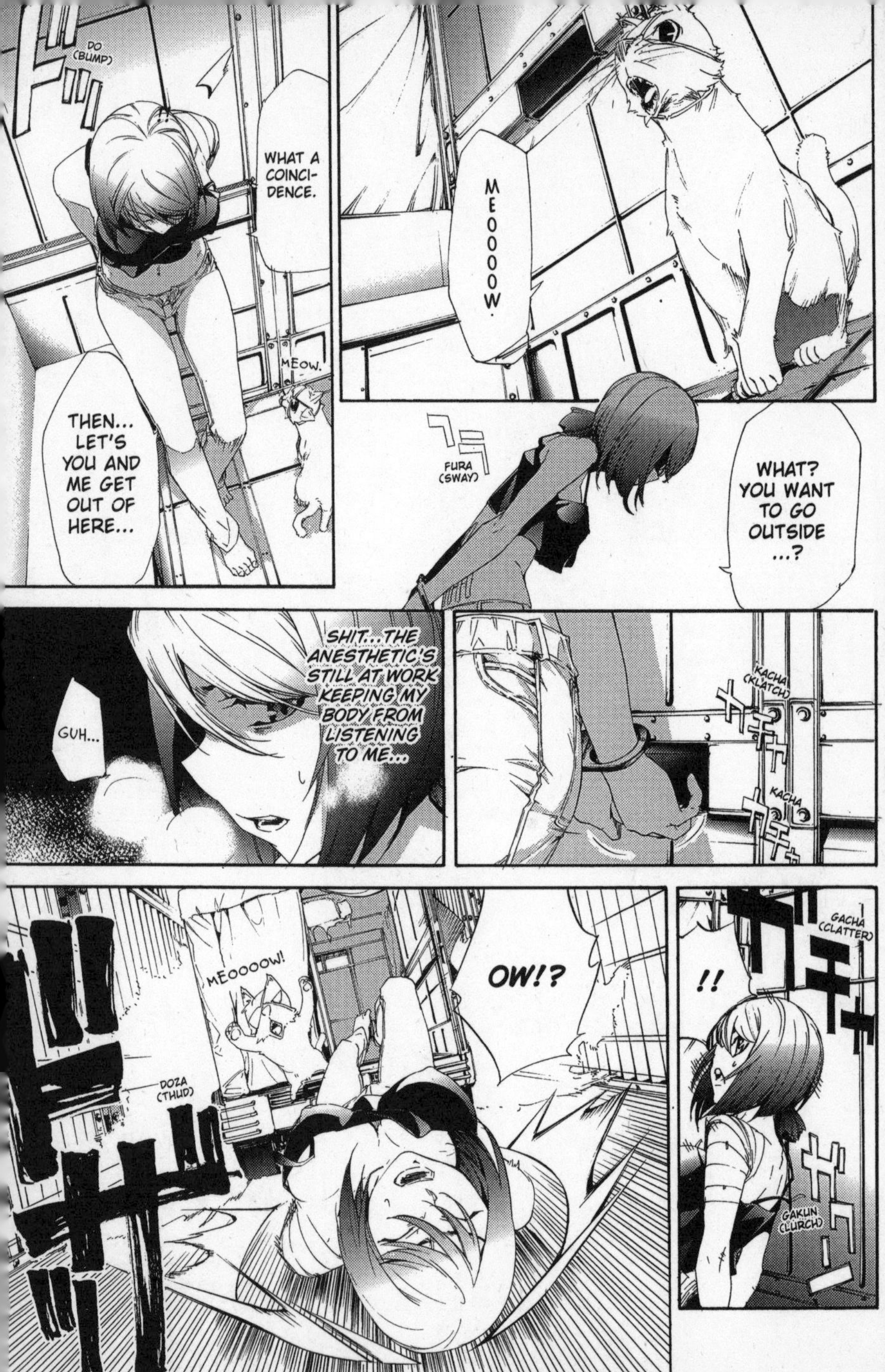
MEOOOOOW.
FURA (SWAY)
WHAT? YOU WANT TO GO OUTSIDE ...?
DO (BUMP)
WHAT A COINCIDENCE.
MEOW.
THEN... LET'S YOU AND ME GET OUT OF HERE...
KACHA (KLATCH)
KACHA
SHIT...THE ANESTHETIC'S STILL AT WORK KEEPING MY BODY FROM LISTENING TO ME...
GUH...
GACHA (CLATTER)
!!
GAKUN (LURCH)
OW!?
MEOOOOW!
DOZA (THUD)

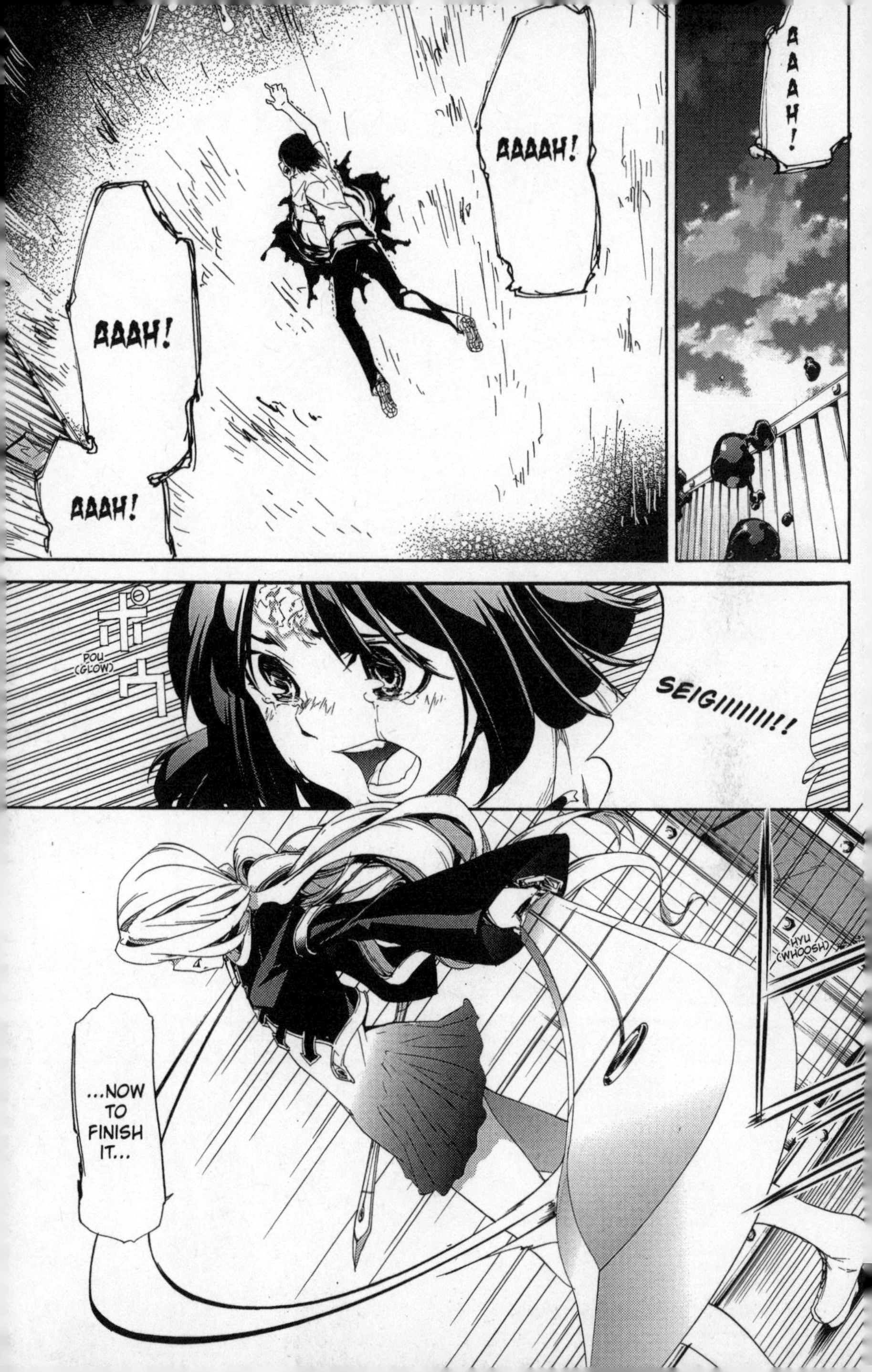
AAAH!
AAAAH!
AAAH!
AAAH!
SEIGIIIIII!!
ポウ
POU (GLOW)
HYU (WHOOSH)
...NOW TO FINISH IT...

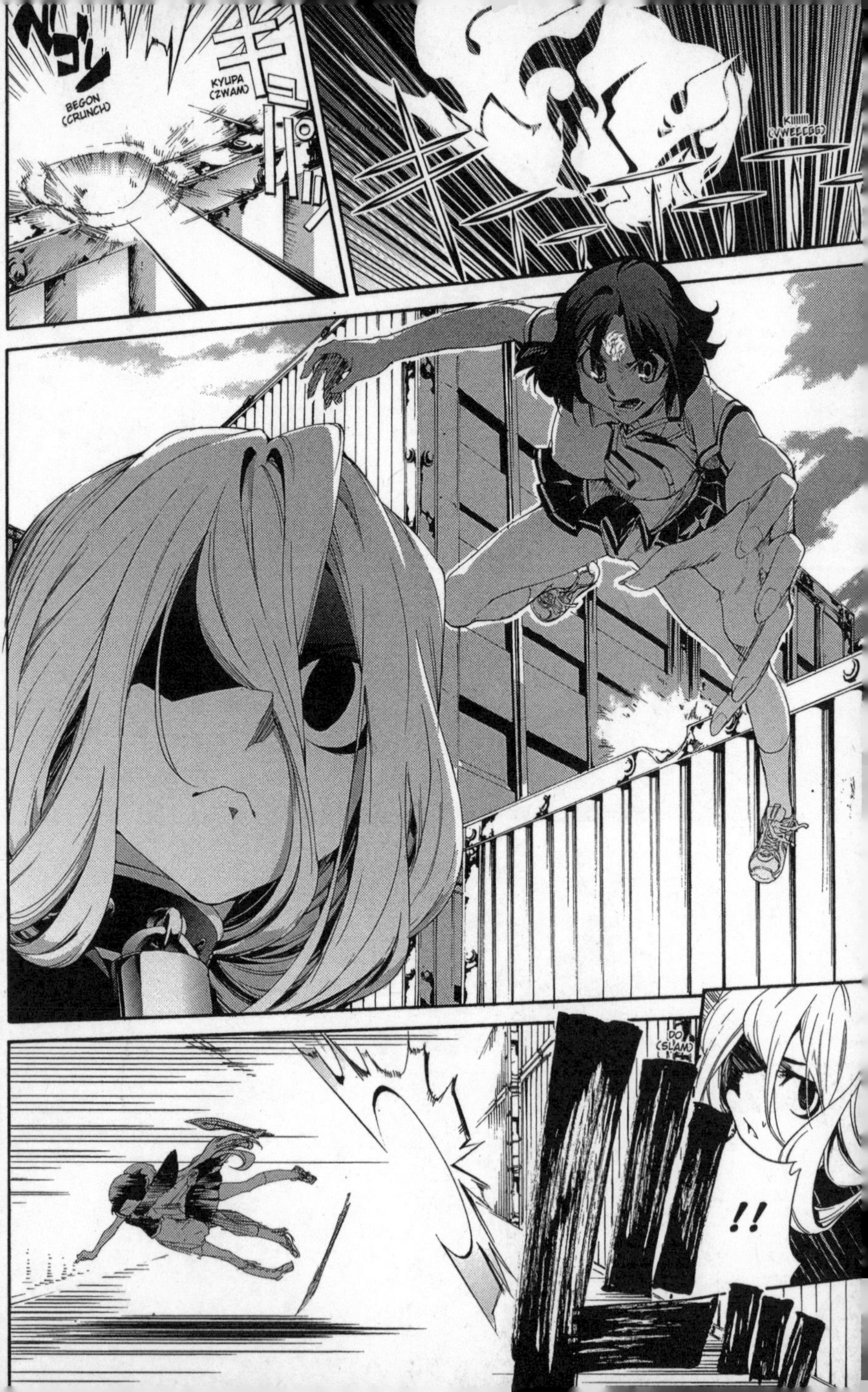
KIIIIII
(VWEEEEE)
KYUPA
(ZWAM)
BEGON
(CRUNCH)
DO
(SLAM)
!!

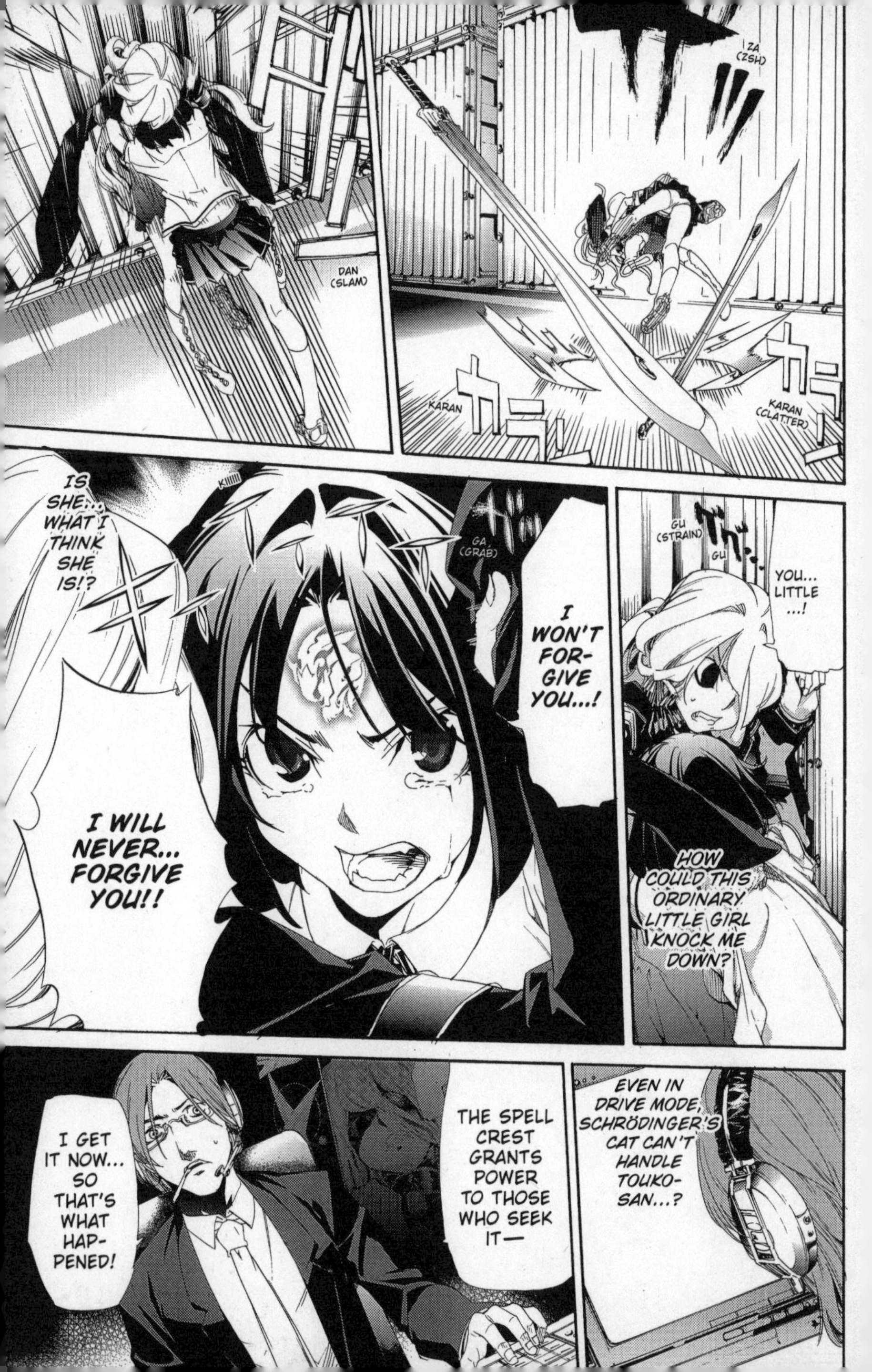
ZA (ZSH)
KARAN (CLATTER)
KARAN
DAN (SLAM)
GU (STRAIN)
GU
YOU... LITTLE ...!
HOW COULD THIS ORDINARY LITTLE GIRL KNOCK ME DOWN?
GA (GRAB)
I WON'T FORGIVE YOU...!
IS SHE... WHAT I THINK SHE IS!?
I WILL NEVER... FORGIVE YOU!!
EVEN IN DRIVE MODE, SCHRÖDINGER'S CAT CAN'T HANDLE TOUKO-SAN...?
THE SPELL CREST GRANTS POWER TO THOSE WHO SEEK IT—
I GET IT NOW... SO THAT'S WHAT HAPPENED!

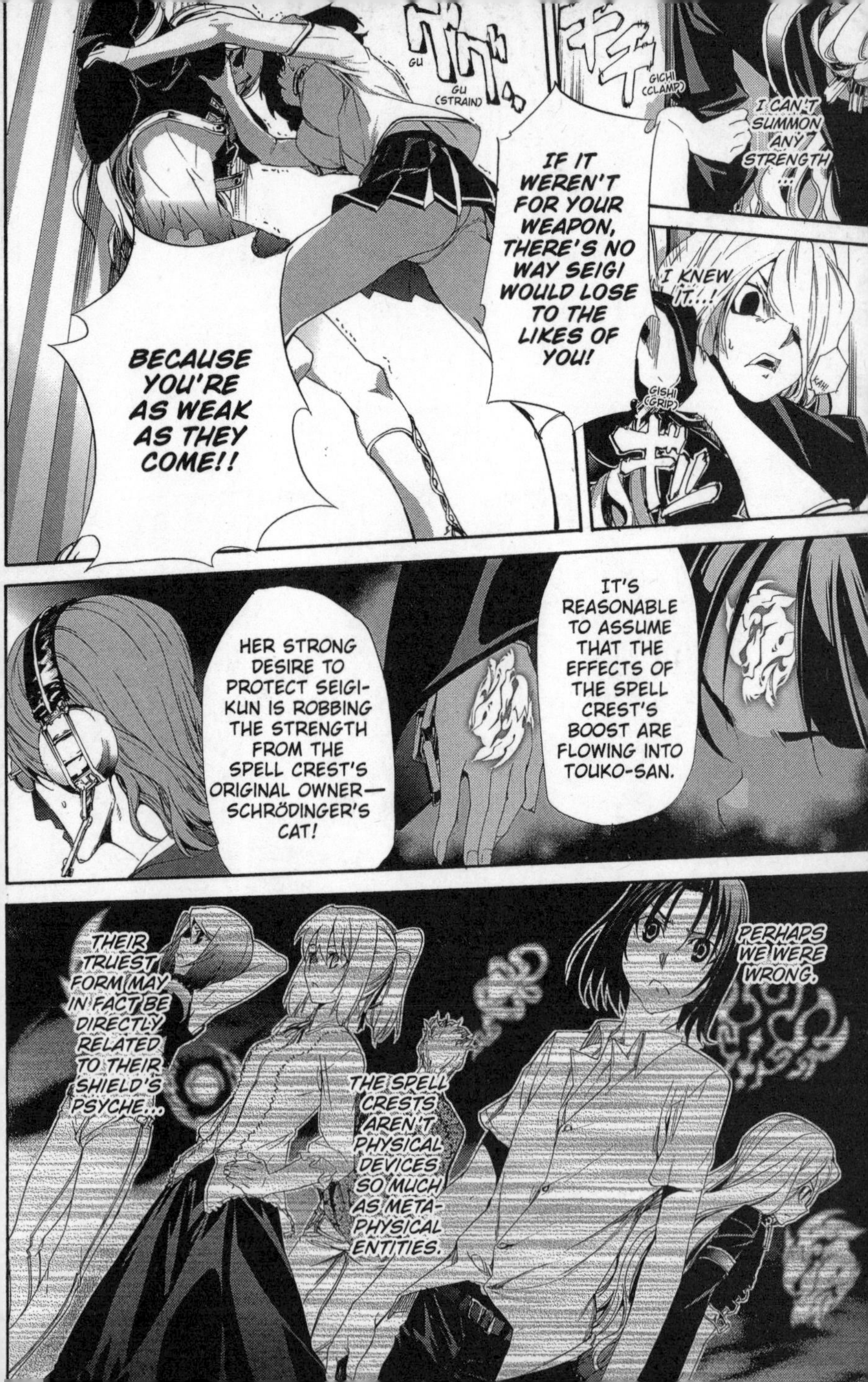
I CAN'T SUMMON ANY STRENGTH...
GICHI (CLAMP)
I KNEW IT...!
KAH!
GISHI (GRIP)
GU GU (STRAIN)
IF IT WEREN'T FOR YOUR WEAPON, THERE'S NO WAY SEIGI WOULD LOSE TO THE LIKES OF YOU!
BECAUSE YOU'RE AS WEAK AS THEY COME!!
IT'S REASONABLE TO ASSUME THAT THE EFFECTS OF THE SPELL CREST'S BOOST ARE FLOWING INTO TOUKO-SAN.
HER STRONG DESIRE TO PROTECT SEIGI-KUN IS ROBBING THE STRENGTH FROM THE SPELL CREST'S ORIGINAL OWNER—SCHRÖDINGER'S CAT!
PERHAPS WE WERE WRONG.
THE SPELL CRESTS AREN'T PHYSICAL DEVICES SO MUCH AS META-PHYSICAL ENTITIES.
THEIR TRUEST FORM MAY IN FACT BE DIRECTLY RELATED TO THEIR SHIELD'S PSYCHE...

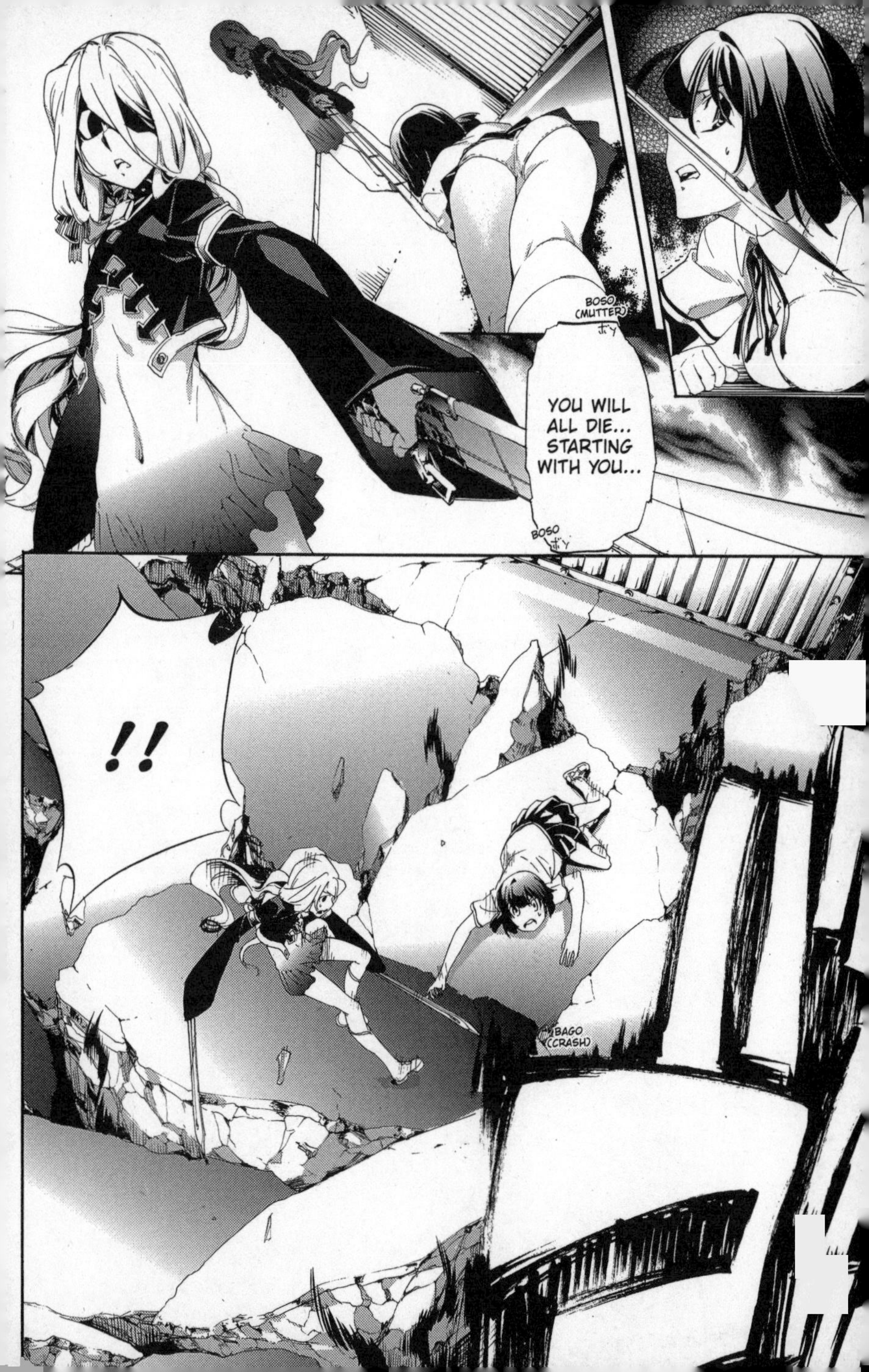
BOSO (MUTTER)
YOU WILL ALL DIE... STARTING WITH YOU...
BOSO
!!
BAGO (CRASH)

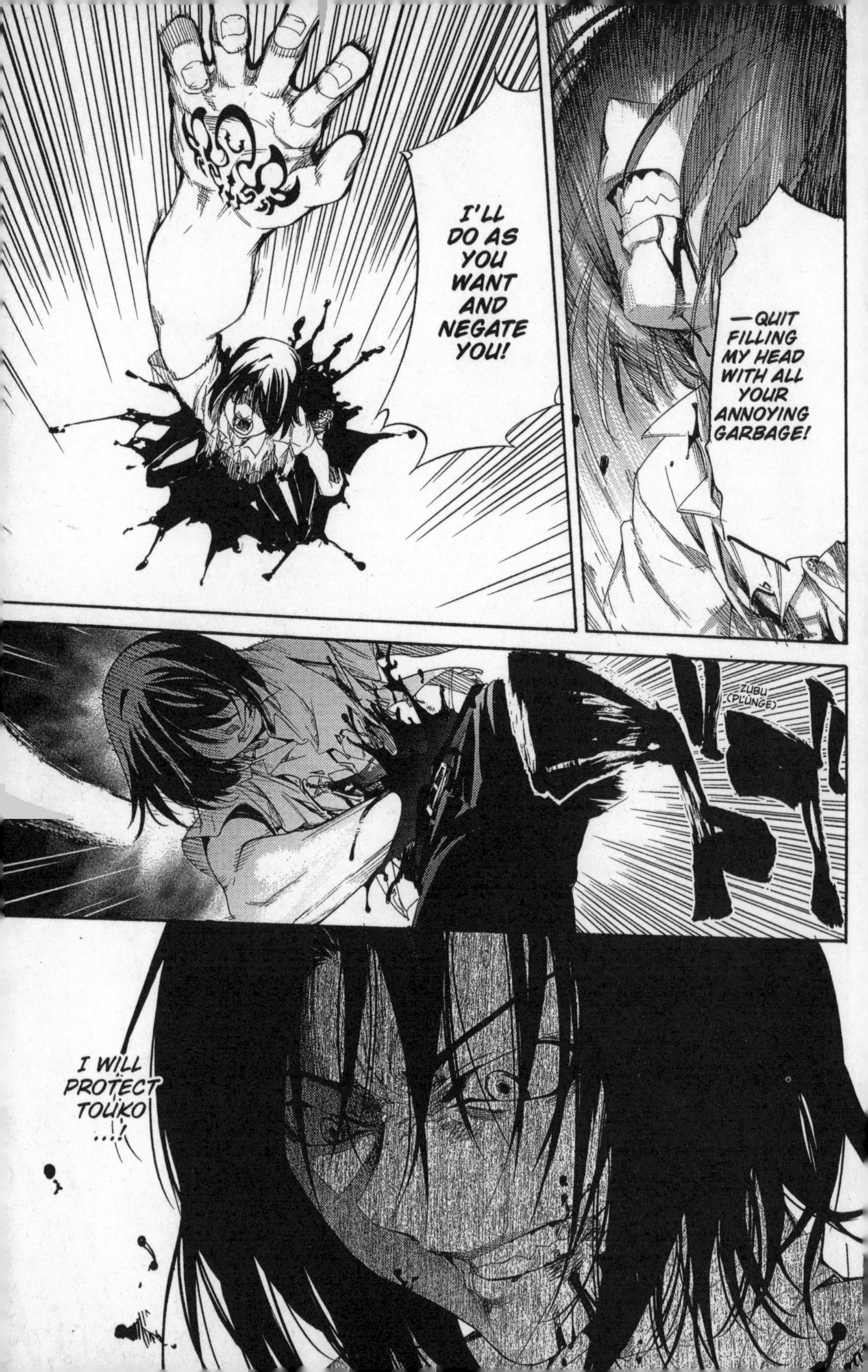
—QUIT FILLING MY HEAD WITH ALL YOUR ANNOYING GARBAGE!
I'LL DO AS YOU WANT AND NEGATE YOU!
ZUBU (PLUNGE)
I WILL PROTECT TOUKO ...!

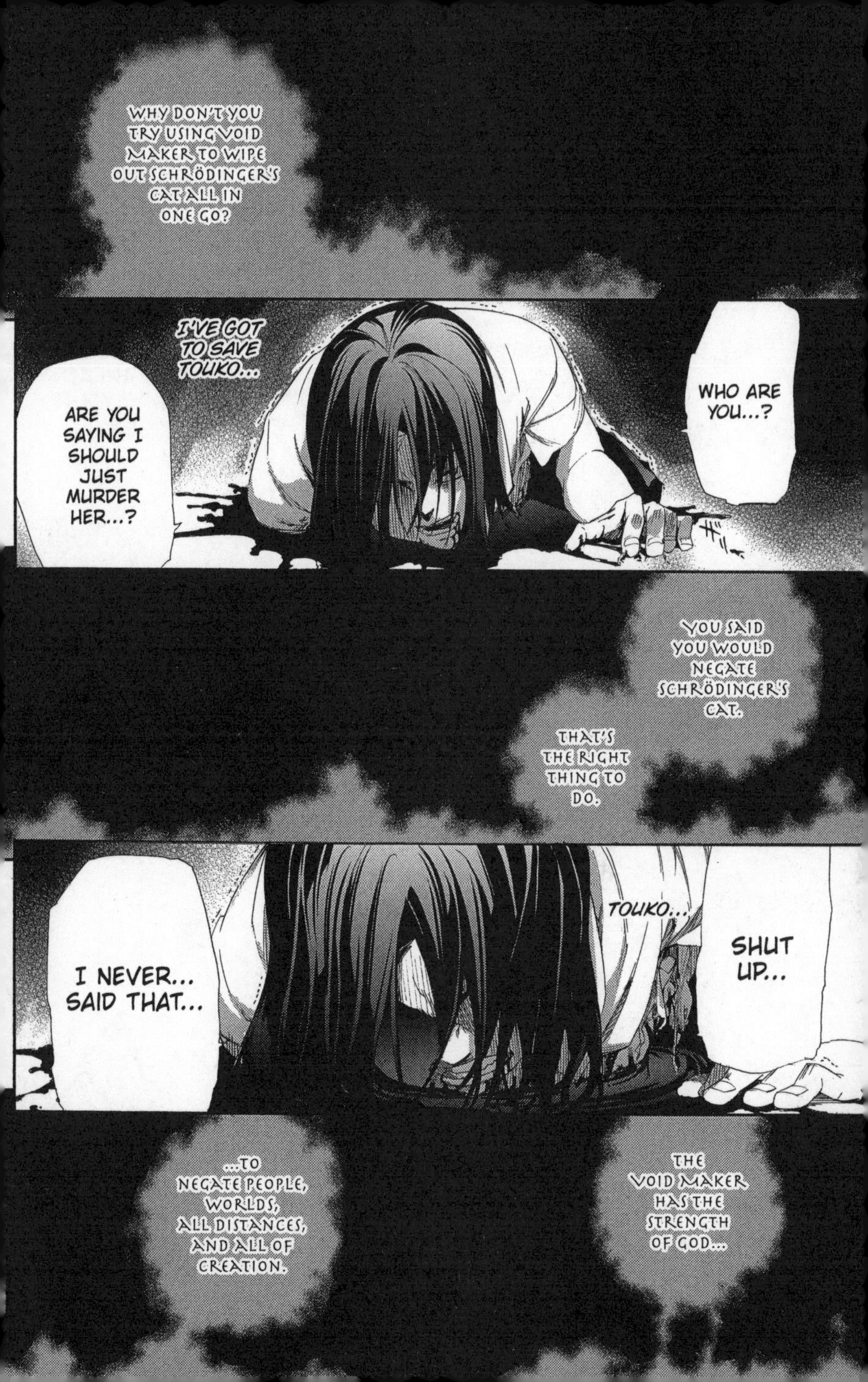
WHY DON'T YOU TRY USING VOID MAKER TO WIPE OUT SCHRÖDINGER'S CAT ALL IN ONE GO?
WHO ARE YOU...?
I'VE GOT TO SAVE TOUKO...
ARE YOU SAYING I SHOULD JUST MURDER HER...?
YOU SAID YOU WOULD NEGATE SCHRÖDINGER'S CAT.
THAT'S THE RIGHT THING TO DO.
SHUT UP...
TOUKO...
I NEVER... SAID THAT...
THE VOID MAKER HAS THE STRENGTH OF GOD...
...TO NEGATE PEOPLE, WORLDS, ALL DISTANCES, AND ALL OF CREATION.

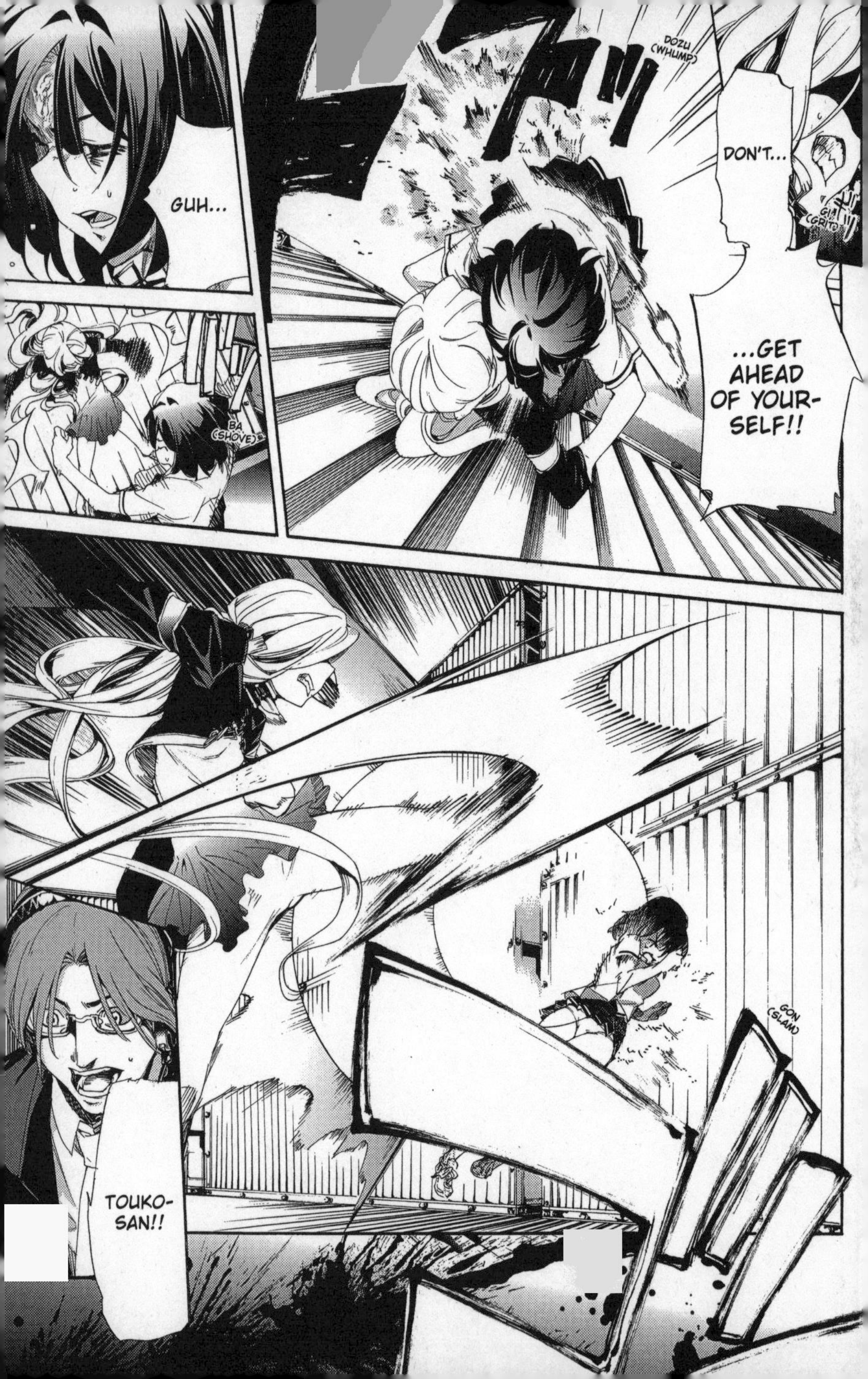
DON'T...
GI (GRIT)
...GET AHEAD OF YOUR-SELF!!
DOZU (WHUMP)
GUH...
BA (SHOVE)
GON (SLAM)
TOUKO-SAN!!

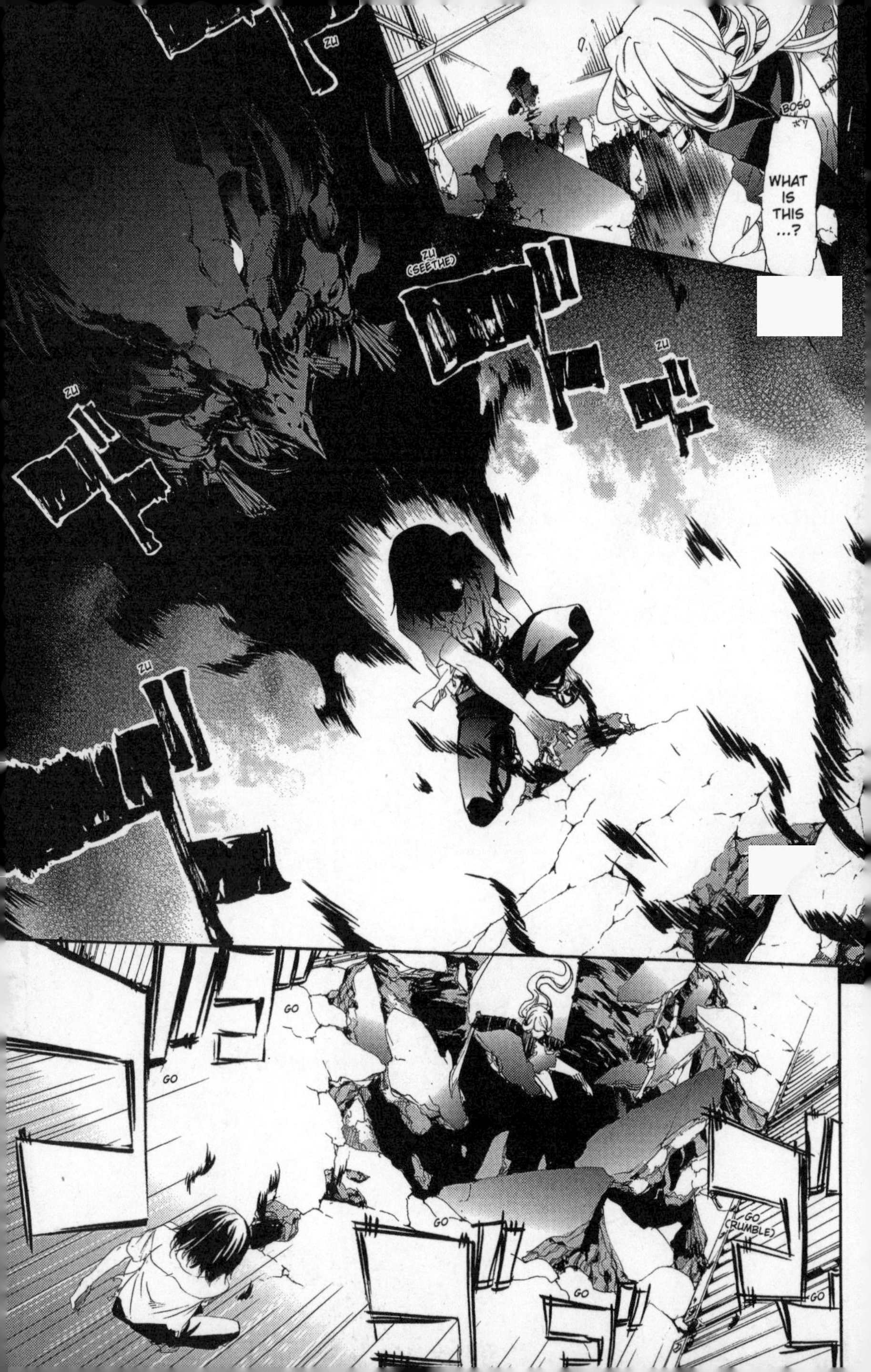
BOSO
ボソ
WHAT IS THIS ...?
ZU (SEETHE)
ZU
ZU
ZU
ZU
GO (CRUMBLE)
GO
GO
GO
GO
GO

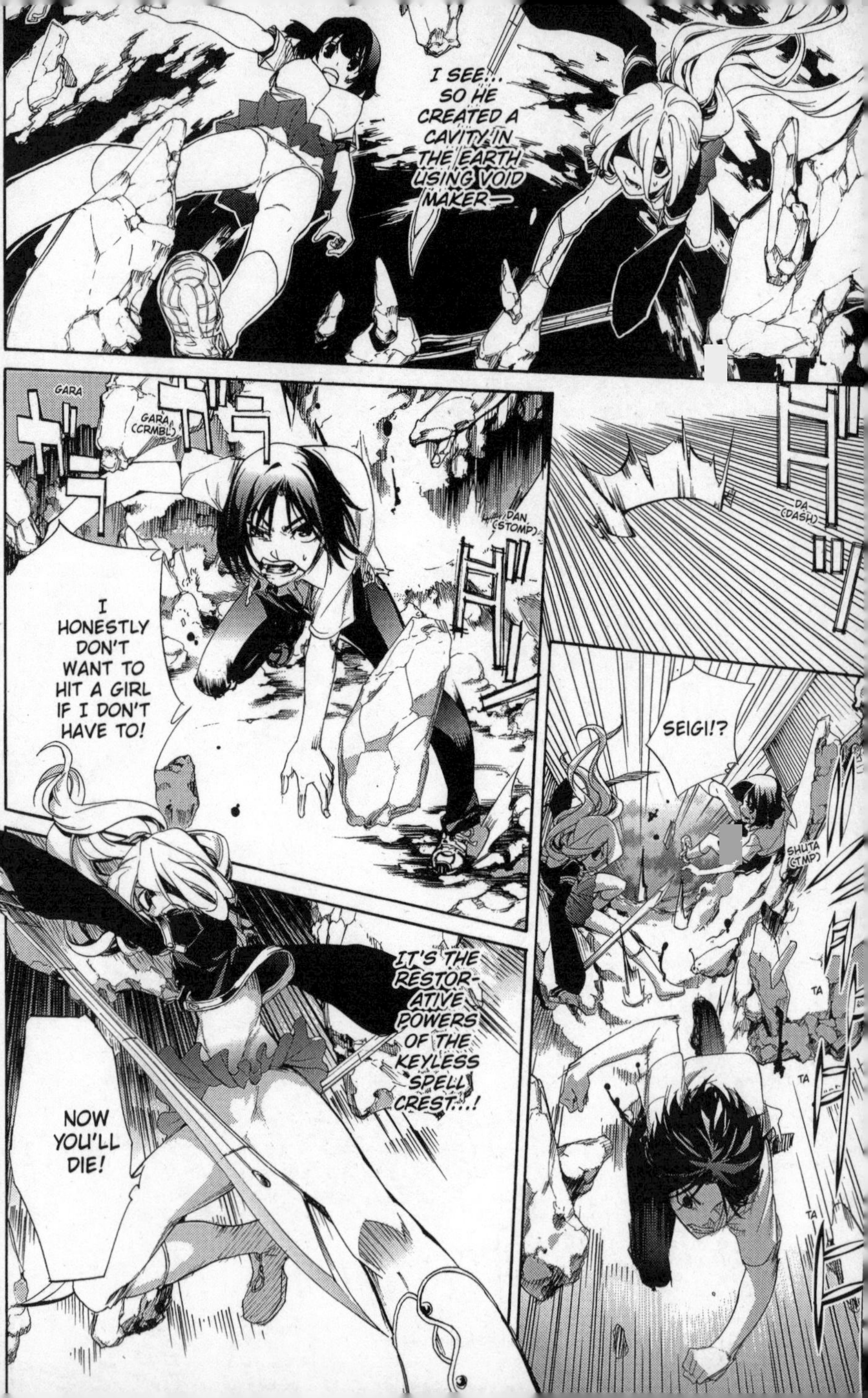
I SEE... SO HE CREATED A CAVITY IN THE EARTH USING VOID MAKER—
DA (DASH)
GARA
GARA (CRMBL)
DAN (STOMP)
I HONESTLY DON'T WANT TO HIT A GIRL IF I DON'T HAVE TO!
SEIGI!?
SHUTA (STMP)
IT'S THE RESTOR-ATIVE POWERS OF THE KEYLESS SPELL CREST...!
NOW YOU'LL DIE!
TA
TA
TA

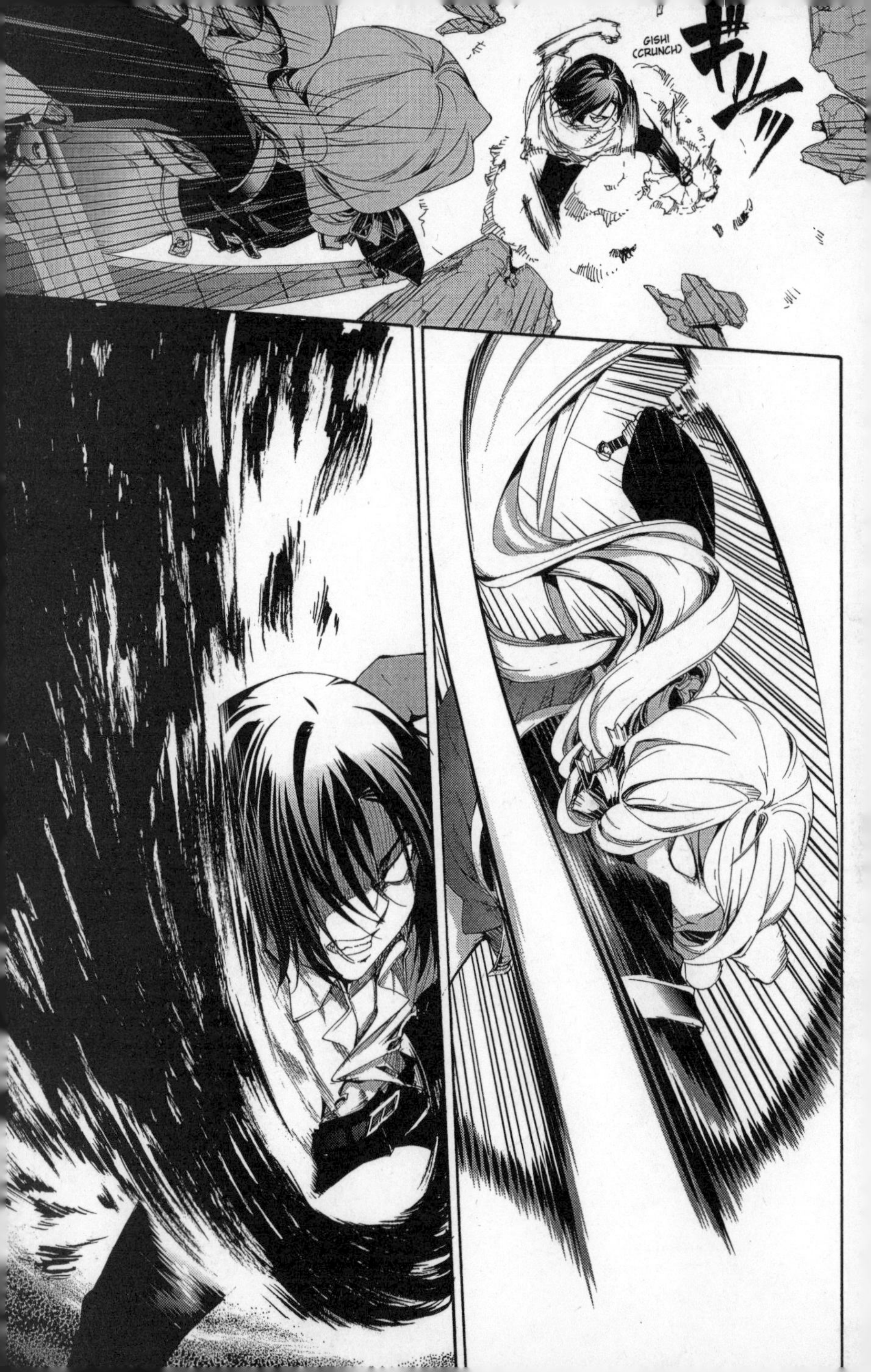
GISHI
(CRUNCH)

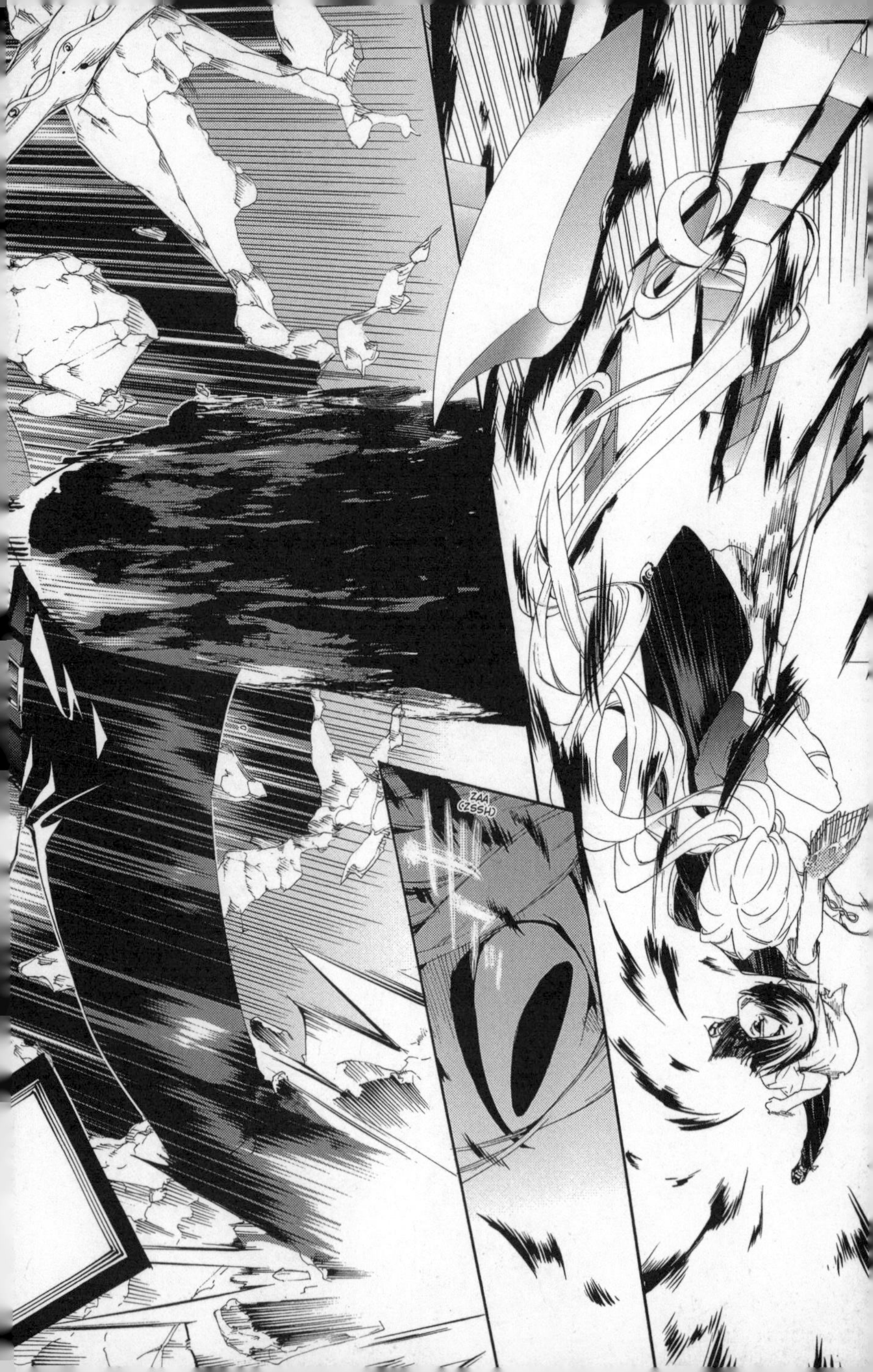
ZAA (ZSSH)

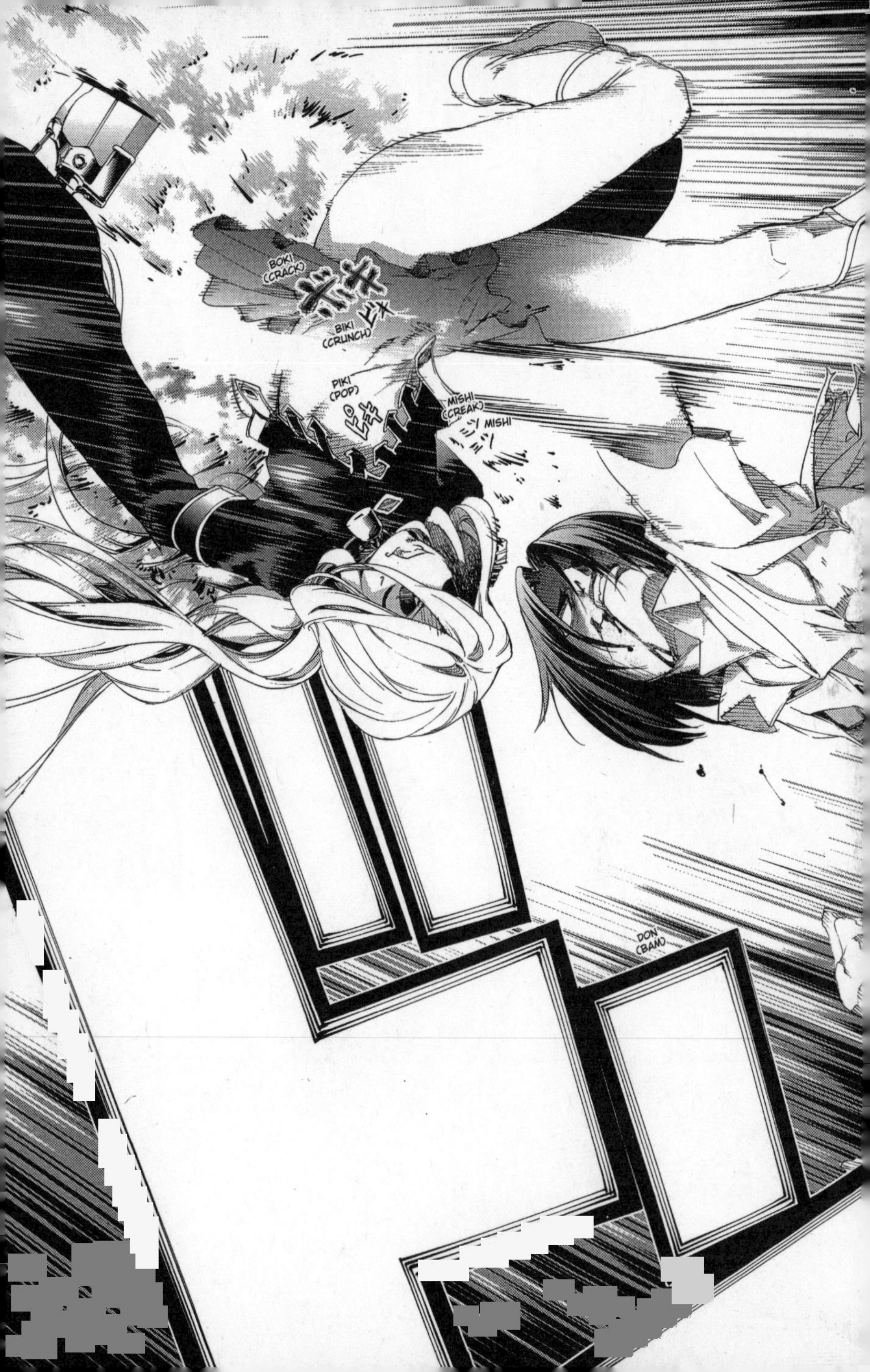
BOKI (CRACK)
BIKI (CRUNCH)
PIKI (POP)
MISHI (CREAK)
MISHI
DON (BAM)

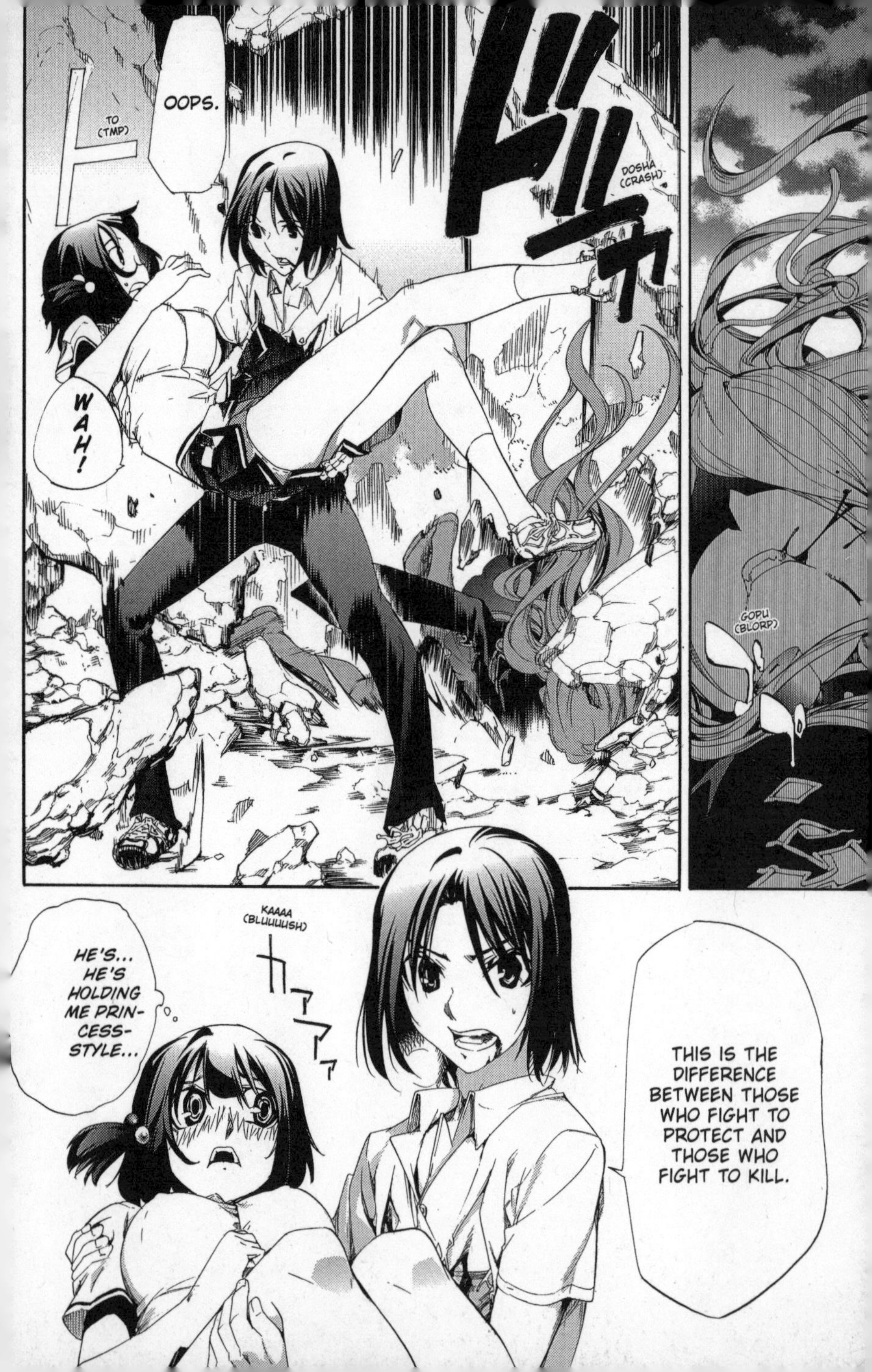
GOPU (BLORP)
DOSHA (CRASH)
OOPS.
TO (TMP)
WAH!
THIS IS THE DIFFERENCE BETWEEN THOSE WHO FIGHT TO PROTECT AND THOSE WHO FIGHT TO KILL.
KAAAA (BLUUUUSH)
HE'S... HE'S HOLDING ME PRIN-CESS-STYLE...

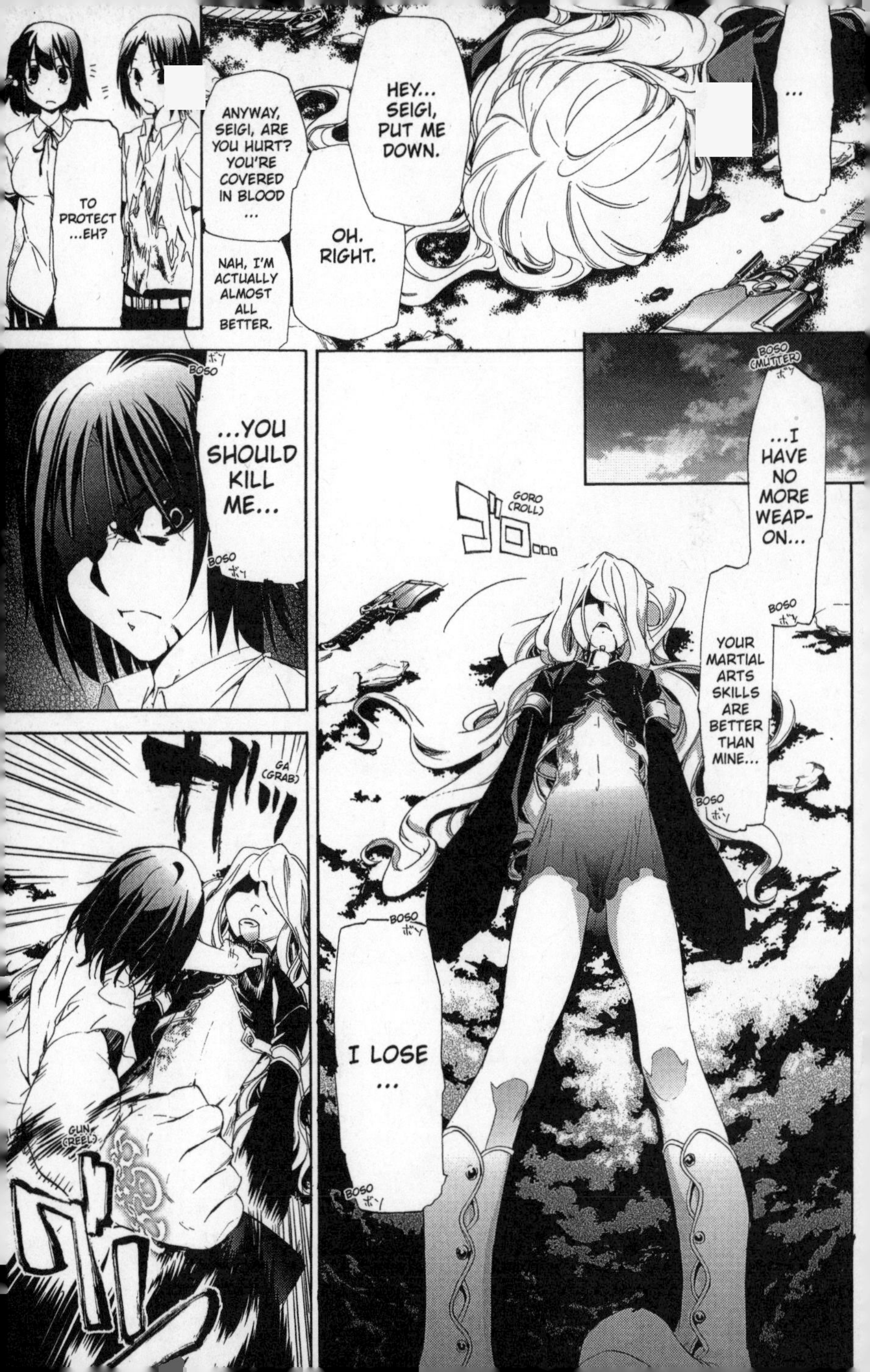
...
HEY... SEIGI, PUT ME DOWN.
OH. RIGHT.
ANYWAY, SEIGI, ARE YOU HURT? YOU'RE COVERED IN BLOOD...
NAH, I'M ACTUALLY ALMOST ALL BETTER.
TO PROTECT ...EH?
BOSO (MUTTER)
...I HAVE NO MORE WEAP-ON...
GORO (ROLL)
BOSO
YOUR MARTIAL ARTS SKILLS ARE BETTER THAN MINE...
BOSO
BOSO
I LOSE...
BOSO
BOSO
...YOU SHOULD KILL ME...
BOSO
GA (GRAB)
GUN (REEL)

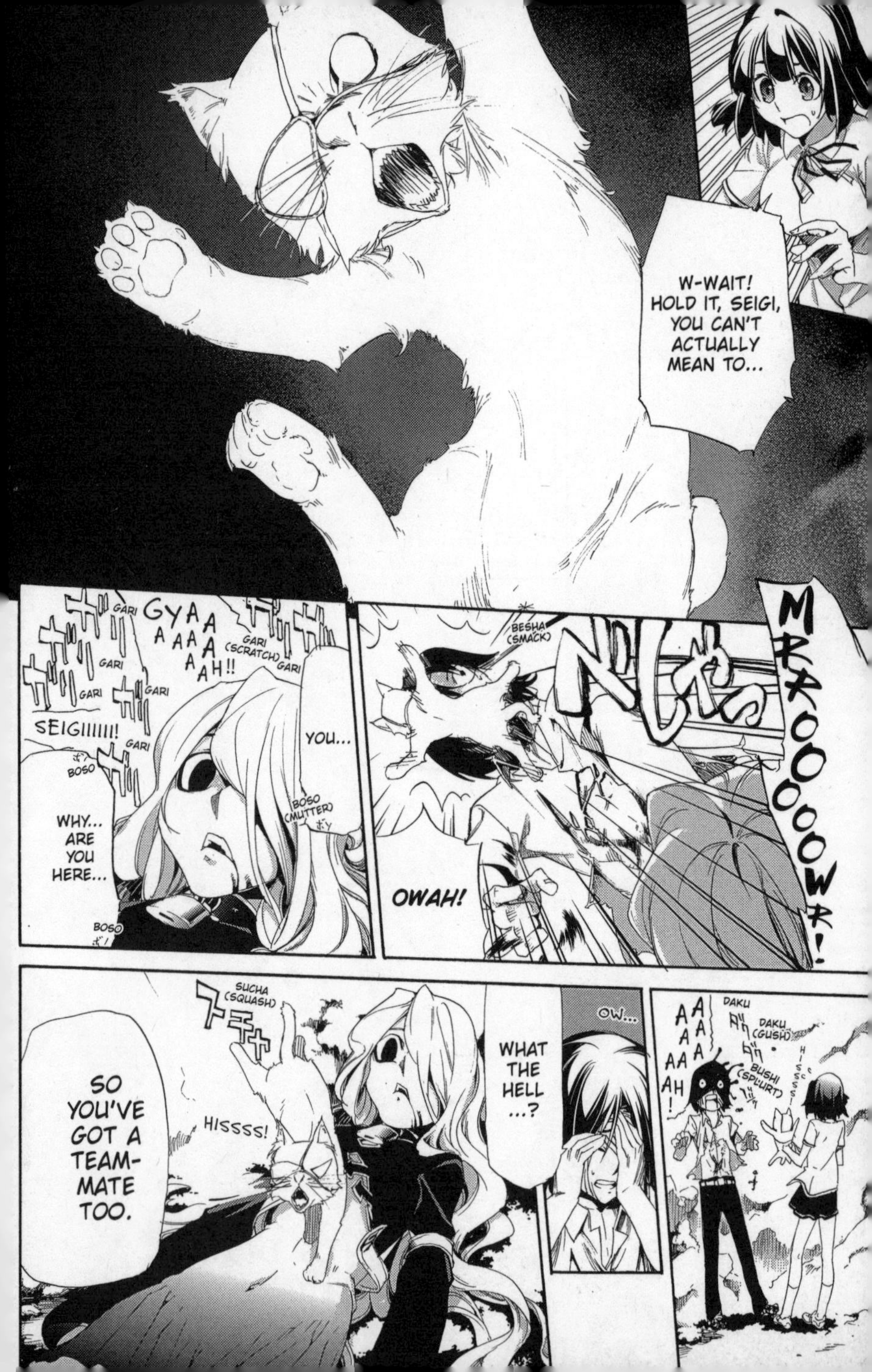
W-WAIT! HOLD IT, SEIGI, YOU CAN'T ACTUALLY MEAN TO...
MRROOOOOOWR!
BESHA (SMACK)
OWAH!
GARI
GYAAAAAAAAH!!
GARI (SCRATCH) GARI
GARI
GARI
GARI
SEIGIIIIII!
GARI
BOSO
YOU...
BOSO (MUTTER)
WHY... ARE YOU HERE...
BOSO
AAAAAAAAH!
DAKU
DAKU (GUSH)
BUSHI (SPLURT)
HISSSS!
OW...
WHAT THE HELL ...?
SUCHA (SQUASH)
HISSSS!
SO YOU'VE GOT A TEAM-MATE TOO.

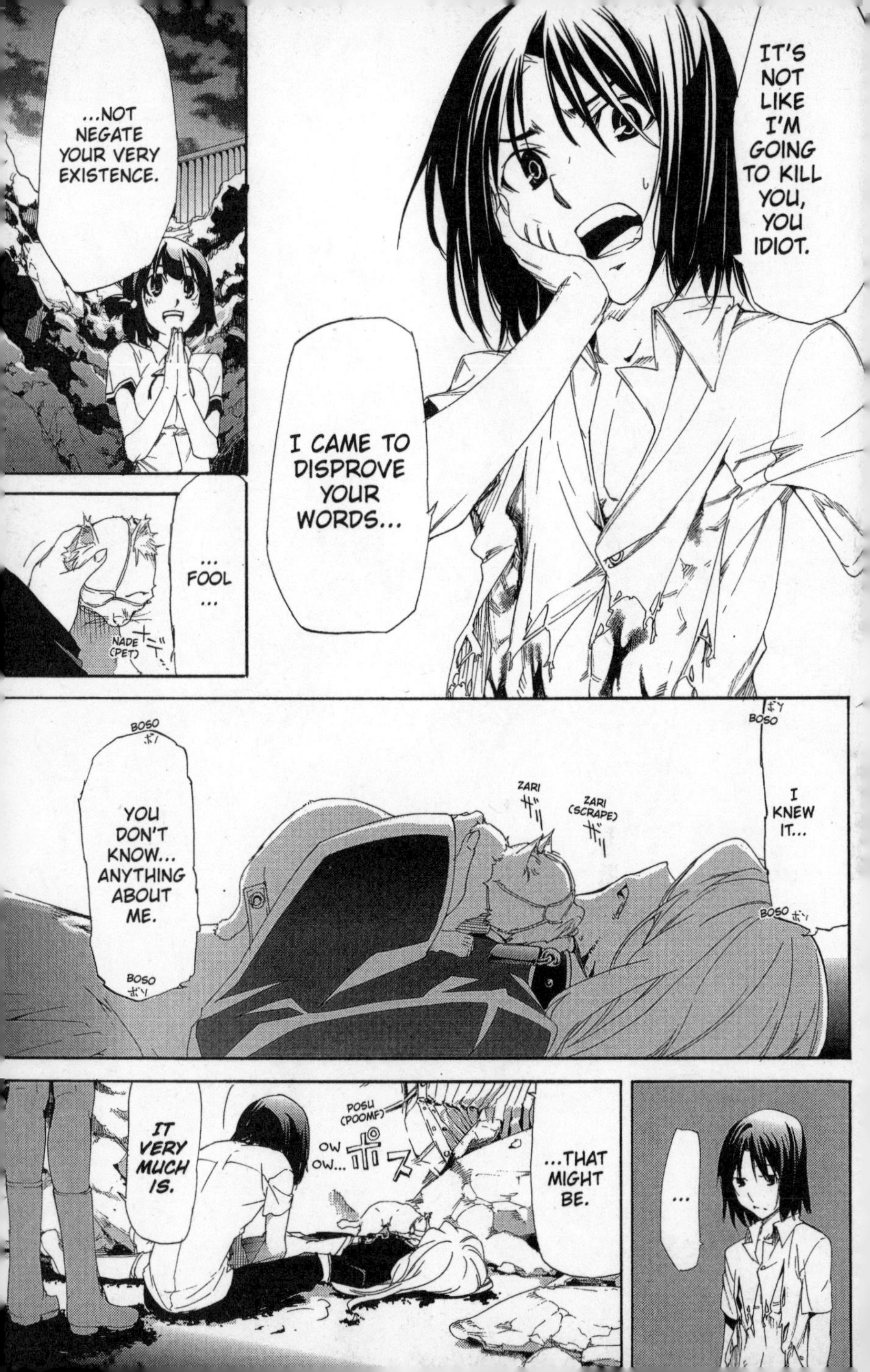
IT'S NOT LIKE I'M GOING TO KILL YOU, YOU IDIOT.
I CAME TO DISPROVE YOUR WORDS...
...NOT NEGATE YOUR VERY EXISTENCE.
... FOOL ...
NADE (PET)
BOSO
I KNEW IT...
BOSO
ZARI (SCRAPE)
ZARI
BOSO
YOU DON'T KNOW... ANYTHING ABOUT ME.
BOSO
...
...THAT MIGHT BE.
POSU (POOMF)
OW OW...
IT VERY MUCH IS.

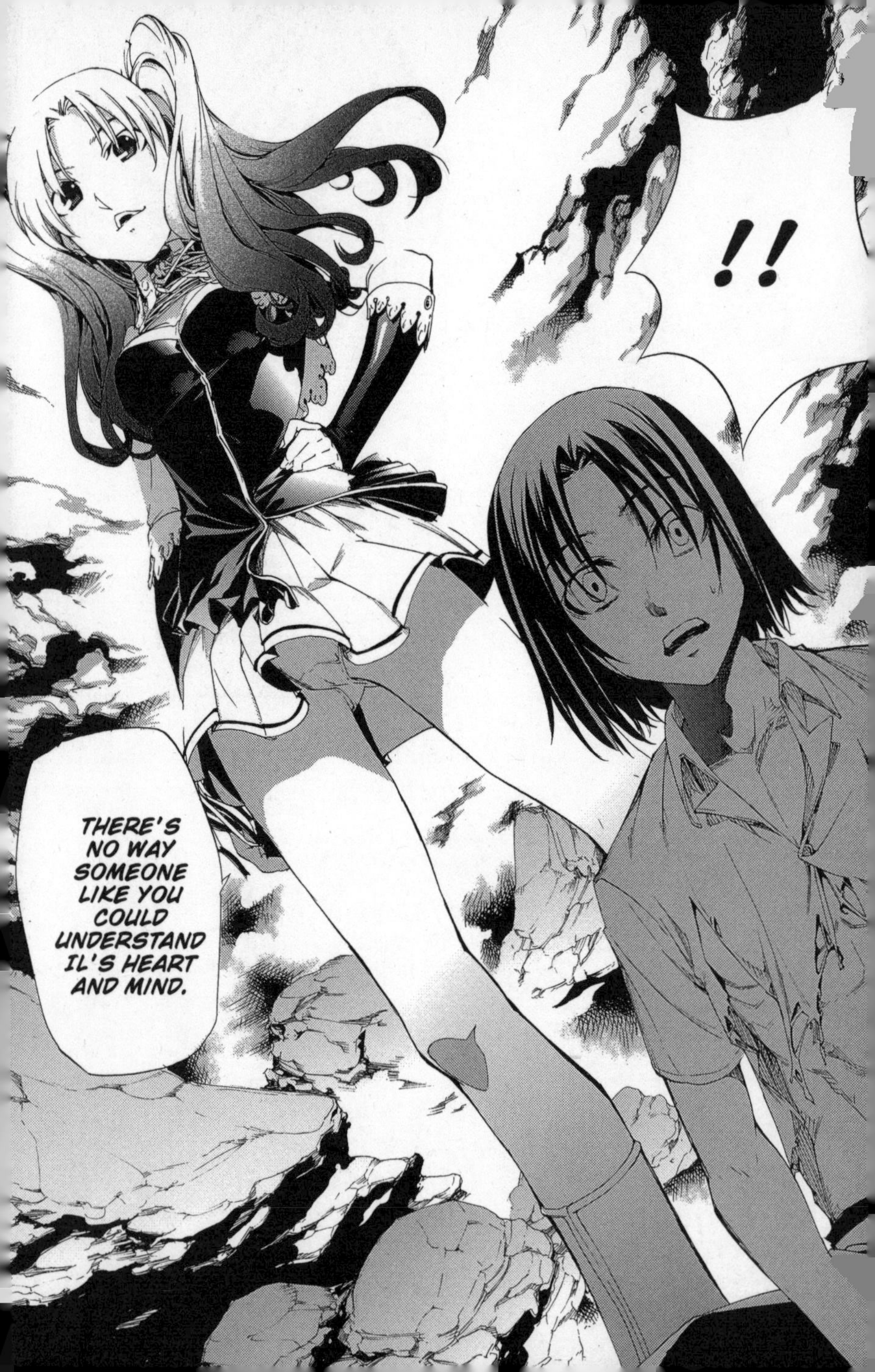
!!
THERE'S NO WAY SOMEONE LIKE YOU COULD UNDERSTAND IL'S HEART AND MIND.

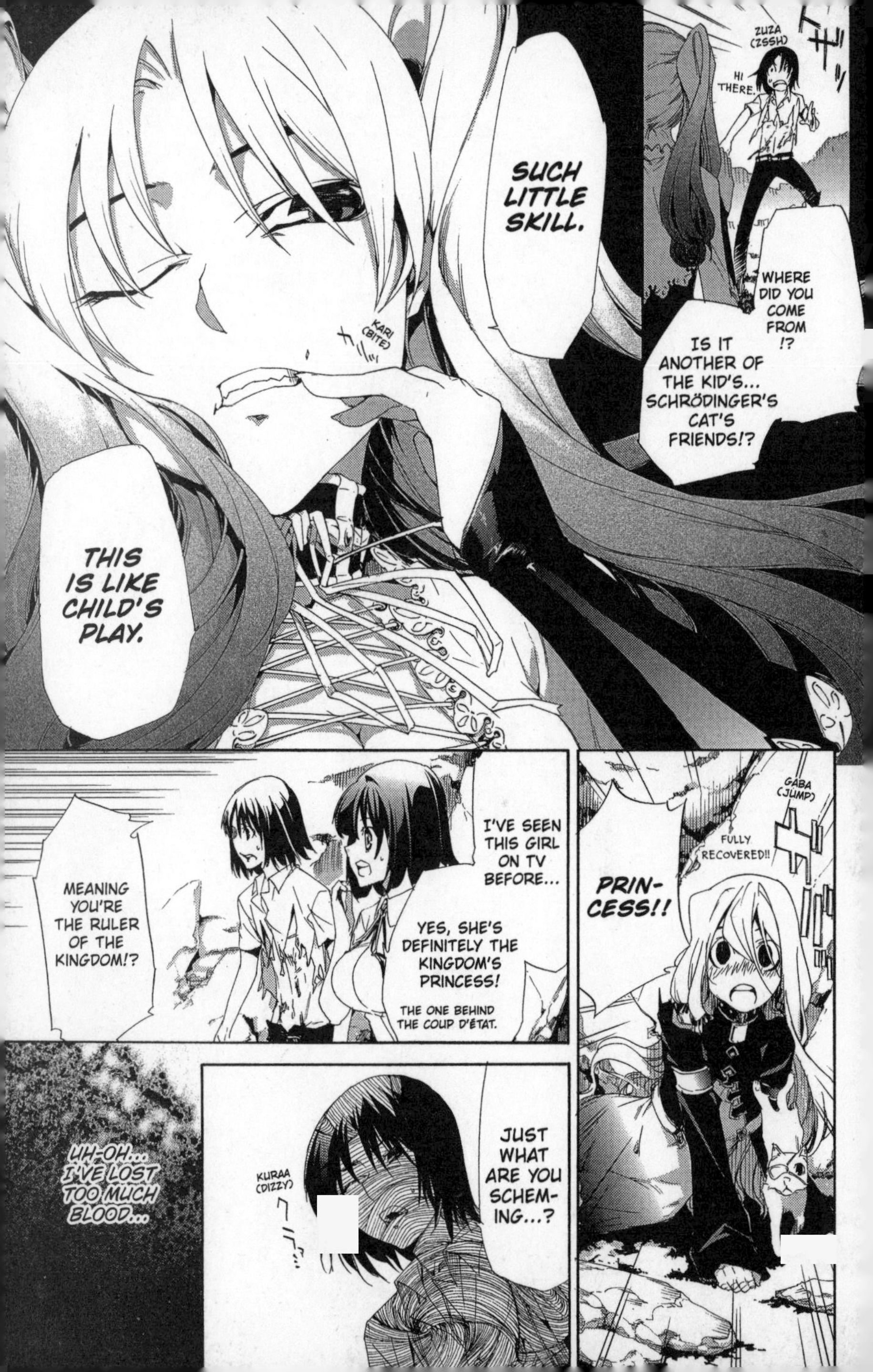
ZUZA (ZSSH)
HI THERE.
WHERE DID YOU COME FROM !?
IS IT ANOTHER OF THE KID'S... SCHRÖDINGER'S CAT'S FRIENDS!?
SUCH LITTLE SKILL.
KARI (BITE)
THIS IS LIKE CHILD'S PLAY.
GABA (JUMP)
FULLY RECOVERED!!
PRIN-CESS!!
I'VE SEEN THIS GIRL ON TV BEFORE...
YES, SHE'S DEFINITELY THE KINGDOM'S PRINCESS!
THE ONE BEHIND THE COUP D'ÉTAT.
MEANING YOU'RE THE RULER OF THE KINGDOM!?
JUST WHAT ARE YOU SCHEM-ING...?
KURAA (DIZZY)
UH-OH... I'VE LOST TOO MUCH BLOOD...

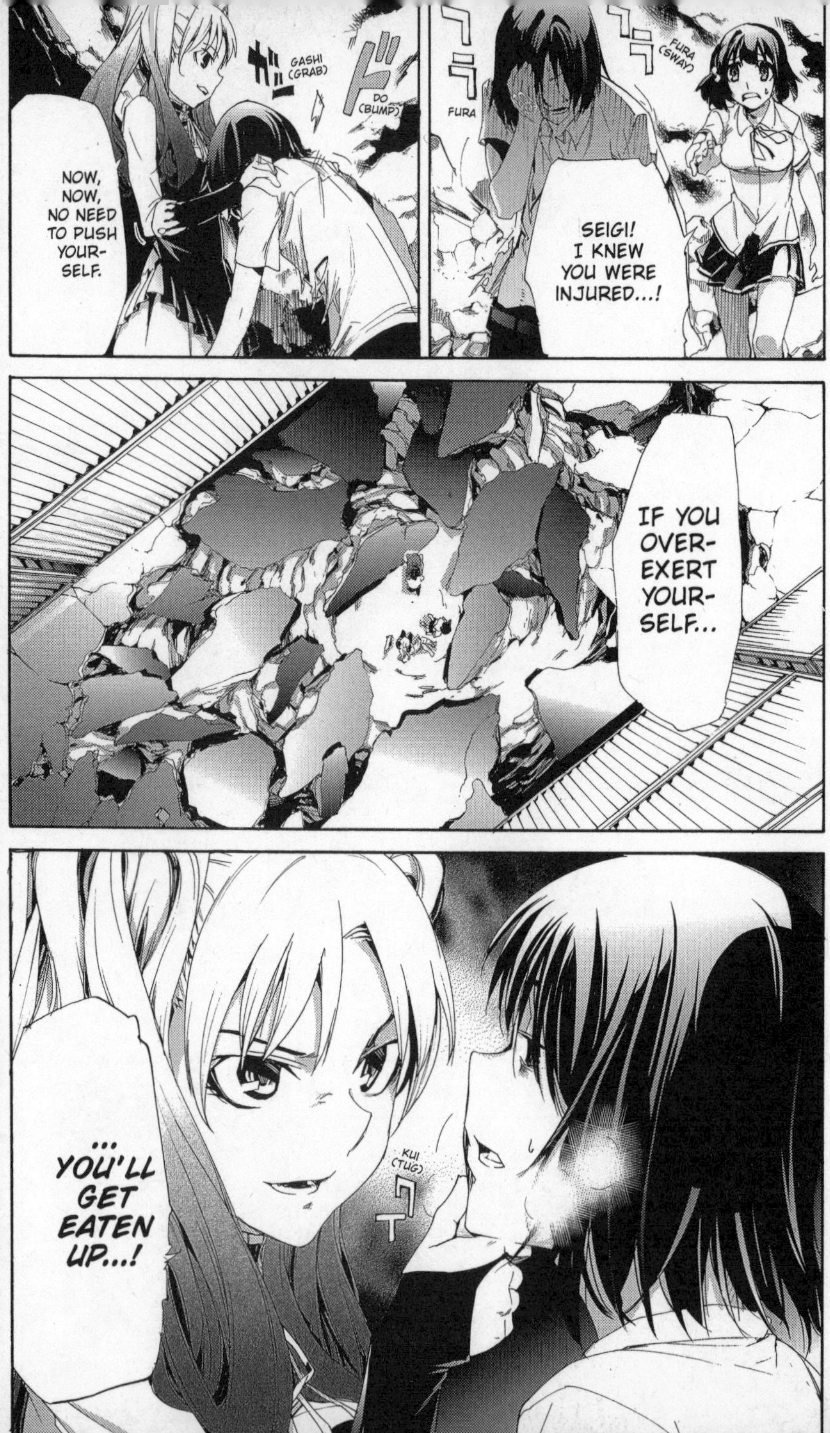
FURA (SWAY)
FURA
SEIGI! I KNEW YOU WERE INJURED...!
GASHI (GRAB)
DO (BUMP)
NOW, NOW, NO NEED TO PUSH YOURSELF.
IF YOU OVER-EXERT YOURSELF...
KUI (TUG)
...YOU'LL GET EATEN UP...!

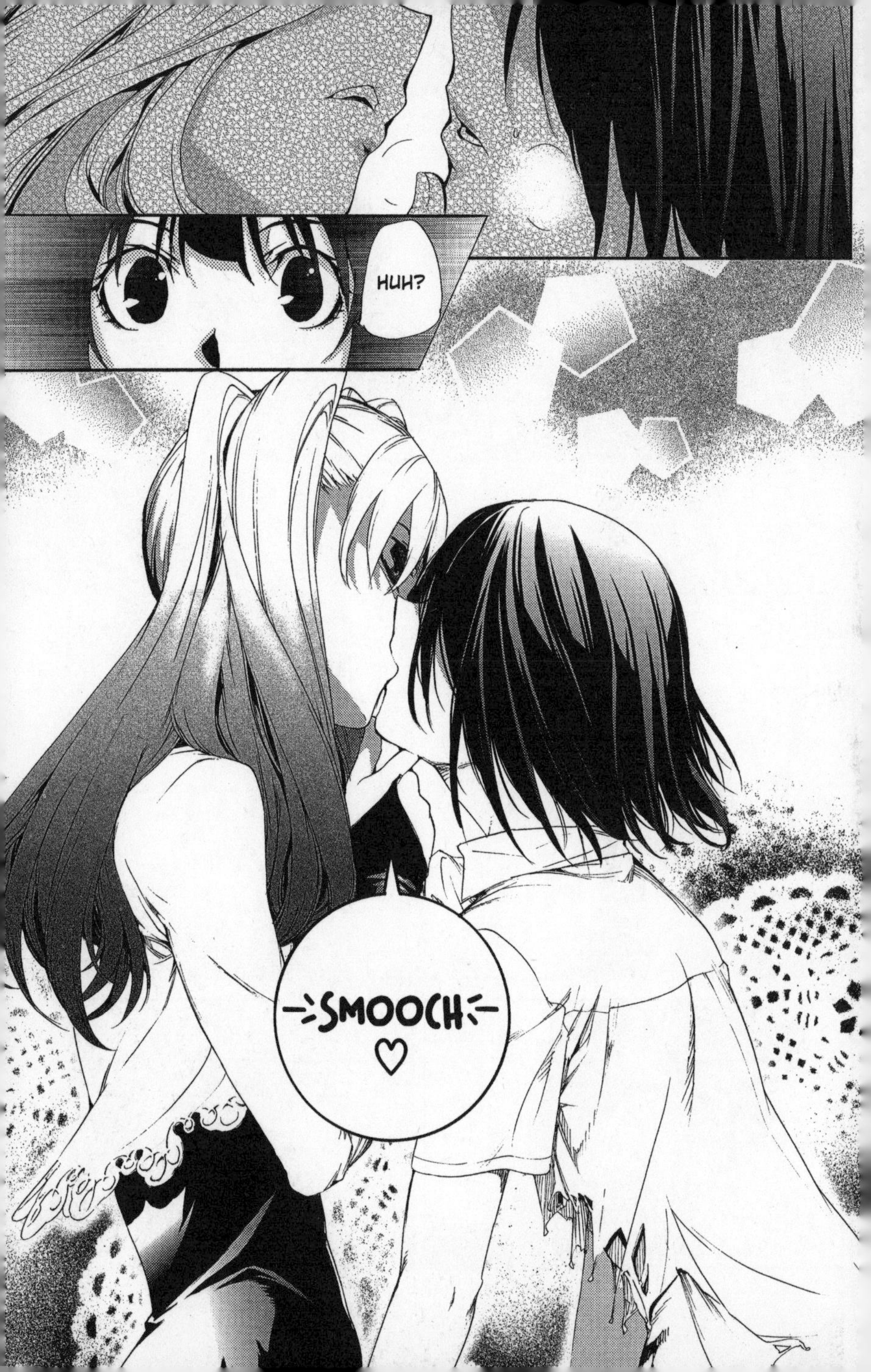
HUH?
SMOOCH
♡

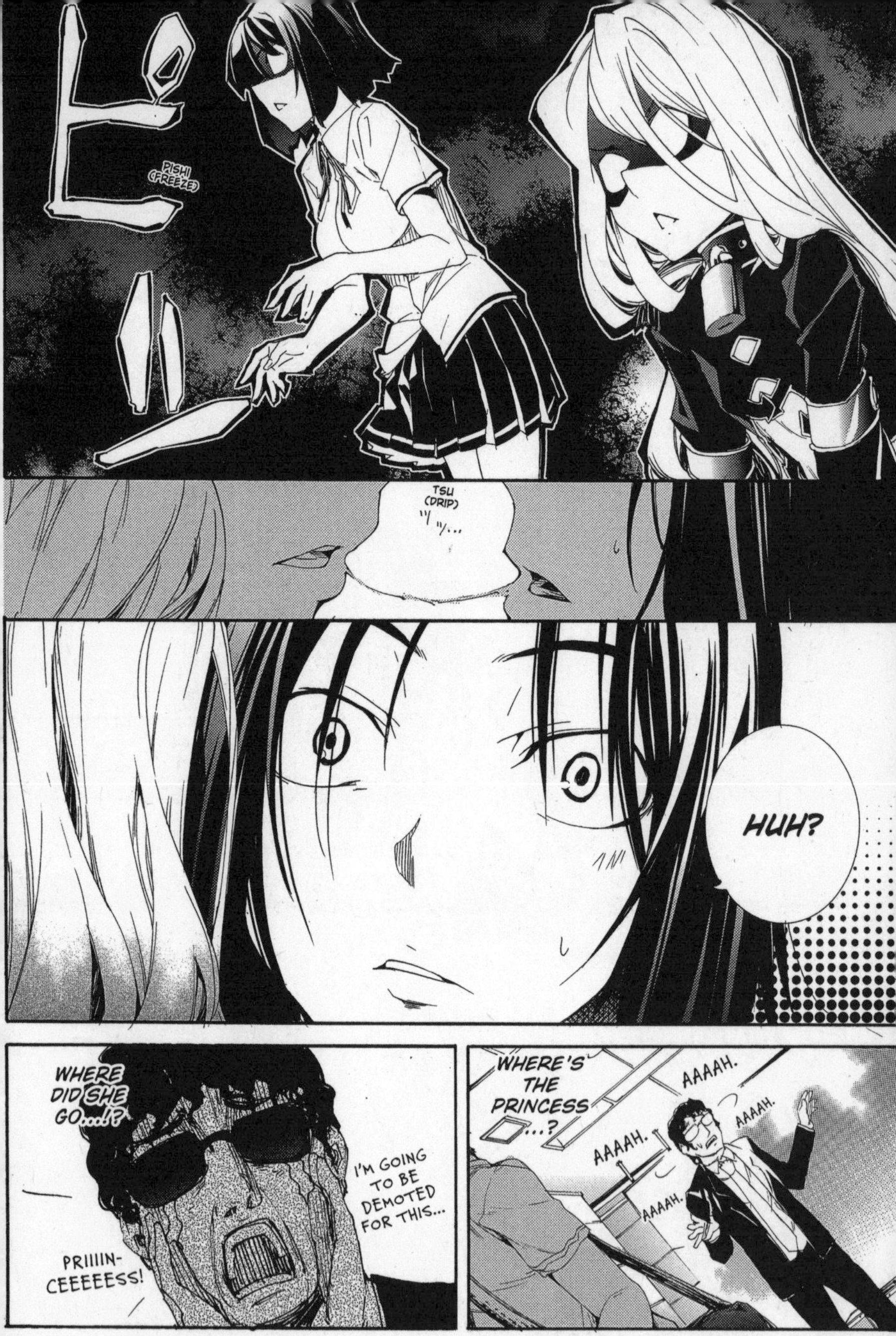
PISHI (FREEZE)
TSU (DRIP)
HUH?
WHERE'S THE PRINCESS...?
AAAAH.
AAAAH.
AAAAH.
AAAAH.
WHERE DID SHE GO...!?
I'M GOING TO BE DEMOTED FOR THIS...
PRIIIIN-CEEEEEESS!

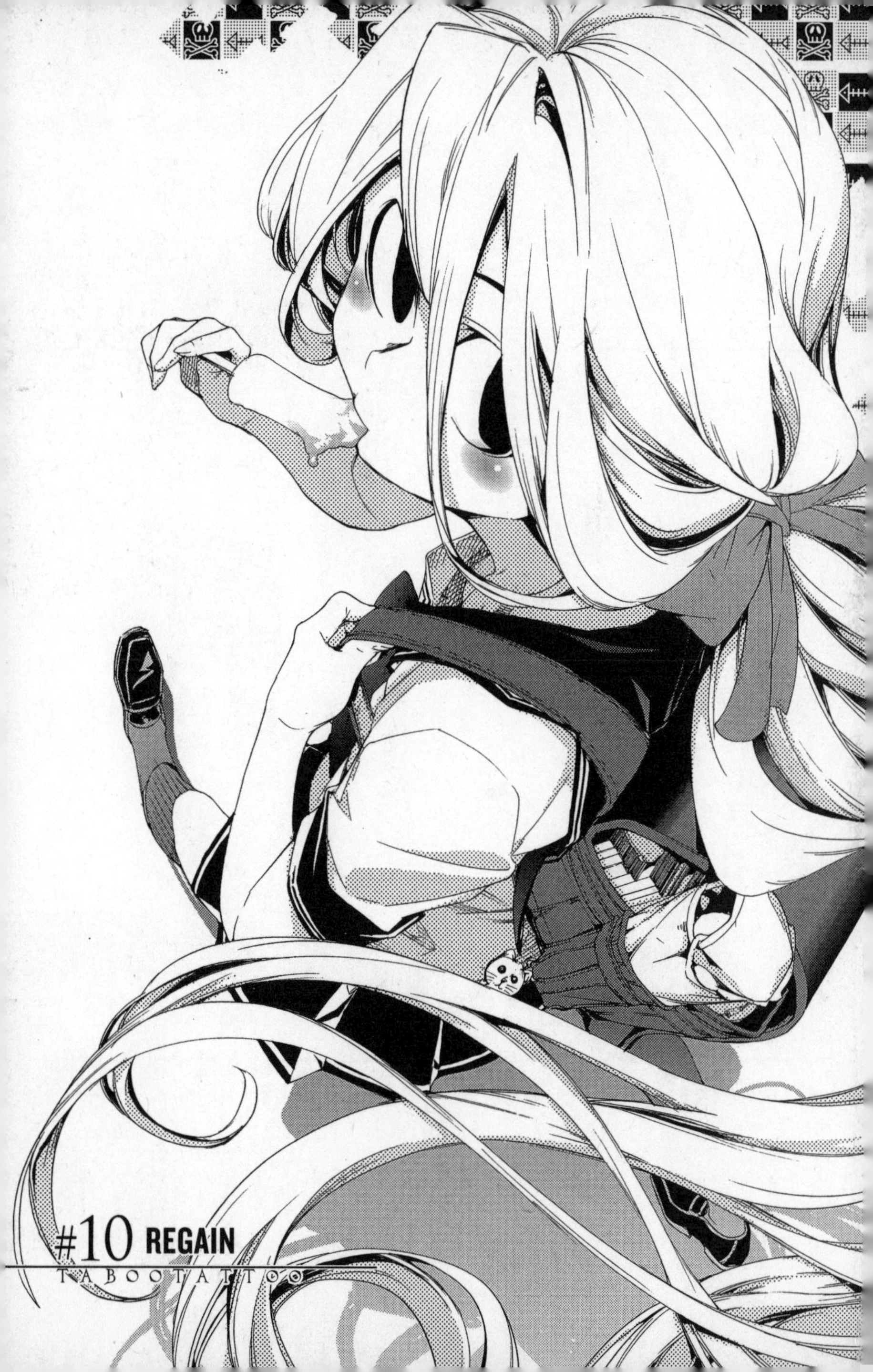
#10 REGAIN
TABOOTATTOO

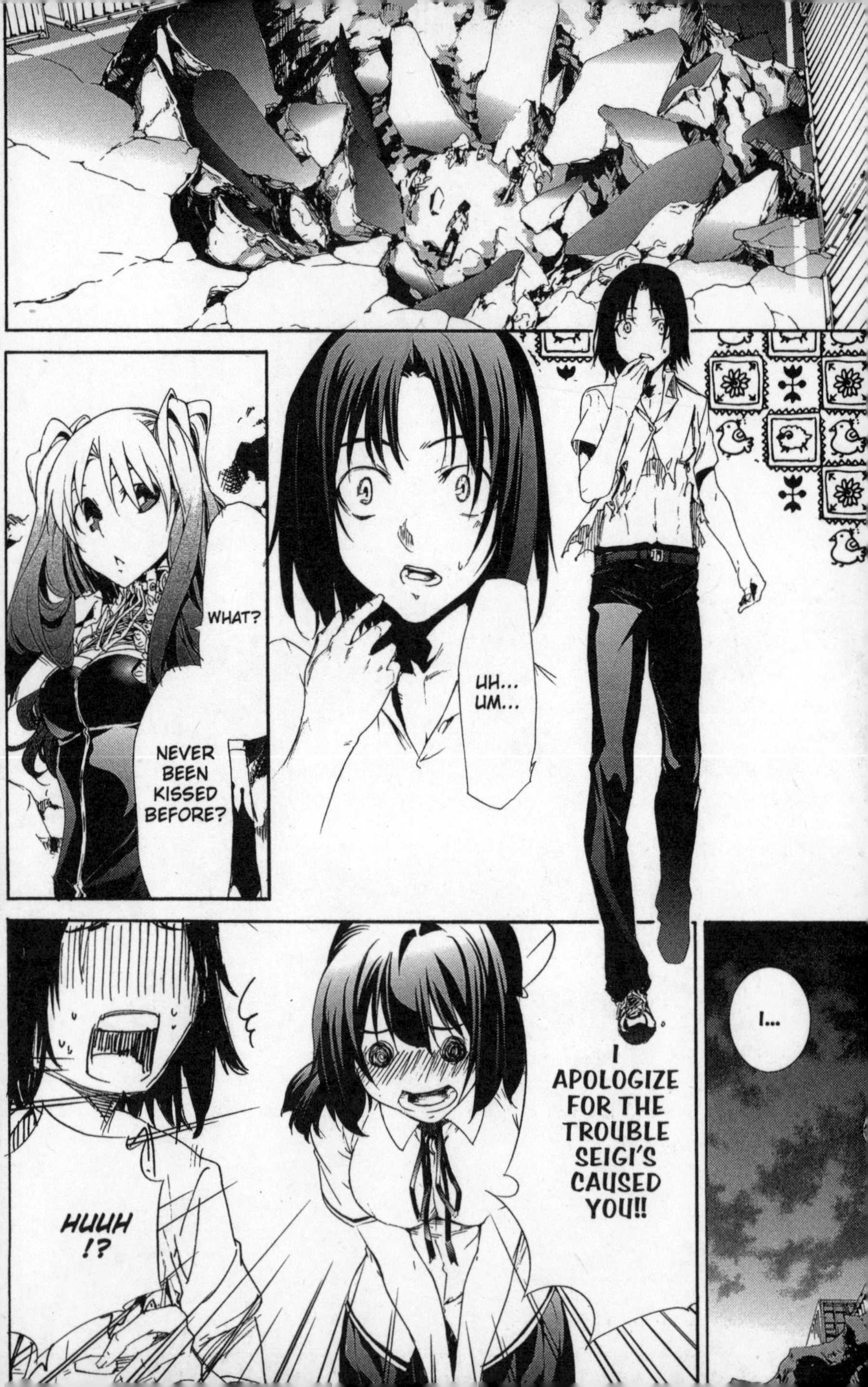
UH... UM...
WHAT?
NEVER BEEN KISSED BEFORE?
I...
I APOLOGIZE FOR THE TROUBLE SEIGI'S CAUSED YOU!!
HUUH !?

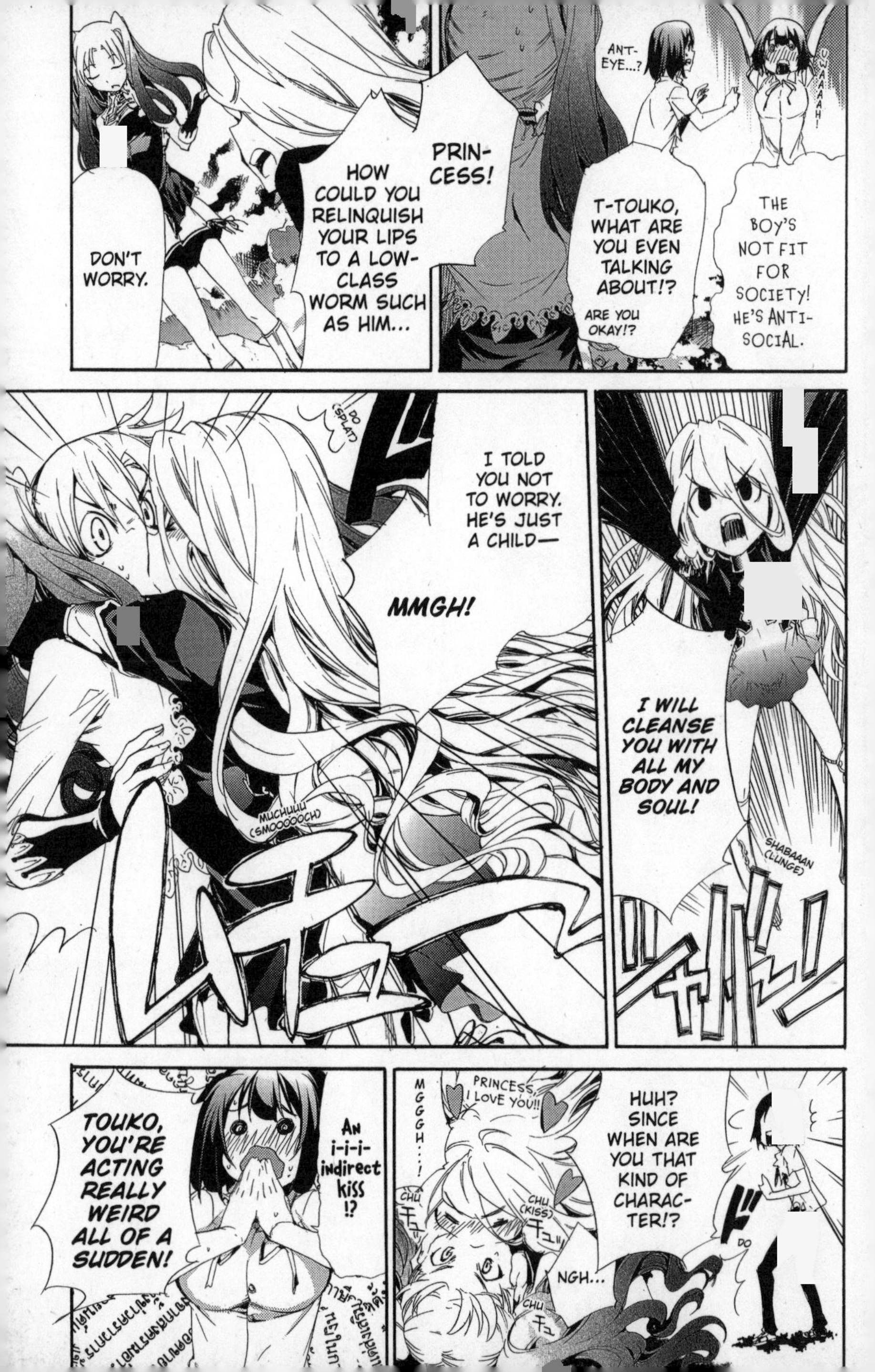

ANT-EYE...?
UWAAAAAH!
THE BOY'S NOT FIT FOR SOCIETY! HE'S ANTI-SOCIAL.
T-TOUKO, WHAT ARE YOU EVEN TALKING ABOUT!?
ARE YOU OKAY!?
PRIN-CESS!
HOW COULD YOU RELINQUISH YOUR LIPS TO A LOW-CLASS WORM SUCH AS HIM...
DON'T WORRY.
I WILL CLEANSE YOU WITH ALL MY BODY AND SOUL!
SHABAAAN (LUNGE)
DO (SPLAT)
I TOLD YOU NOT TO WORRY. HE'S JUST A CHILD—
MMGH!
MUCHUUU (SMOOOOOCH)
HUH? SINCE WHEN ARE YOU THAT KIND OF CHARAC-TER!?
DO
PRINCESS, I LOVE YOU!!
MGGGH...!
CHU
CHU (KISS)
NGH...
CHU
An i-i-i-indirect kiss!?
TOUKO, YOU'RE ACTING REALLY WEIRD ALL OF A SUDDEN!

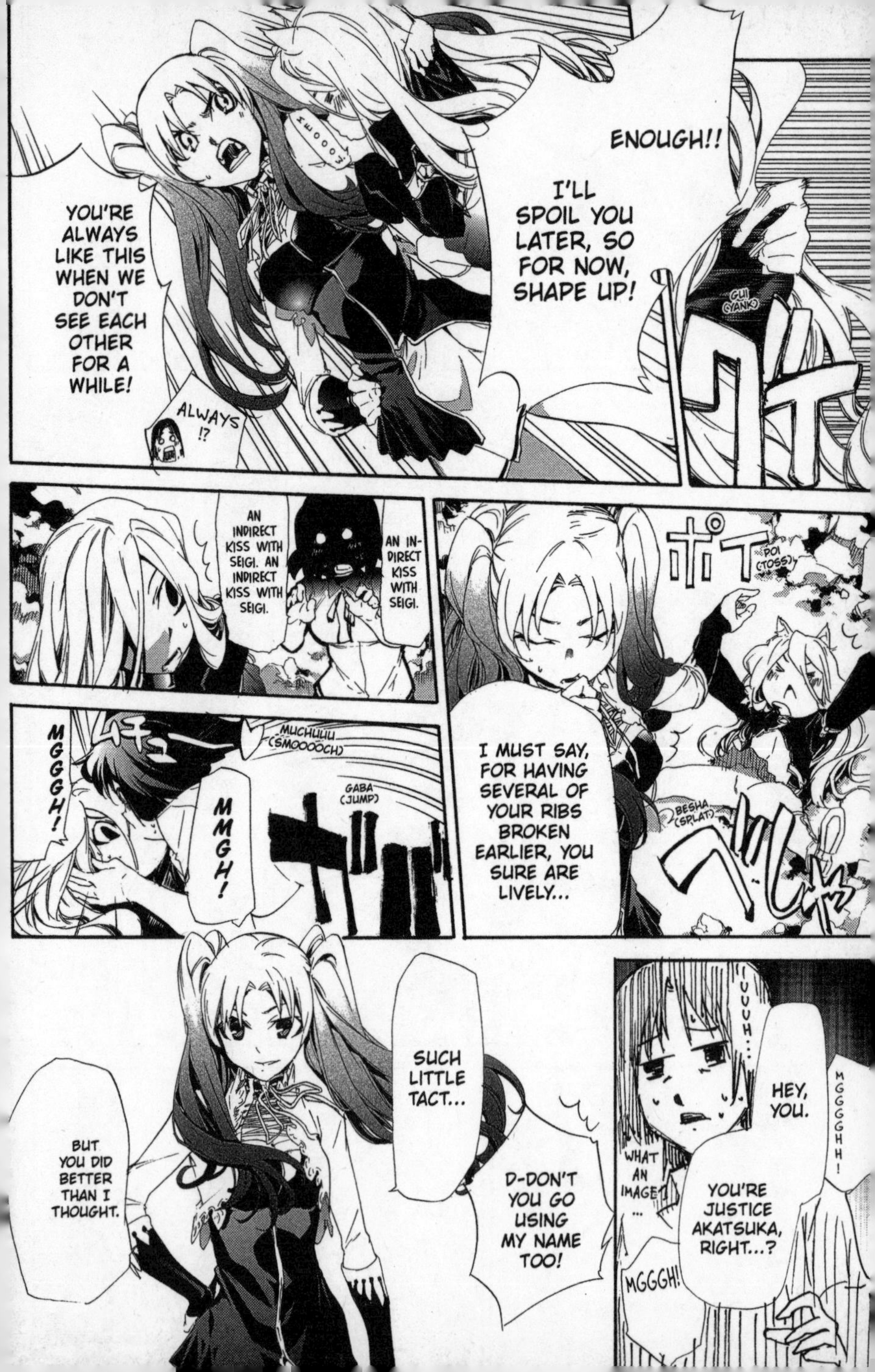
ENOUGH!!
I'LL SPOIL YOU LATER, SO FOR NOW, SHAPE UP!
GUI (YANK)
YOU'RE ALWAYS LIKE THIS WHEN WE DON'T SEE EACH OTHER FOR A WHILE!
ALWAYS !?
POI (TOSS)
I MUST SAY, FOR HAVING SEVERAL OF YOUR RIBS BROKEN EARLIER, YOU SURE ARE LIVELY...
BESHA (SPLAT)
AN IN-DIRECT KISS WITH SEIGI.
AN INDIRECT KISS WITH SEIGI. AN INDIRECT KISS WITH SEIGI.
MUCHUUU (SMOOOOCH)
GABA (JUMP)
MMGH!
MGGGH!
UUUH...
MGGGGHH!
HEY, YOU.
YOU'RE JUSTICE AKATSUKA, RIGHT...?
WHAT AN IMAGE...
MGGGH!
SUCH LITTLE TACT...
D-DON'T YOU GO USING MY NAME TOO!
BUT YOU DID BETTER THAN I THOUGHT.

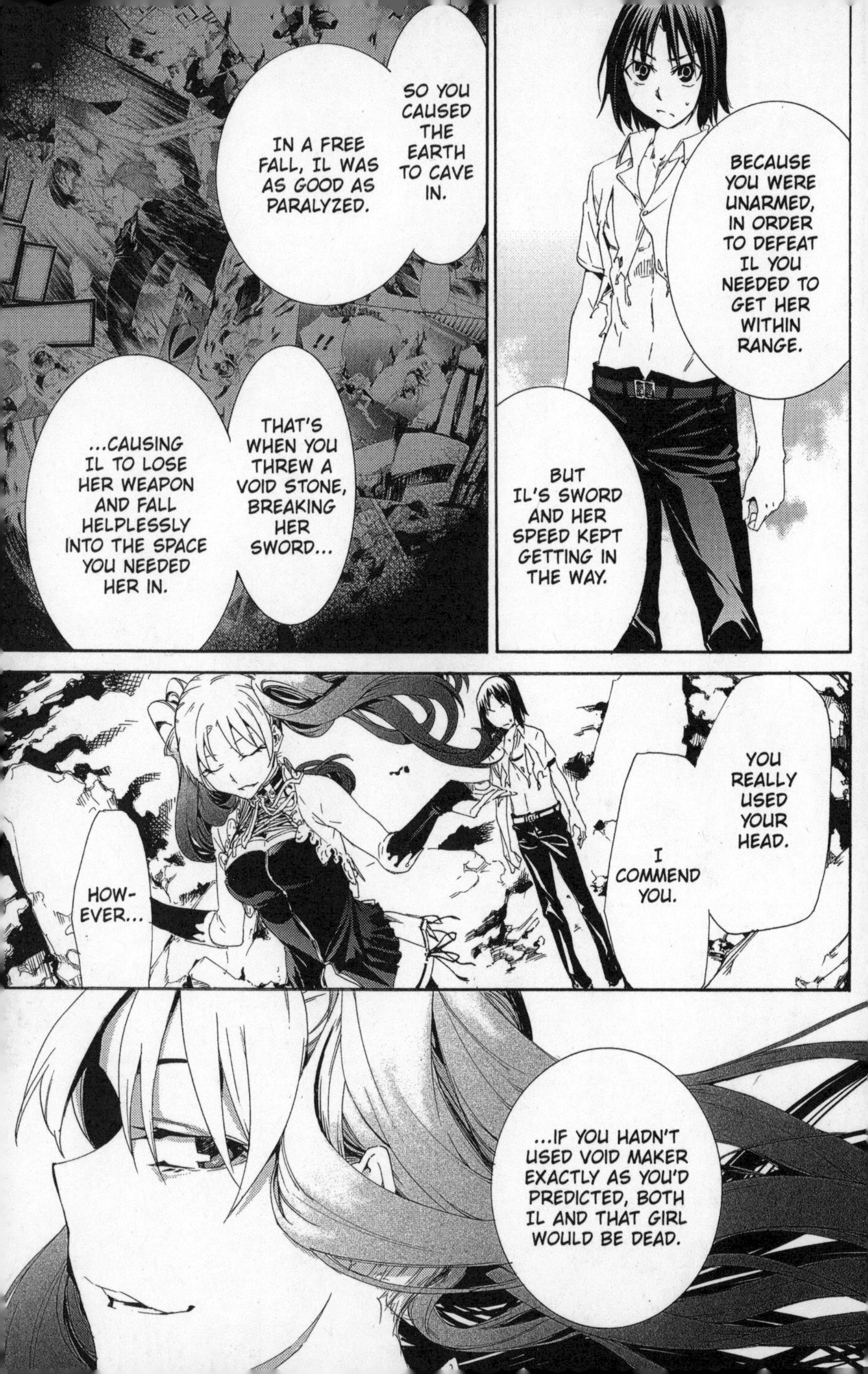
BECAUSE YOU WERE UNARMED, IN ORDER TO DEFEAT IL YOU NEEDED TO GET HER WITHIN RANGE.
BUT IL'S SWORD AND HER SPEED KEPT GETTING IN THE WAY.
SO YOU CAUSED THE EARTH TO CAVE IN.
IN A FREE FALL, IL WAS AS GOOD AS PARALYZED.
!!
THAT'S WHEN YOU THREW A VOID STONE, BREAKING HER SWORD...
...CAUSING IL TO LOSE HER WEAPON AND FALL HELPLESSLY INTO THE SPACE YOU NEEDED HER IN.
YOU REALLY USED YOUR HEAD.
I COMMEND YOU.
HOW-EVER...
...IF YOU HADN'T USED VOID MAKER EXACTLY AS YOU'D PREDICTED, BOTH IL AND THAT GIRL WOULD BE DEAD.

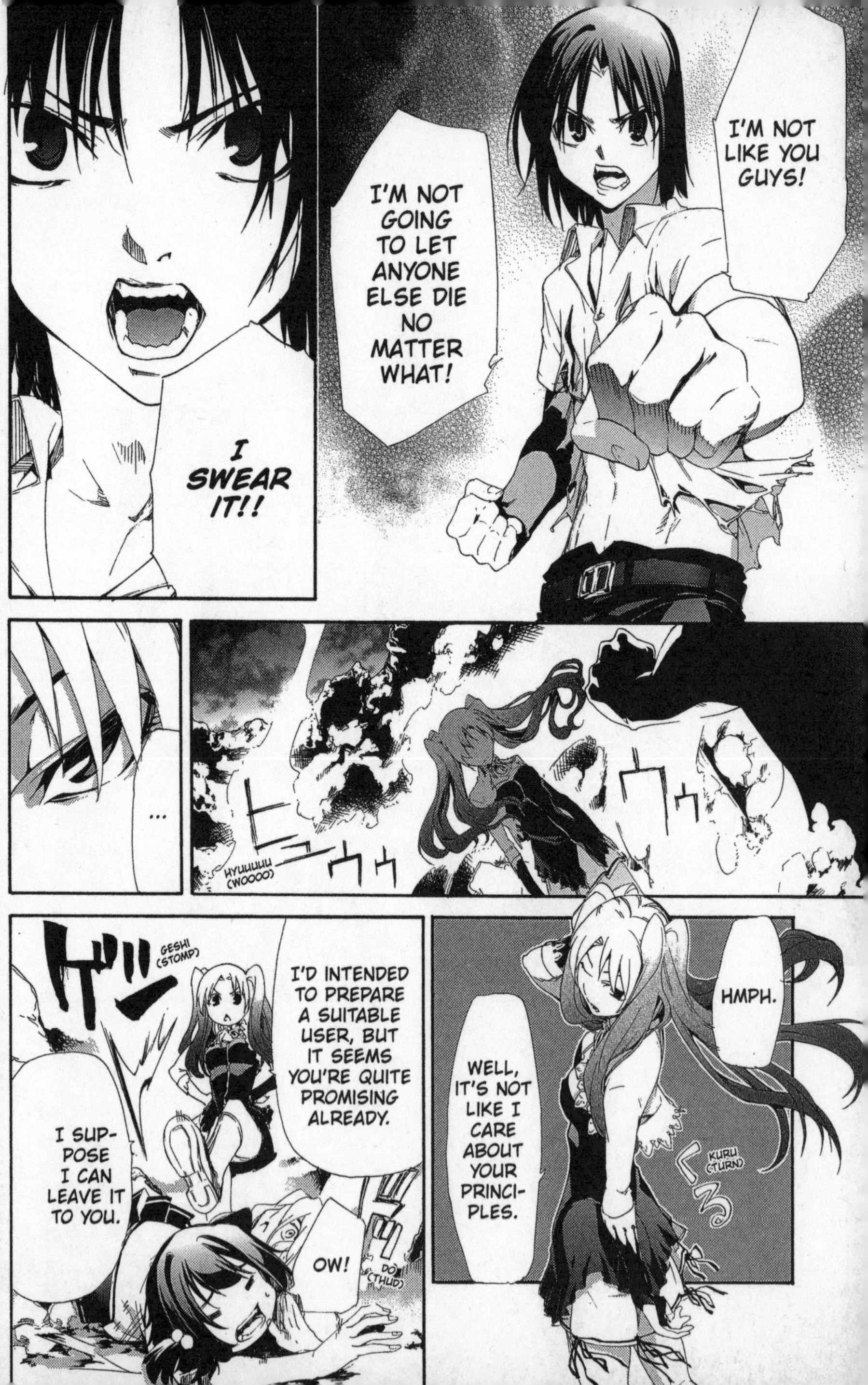
I'M NOT LIKE YOU GUYS!
I'M NOT GOING TO LET ANYONE ELSE DIE NO MATTER WHAT!
I SWEAR IT!!
HYUUUUU (WOOOO)
...
HMPH.
WELL, IT'S NOT LIKE I CARE ABOUT YOUR PRINCIPLES.
KURU (TURN)
GESHI (STOMP)
I'D INTENDED TO PREPARE A SUITABLE USER, BUT IT SEEMS YOU'RE QUITE PROMISING ALREADY.
I SUPPOSE I CAN LEAVE IT TO YOU.
OW!
DO (THUD)

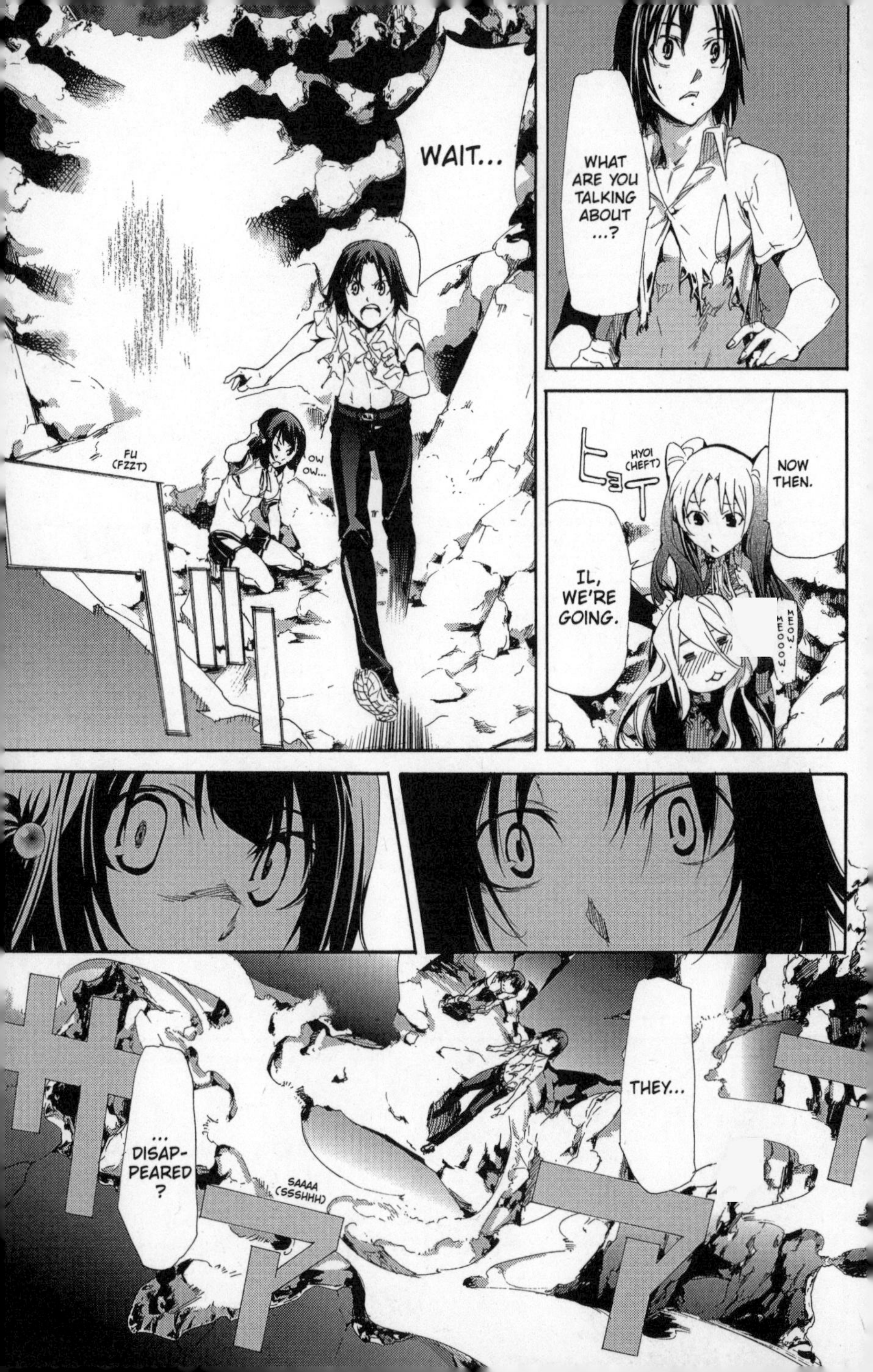
WHAT ARE YOU TALKING ABOUT ...?
NOW THEN.
HYOI (HEFT)
IL, WE'RE GOING.
MEOW. MEOOOOW.
WAIT...
FU (FZZT)
OW OW...
THEY...
... DISAP-PEARED ?
SAAAA (SSSHHH)

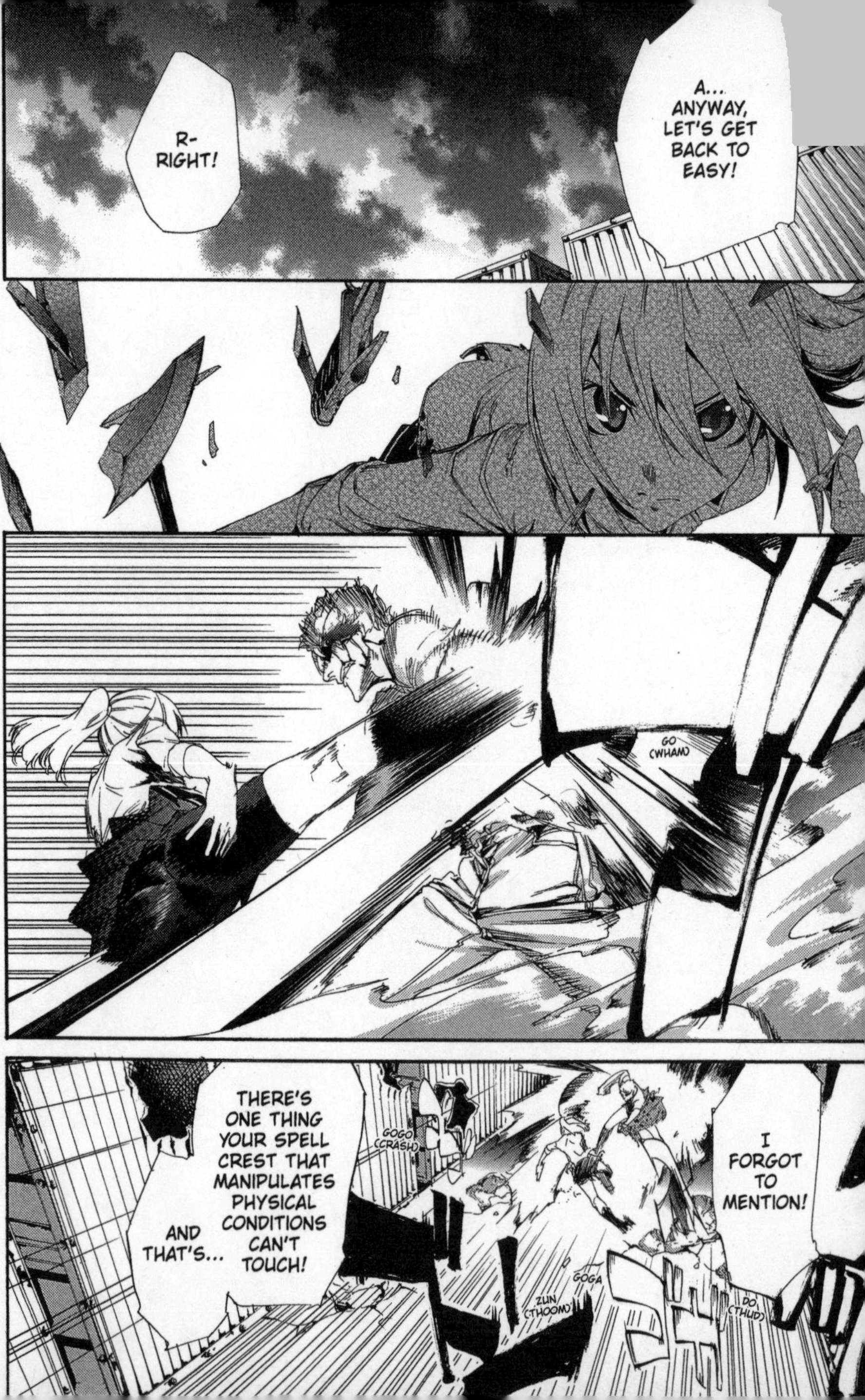
A... ANYWAY, LET'S GET BACK TO EASY!
R-RIGHT!
GO (WHAM)
I FORGOT TO MENTION!
DO (THUD)
GOGA
ZUN (THOOM)
GOGO (CRASH)
THERE'S ONE THING YOUR SPELL CREST THAT MANIPULATES PHYSICAL CONDITIONS CAN'T TOUCH!
AND THAT'S...

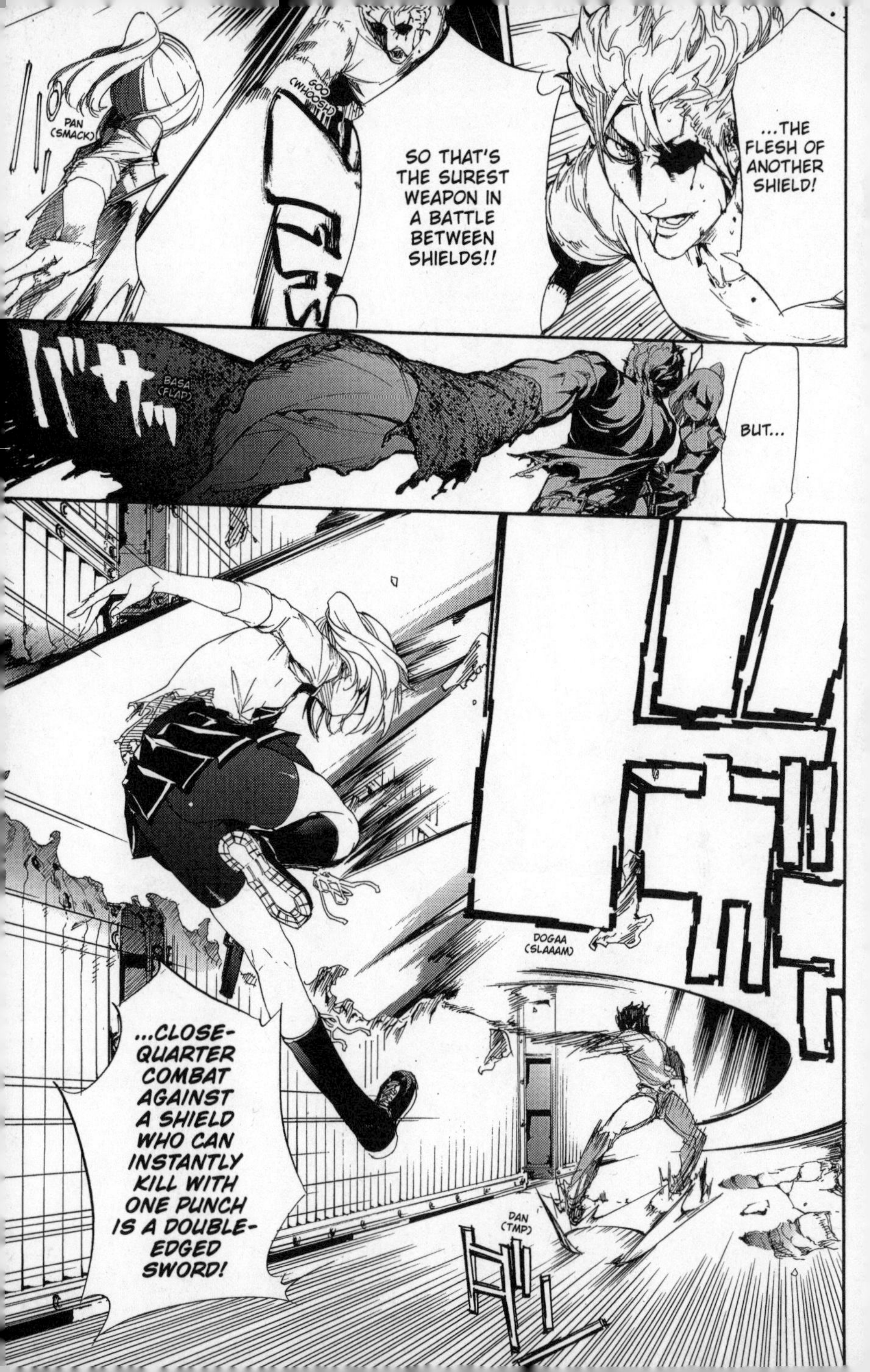
...THE FLESH OF ANOTHER SHIELD!
SO THAT'S THE SUREST WEAPON IN A BATTLE BETWEEN SHIELDS!!
GOO (WHOOSH)
PAN (SMACK)
BUT...
BASA (FLAP)
DOGAA (SLAAAM)
DAN (TMP)
...CLOSE-QUARTER COMBAT AGAINST A SHIELD WHO CAN INSTANTLY KILL WITH ONE PUNCH IS A DOUBLE-EDGED SWORD!

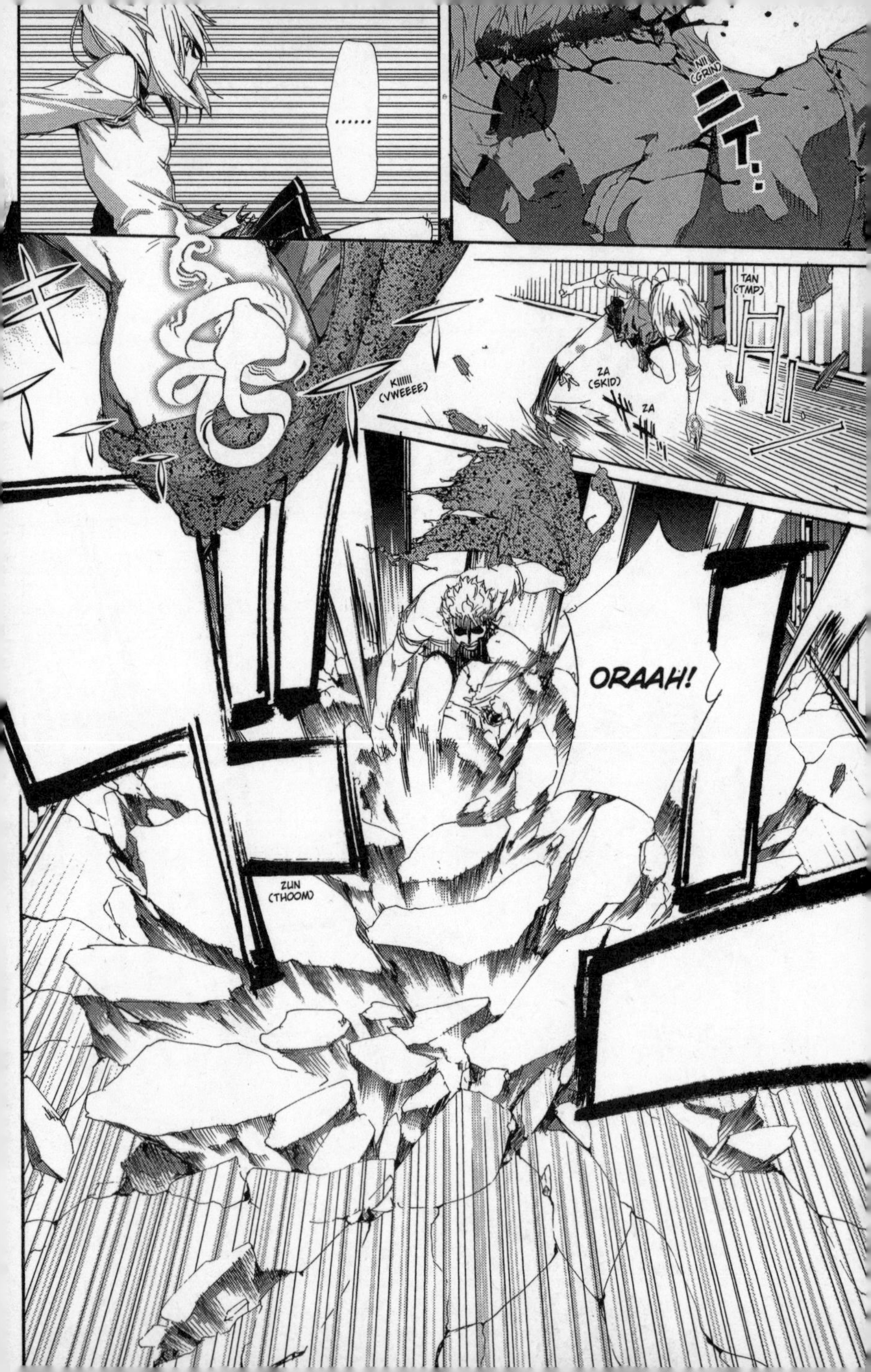
NII (GRIN)
……
TAN (TMP)
ZA (SKID)
ZA
KIIIII (VWEEEE)
ORAAH!
ZUN (THOOM)

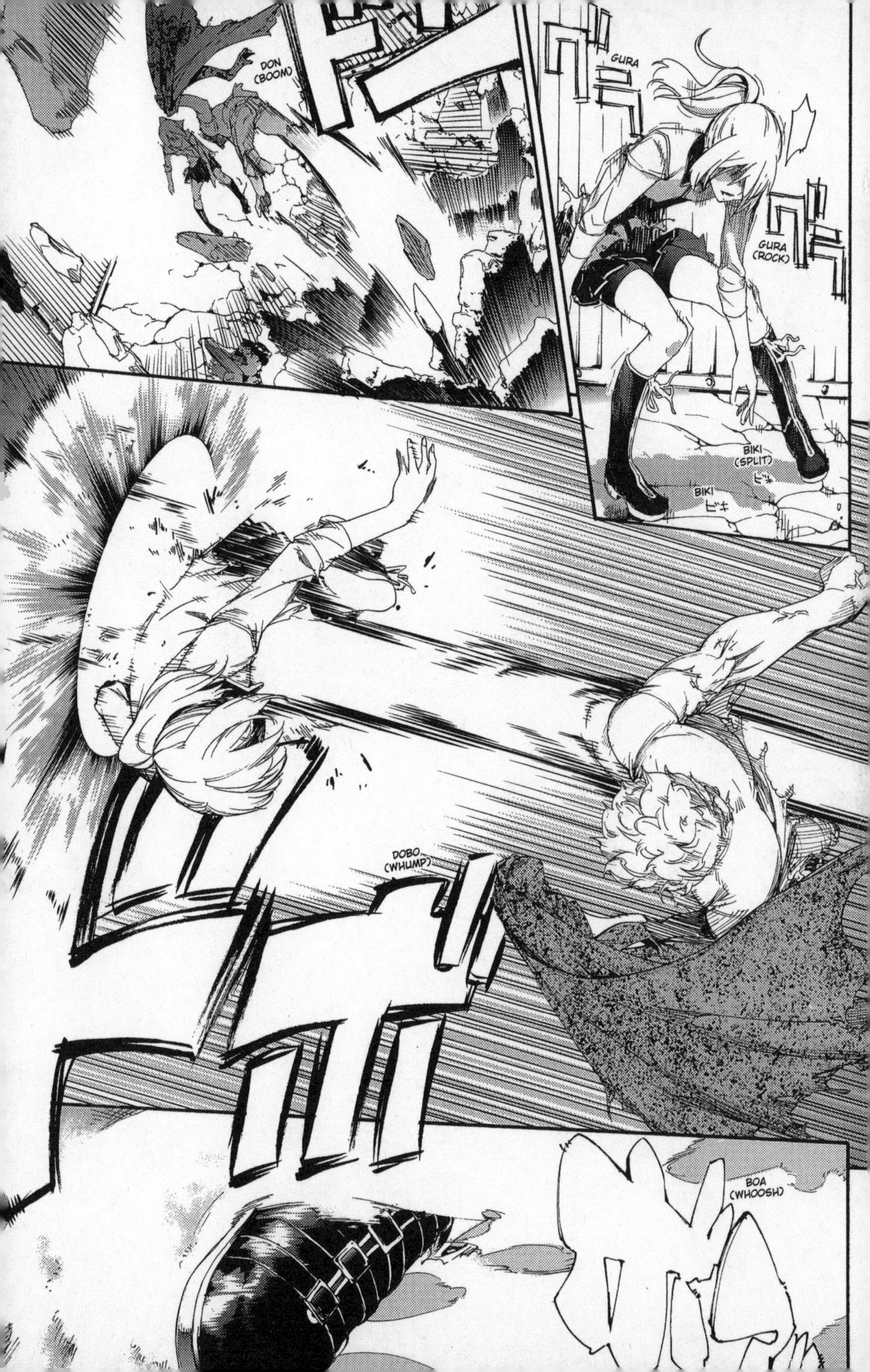
GURA
GURA (ROCK)
BIKI (SPLIT)
ビキ
BIKI
ビキ
DON (BOOM)
DOBO (WHUMP)
BOA (WHOOSH)

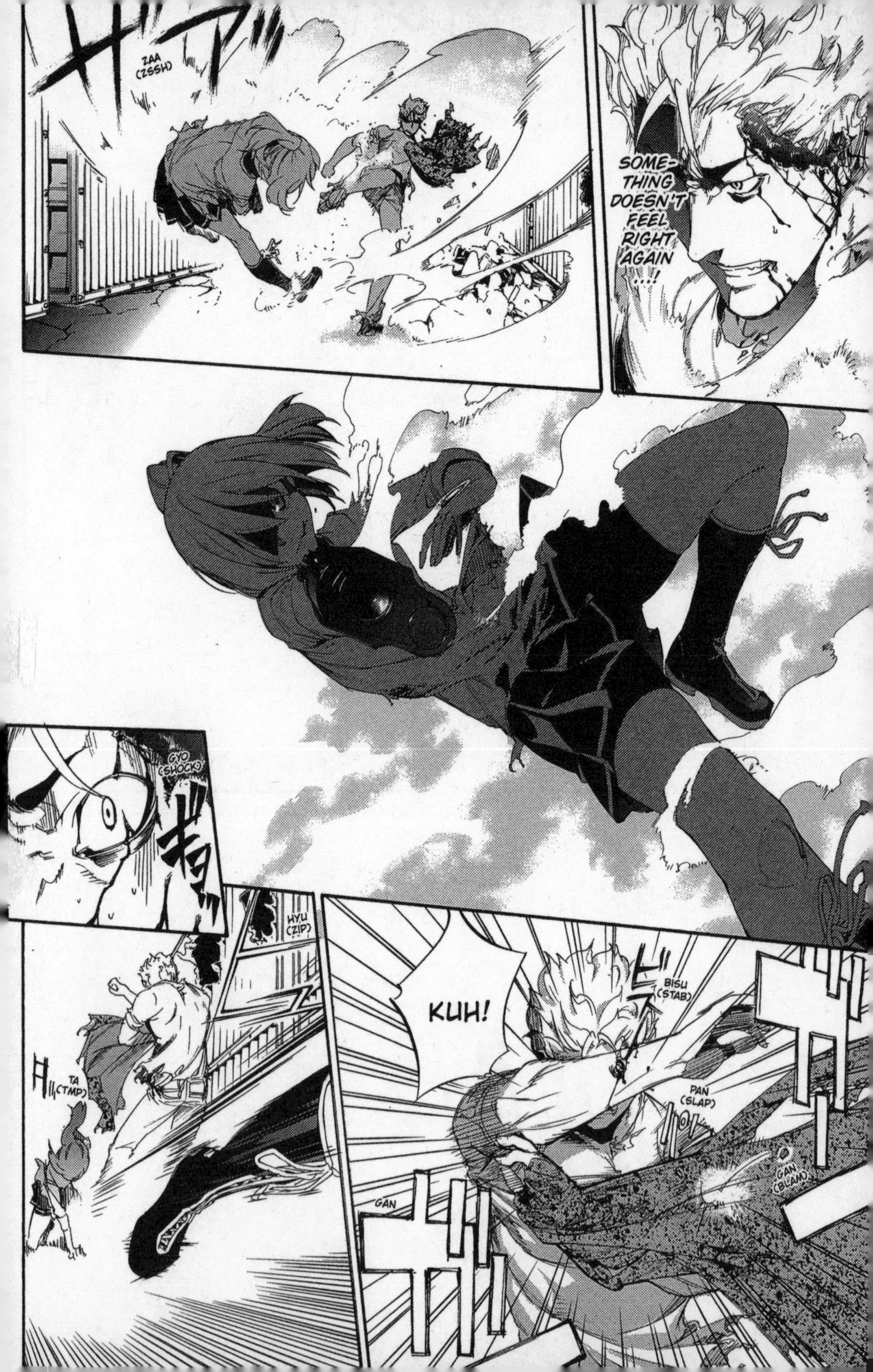
SOMETHING DOESN'T FEEL RIGHT AGAIN ...!
ZAA (ZSSH)
GYO (SHOCK)
KUH!
BISU (STAB)
PAN (SLAP)
GAN (BLAM)
GAN
HYU (ZIP)
TA (TMP)

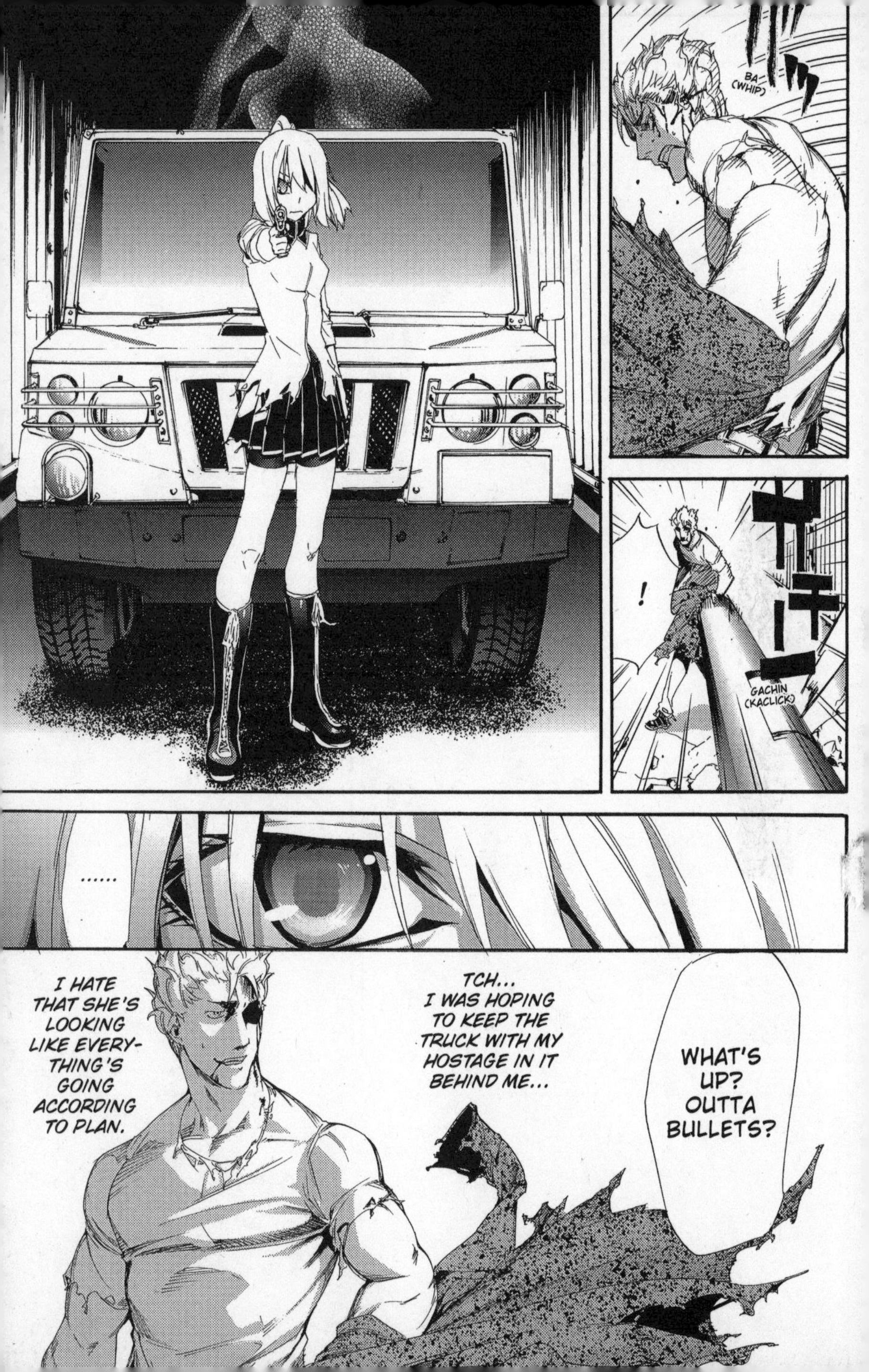
BA-
(WHIP)
!
GACHIN
(KACLICK)
......
WHAT'S UP? OUTTA BULLETS?
TCH... I WAS HOPING TO KEEP THE TRUCK WITH MY HOSTAGE IN IT BEHIND ME...
I HATE THAT SHE'S LOOKING LIKE EVERY-THING'S GOING ACCORDING TO PLAN.

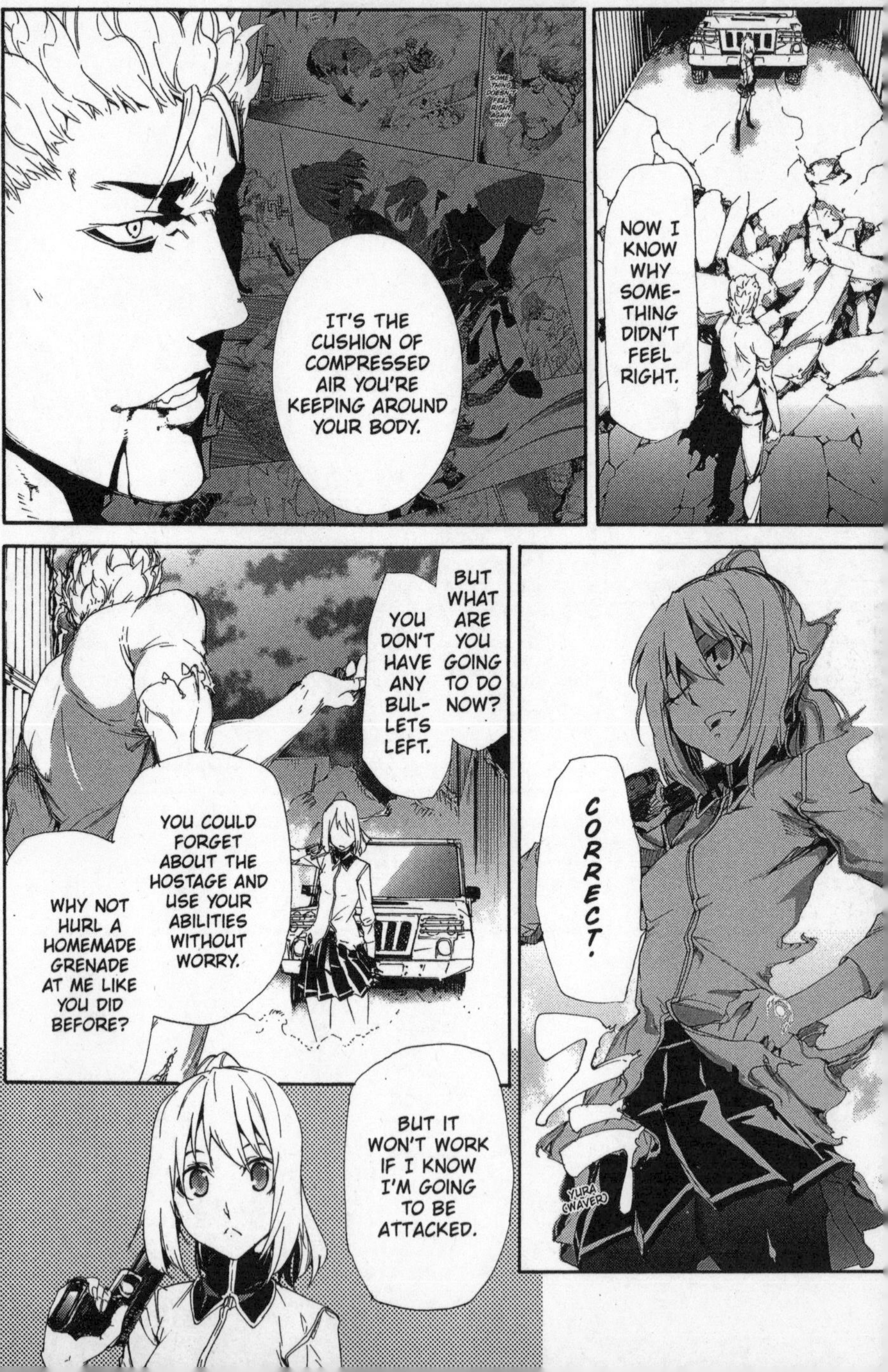
NOW I KNOW WHY SOMETHING DIDN'T FEEL RIGHT.
SOMETHING DOESN'T FEEL RIGHT AGAIN...!
IT'S THE CUSHION OF COMPRESSED AIR YOU'RE KEEPING AROUND YOUR BODY.
CORRECT.
YURA (WAVER)
BUT WHAT ARE YOU GOING TO DO NOW?
YOU DON'T HAVE ANY BULLETS LEFT.
YOU COULD FORGET ABOUT THE HOSTAGE AND USE YOUR ABILITIES WITHOUT WORRY.
WHY NOT HURL A HOMEMADE GRENADE AT ME LIKE YOU DID BEFORE?
BUT IT WON'T WORK IF I KNOW I'M GOING TO BE ATTACKED.

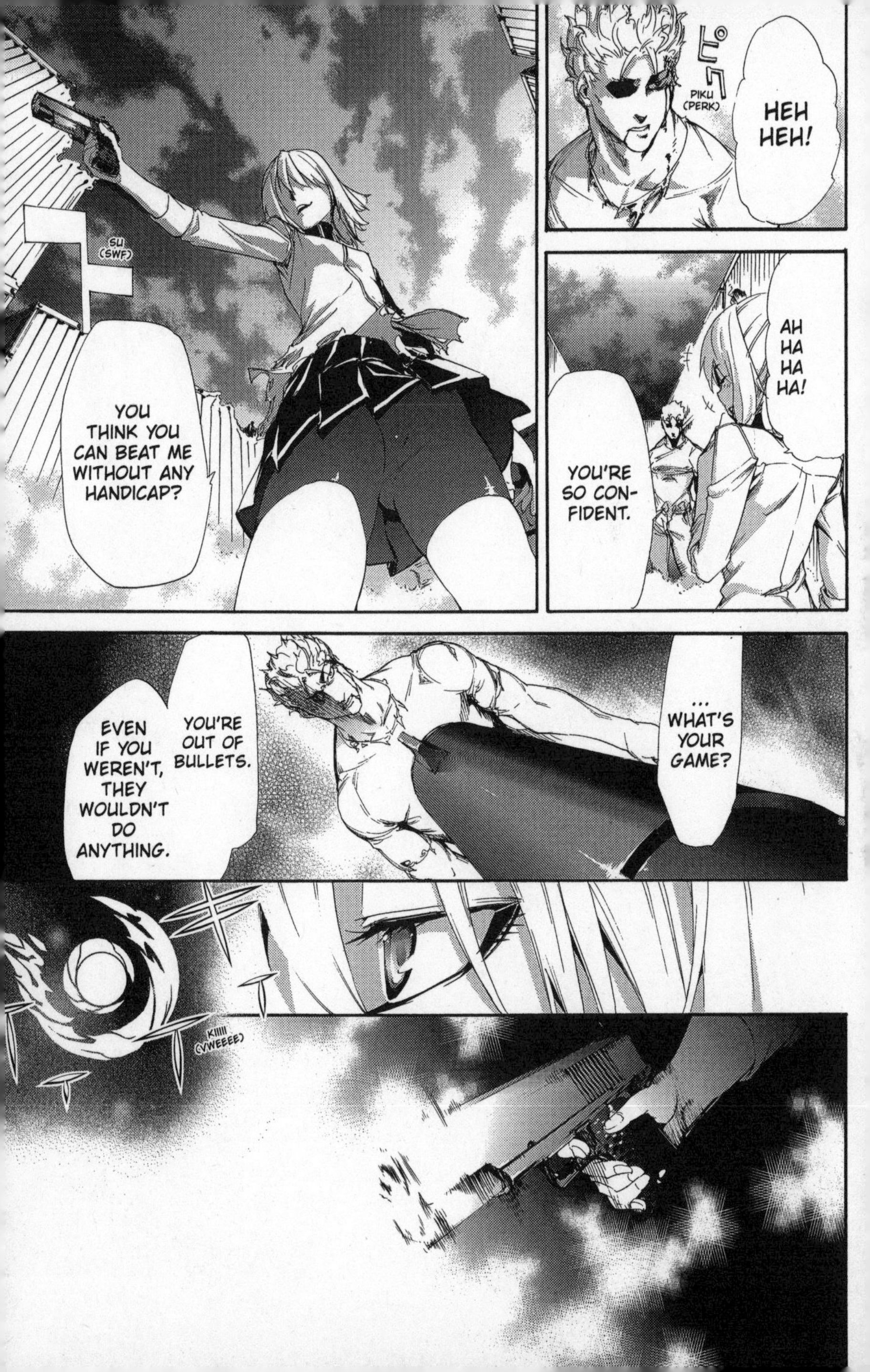
PIKU (PERK)
HEH HEH!
AH HA HA HA!
YOU'RE SO CON-FIDENT.
SU (SWF)
YOU THINK YOU CAN BEAT ME WITHOUT ANY HANDICAP?
... WHAT'S YOUR GAME?
YOU'RE OUT OF BULLETS.
EVEN IF YOU WEREN'T, THEY WOULDN'T DO ANYTHING.
KIIII (VWEEEE)

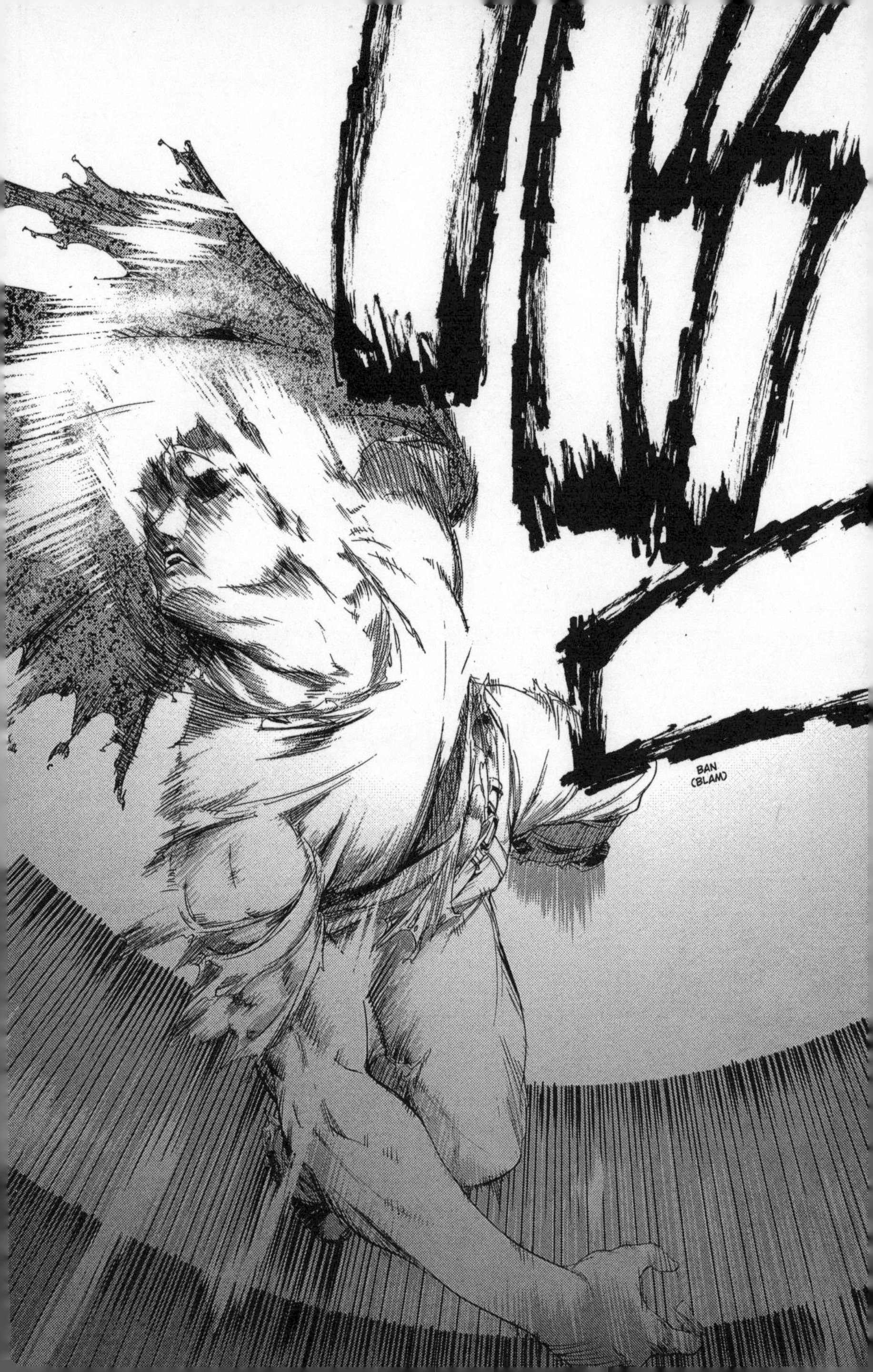
BAN
(BLAM)

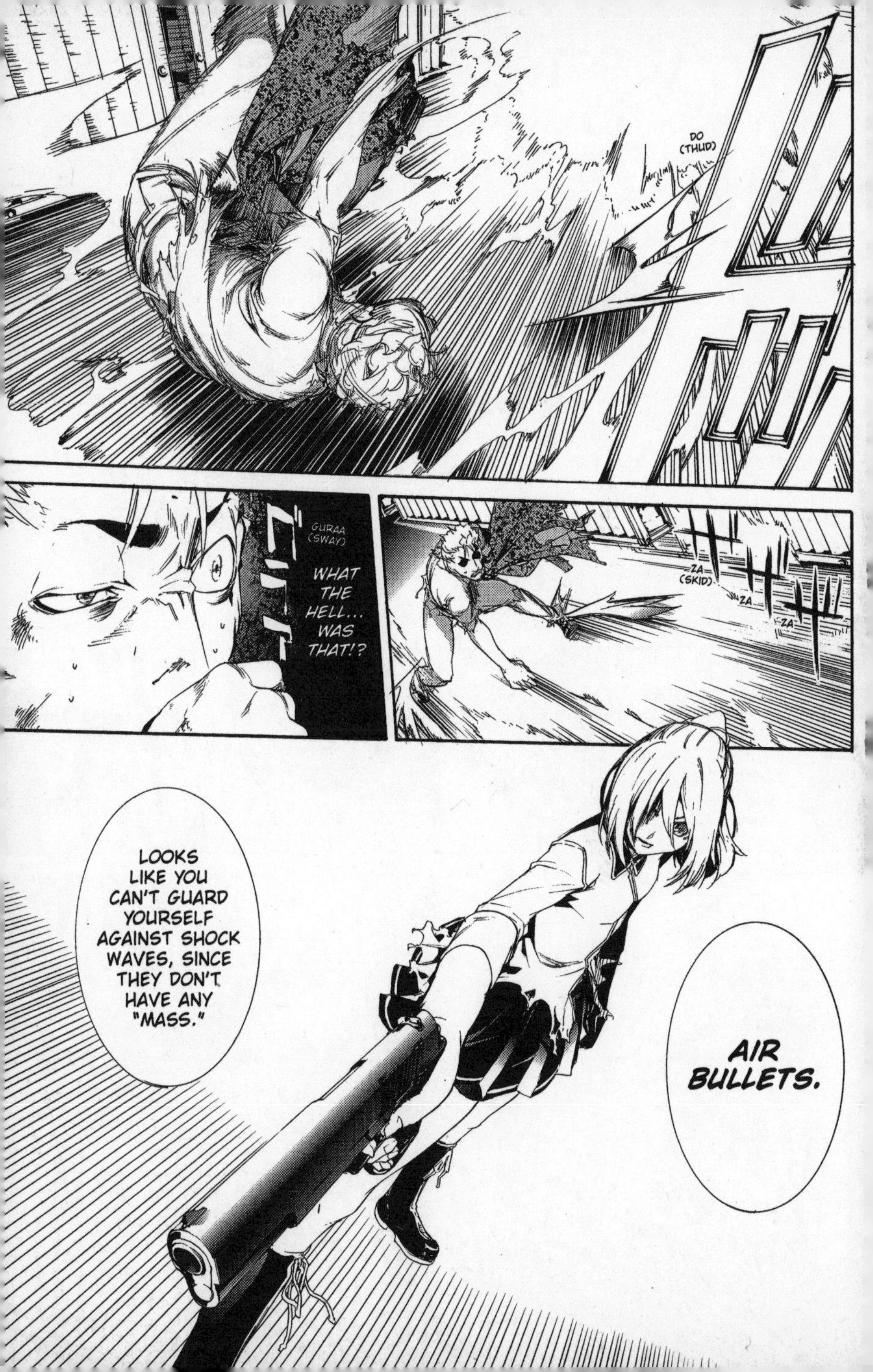
DO
(THUD)
ZA
(SKID)
ZA
ZA
GURAA
(SWAY)
WHAT THE HELL... WAS THAT!?
AIR BULLETS.
LOOKS LIKE YOU CAN'T GUARD YOURSELF AGAINST SHOCK WAVES, SINCE THEY DON'T HAVE ANY "MASS."

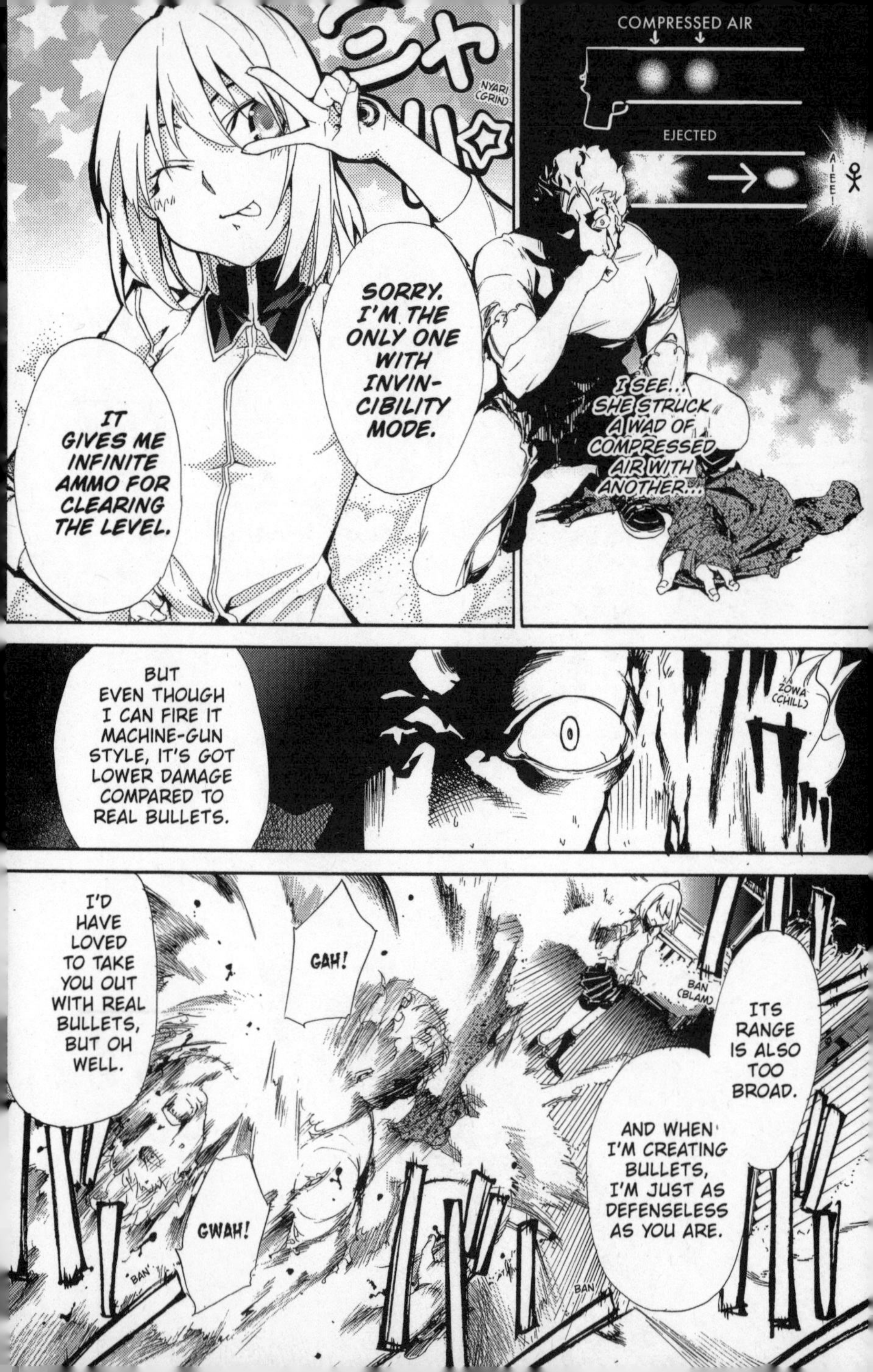
COMPRESSED AIR
EJECTED
AIEE!
I SEE... SHE STRUCK A WAD OF COMPRESSED AIR WITH ANOTHER...
NYARI (GRIN)
SORRY. I'M THE ONLY ONE WITH INVIN-CIBILITY MODE.
IT GIVES ME INFINITE AMMO FOR CLEARING THE LEVEL.
ZOWA (CHILL)
BUT EVEN THOUGH I CAN FIRE IT MACHINE-GUN STYLE, IT'S GOT LOWER DAMAGE COMPARED TO REAL BULLETS.
ITS RANGE IS ALSO TOO BROAD.
BAN (BLAM)
AND WHEN I'M CREATING BULLETS, I'M JUST AS DEFENSELESS AS YOU ARE.
GAH!
I'D HAVE LOVED TO TAKE YOU OUT WITH REAL BULLETS, BUT OH WELL.
GWAH!
BAN
BAN

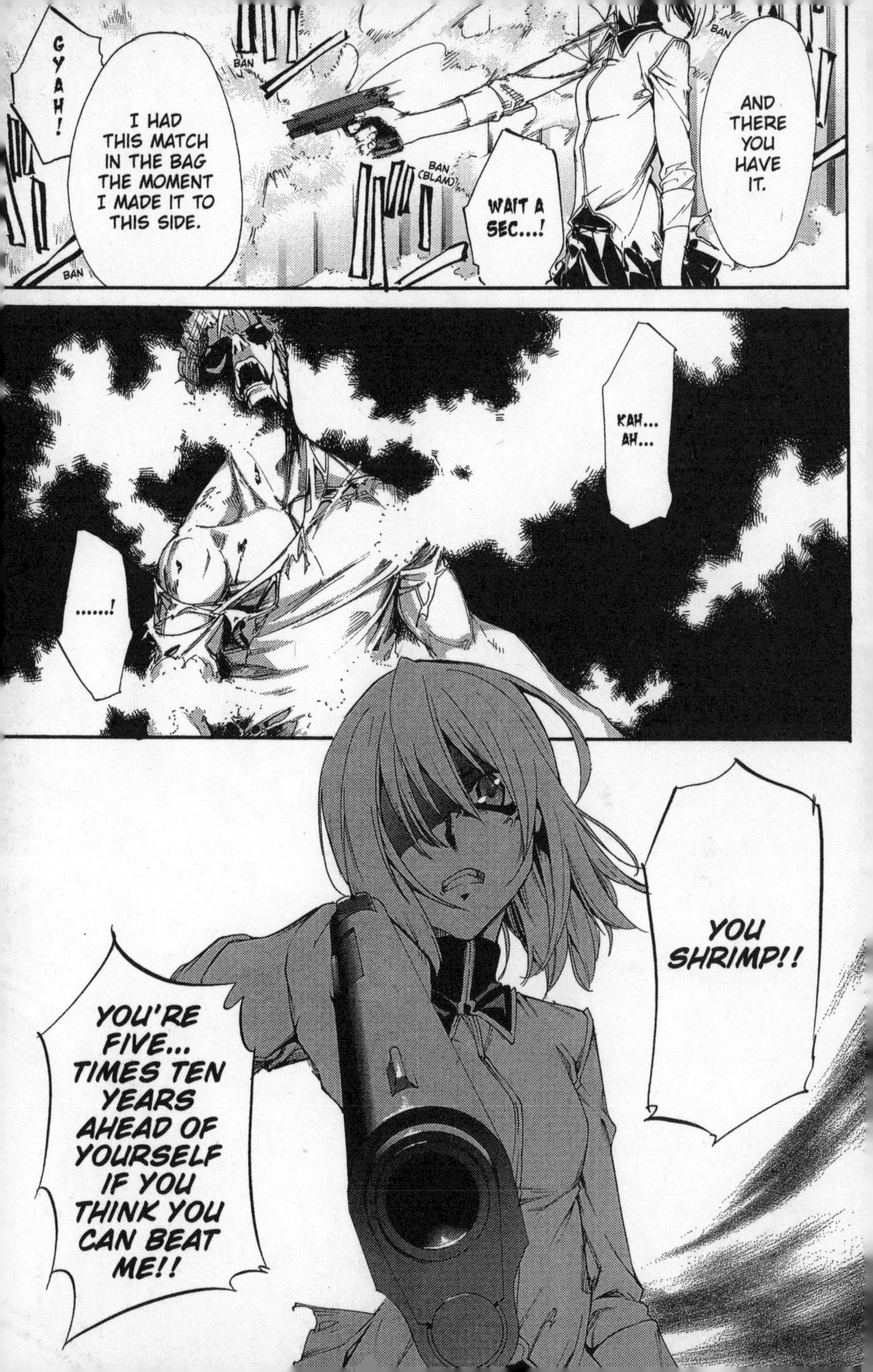
AND THERE YOU HAVE IT.
BAN
WAIT A SEC...!
BAN (BLAM)
BAN
I HAD THIS MATCH IN THE BAG THE MOMENT I MADE IT TO THIS SIDE.
GYAH!
BAN
KAH... AH...
......!
YOU SHRIMP!!
YOU'RE FIVE... TIMES TEN YEARS AHEAD OF YOURSELF IF YOU THINK YOU CAN BEAT ME!!

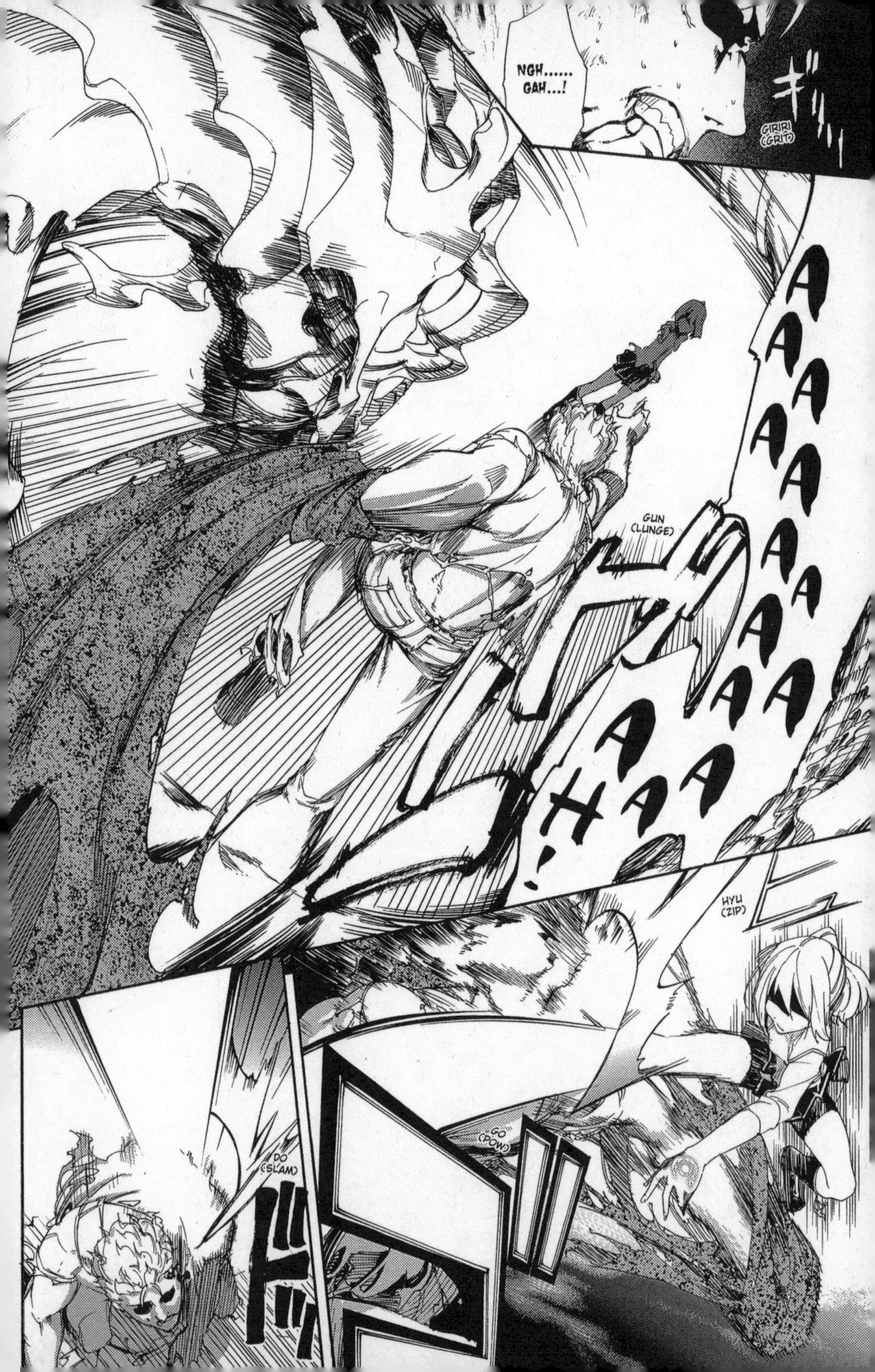
GIRIRI (GRIT)
NGH...... GAH...!
GUN (LUNGE)
AAAAAAAAAAAAAAH!
HYU (ZIP)
GO (POW)
DO (SLAM)

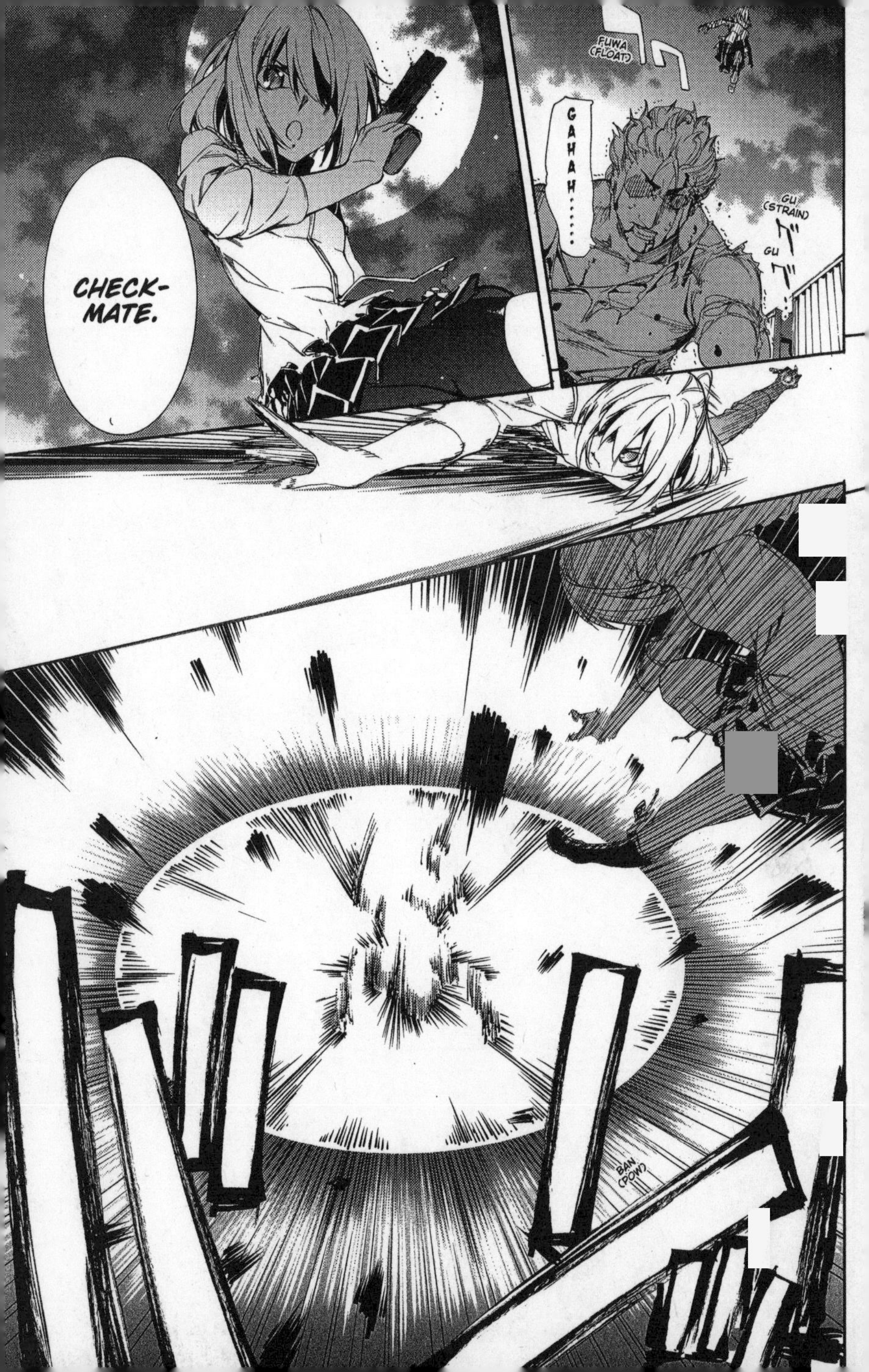
FUWA (FLOAT)
GAHAH......
GU (STRAIN)
GU
CHECK-MATE.
BAN (POW)

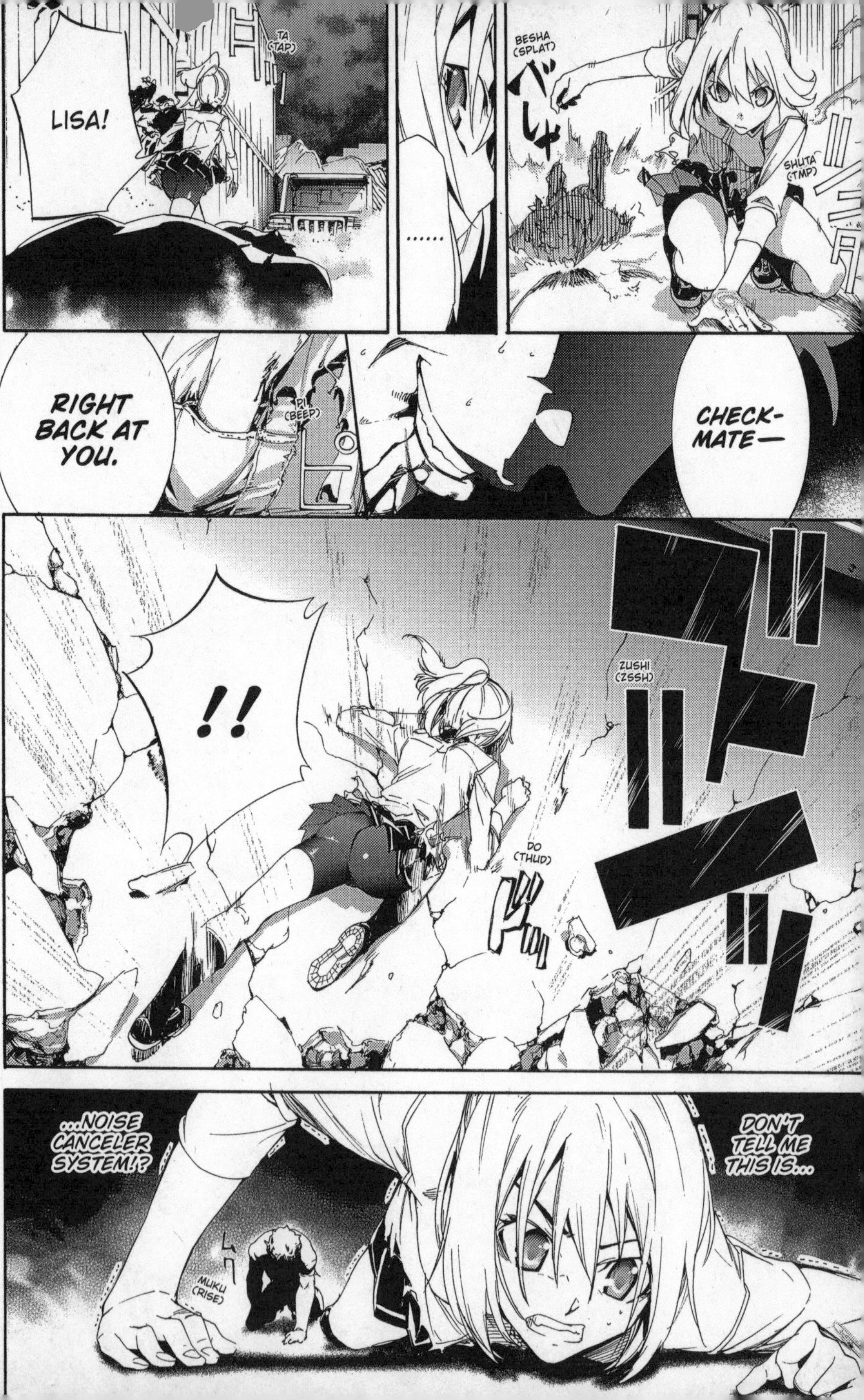
BESHA (SPLAT)
SHUTA (TMP)
......
TA (TAP)
LISA!
CHECK-MATE—
PI (BEEP)
RIGHT BACK AT YOU.
ZUSHI (ZSSH)
DO (THUD)
!!
DON'T TELL ME THIS IS...
...NOISE CANCELER SYSTEM!?
MUKU (RISE)

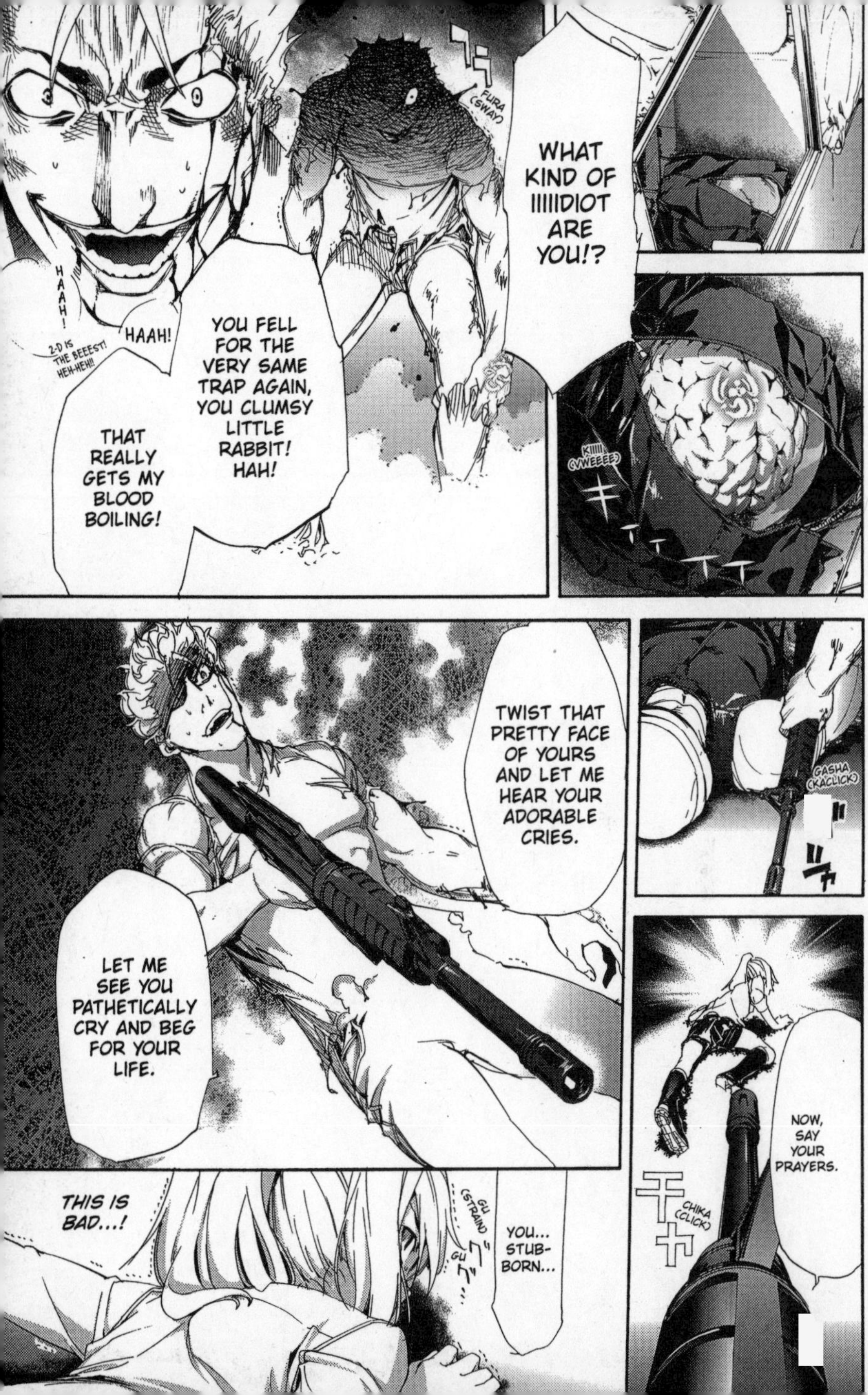
KIIII (VWEEEE)
FURA (SWAY)
WHAT KIND OF IIIIIDIOT ARE YOU!?
HAAAH!
HAAH!
2-D IS THE BEEEST! HEH-HEH!!
YOU FELL FOR THE VERY SAME TRAP AGAIN, YOU CLUMSY LITTLE RABBIT! HAH!
THAT REALLY GETS MY BLOOD BOILING!
GASHA (KACLICK)
TWIST THAT PRETTY FACE OF YOURS AND LET ME HEAR YOUR ADORABLE CRIES.
LET ME SEE YOU PATHETICALLY CRY AND BEG FOR YOUR LIFE.
NOW, SAY YOUR PRAYERS.
CHIKA (CLICK)
GU (STRAIN) GU
YOU... STUBBORN...
THIS IS BAD...!

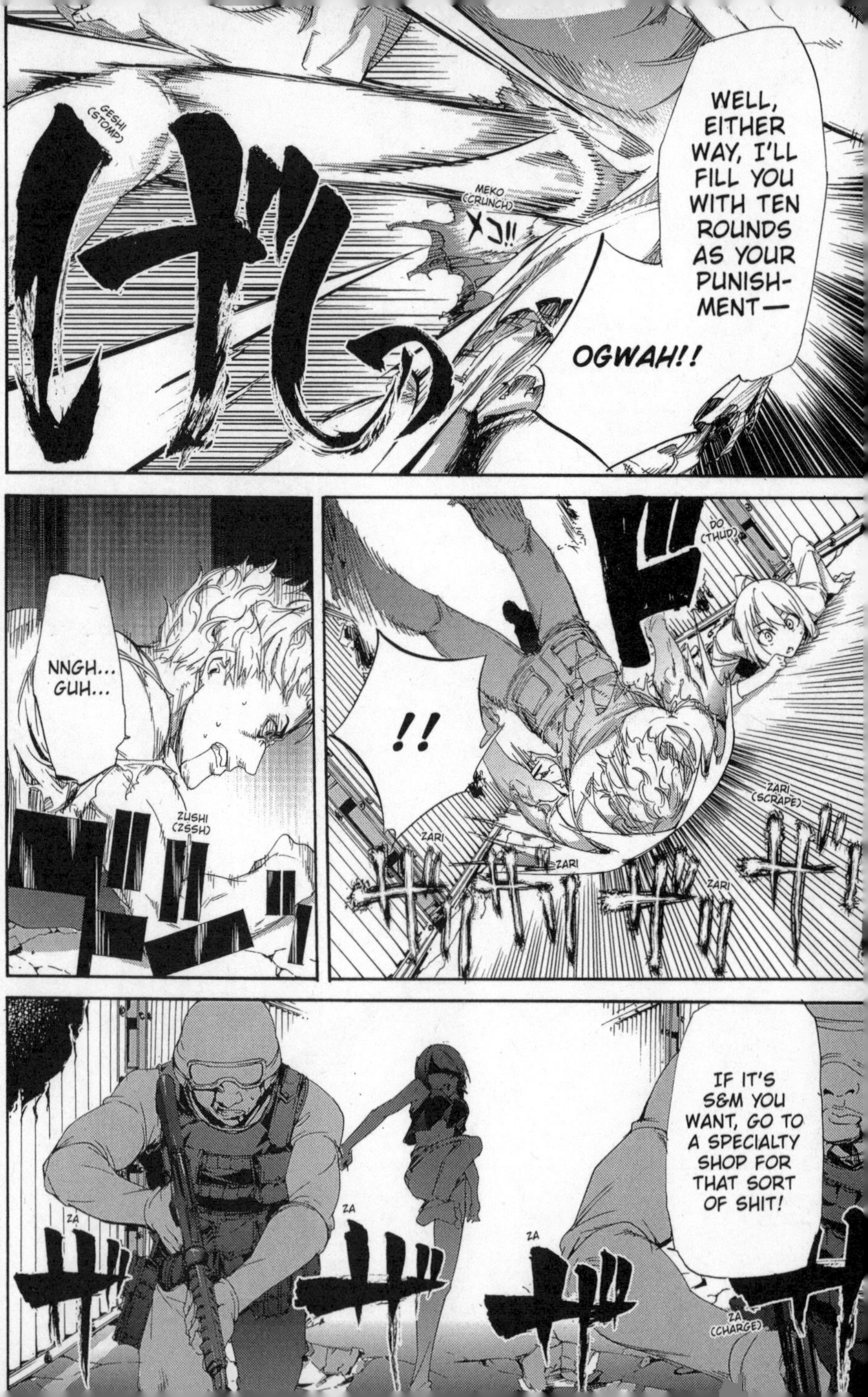
WELL, EITHER WAY, I'LL FILL YOU WITH TEN ROUNDS AS YOUR PUNISHMENT—
MEKO (CRUNCH)
メコ!!
OGWAH!!
GESHI (STOMP)
DO (THUD)
!!
ZARI (SCRAPE)
ZARI
ZARI
ZARI
NNGH... GUH...
ZUSHI (ZSSH)
IF IT'S S&M YOU WANT, GO TO A SPECIALTY SHOP FOR THAT SORT OF SHIT!
ZA (CHARGE)
ZA
ZA
ZA

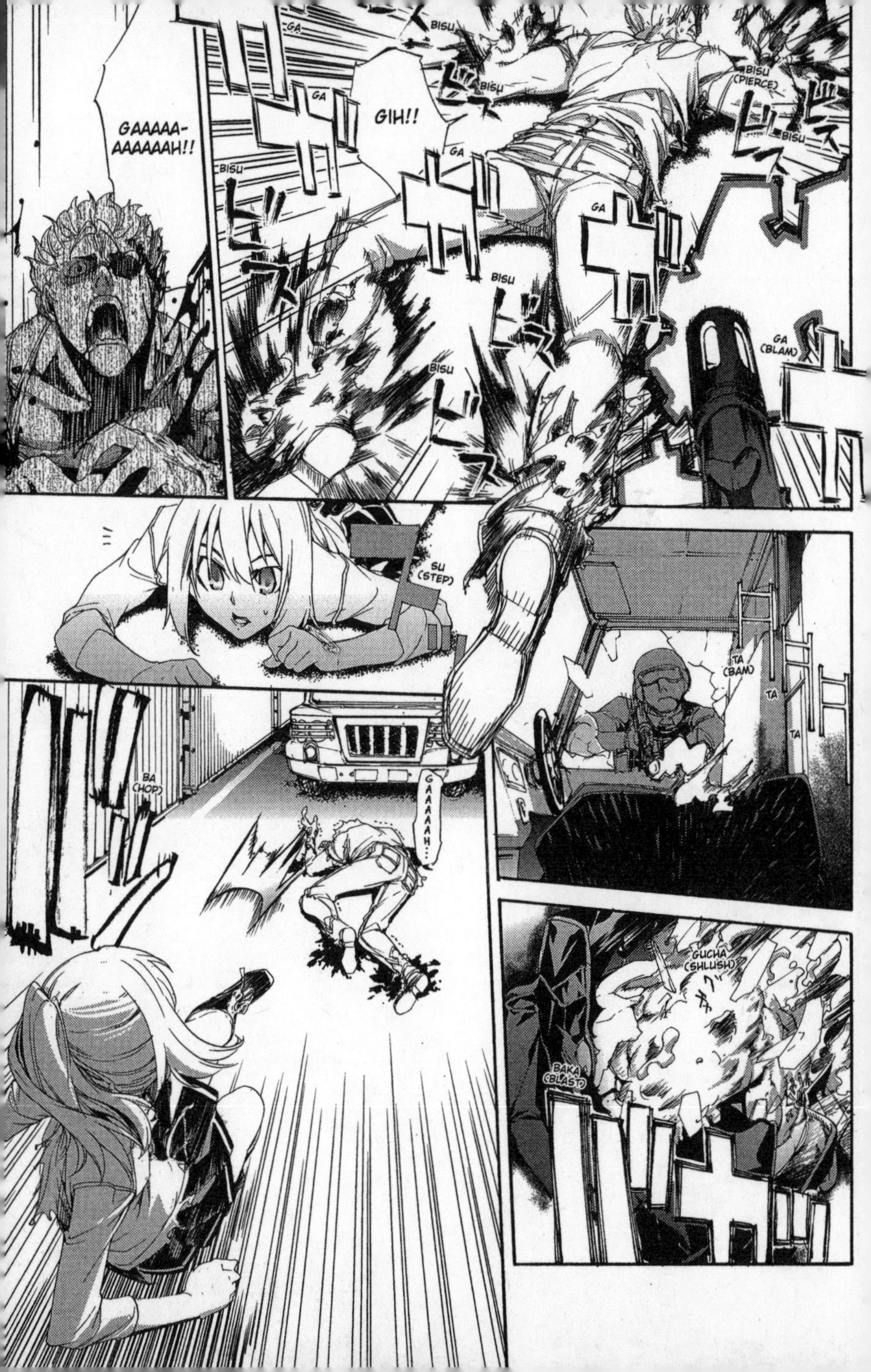
BISU (PIERCE)
BISU
BISU
BISU
GA
GA
GIH!!
GA
GA
BISU
BISU
BISU
BISU
GA (BLAM)
GAAAAA-AAAAAAH!!
TA (BAM)
TA
TA
SU (STEP)
GUCHA (SHLUSH)
BAKA (BLAST)
BA (HOP)
GAAAAAAH...

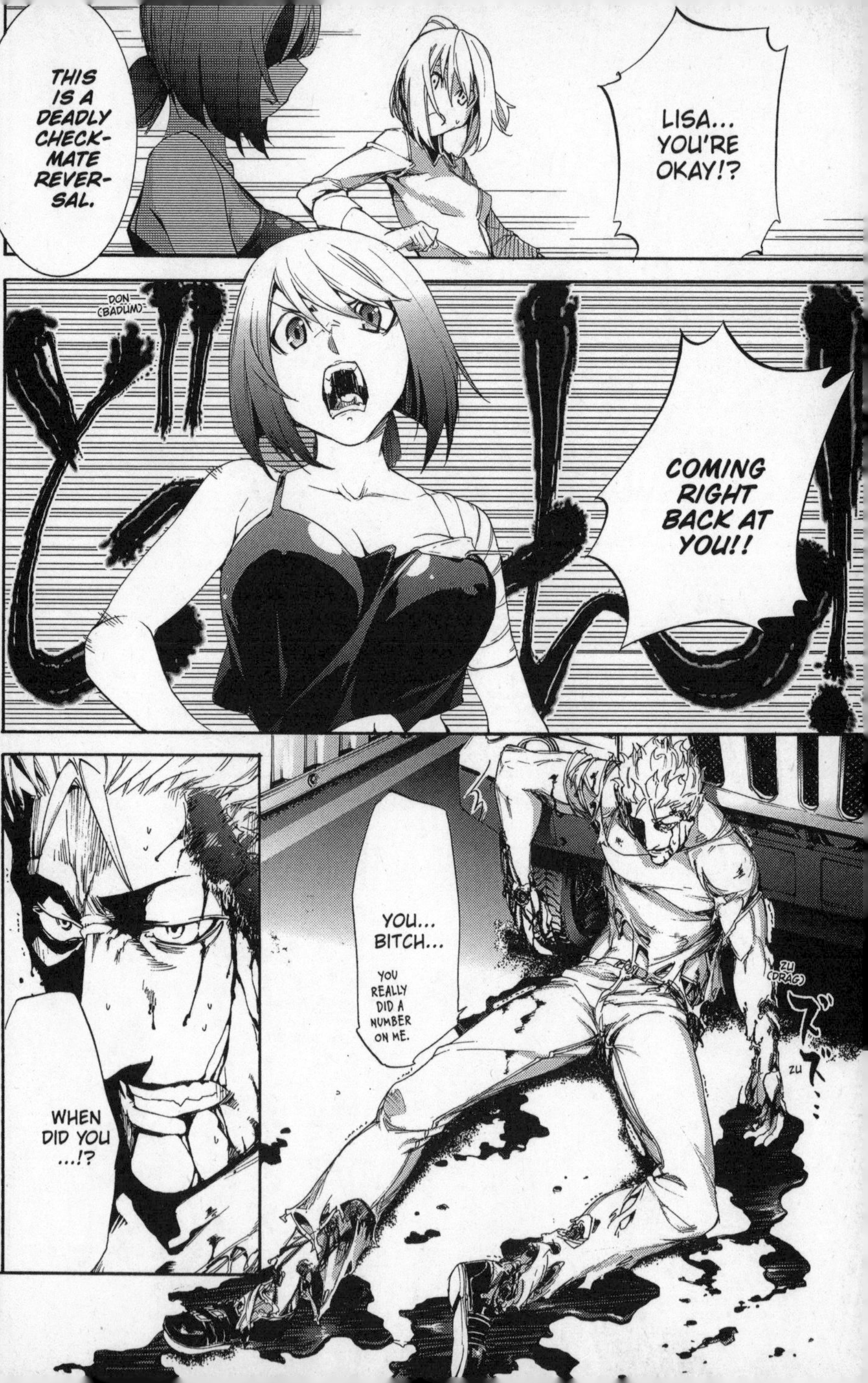
LISA... YOU'RE OKAY!?
THIS IS A DEADLY CHECK-MATE REVER-SAL.
COMING RIGHT BACK AT YOU!!
DON (BADUM)
YOU... BITCH...
YOU REALLY DID A NUMBER ON ME.
ZU (DRAG)
ZU
WHEN DID YOU ...!?

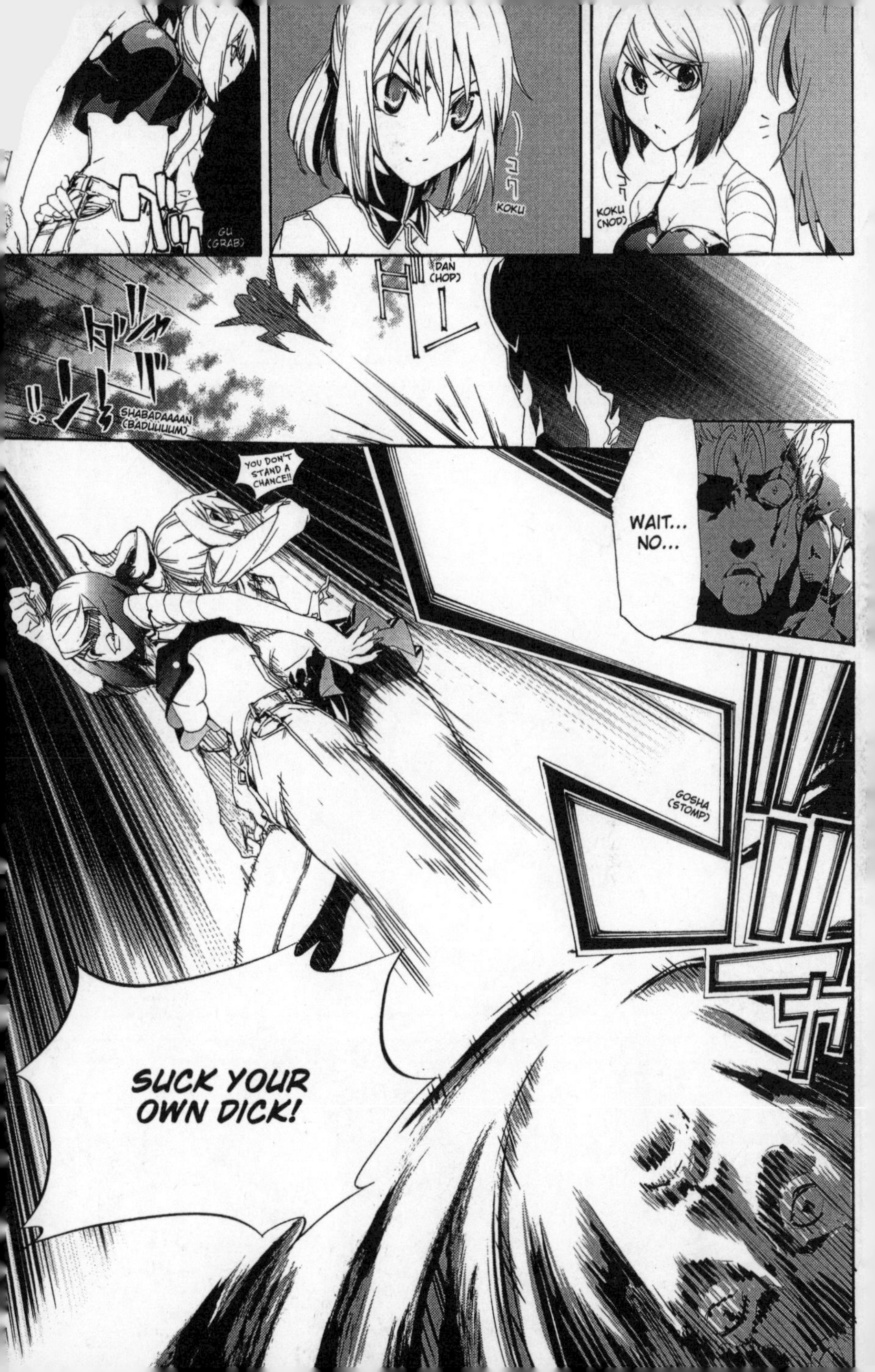
KOKU (NOD)
KOKU
GU (GRAB)
DAN (HOP)
SHABADAAAAN (BADUUUUM)
WAIT... NO...
YOU DON'T STAND A CHANCE!!
GOSHA (STOMP)
SUCK YOUR OWN DICK!

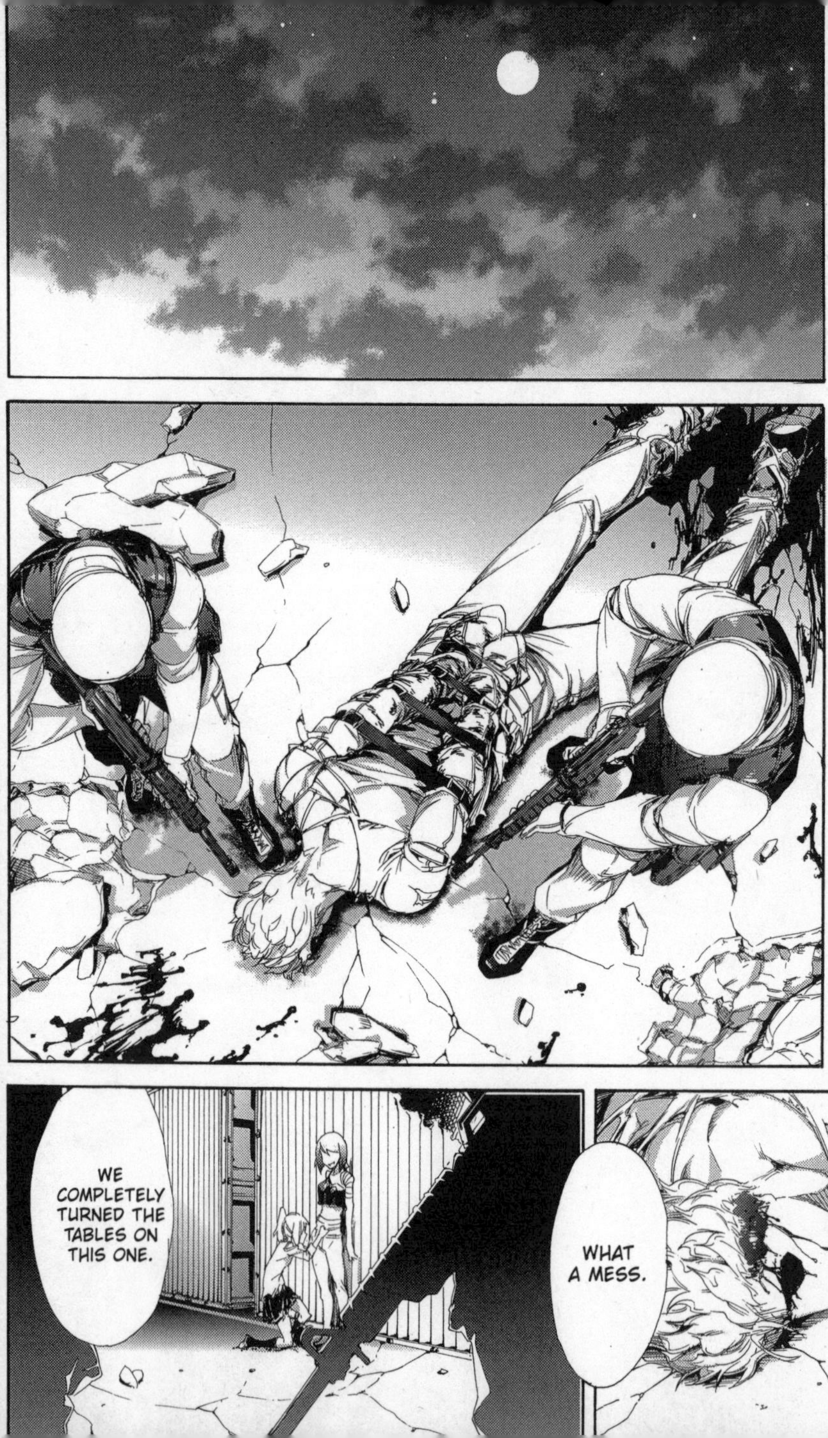
WHAT A MESS.
WE COMPLETELY TURNED THE TABLES ON THIS ONE.

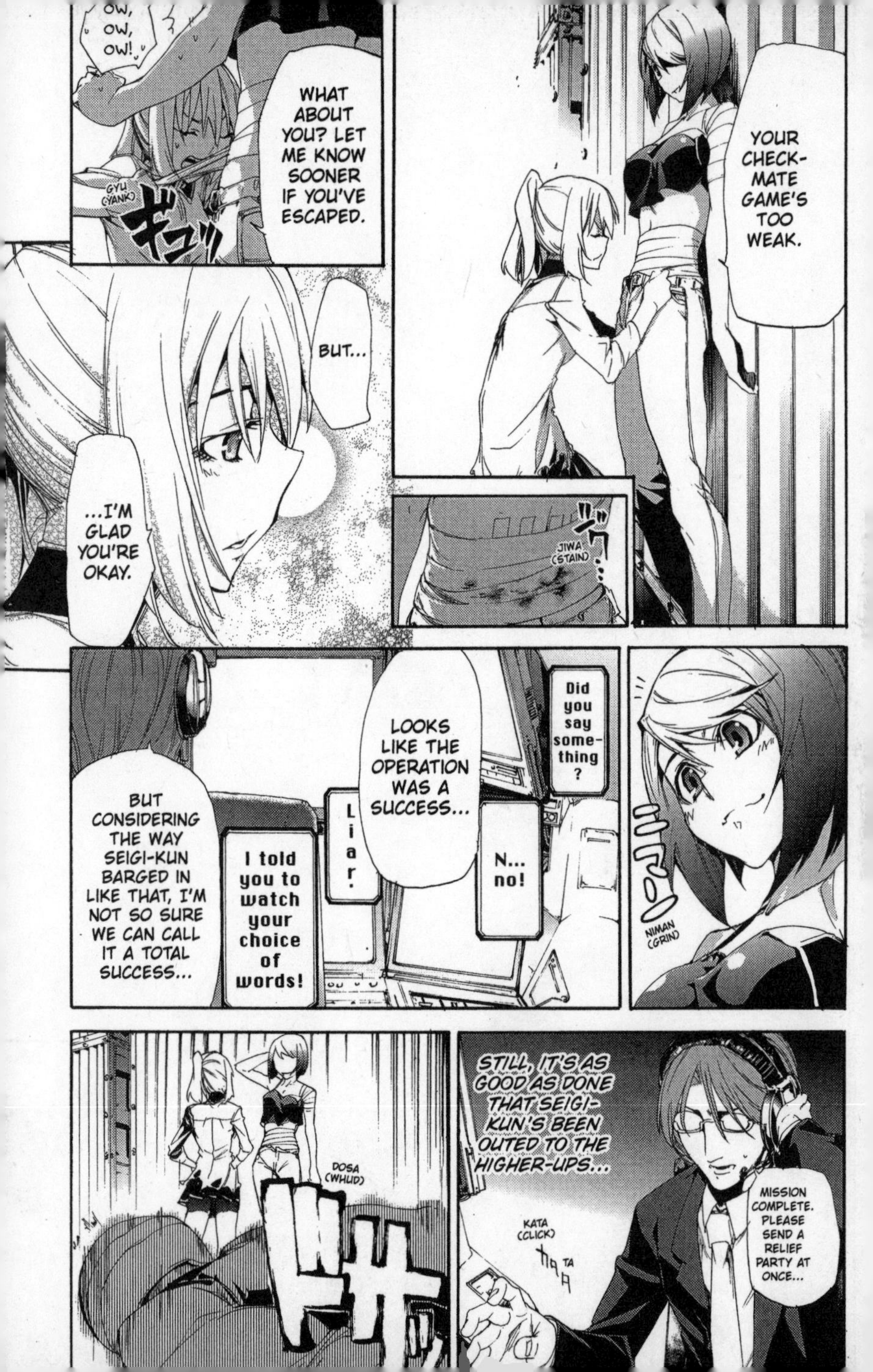
YOUR CHECKMATE GAME'S TOO WEAK.
OW, OW, OW!
WHAT ABOUT YOU? LET ME KNOW SOONER IF YOU'VE ESCAPED.
GYU (YANK)
JIWA (STAIN)
BUT...
...I'M GLAD YOU'RE OKAY.
Did you say something?
NIMAN (GRIN)
LOOKS LIKE THE OPERATION WAS A SUCCESS...
N... no!
Liar.
I told you to watch your choice of words!
BUT CONSIDERING THE WAY SEIGI-KUN BARGED IN LIKE THAT, I'M NOT SO SURE WE CAN CALL IT A TOTAL SUCCESS...
STILL, IT'S AS GOOD AS DONE THAT SEIGI-KUN'S BEEN OUTED TO THE HIGHER-UPS...
MISSION COMPLETE. PLEASE SEND A RELIEF PARTY AT ONCE...
KATA (CLICK)
DOSA (WHUD)

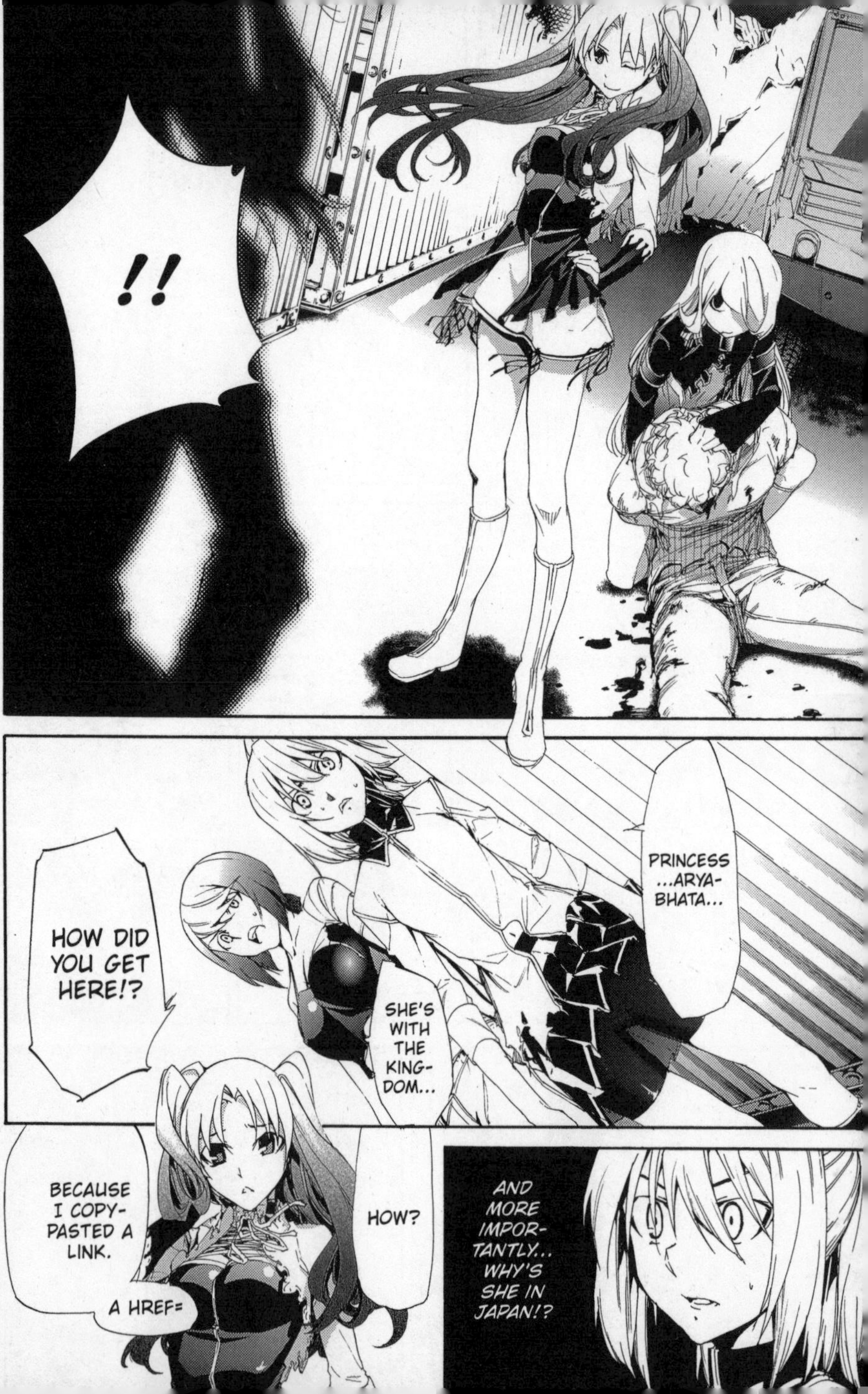
!!
PRINCESS ...ARYA-BHATA...
SHE'S WITH THE KING-DOM...
HOW DID YOU GET HERE!?
AND MORE IMPOR-TANTLY... WHY'S SHE IN JAPAN!?
HOW?
BECAUSE I COPY-PASTED A LINK.
A HREF=

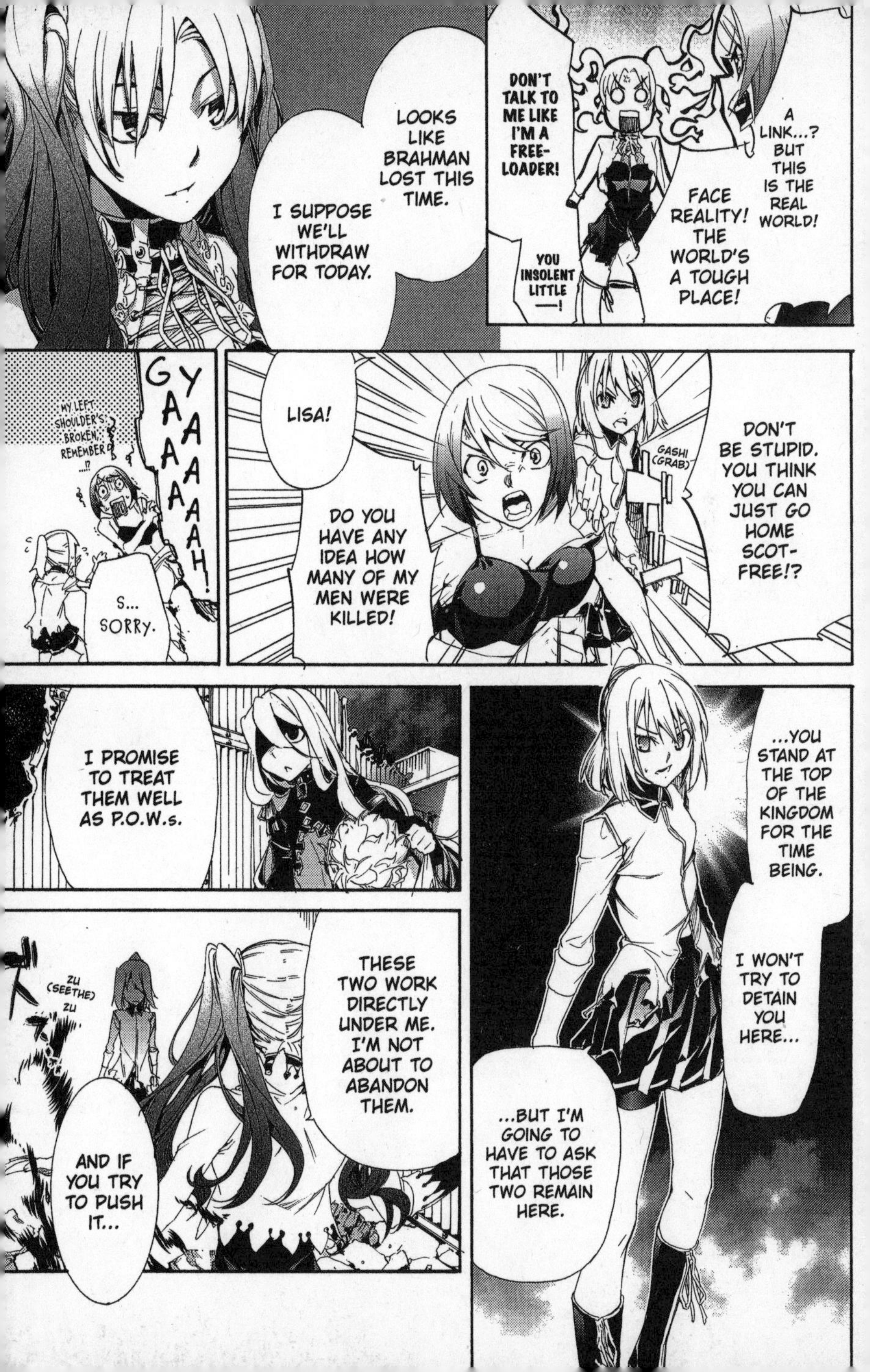
A LINK...? BUT THIS IS THE REAL WORLD!
FACE REALITY! THE WORLD'S A TOUGH PLACE!
DON'T TALK TO ME LIKE I'M A FREE-LOADER!
YOU INSOLENT LITTLE —!
LOOKS LIKE BRAHMAN LOST THIS TIME.
I SUPPOSE WE'LL WITHDRAW FOR TODAY.
DON'T BE STUPID. YOU THINK YOU CAN JUST GO HOME SCOT-FREE!?
GASHI (GRAB)
LISA!
DO YOU HAVE ANY IDEA HOW MANY OF MY MEN WERE KILLED!
GYAAAAAAAAH!
MY LEFT SHOULDER'S BROKEN, REMEMBER ...!?
S... SORRY.
...YOU STAND AT THE TOP OF THE KINGDOM FOR THE TIME BEING.
I WON'T TRY TO DETAIN YOU HERE...
...BUT I'M GOING TO HAVE TO ASK THAT THOSE TWO REMAIN HERE.
I PROMISE TO TREAT THEM WELL AS P.O.W.s.
THESE TWO WORK DIRECTLY UNDER ME. I'M NOT ABOUT TO ABANDON THEM.
ZU (SEETHE) ZU
AND IF YOU TRY TO PUSH IT...

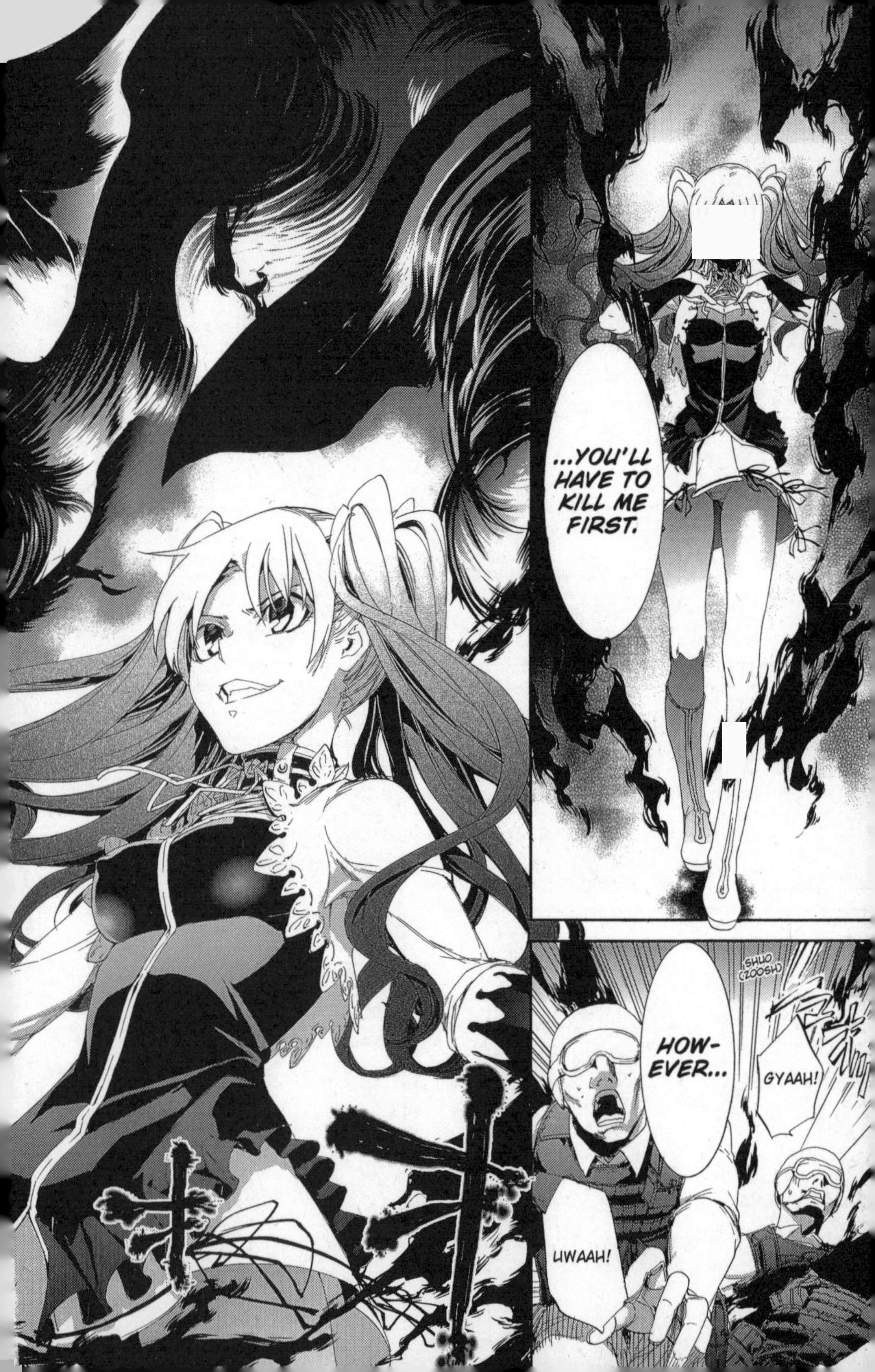
...YOU'LL HAVE TO KILL ME FIRST.
SHUO (ZOOSH)
HOW-EVER...
GYAAH!
UWAAH!

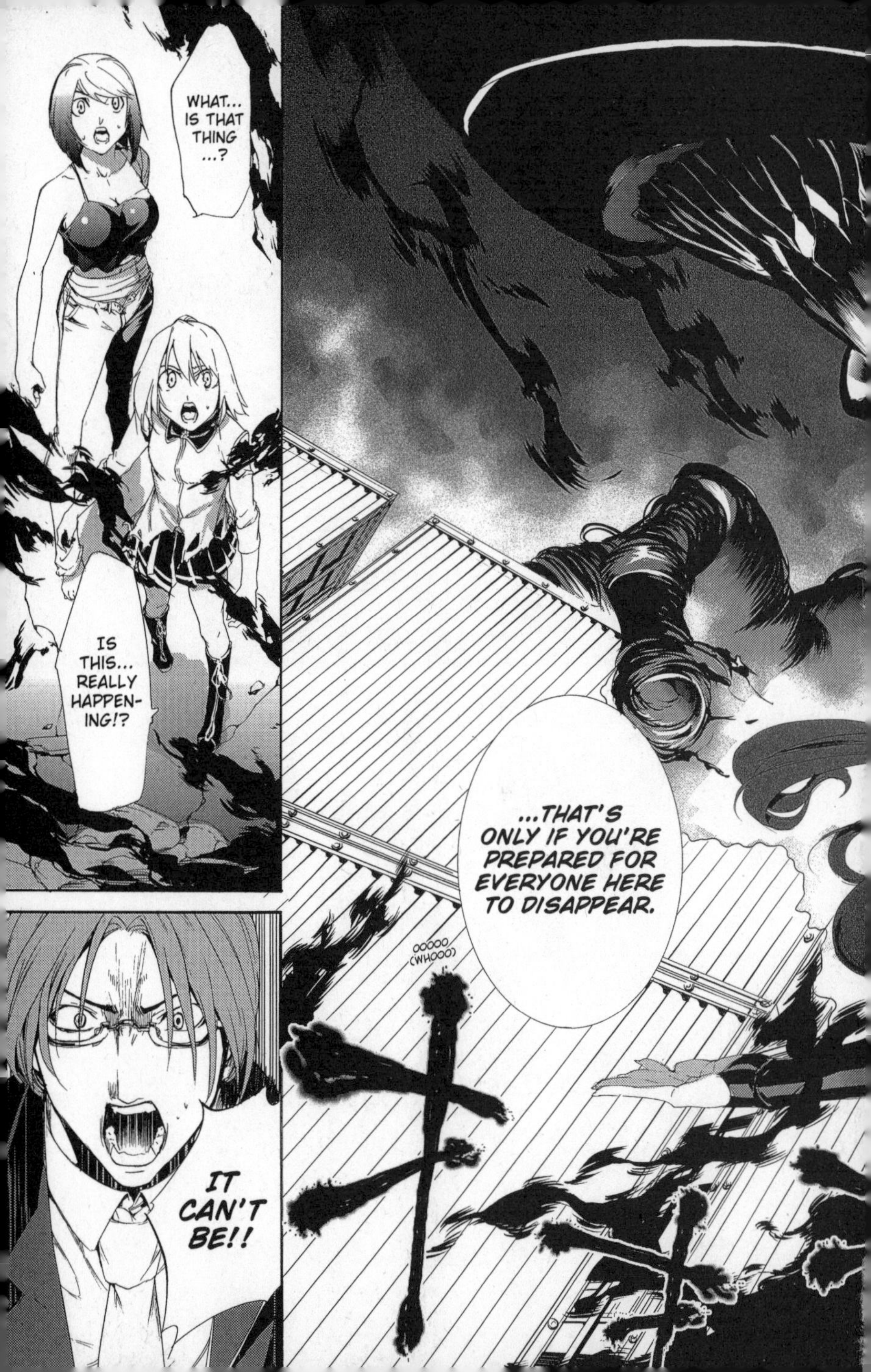
...THAT'S ONLY IF YOU'RE PREPARED FOR EVERYONE HERE TO DISAPPEAR.
OOOOO (WHOOO)
WHAT... IS THAT THING ...?
IS THIS... REALLY HAPPEN-ING!?
IT CAN'T BE!!

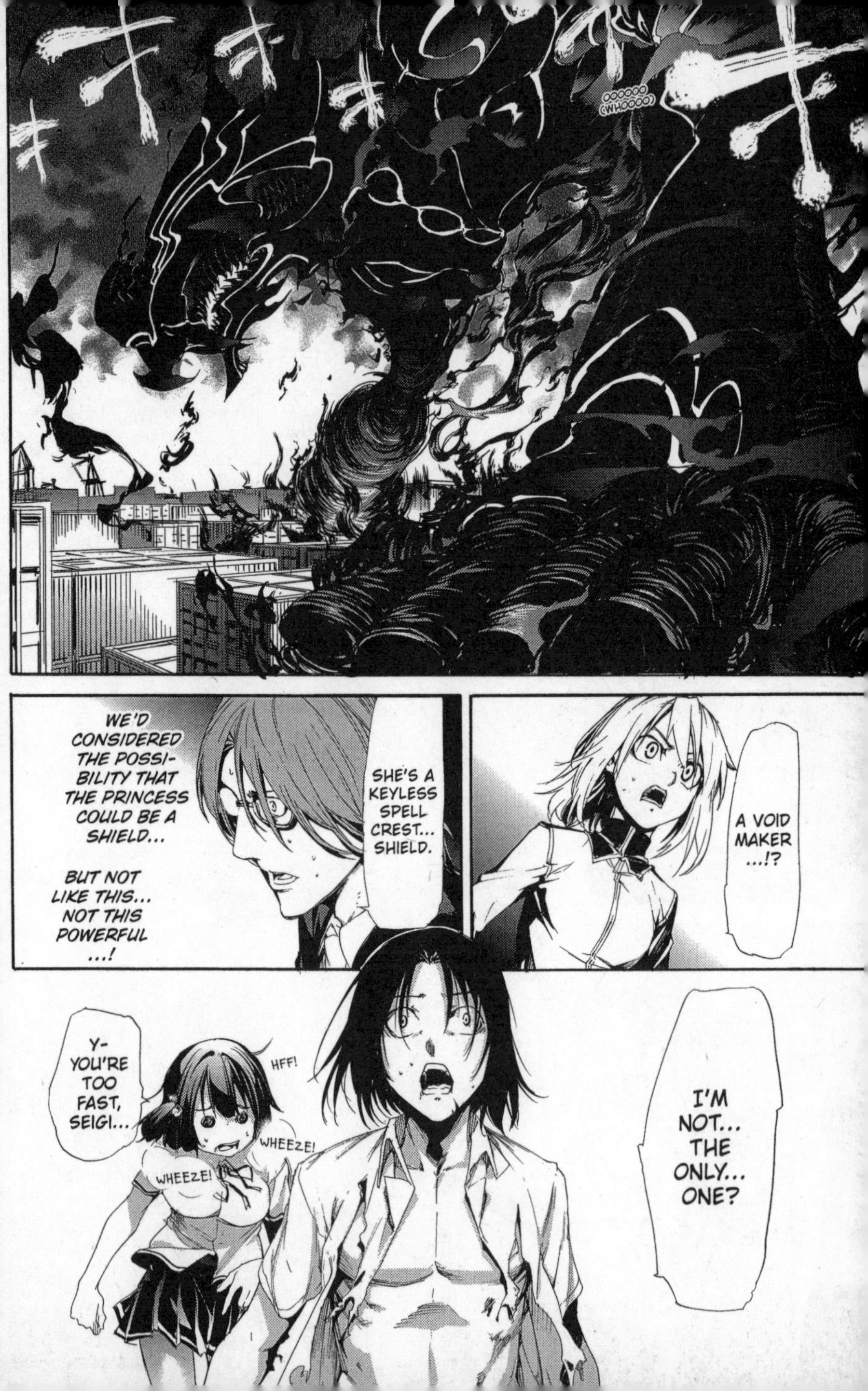
OOOOOO
(WHOOOO)
A VOID MAKER ...!?
SHE'S A KEYLESS SPELL CREST... SHIELD.
WE'D CONSIDERED THE POSSI-BILITY THAT THE PRINCESS COULD BE A SHIELD...
BUT NOT LIKE THIS... NOT THIS POWERFUL ...!
I'M NOT... THE ONLY... ONE?
Y-YOU'RE TOO FAST, SEIGI...
HFF!
WHEEZE!
WHEEZE!

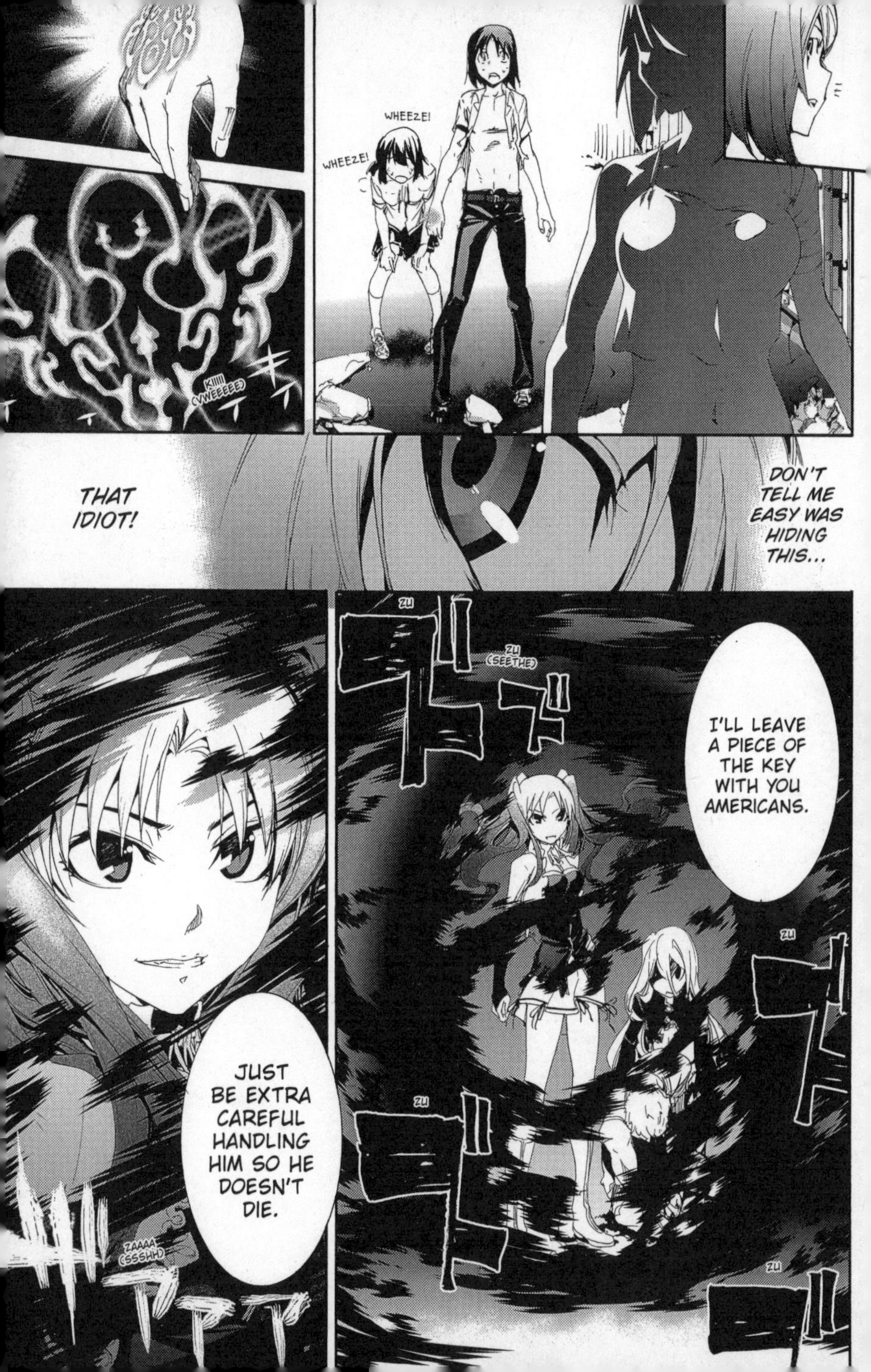
WHEEZE!
WHEEZE!
KIIIII (VWEEEEE)
DON'T TELL ME EASY WAS HIDING THIS...
THAT IDIOT!
ZU
ZU (SEETHE)
I'LL LEAVE A PIECE OF THE KEY WITH YOU AMERICANS.
ZU
ZU
ZU
JUST BE EXTRA CAREFUL HANDLING HIM SO HE DOESN'T DIE.
ZAAAA (SSSHH)

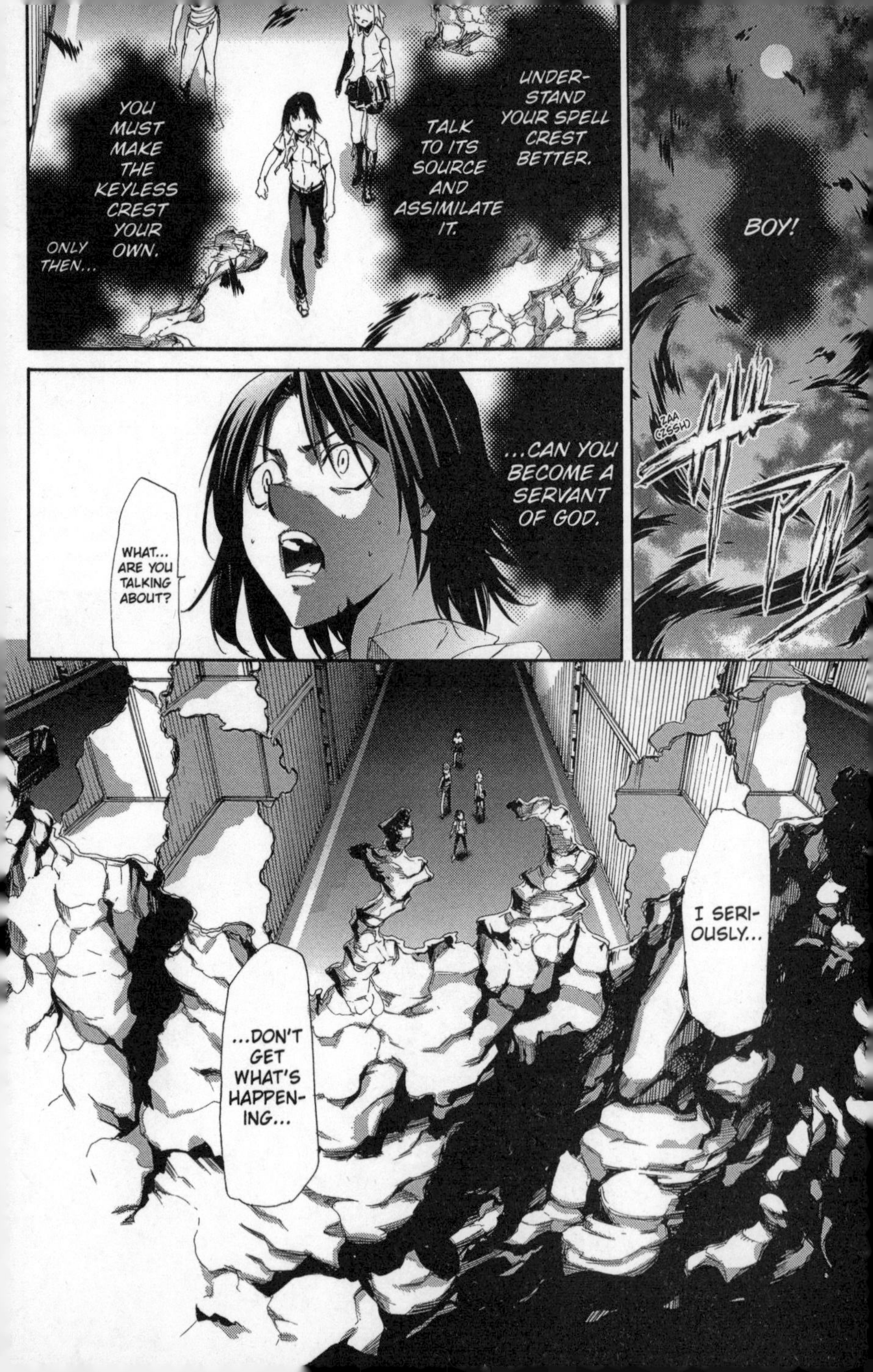
BOY!
ZAA (ZSSH)
UNDER-STAND YOUR SPELL CREST BETTER.
TALK TO ITS SOURCE AND ASSIMILATE IT.
YOU MUST MAKE THE KEYLESS CREST YOUR OWN.
ONLY THEN...
...CAN YOU BECOME A SERVANT OF GOD.
WHAT... ARE YOU TALKING ABOUT?
I SERI-OUSLY...
...DON'T GET WHAT'S HAPPEN-ING...

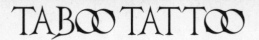

TABOO TATTOO

A PAGE THAT DIDN'T MAKE IT INTO THE SECOND VOLUME DUE TO VARIOUS REASONS.

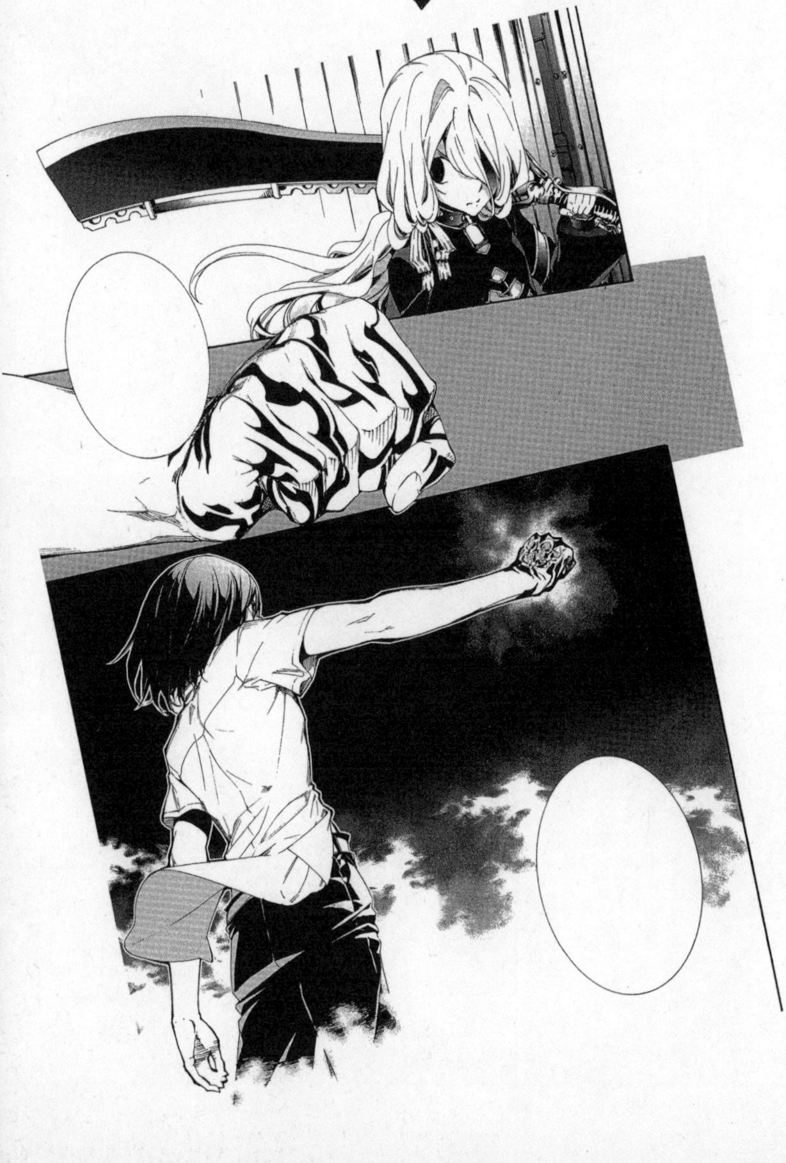

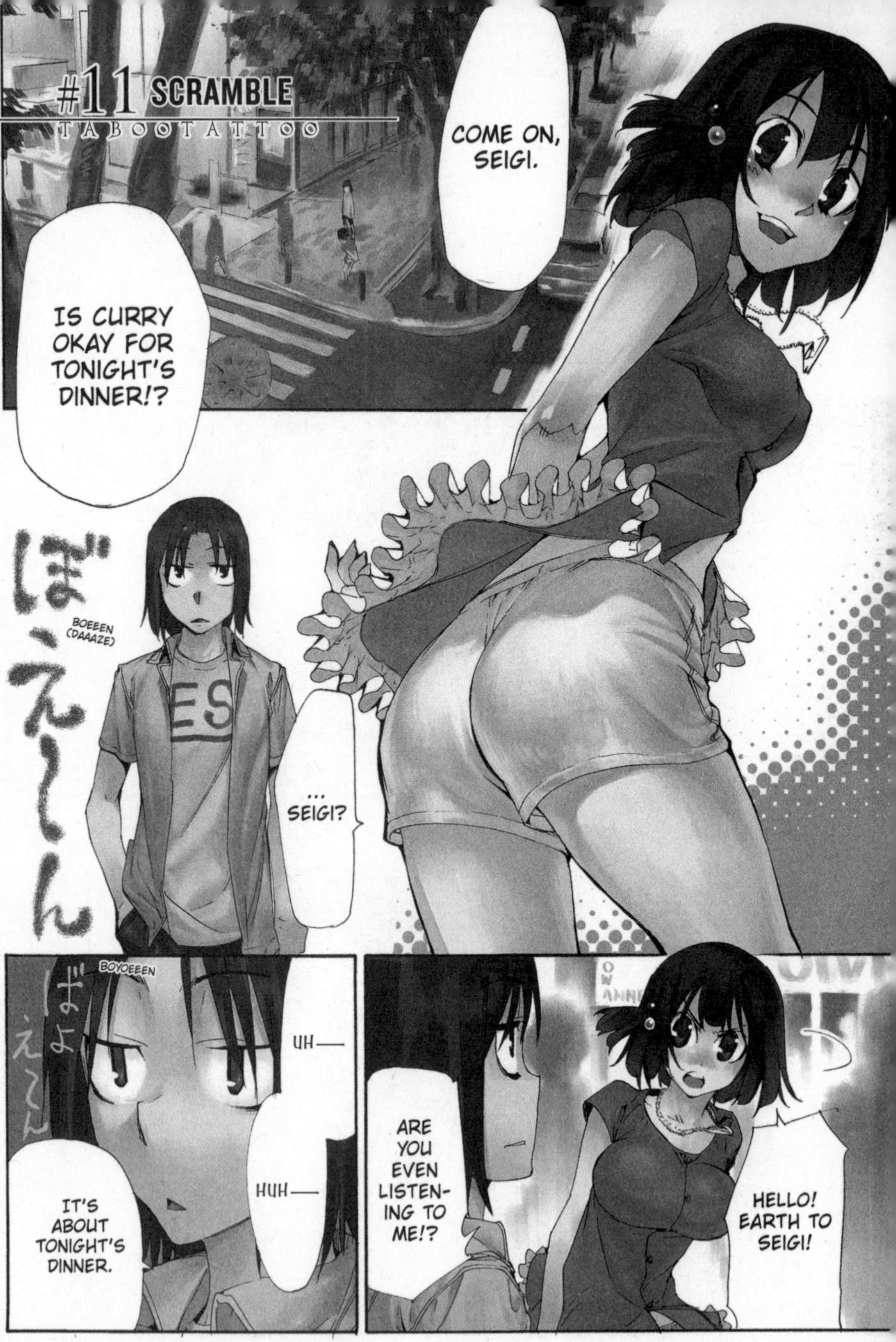

#11 SCRAMBLE
TABOOTATTOO
COME ON, SEIGI.
IS CURRY OKAY FOR TONIGHT'S DINNER!?
ぼえ〜ん
BOEEEN (DAAAZE)
... SEIGI?
HELLO! EARTH TO SEIGI!
ARE YOU EVEN LISTENING TO ME!?
ぼよえ〜ん
BOYOEEEN
UH—
HUH—
IT'S ABOUT TONIGHT'S DINNER.

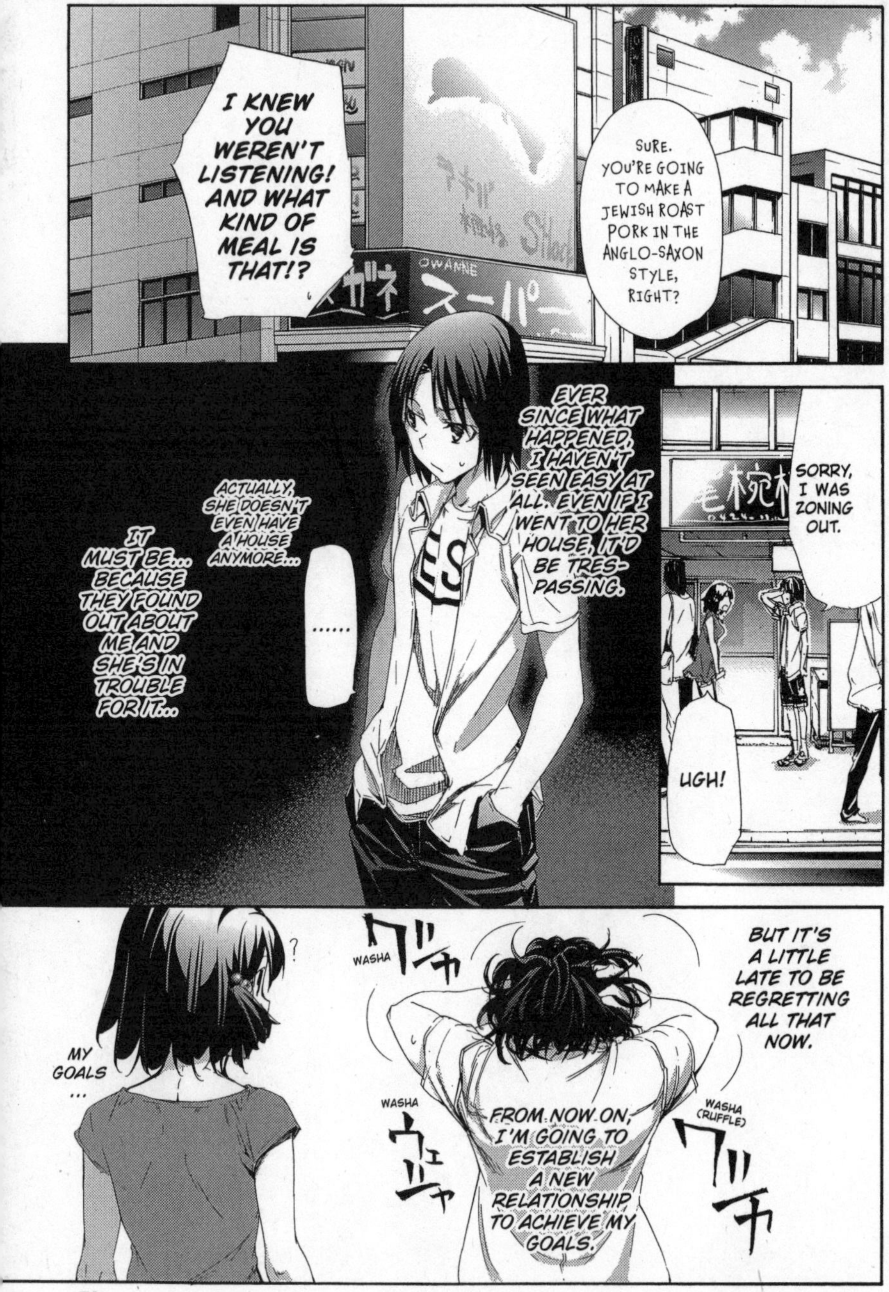
SURE. YOU'RE GOING TO MAKE A JEWISH ROAST PORK IN THE ANGLO-SAXON STYLE, RIGHT?
I KNEW YOU WEREN'T LISTENING! AND WHAT KIND OF MEAL IS THAT!?
OWANNE
SORRY, I WAS ZONING OUT.
UGH!
EVER SINCE WHAT HAPPENED, I HAVEN'T SEEN EASY AT ALL. EVEN IF I WENT TO HER HOUSE, IT'D BE TRES-PASSING.
......
ACTUALLY, SHE DOESN'T EVEN HAVE A HOUSE ANYMORE...
IT MUST BE... BECAUSE THEY FOUND OUT ABOUT ME AND SHE'S IN TROUBLE FOR IT...
BUT IT'S A LITTLE LATE TO BE REGRETTING ALL THAT NOW.
WASHA (RUFFLE)
FROM NOW ON, I'M GOING TO ESTABLISH A NEW RELATIONSHIP TO ACHIEVE MY GOALS.
WASHA
WASHA
?
MY GOALS ...

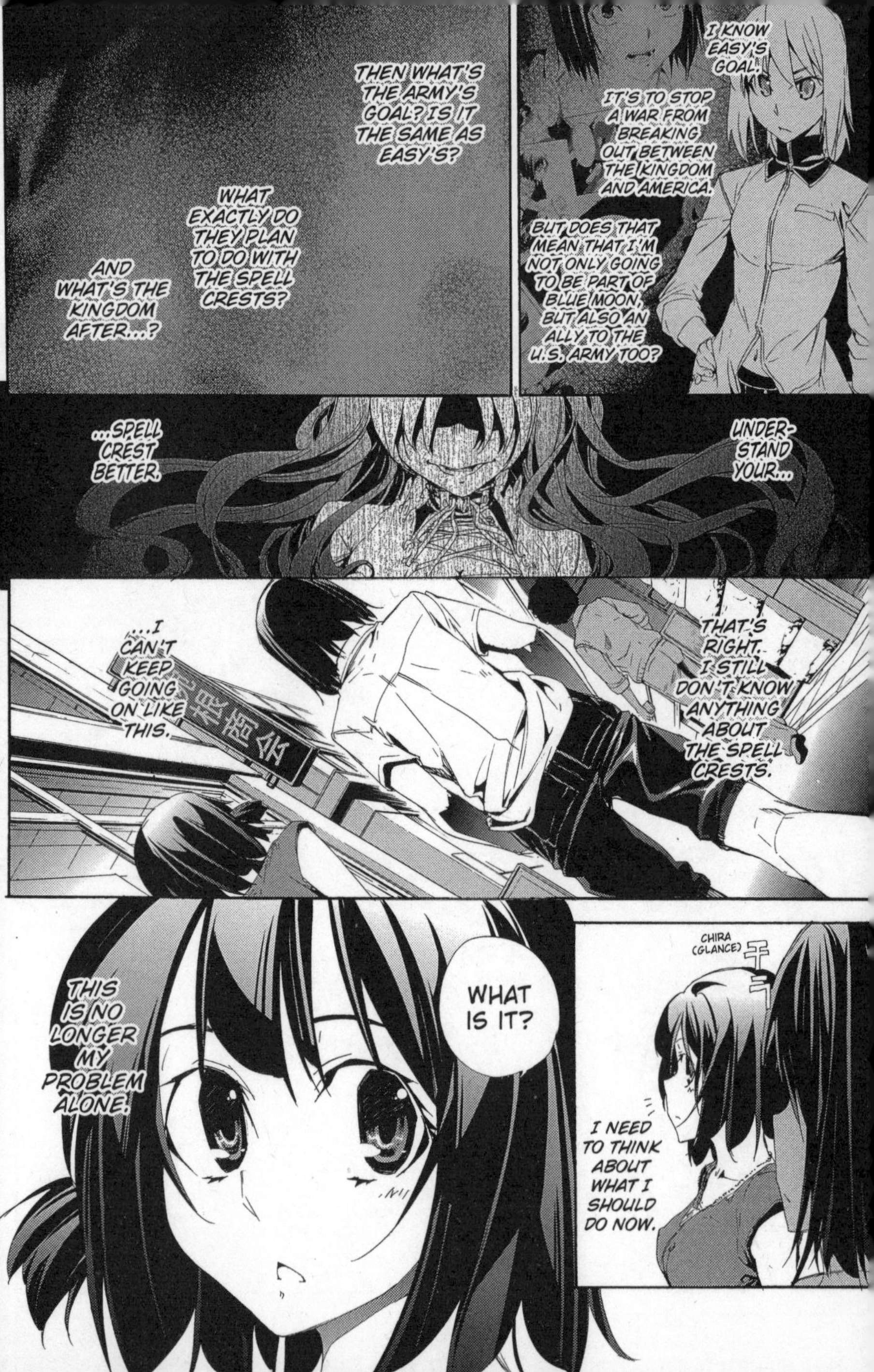
I KNOW EASY'S GOAL.
IT'S TO STOP A WAR FROM BREAKING OUT BETWEEN THE KINGDOM AND AMERICA.
BUT DOES THAT MEAN THAT I'M NOT ONLY GOING TO BE PART OF BLUE MOON, BUT ALSO AN ALLY TO THE U.S. ARMY TOO?
THEN WHAT'S THE ARMY'S GOAL? IS IT THE SAME AS EASY'S?
WHAT EXACTLY DO THEY PLAN TO DO WITH THE SPELL CRESTS?
AND WHAT'S THE KINGDOM AFTER...?
UNDER-STAND YOUR...
...SPELL CREST BETTER.
THAT'S RIGHT. I STILL DON'T KNOW ANYTHING ABOUT THE SPELL CRESTS.
...I CAN'T KEEP GOING ON LIKE THIS.
CHIRA (GLANCE)
I NEED TO THINK ABOUT WHAT I SHOULD DO NOW.
WHAT IS IT?
THIS IS NO LONGER MY PROBLEM ALONE.

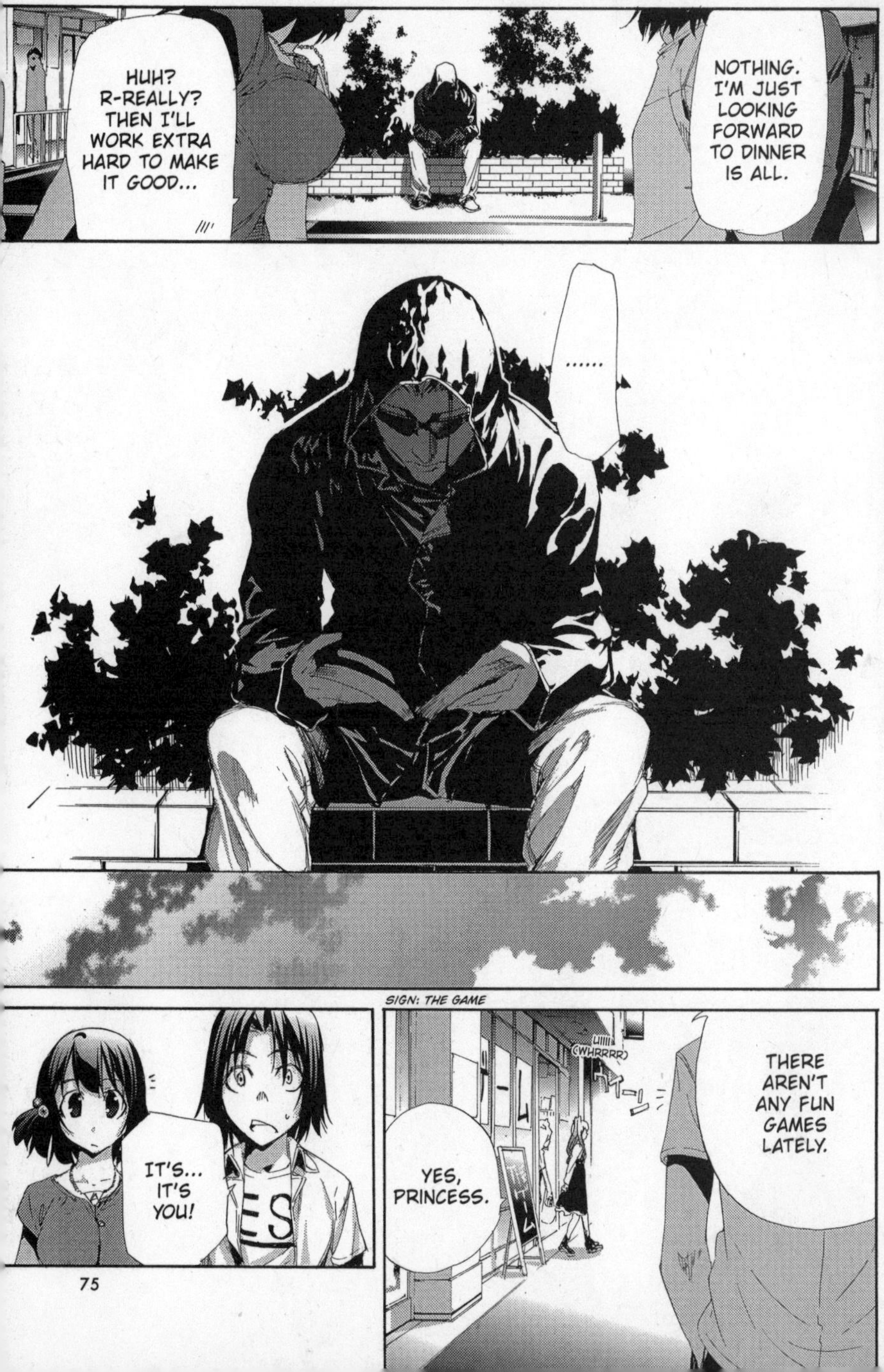
NOTHING. I'M JUST LOOKING FORWARD TO DINNER IS ALL.
HUH? R-REALLY? THEN I'LL WORK EXTRA HARD TO MAKE IT GOOD...
......
SIGN: THE GAME
THERE AREN'T ANY FUN GAMES LATELY.
(WHRRRR)
YES, PRINCESS.
IT'S... IT'S YOU!

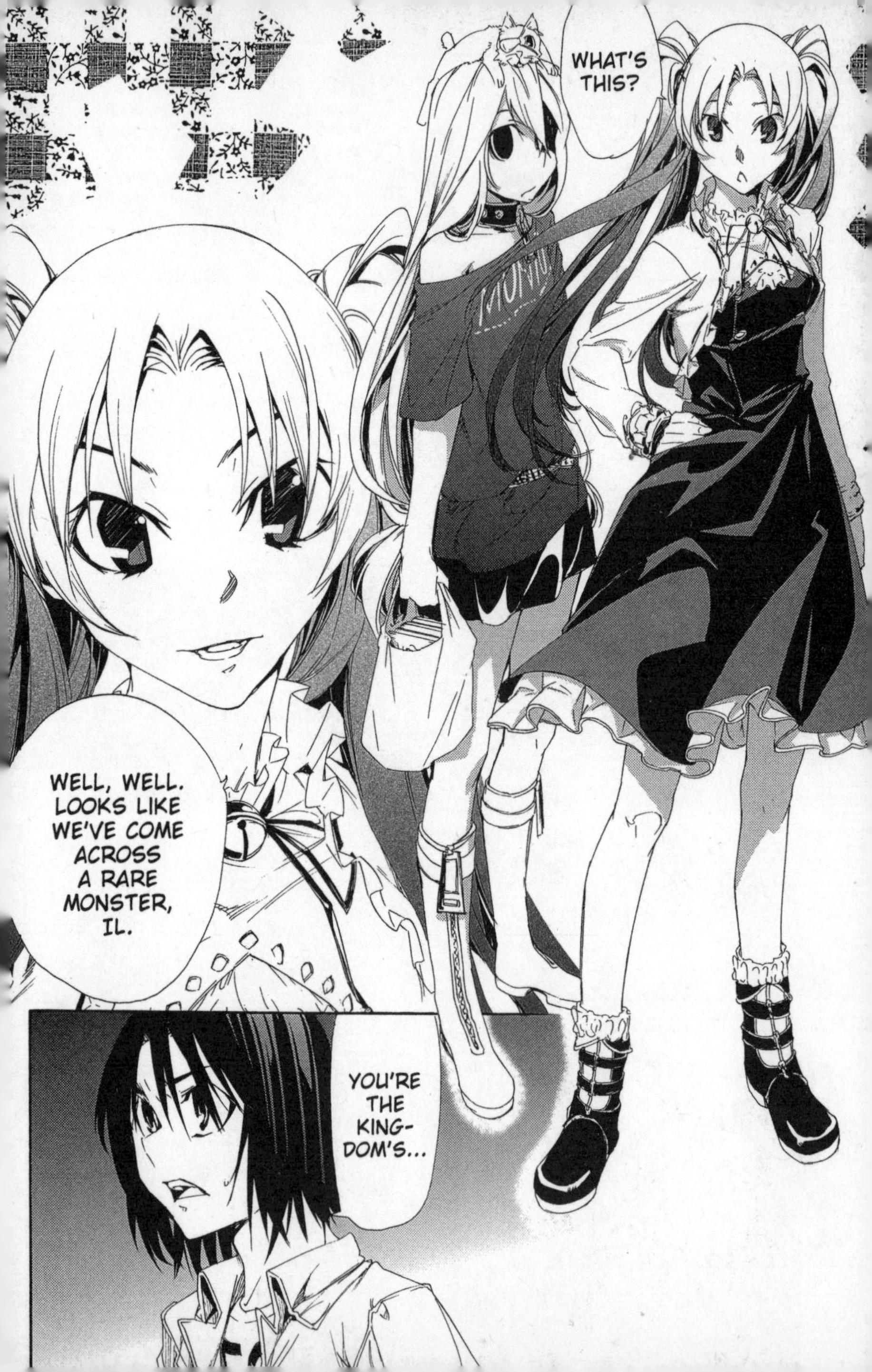
WHAT'S THIS?
WELL, WELL. LOOKS LIKE WE'VE COME ACROSS A RARE MONSTER, IL.
YOU'RE THE KING-DOM'S...

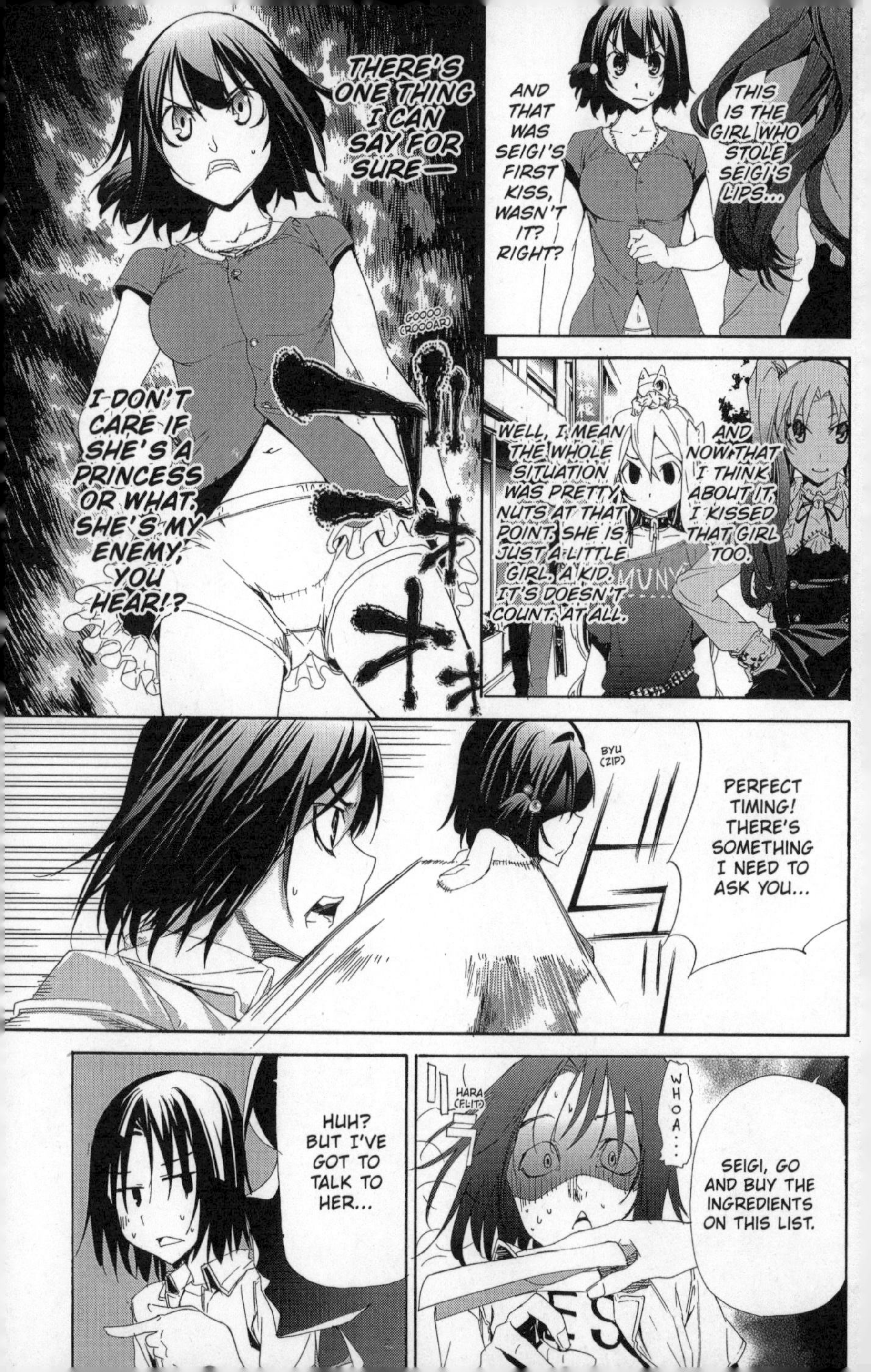
THIS IS THE GIRL WHO STOLE SEIGI'S LIPS...
AND THAT WAS SEIGI'S FIRST KISS, WASN'T IT? RIGHT?
AND NOW THAT I THINK ABOUT IT, I KISSED THAT GIRL TOO.
WELL, I MEAN THE WHOLE SITUATION WAS PRETTY NUTS AT THAT POINT. SHE IS JUST A LITTLE GIRL, A KID. IT'S DOESN'T COUNT AT ALL.
THERE'S ONE THING I CAN SAY FOR SURE—
GOOOO (ROOOAR)
I DON'T CARE IF SHE'S A PRINCESS OR WHAT. SHE'S MY ENEMY, YOU HEAR!?
PERFECT TIMING! THERE'S SOMETHING I NEED TO ASK YOU...
BYU (ZIP)
SEIGI, GO AND BUY THE INGREDIENTS ON THIS LIST.
WHOA...
HARA (FLIT)
HUH? BUT I'VE GOT TO TALK TO HER...

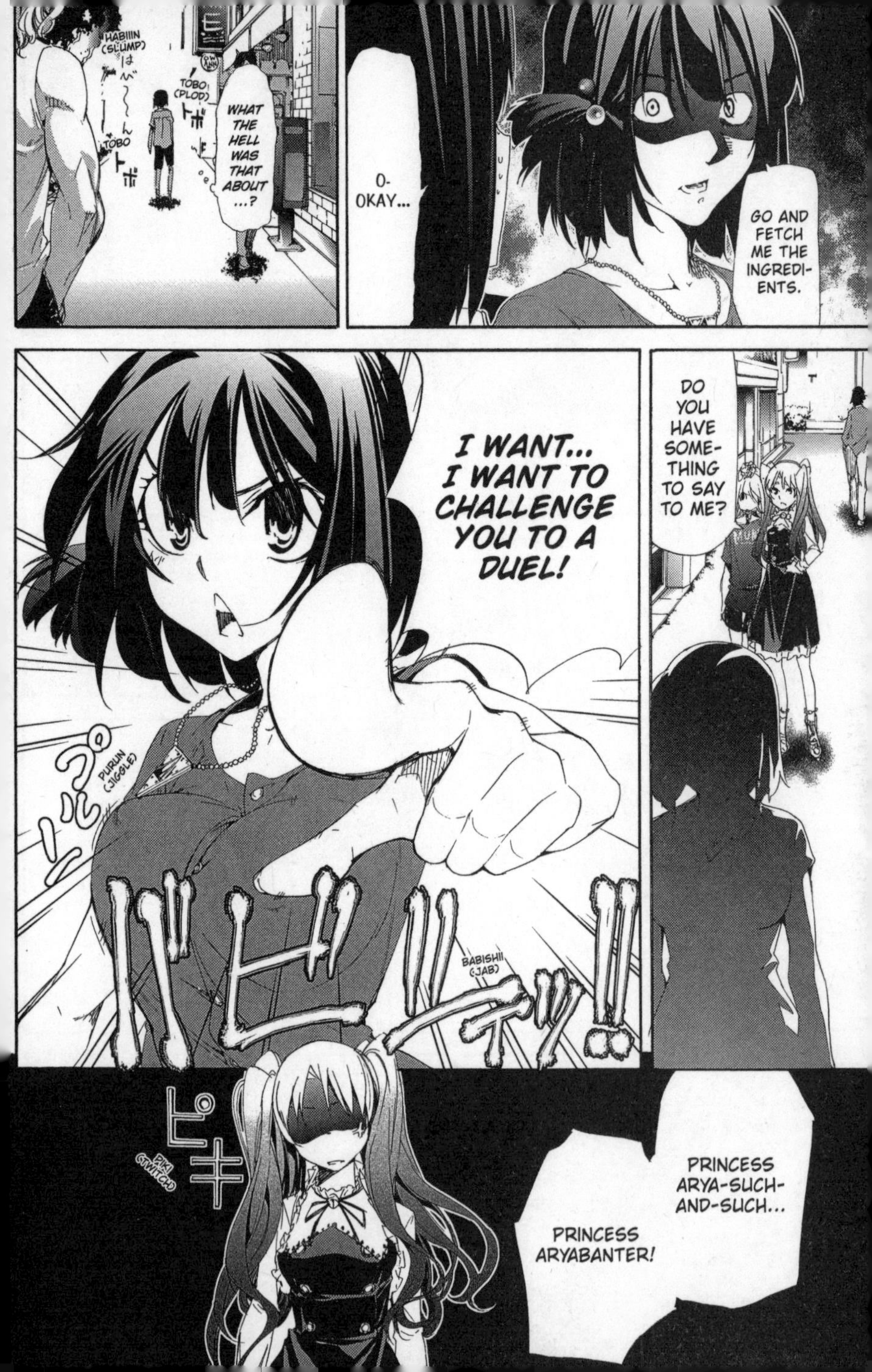
GO AND FETCH ME THE INGREDIENTS.
O-OKAY...
HABIIN (SLUMP)
はべ~ん
TOBO (PLOD)
トボ
TOBO
トボ
WHAT THE HELL WAS THAT ABOUT...?
DO YOU HAVE SOMETHING TO SAY TO ME?
I WANT... I WANT TO CHALLENGE YOU TO A DUEL!
PURUN (JIGGLE)
ぷるん
BABISHII (JAB)
バビシィッ!!
PRINCESS ARYA-SUCH-AND-SUCH...
PRINCESS ARYABANTER!
PIKI (TWITCH)
ピキ

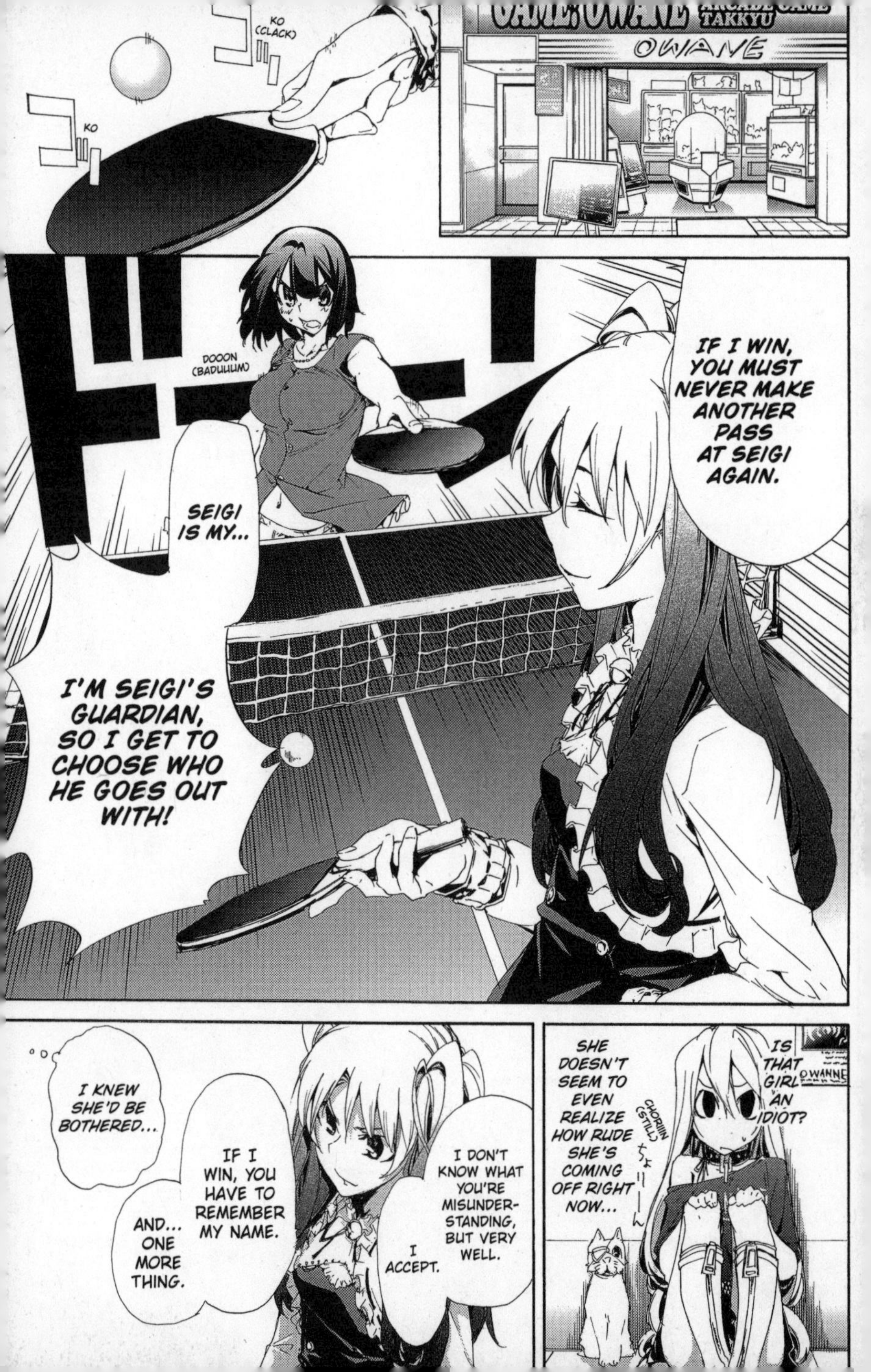
ARCADE GAME TAKKYU
OWANE
KO (CLACK)
KO
IF I WIN, YOU MUST NEVER MAKE ANOTHER PASS AT SEIGI AGAIN.
DOOON (BADUUUM)
SEIGI IS MY...
I'M SEIGI'S GUARDIAN, SO I GET TO CHOOSE WHO HE GOES OUT WITH!
OWANNE
IS THAT GIRL AN IDIOT?
SHE DOESN'T SEEM TO EVEN REALIZE HOW RUDE SHE'S COMING OFF RIGHT NOW...
CHORIIIN (STILL)
I DON'T KNOW WHAT YOU'RE MISUNDER-STANDING, BUT VERY WELL.
I ACCEPT.
IF I WIN, YOU HAVE TO REMEMBER MY NAME.
AND... ONE MORE THING.
I KNEW SHE'D BE BOTHERED...

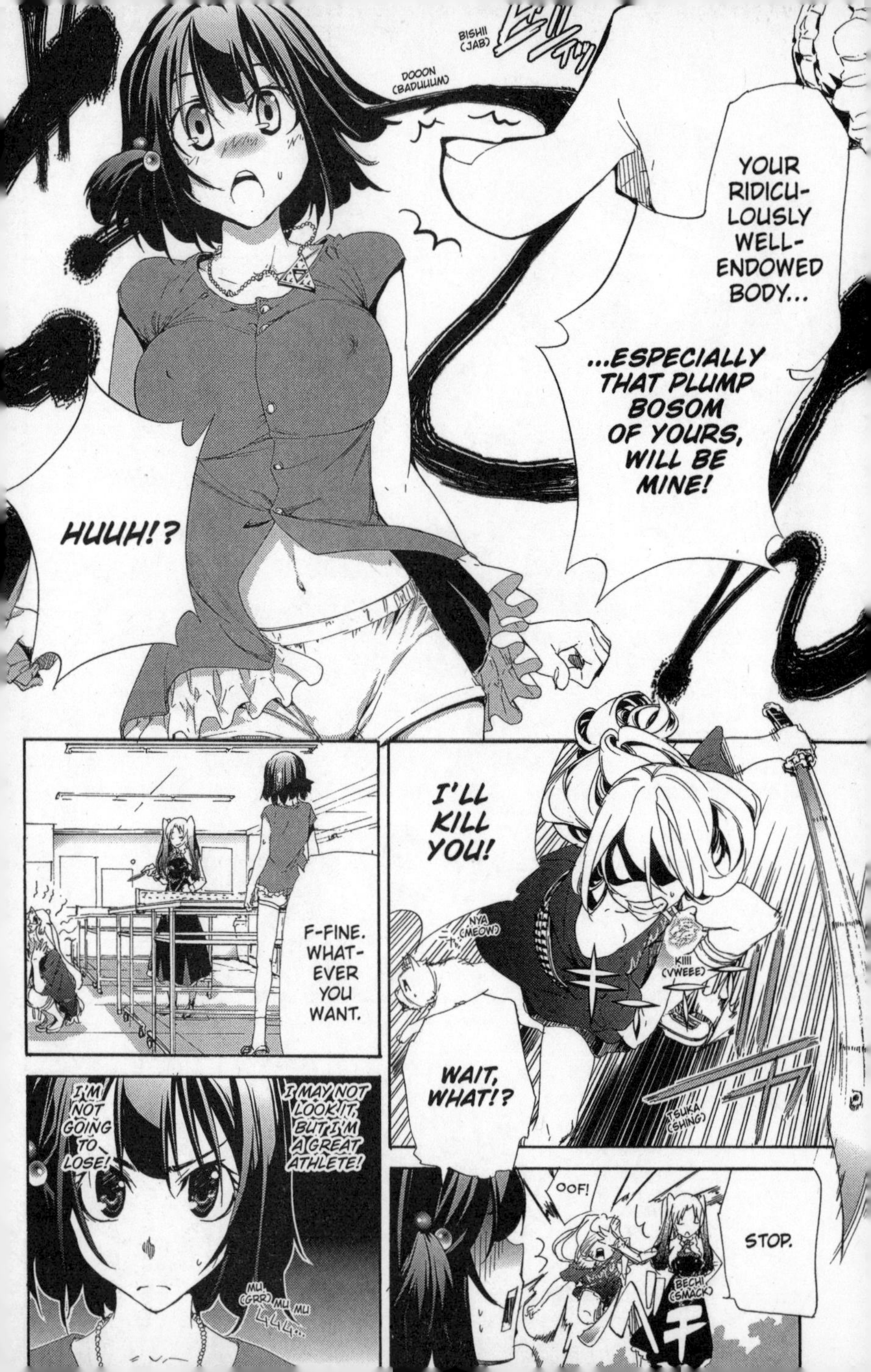
BISHII (JAB)
DOOON (BADUUUM)
YOUR RIDICU-LOUSLY WELL-ENDOWED BODY...
...ESPECIALLY THAT PLUMP BOSOM OF YOURS, WILL BE MINE!
HUUH!?
I'LL KILL YOU!
NYA (MEOW)
KIIII (VWEEE)
WAIT, WHAT!?
TSUKA (SHING)
F-FINE. WHAT-EVER YOU WANT.
OOF!
STOP.
BECHI (SMACK)
I MAY NOT LOOK IT, BUT I'M A GREAT ATHLETE!
I'M NOT GOING TO LOSE!
MU (GRR) MU MU

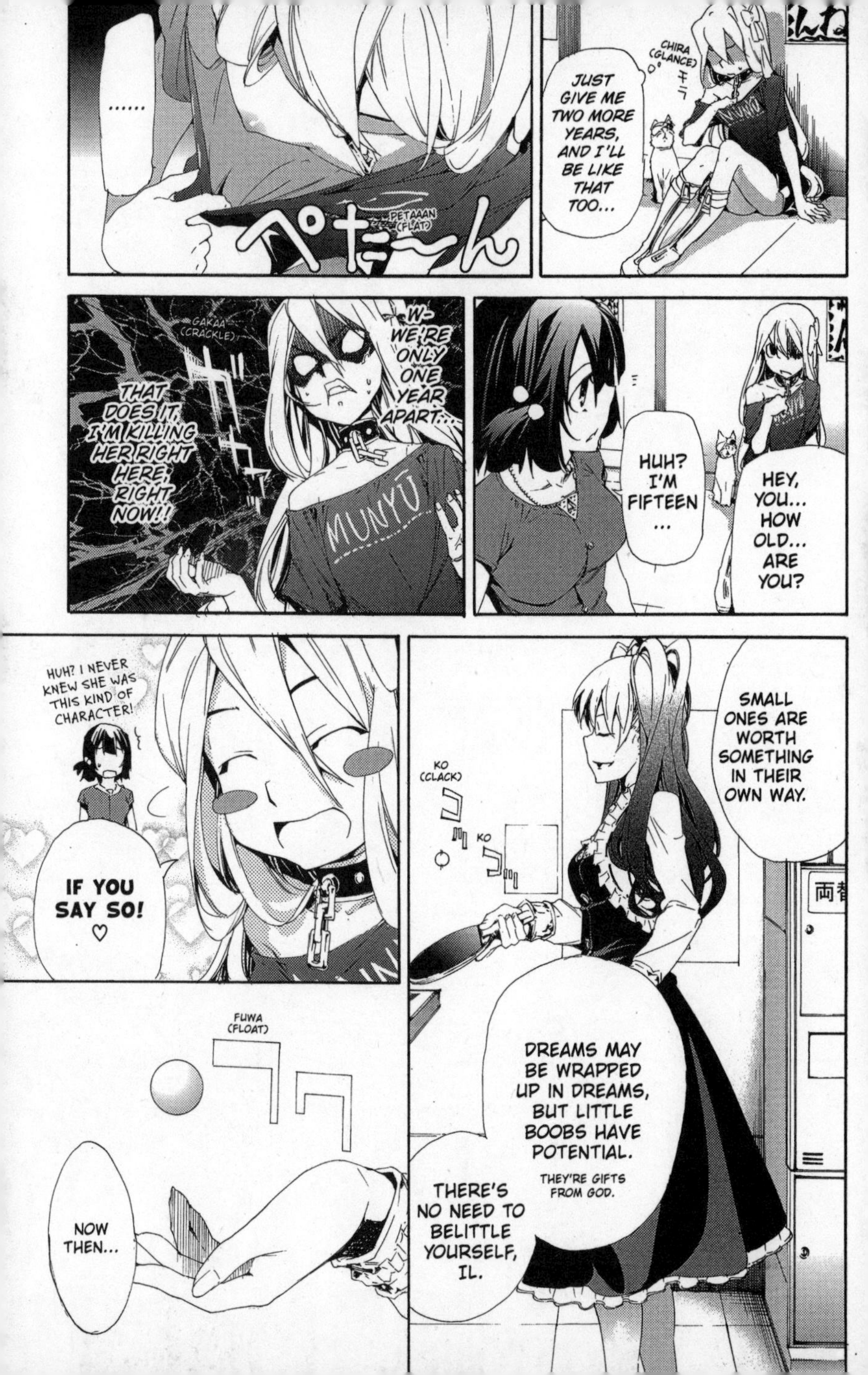
CHIRA (GLANCE)
チラ
JUST GIVE ME TWO MORE YEARS, AND I'LL BE LIKE THAT TOO...
......
PETAAAN (FLAT)
ぺた~ん
HEY, YOU... HOW OLD... ARE YOU?
HUH? I'M FIFTEEN...
W-WE'RE ONLY ONE YEAR APART...
GAKAA (CRACKLE)
THAT DOES IT. I'M KILLING HER RIGHT HERE, RIGHT NOW!!
SMALL ONES ARE WORTH SOMETHING IN THEIR OWN WAY.
KO (CLACK)
KO
DREAMS MAY BE WRAPPED UP IN DREAMS, BUT LITTLE BOOBS HAVE POTENTIAL.
THEY'RE GIFTS FROM GOD.
THERE'S NO NEED TO BELITTLE YOURSELF, IL.
HUH? I NEVER KNEW SHE WAS THIS KIND OF CHARACTER!
IF YOU SAY SO! ♡
FUWA (FLOAT)
NOW THEN...

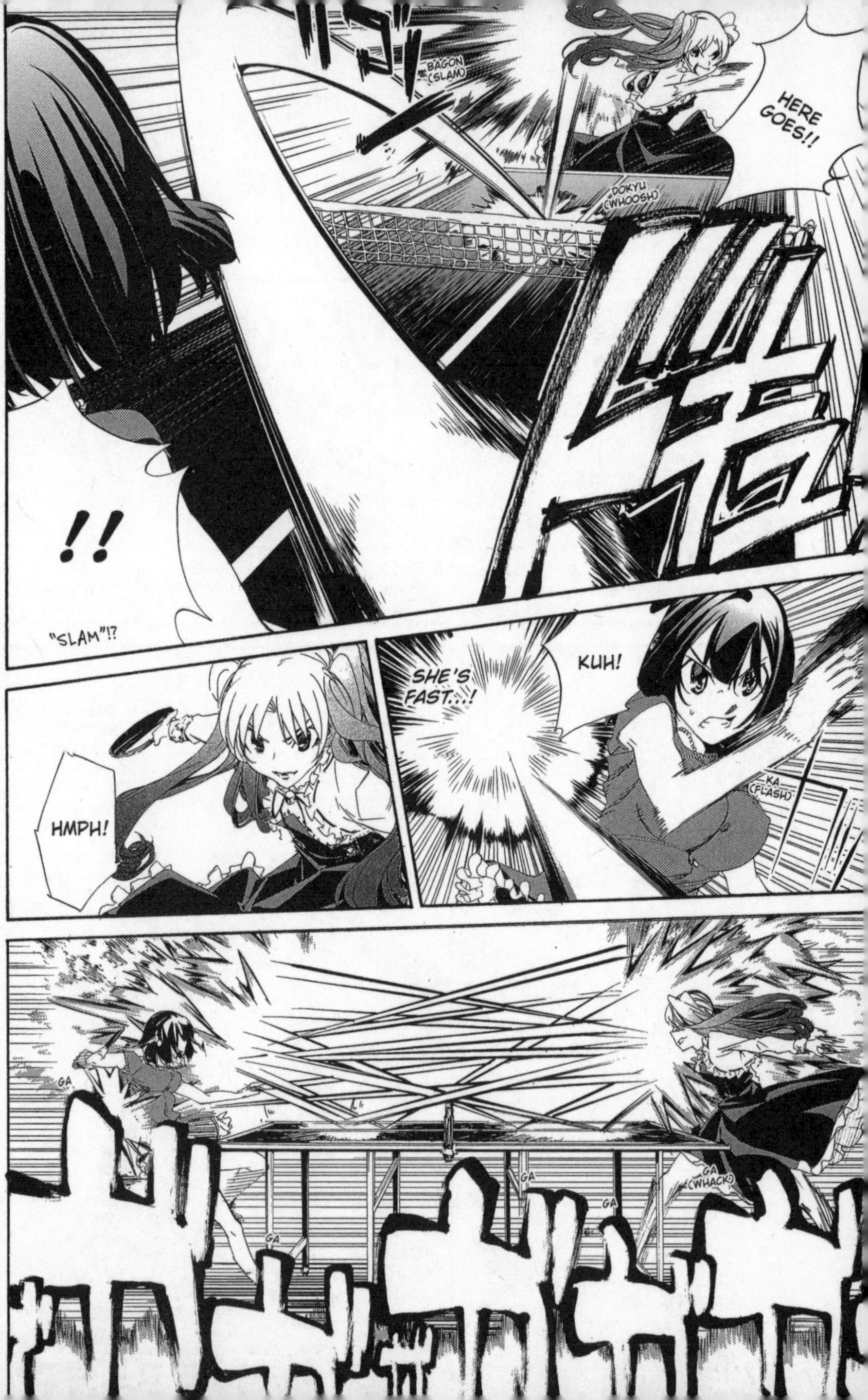

HERE GOES!!
BAGON (SLAM)
DOKYU (WHOOSH)
!!
"SLAM"!?
KUH!
KA (FLASH)
SHE'S FAST...!
HMPH!
GA (WHACK)
GA
GA
GA
GA

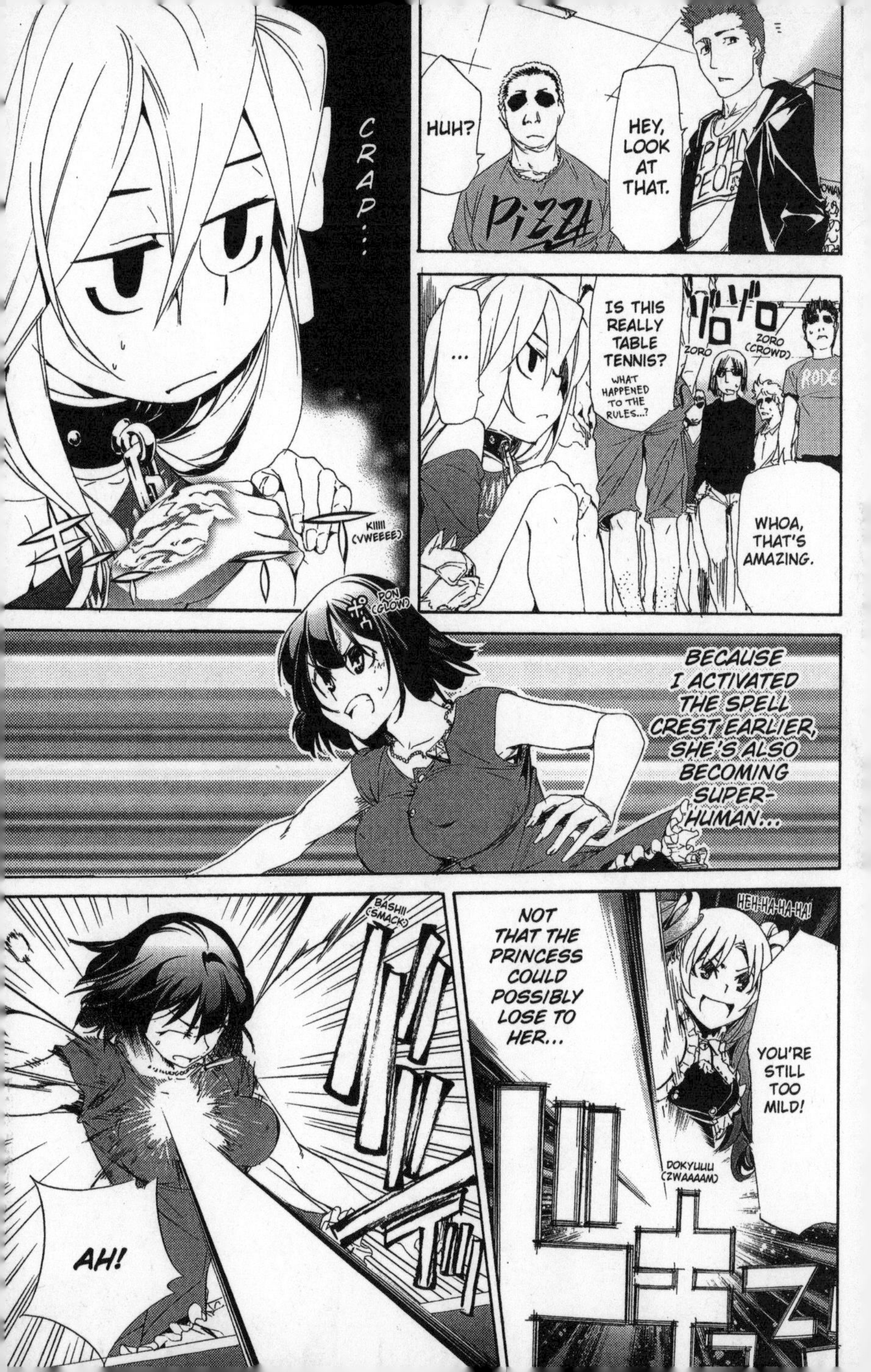
HEY, LOOK AT THAT.
HUH?
IS THIS REALLY TABLE TENNIS?
WHAT HAPPENED TO THE RULES...?
ZORO (CROWD)
ZORO
...
WHOA, THAT'S AMAZING.
CRAP...
KIIIII (VWEEEE)
PON (GLOW)
BECAUSE I ACTIVATED THE SPELL CREST EARLIER, SHE'S ALSO BECOMING SUPER-HUMAN...
HEH-HA-HA-HA!
NOT THAT THE PRINCESS COULD POSSIBLY LOSE TO HER...
YOU'RE STILL TOO MILD!
DOKYUUU (ZWAAAAM)
BASHI! (SMACK)
AH!

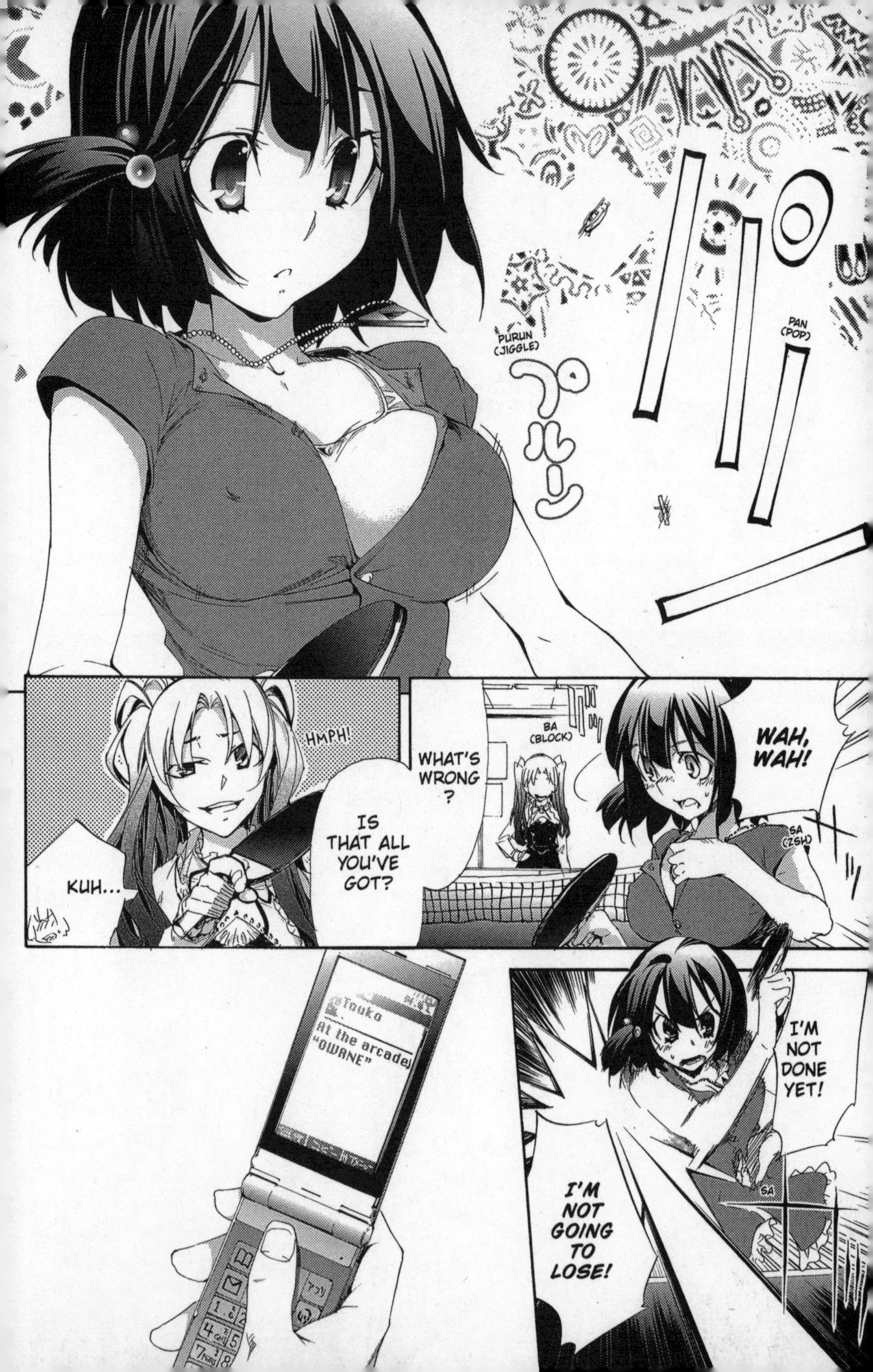
PAN (POP)
PURUN (JIGGLE)
WAH, WAH!
SA (ZSH)
BA (BLOCK)
WHAT'S WRONG?
IS THAT ALL YOU'VE GOT?
HMPH!
KUH...
I'M NOT DONE YET!
SA
I'M NOT GOING TO LOSE!
Touko
At the arcade)
"OWANE"

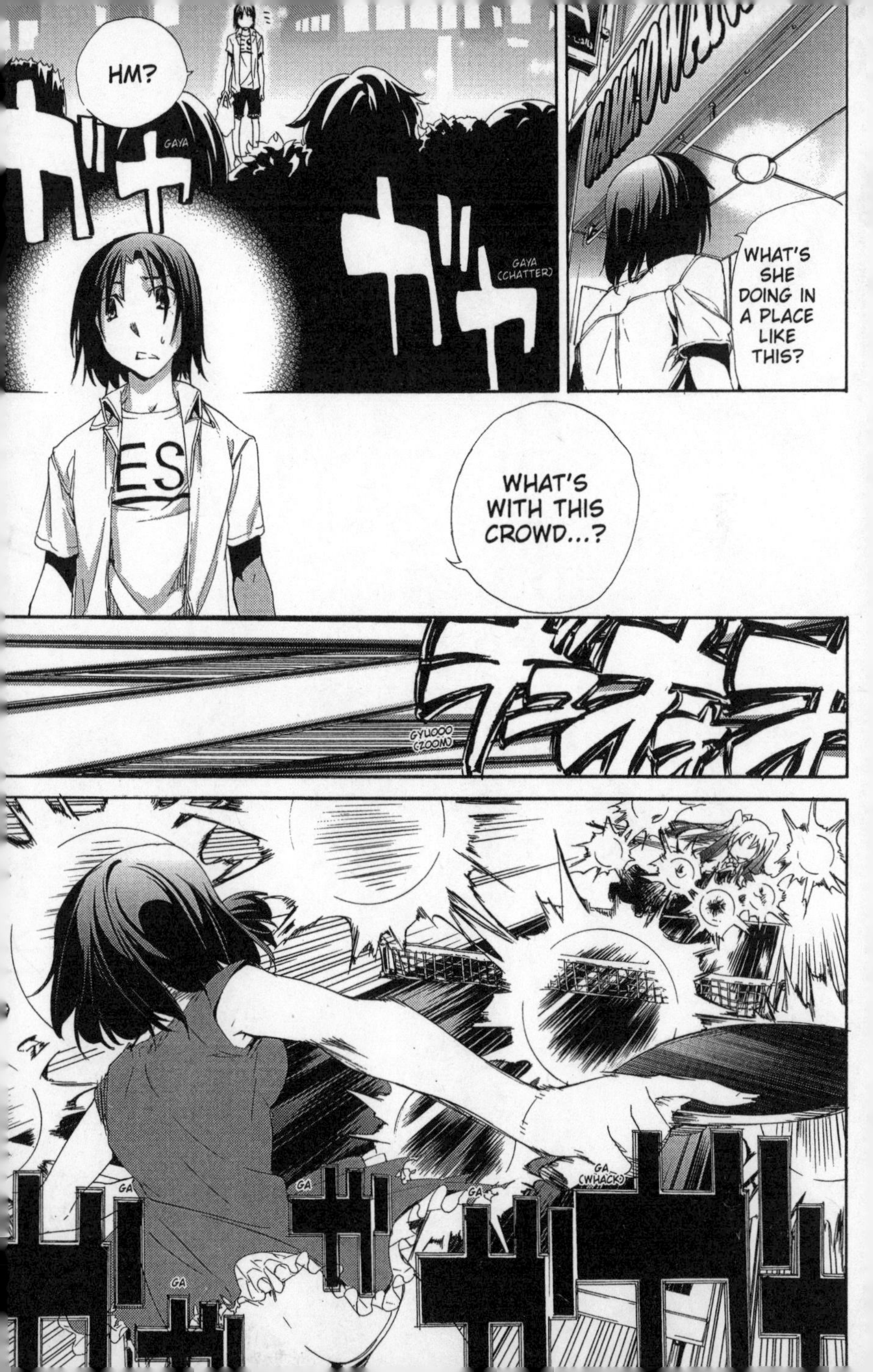
WHAT'S SHE DOING IN A PLACE LIKE THIS?
HM?
GAYA
GAYA (CHATTER)
WHAT'S WITH THIS CROWD...?
GYUOOO (ZOOM)
GA (WHACK)
GA
GA
GA
GA

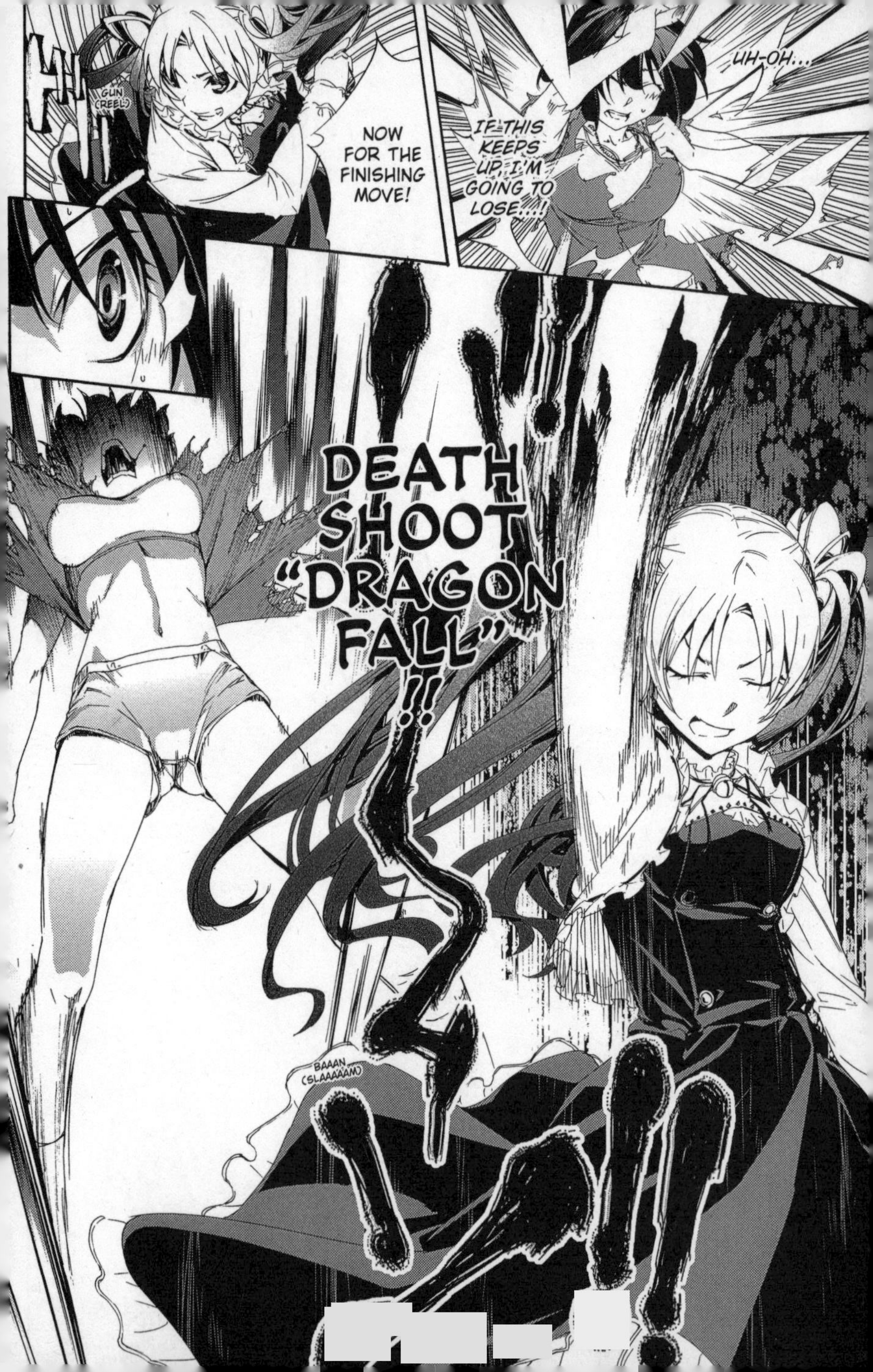
UH-OH...
IF THIS KEEPS UP, I'M GOING TO LOSE...!
GUN (REEL)
NOW FOR THE FINISHING MOVE!
DEATH SHOOT "DRAGON FALL"!!
BAAAN (SLAAAAAM)

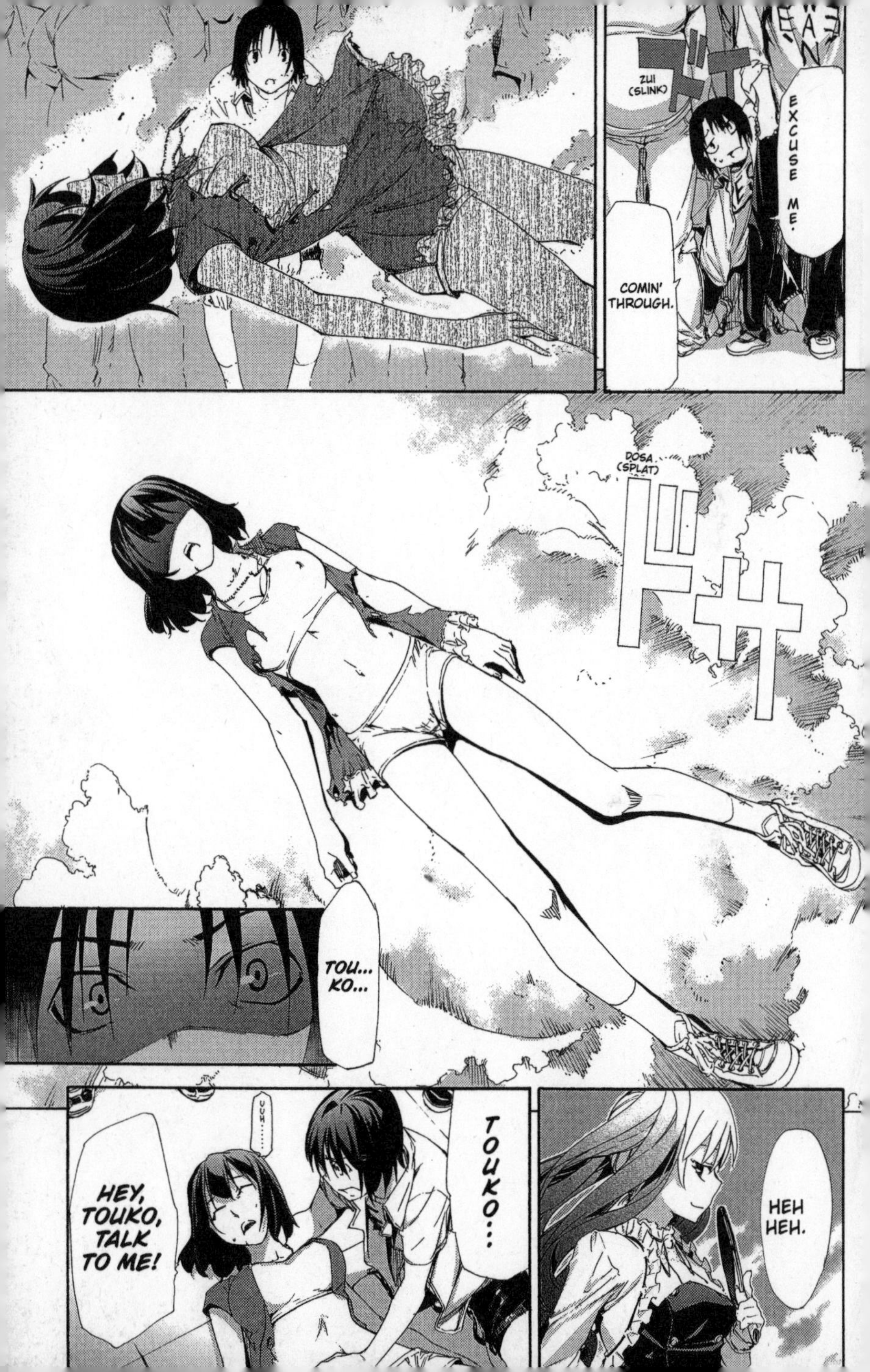
EXCUSE ME.
ZUI (SLINK)
COMIN' THROUGH.
DOSA (SPLAT)
TOU... KO...
HEH HEH.
TOUKO...
UUH......
HEY, TOUKO, TALK TO ME!

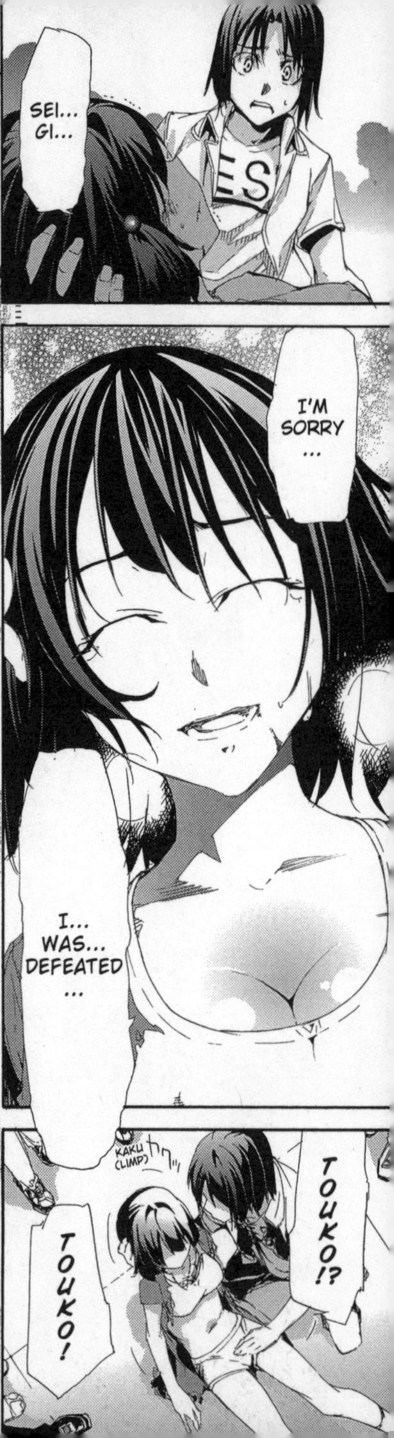
SEI... GI...
I'M SORRY ...
I... WAS... DEFEATED ...
KAKU (LIMP)
TOUKO!?
TOUKO!
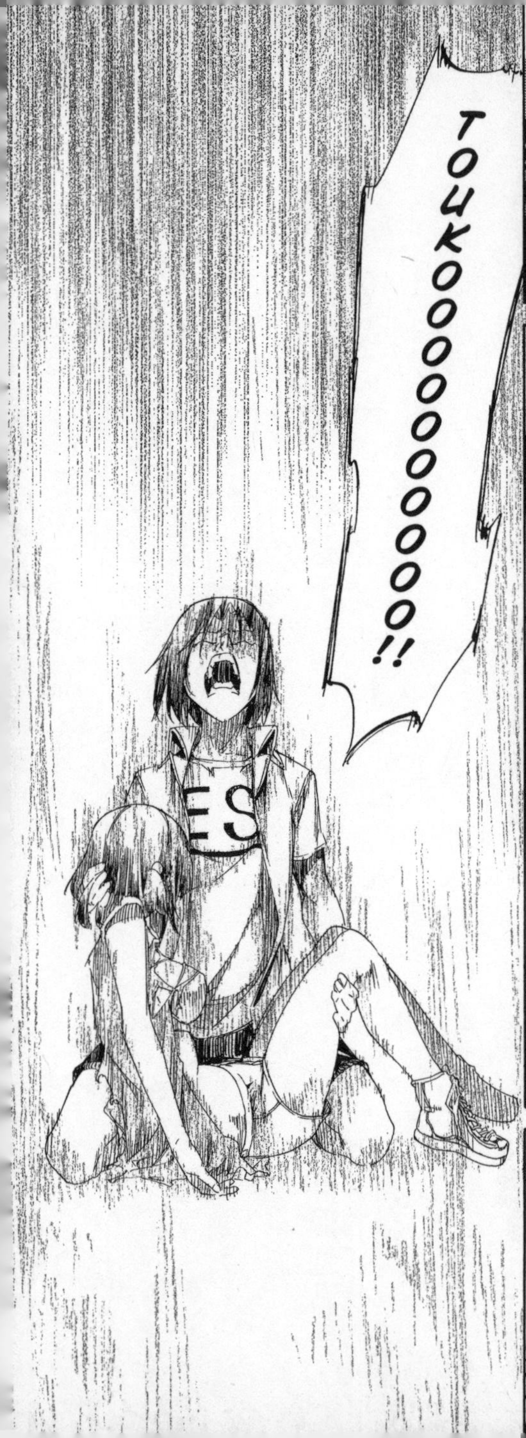
TOUKOOOOOOOOOO!!

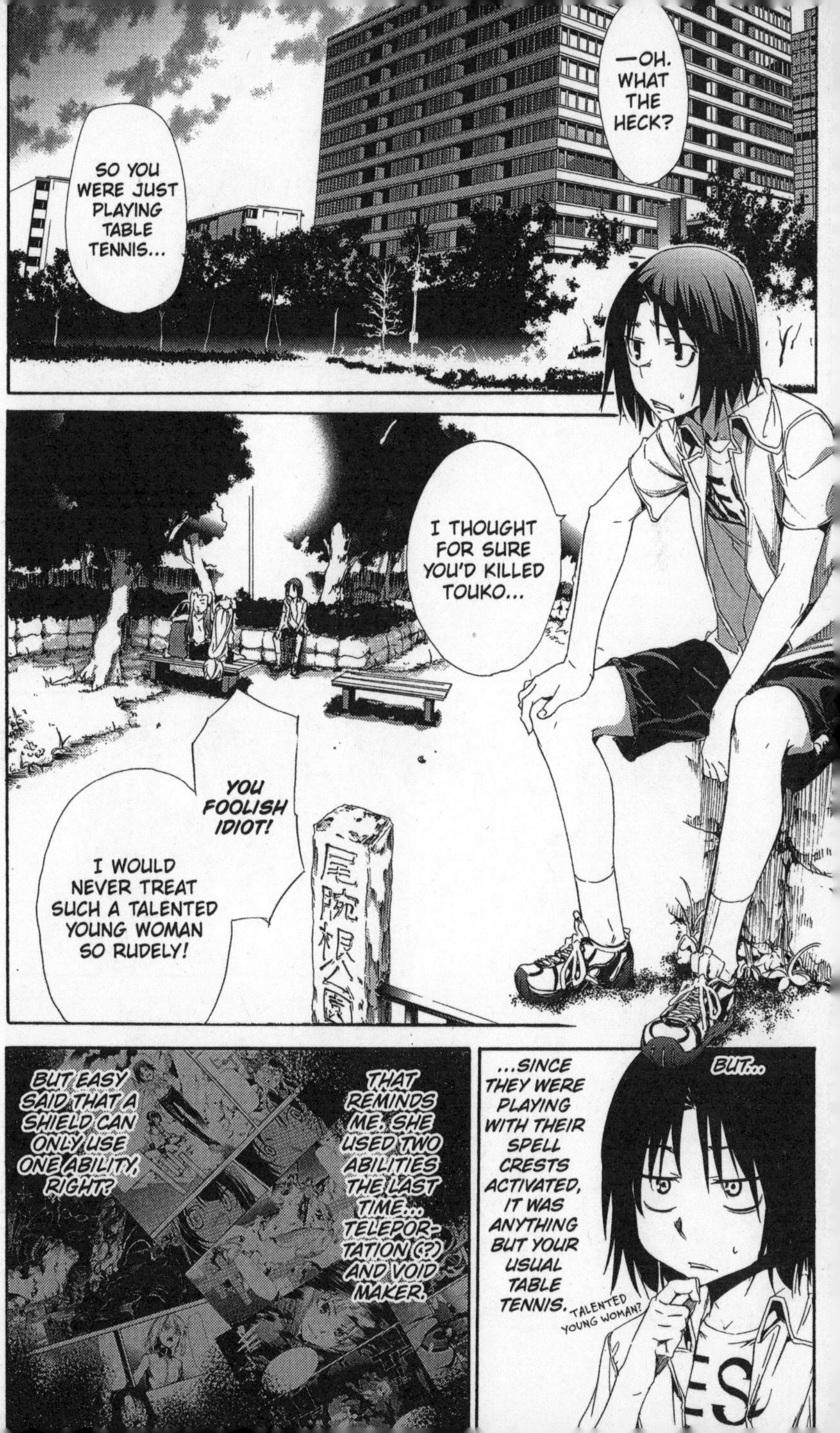
—OH. WHAT THE HECK?
SO YOU WERE JUST PLAYING TABLE TENNIS...
I THOUGHT FOR SURE YOU'D KILLED TOUKO...
YOU FOOLISH IDIOT!
I WOULD NEVER TREAT SUCH A TALENTED YOUNG WOMAN SO RUDELY!
BUT...
...SINCE THEY WERE PLAYING WITH THEIR SPELL CRESTS ACTIVATED, IT WAS ANYTHING BUT YOUR USUAL TABLE TENNIS.
TALENTED YOUNG WOMAN?
THAT REMINDS ME. SHE USED TWO ABILITIES THE LAST TIME... TELEPORTATION (?) AND VOID MAKER.
BUT EASY SAID THAT A SHIELD CAN ONLY USE ONE ABILITY, RIGHT?

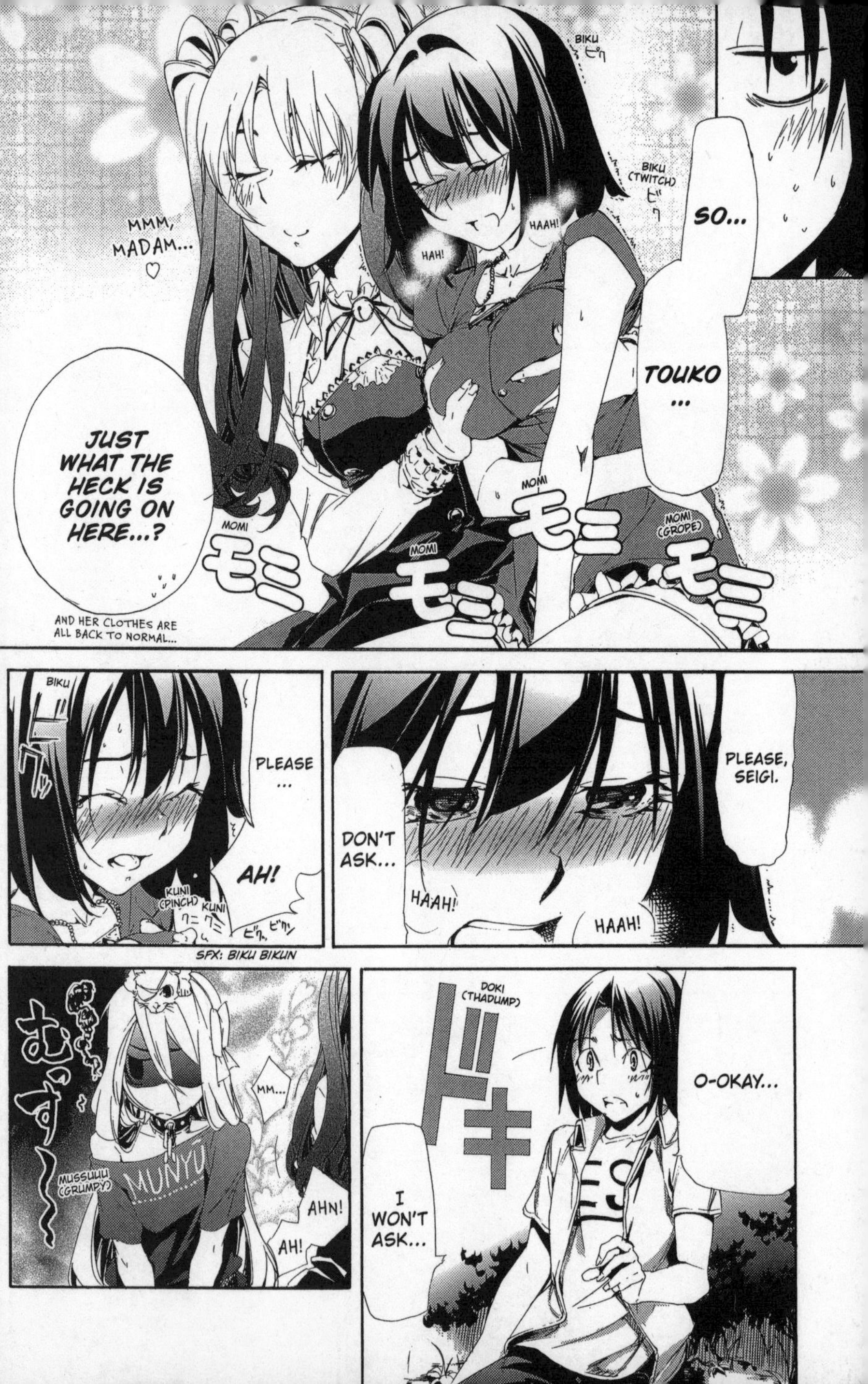
SO...
TOUKO...
BIKU
BIKU (TWITCH)
HAAH!
HAH!
MMM, MADAM... ♡
JUST WHAT THE HECK IS GOING ON HERE...?
MOMI
MOMI (GROPE)
MOMI
MOMI
AND HER CLOTHES ARE ALL BACK TO NORMAL...
PLEASE, SEIGI.
DON'T ASK...
HAAH!
HAAH!
BIKU
PLEASE...
AH!
KUNI (PINCH) KUNI
SFX: BIKU BIKUN
DOKI (THADUMP)
O-OKAY...
I WON'T ASK...
MM...
MUSSUUU (GRUMPY)
MUNYU
AHN!
AH!

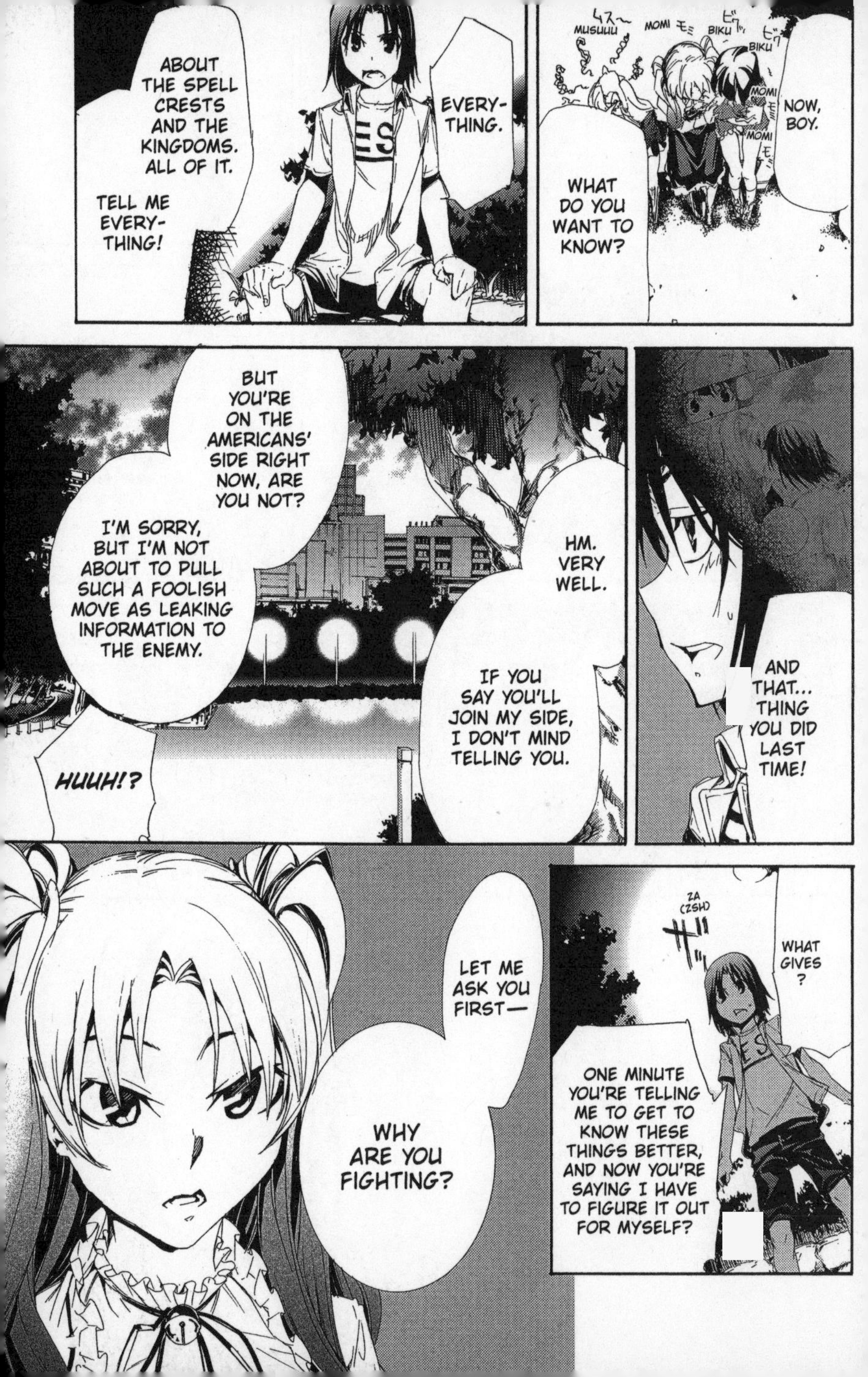
ムス～ MUSUUU
MOMI モミ
BIKU ビク
ビク BIKU
MOMI モ
MOMI モ
NOW, BOY.
WHAT DO YOU WANT TO KNOW?
EVERY-THING.
ABOUT THE SPELL CRESTS AND THE KINGDOMS. ALL OF IT.
TELL ME EVERY-THING!
AND THAT... THING YOU DID LAST TIME!
BUT YOU'RE ON THE AMERICANS' SIDE RIGHT NOW, ARE YOU NOT?
I'M SORRY, BUT I'M NOT ABOUT TO PULL SUCH A FOOLISH MOVE AS LEAKING INFORMATION TO THE ENEMY.
HUUH!?
HM. VERY WELL.
IF YOU SAY YOU'LL JOIN MY SIDE, I DON'T MIND TELLING YOU.
ZA (ZSH)
WHAT GIVES?
ONE MINUTE YOU'RE TELLING ME TO GET TO KNOW THESE THINGS BETTER, AND NOW YOU'RE SAYING I HAVE TO FIGURE IT OUT FOR MYSELF?
LET ME ASK YOU FIRST—
WHY ARE YOU FIGHTING?

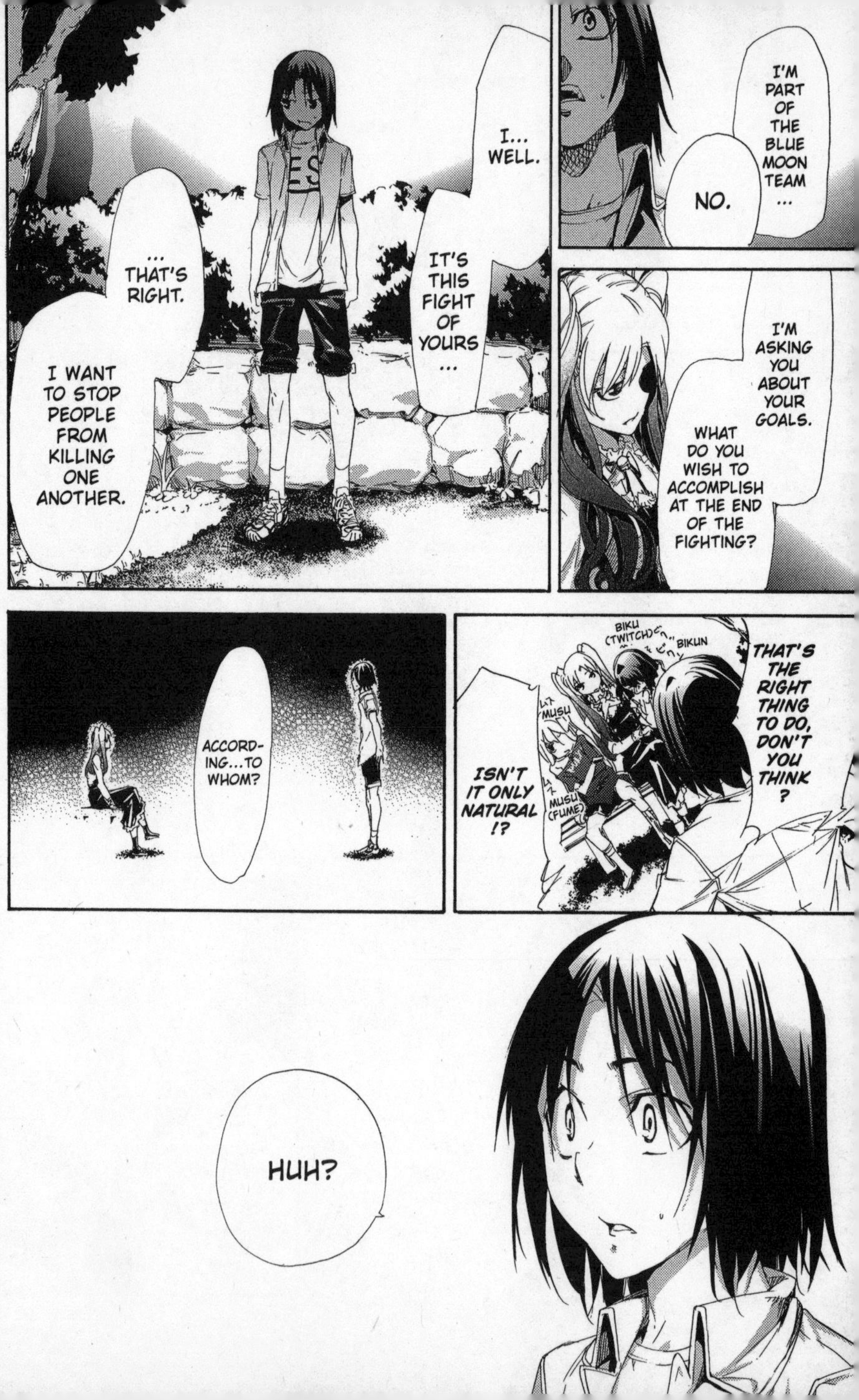
I'M PART OF THE BLUE MOON TEAM...
NO.
I'M ASKING YOU ABOUT YOUR GOALS.
WHAT DO YOU WISH TO ACCOMPLISH AT THE END OF THE FIGHTING?
I... WELL.
IT'S THIS FIGHT OF YOURS...
...THAT'S RIGHT.
I WANT TO STOP PEOPLE FROM KILLING ONE ANOTHER.
THAT'S THE RIGHT THING TO DO, DON'T YOU THINK?
BIKU (TWITCH)
BIKUN
MUSU
MUSU (FUME)
ISN'T IT ONLY NATURAL!?
ACCORDING...TO WHOM?
HUH?

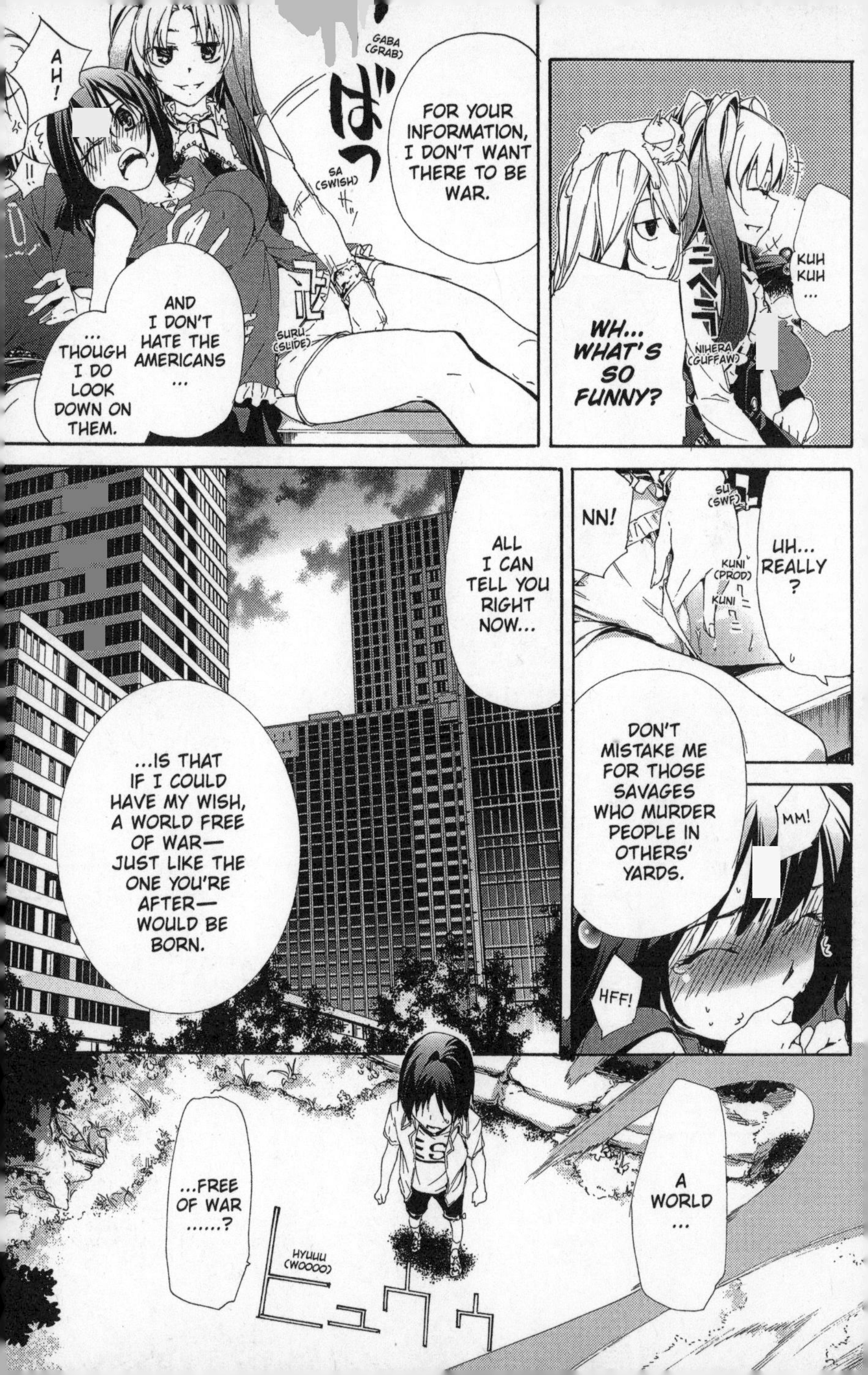
KUH KUH ...
WH... WHAT'S SO FUNNY?
NIHERA (GUFFAW)
GABA (GRAB)
FOR YOUR INFORMATION, I DON'T WANT THERE TO BE WAR.
SA (SWISH)
AH!
AND I DON'T HATE THE AMERICANS ...
... THOUGH I DO LOOK DOWN ON THEM.
SURU (SLIDE)
SU (SWF)
UH... REALLY ?
NN!
KUNI (PROD)
KUNI
DON'T MISTAKE ME FOR THOSE SAVAGES WHO MURDER PEOPLE IN OTHERS' YARDS.
MM!
HFF!
ALL I CAN TELL YOU RIGHT NOW...
...IS THAT IF I COULD HAVE MY WISH, A WORLD FREE OF WAR—JUST LIKE THE ONE YOU'RE AFTER—WOULD BE BORN.
A WORLD ...
...FREE OF WAR ......?
HYUUU (WOOOO)

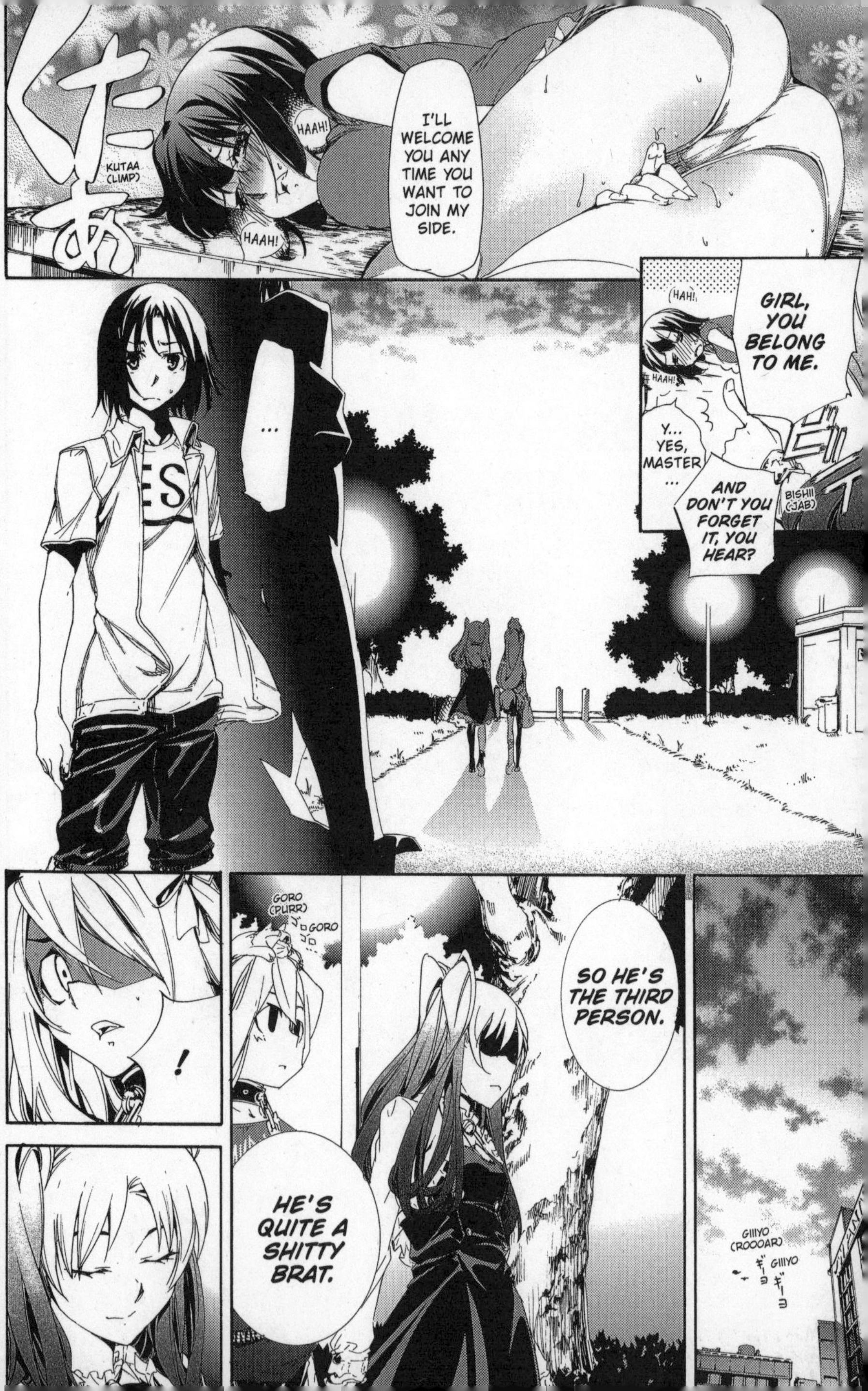
HAAH!
I'LL WELCOME YOU ANY TIME YOU WANT TO JOIN MY SIDE.
KUTAA (LIMP)
HAAH!
GIRL, YOU BELONG TO ME.
(HAH!)
HAAH!
Y... YES, MASTER ...
AND DON'T YOU FORGET IT, YOU HEAR?
BISHII (JAB)
...
GIIIYO (ROOOAR)
GIIIYO
SO HE'S THE THIRD PERSON.
GORO (PURR)
GORO
HE'S QUITE A SHITTY BRAT.
!

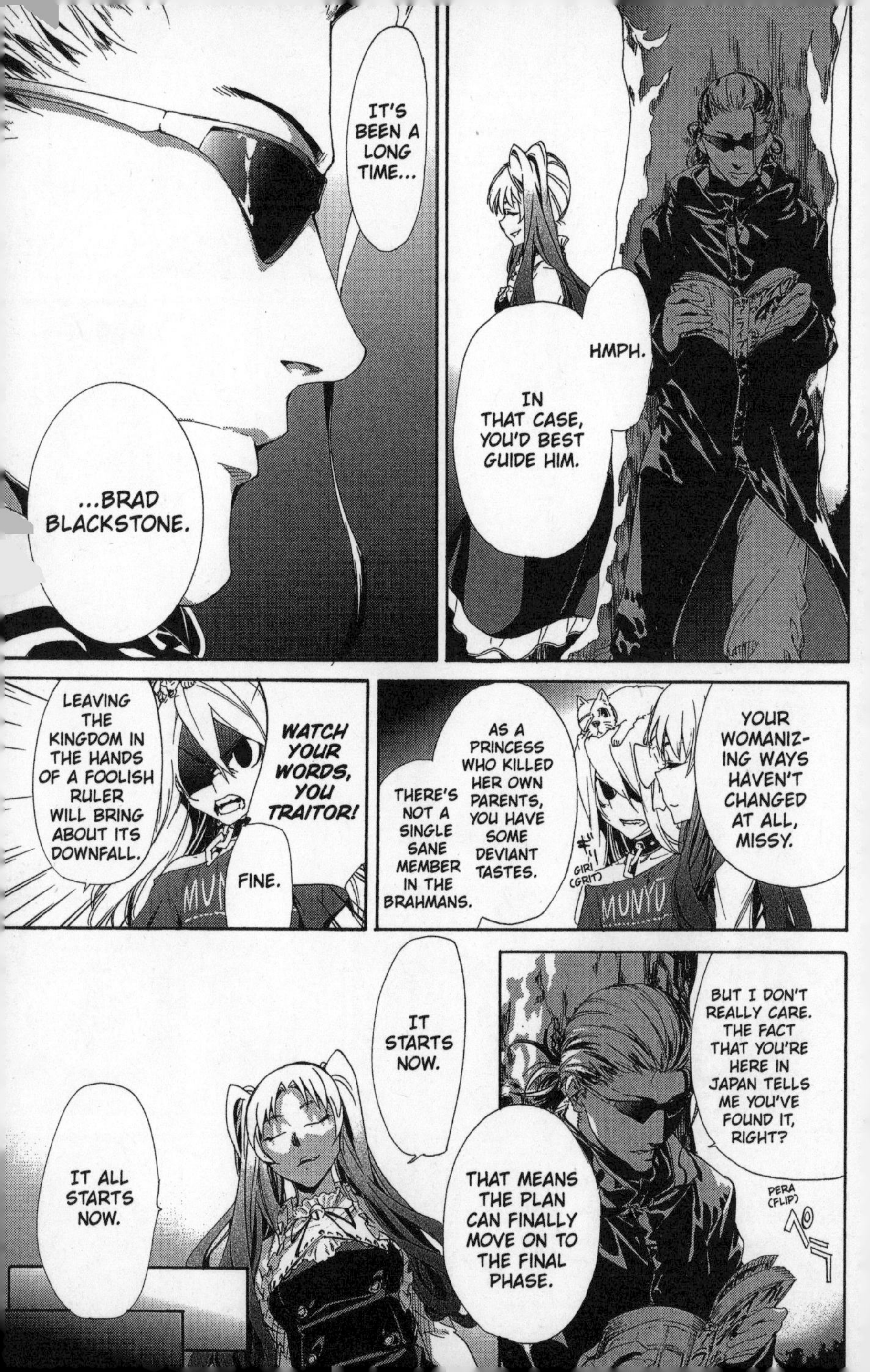
HMPH.
IN THAT CASE, YOU'D BEST GUIDE HIM.
IT'S BEEN A LONG TIME...
...BRAD BLACKSTONE.
YOUR WOMANIZING WAYS HAVEN'T CHANGED AT ALL, MISSY.
AS A PRINCESS WHO KILLED HER OWN PARENTS, YOU HAVE SOME DEVIANT TASTES.
GIRI (GRIT)
MUNYU
THERE'S NOT A SINGLE SANE MEMBER IN THE BRAHMANS.
WATCH YOUR WORDS, YOU TRAITOR!
LEAVING THE KINGDOM IN THE HANDS OF A FOOLISH RULER WILL BRING ABOUT ITS DOWNFALL.
FINE.
BUT I DON'T REALLY CARE. THE FACT THAT YOU'RE HERE IN JAPAN TELLS ME YOU'VE FOUND IT, RIGHT?
PERA (FLIP)
THAT MEANS THE PLAN CAN FINALLY MOVE ON TO THE FINAL PHASE.
IT STARTS NOW.
IT ALL STARTS NOW.

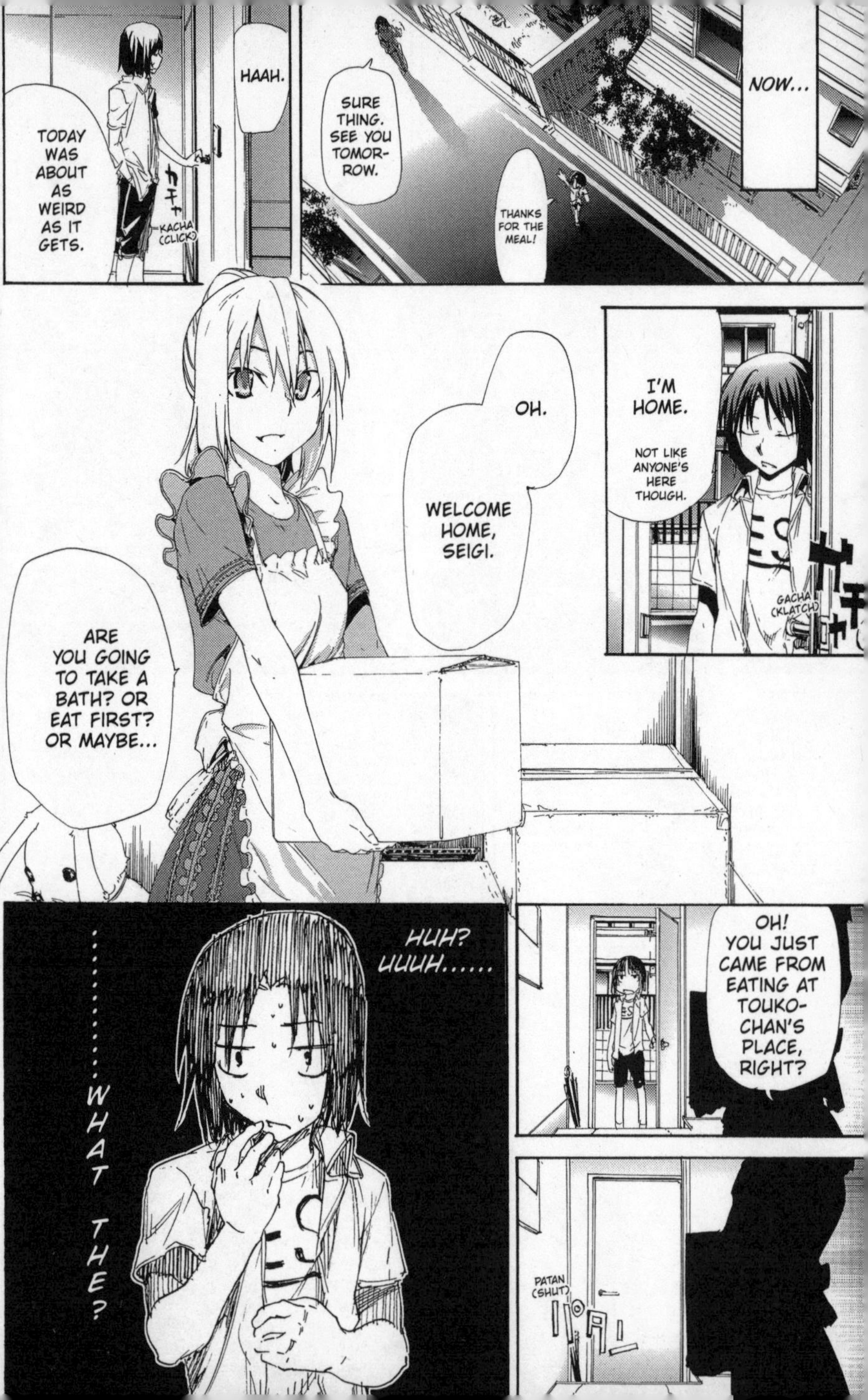
NOW...
THANKS FOR THE MEAL!
SURE THING. SEE YOU TOMORROW.
HAAH.
TODAY WAS ABOUT AS WEIRD AS IT GETS.
KACHA (CLICK)
I'M HOME.
NOT LIKE ANYONE'S HERE THOUGH.
GACHA (KLATCH)
OH.
WELCOME HOME, SEIGI.
ARE YOU GOING TO TAKE A BATH? OR EAT FIRST? OR MAYBE...
OH! YOU JUST CAME FROM EATING AT TOUKO-CHAN'S PLACE, RIGHT?
PATAN (SHUT)
HUH? UUUH......
..........WHAT THE?

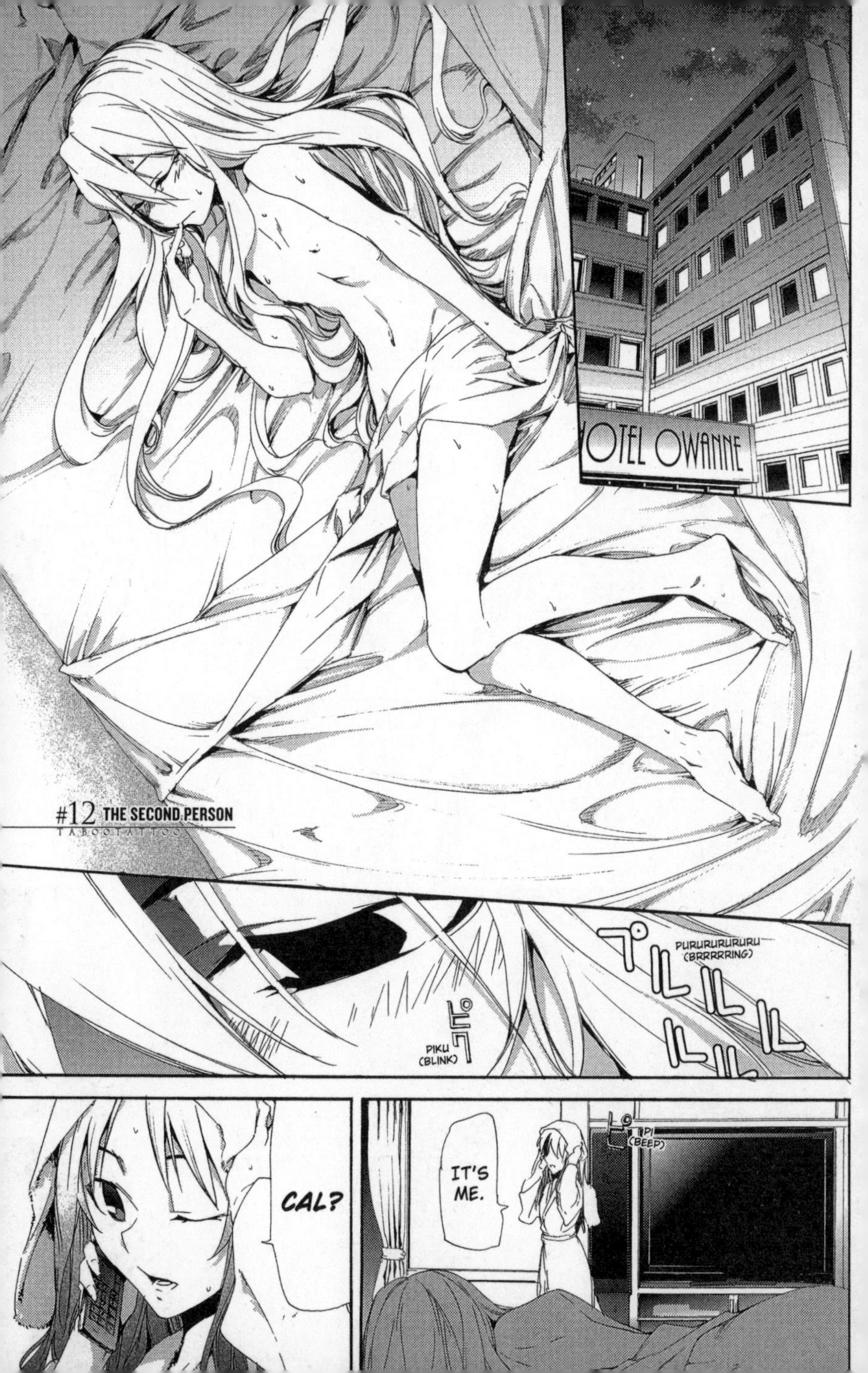
HOTEL OWANNE
#12 THE SECOND PERSON
TABOOTATTOO
プルルルルル
PURURURURURU
(BRRRRRING)
ピク
PIKU
(BLINK)
ピ
PI
(BEEP)
IT'S ME.
CAL?

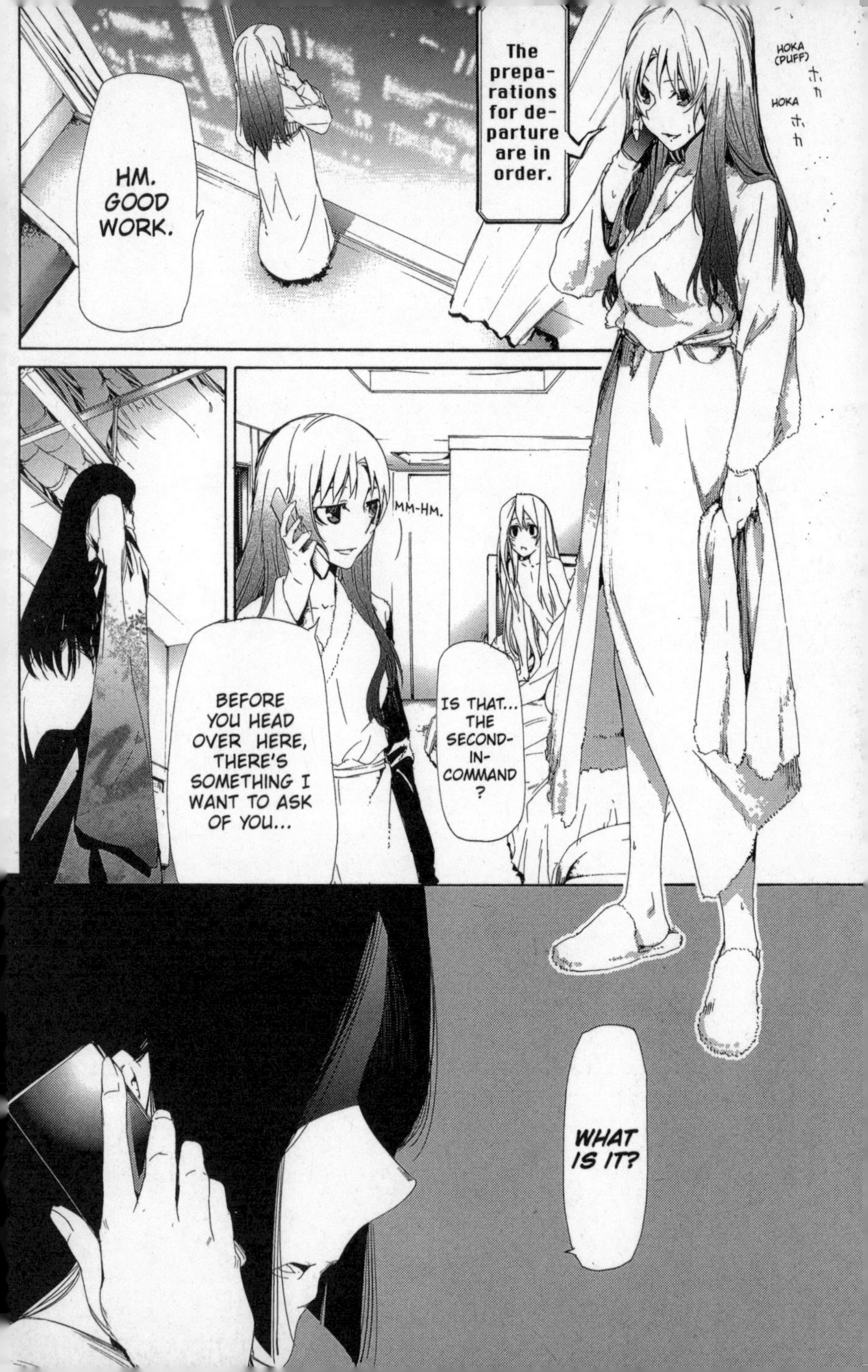
HOKA (PUFF)
HOKA
The preparations for departure are in order.
HM. GOOD WORK.
MM-HM.
IS THAT... THE SECOND-IN-COMMAND?
BEFORE YOU HEAD OVER HERE, THERE'S SOMETHING I WANT TO ASK OF YOU...
WHAT IS IT?

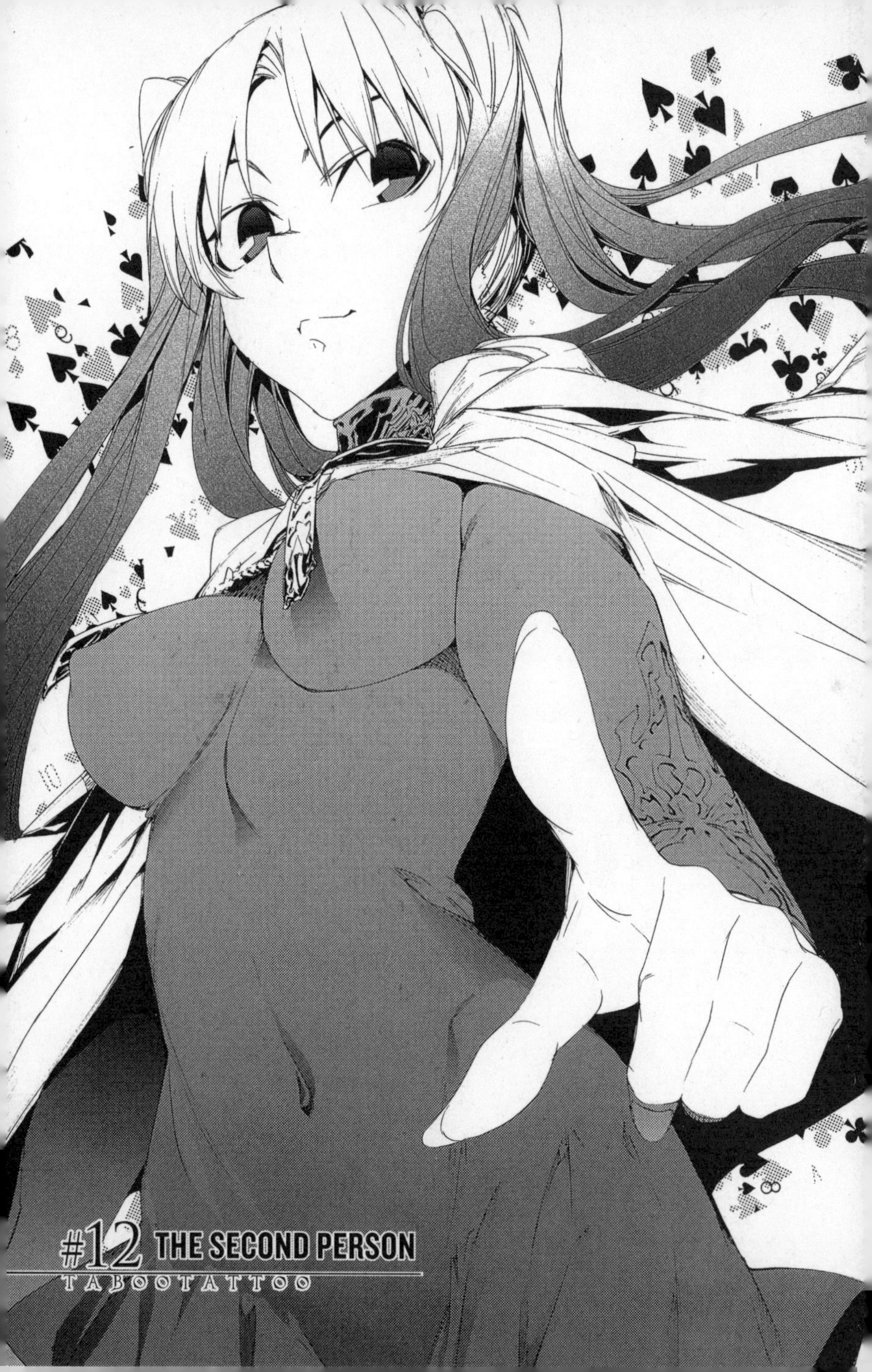
#12 THE SECOND PERSON
TABOOTATTOO

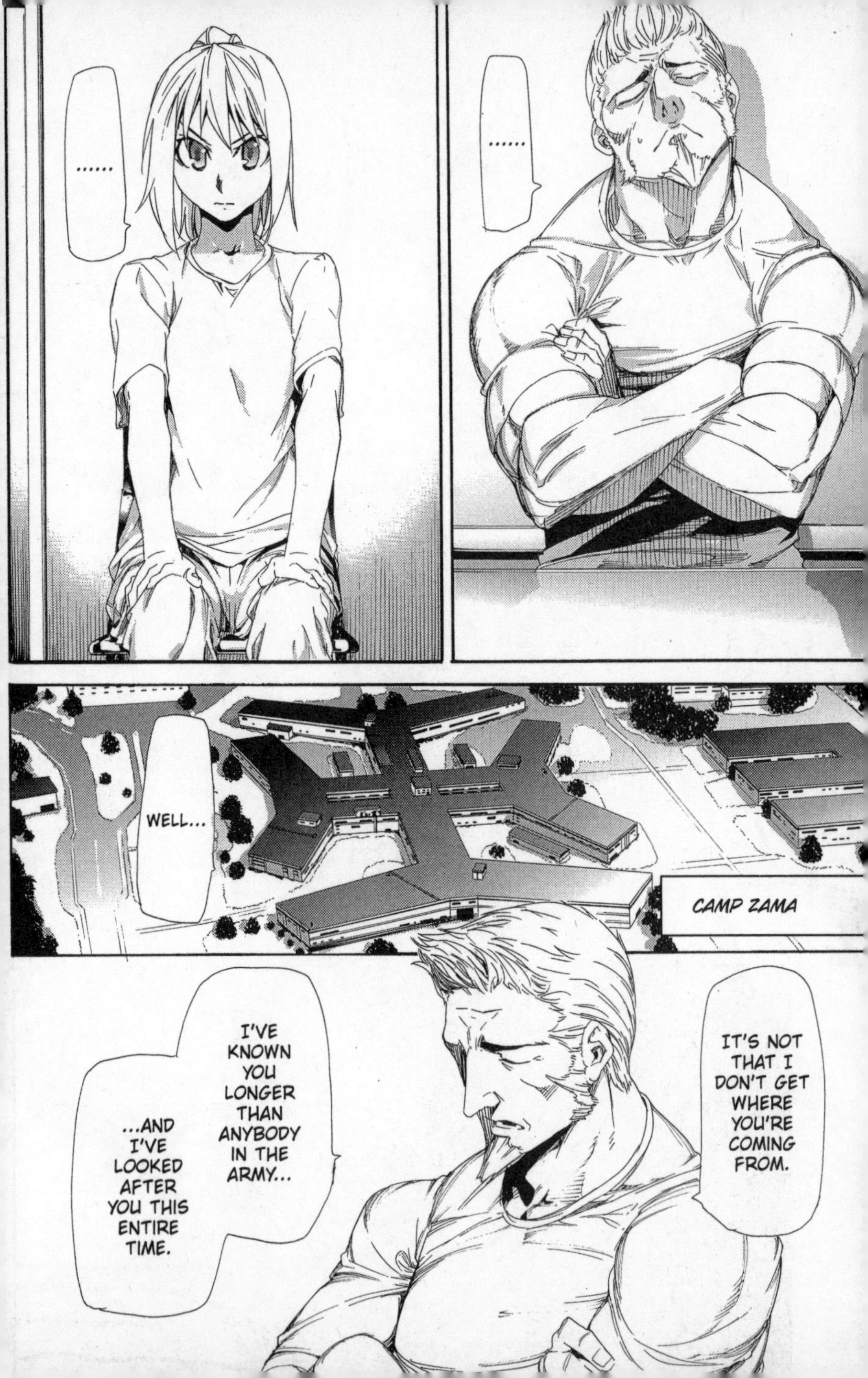
......
......
CAMP ZAMA
WELL...
IT'S NOT THAT I DON'T GET WHERE YOU'RE COMING FROM.
I'VE KNOWN YOU LONGER THAN ANYBODY IN THE ARMY...
...AND I'VE LOOKED AFTER YOU THIS ENTIRE TIME.

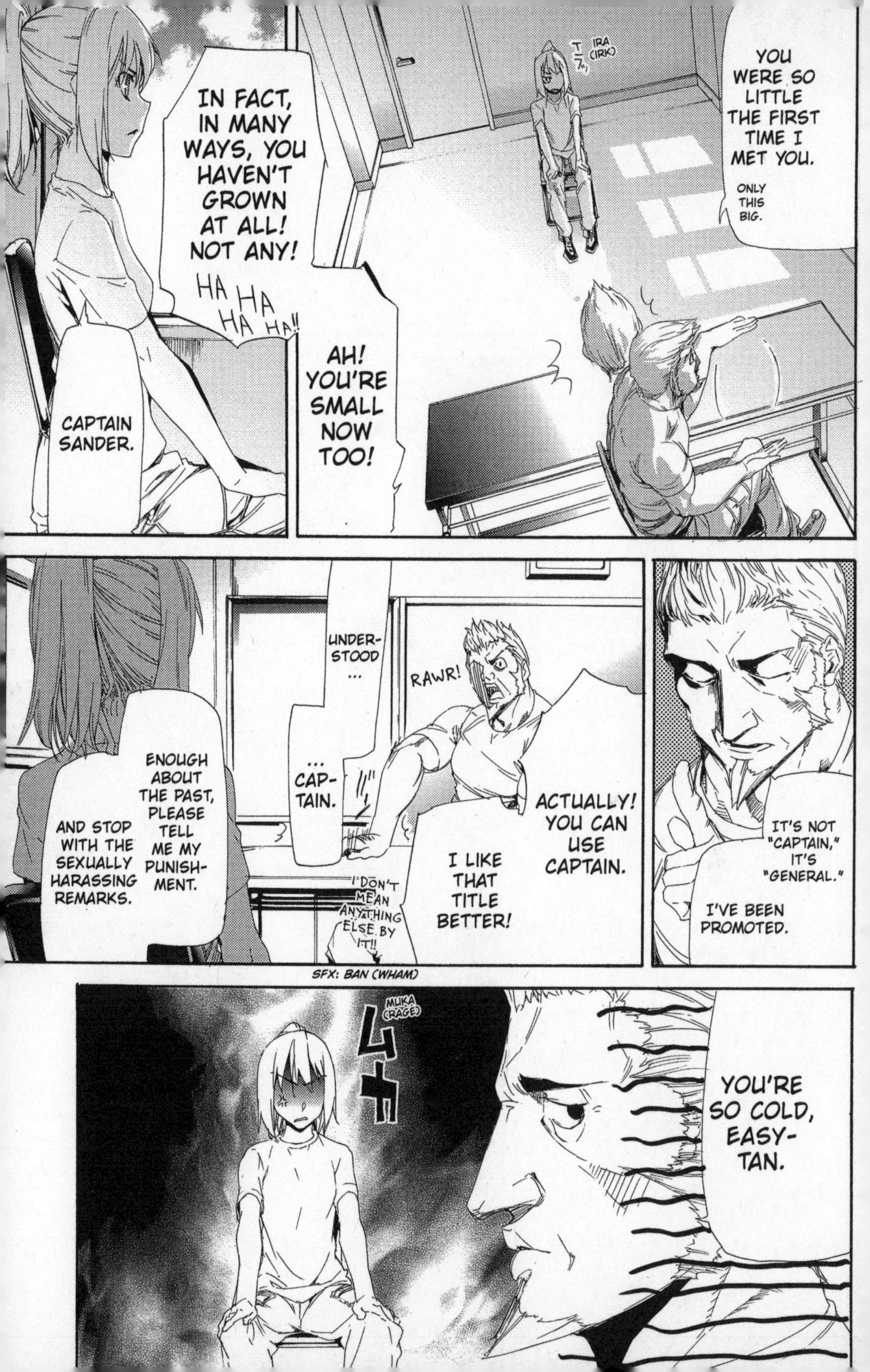
YOU WERE SO LITTLE THE FIRST TIME I MET YOU.
ONLY THIS BIG.
IRA (IRK)
AH! YOU'RE SMALL NOW TOO!
IN FACT, IN MANY WAYS, YOU HAVEN'T GROWN AT ALL! NOT ANY!
HA HA HA HA!!
CAPTAIN SANDER.
IT'S NOT "CAPTAIN," IT'S "GENERAL."
I'VE BEEN PROMOTED.
UNDER-STOOD ...
... CAP-TAIN.
RAWR!
ACTUALLY! YOU CAN USE CAPTAIN.
I LIKE THAT TITLE BETTER!
I DON'T MEAN ANYTHING ELSE BY IT!!
ENOUGH ABOUT THE PAST, PLEASE TELL ME MY PUNISH-MENT.
AND STOP WITH THE SEXUALLY HARASSING REMARKS.
SFX: BAN (WHAM)
MUKA (RAGE)
YOU'RE SO COLD, EASY-TAN.

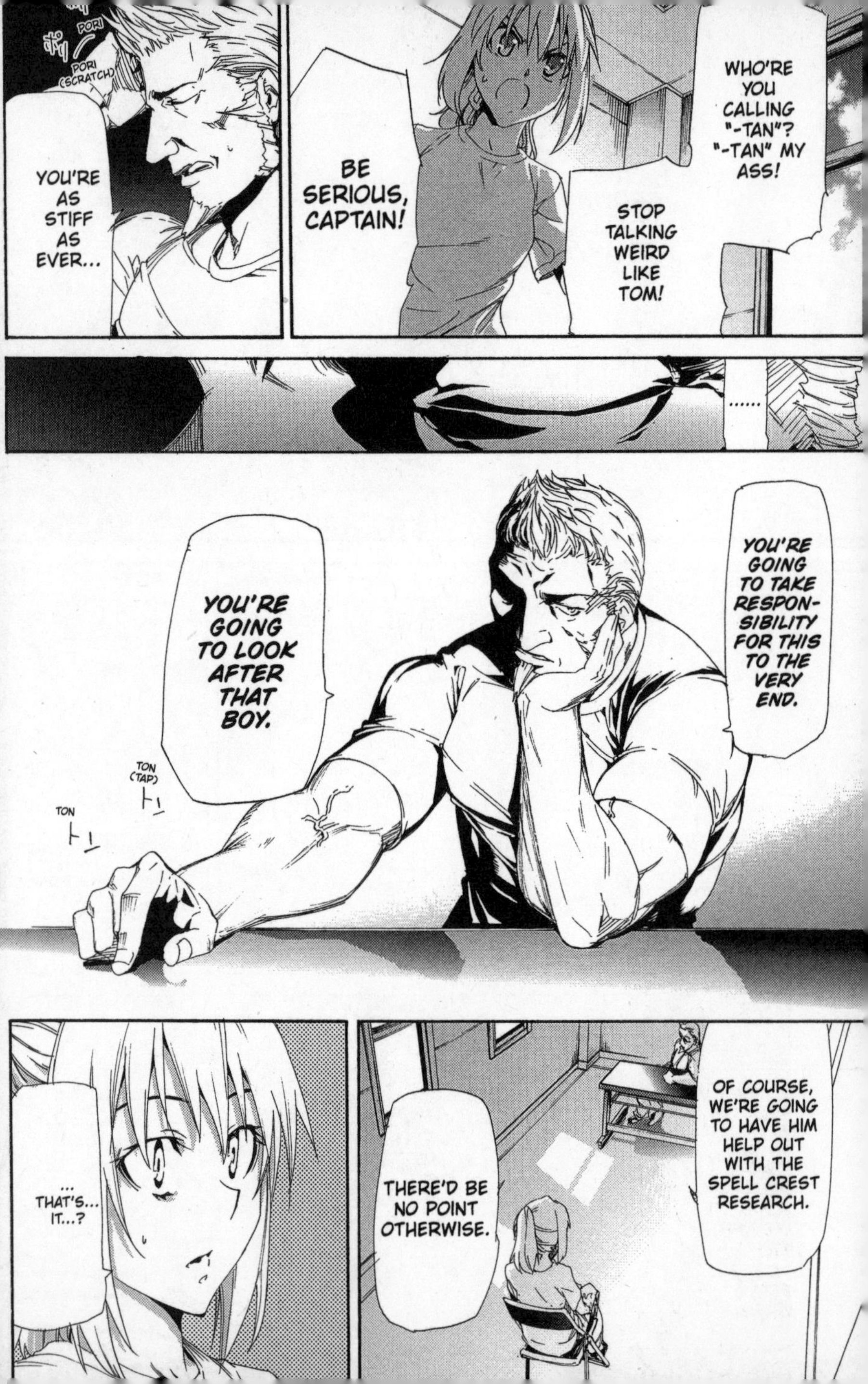
WHO'RE YOU CALLING "-TAN"? "-TAN" MY ASS!
STOP TALKING WEIRD LIKE TOM!
BE SERIOUS, CAPTAIN!
PORI
PORI (SCRATCH)
YOU'RE AS STIFF AS EVER...
......
YOU'RE GOING TO TAKE RESPON-SIBILITY FOR THIS TO THE VERY END.
YOU'RE GOING TO LOOK AFTER THAT BOY.
TON (TAP)
TON
OF COURSE, WE'RE GOING TO HAVE HIM HELP OUT WITH THE SPELL CREST RESEARCH.
THERE'D BE NO POINT OTHERWISE.
... THAT'S... IT...?

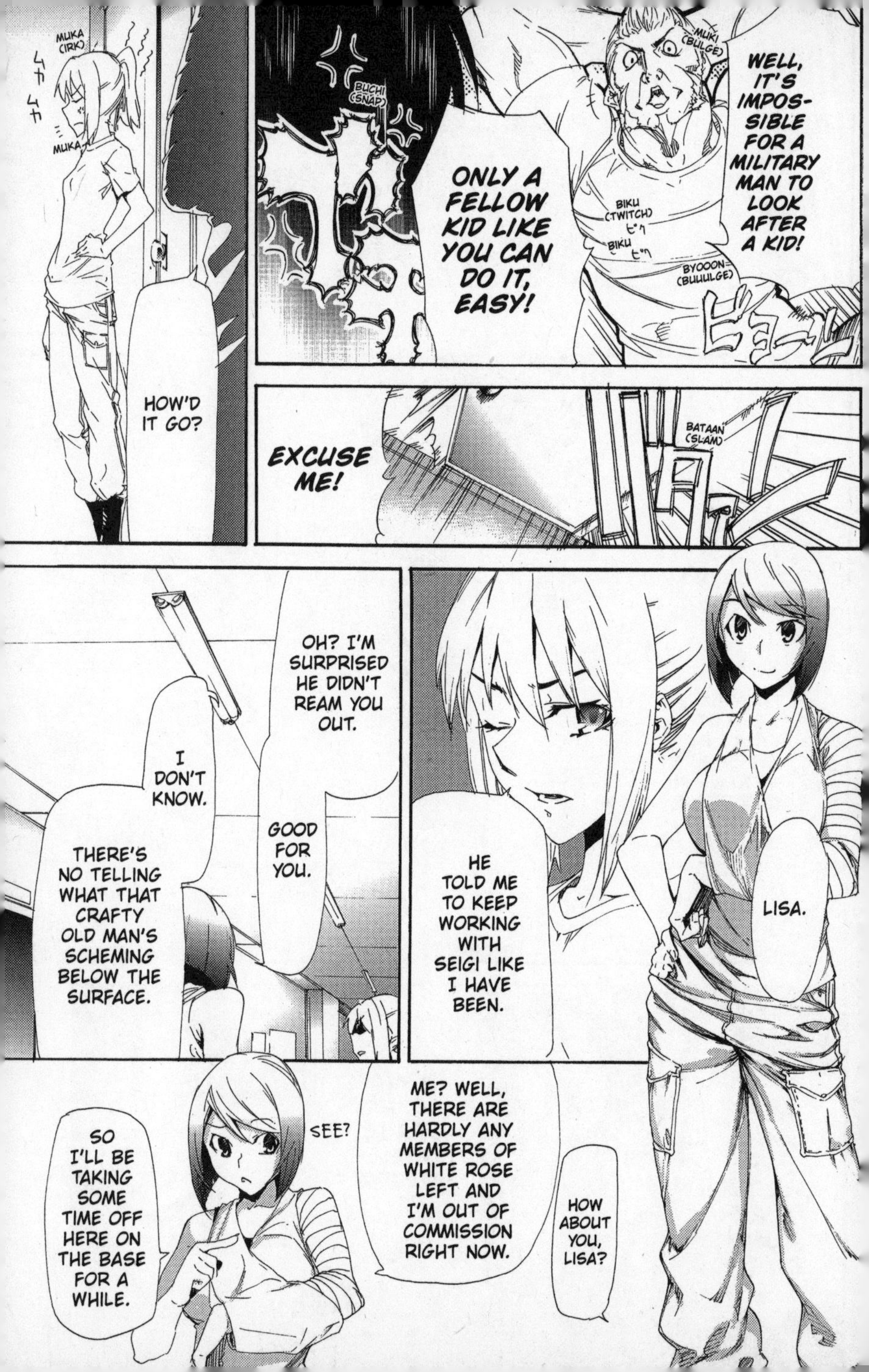
MUKI (BULGE)
WELL, IT'S IMPOSSIBLE FOR A MILITARY MAN TO LOOK AFTER A KID!
BIKU (TWITCH)
BIKU
BYOOON (BUUULGE)
BUCHI (SNAP)
ONLY A FELLOW KID LIKE YOU CAN DO IT, EASY!
BATAAN (SLAM)
EXCUSE ME!
MUKA (IRK)
MUKA
HOW'D IT GO?
LISA.
HE TOLD ME TO KEEP WORKING WITH SEIGI LIKE I HAVE BEEN.
OH? I'M SURPRISED HE DIDN'T REAM YOU OUT.
GOOD FOR YOU.
I DON'T KNOW.
THERE'S NO TELLING WHAT THAT CRAFTY OLD MAN'S SCHEMING BELOW THE SURFACE.
HOW ABOUT YOU, LISA?
ME? WELL, THERE ARE HARDLY ANY MEMBERS OF WHITE ROSE LEFT AND I'M OUT OF COMMISSION RIGHT NOW.
SEE?
SO I'LL BE TAKING SOME TIME OFF HERE ON THE BASE FOR A WHILE.

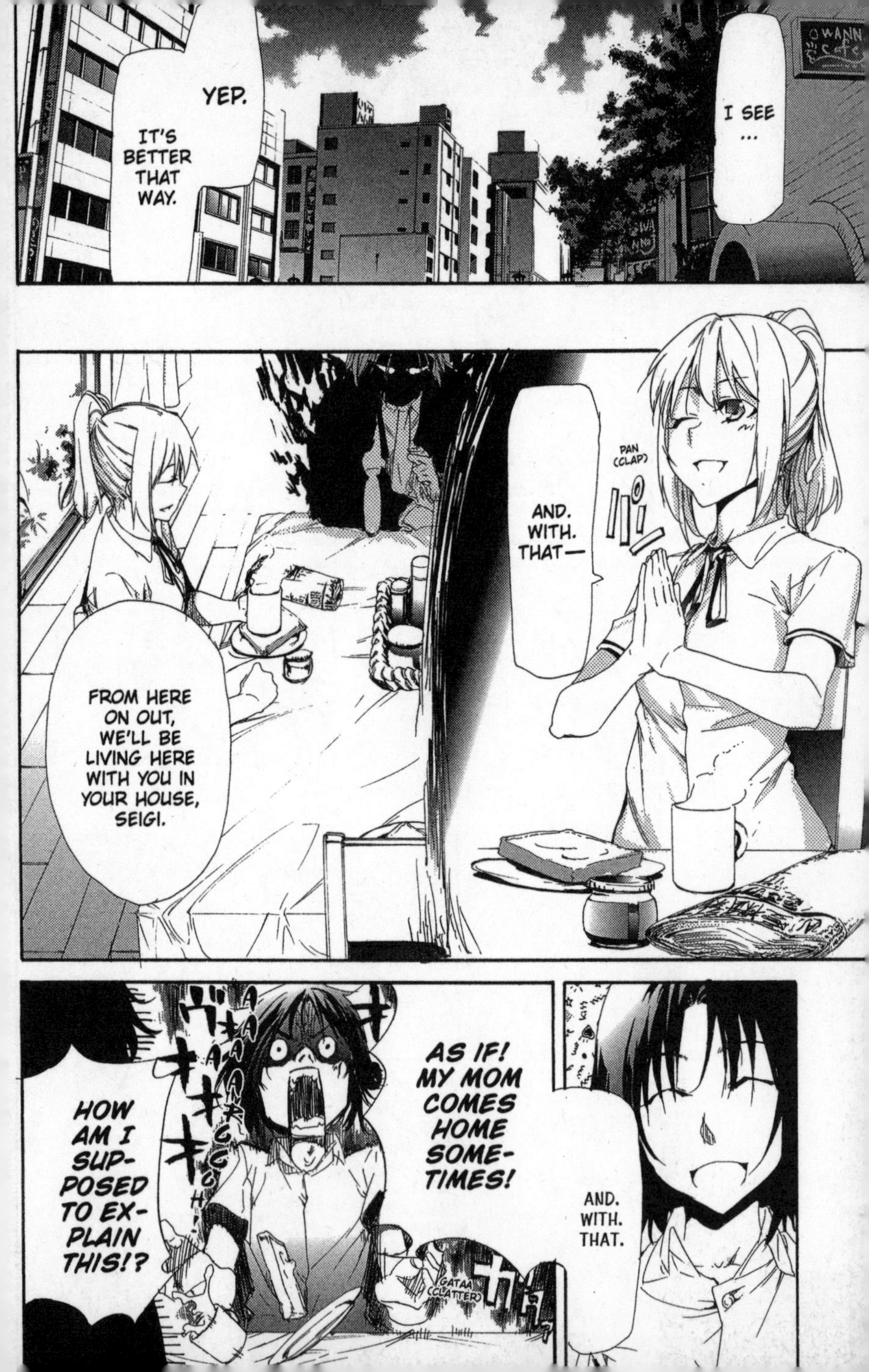
I SEE ...
YEP.
IT'S BETTER THAT WAY.
PAN (CLAP)
AND. WITH. THAT—
FROM HERE ON OUT, WE'LL BE LIVING HERE WITH YOU IN YOUR HOUSE, SEIGI.
AND. WITH. THAT.
AS IF! MY MOM COMES HOME SOMETIMES!
AAAARGGH!
HOW AM I SUPPOSED TO EXPLAIN THIS!?
GATAA (CLATTER)

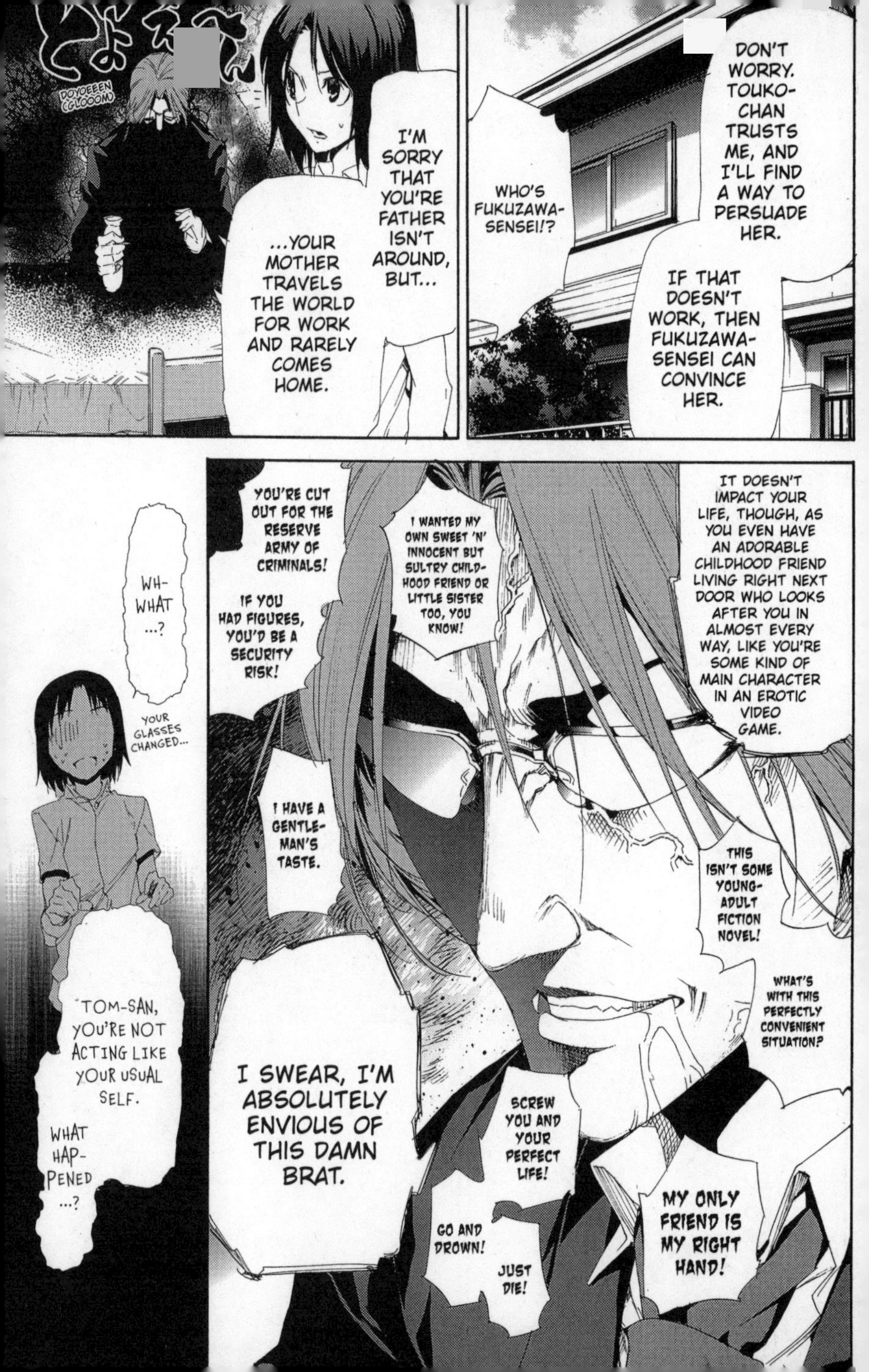
DON'T WORRY. TOUKO-CHAN TRUSTS ME, AND I'LL FIND A WAY TO PERSUADE HER.
IF THAT DOESN'T WORK, THEN FUKUZAWA-SENSEI CAN CONVINCE HER.
WHO'S FUKUZAWA-SENSEI!?
I'M SORRY THAT YOU'RE FATHER ISN'T AROUND, BUT...
...YOUR MOTHER TRAVELS THE WORLD FOR WORK AND RARELY COMES HOME.
DOYOEEEN (GLOOOM)
IT DOESN'T IMPACT YOUR LIFE, THOUGH, AS YOU EVEN HAVE AN ADORABLE CHILDHOOD FRIEND LIVING RIGHT NEXT DOOR WHO LOOKS AFTER YOU IN ALMOST EVERY WAY, LIKE YOU'RE SOME KIND OF MAIN CHARACTER IN AN EROTIC VIDEO GAME.
I WANTED MY OWN SWEET 'N' INNOCENT BUT SULTRY CHILD-HOOD FRIEND OR LITTLE SISTER TOO, YOU KNOW!
YOU'RE CUT OUT FOR THE RESERVE ARMY OF CRIMINALS!
IF YOU HAD FIGURES, YOU'D BE A SECURITY RISK!
I HAVE A GENTLE-MAN'S TASTE.
THIS ISN'T SOME YOUNG-ADULT FICTION NOVEL!
WHAT'S WITH THIS PERFECTLY CONVENIENT SITUATION?
I SWEAR, I'M ABSOLUTELY ENVIOUS OF THIS DAMN BRAT.
SCREW YOU AND YOUR PERFECT LIFE!
MY ONLY FRIEND IS MY RIGHT HAND!
GO AND DROWN!
JUST DIE!
WH-WHAT ...?
YOUR GLASSES CHANGED...
TOM-SAN, YOU'RE NOT ACTING LIKE YOUR USUAL SELF.
WHAT HAP-PENED ...?

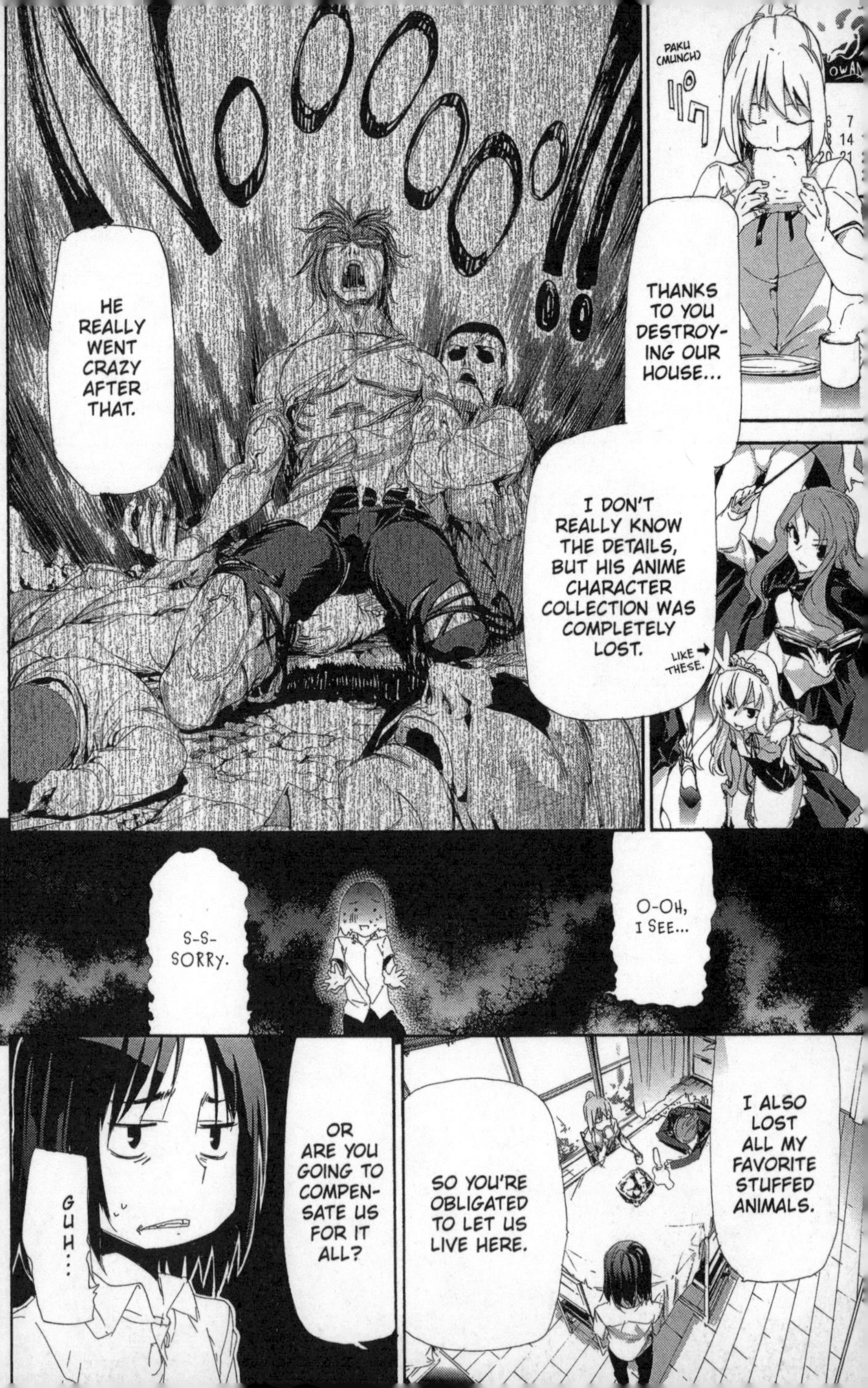
PAKU (MUNCH)
THANKS TO YOU DESTROYING OUR HOUSE...
I DON'T REALLY KNOW THE DETAILS, BUT HIS ANIME CHARACTER COLLECTION WAS COMPLETELY LOST.
LIKE THESE.
NOOOOOOOO!!
HE REALLY WENT CRAZY AFTER THAT.
O-OH, I SEE...
S-S-SORRY.
I ALSO LOST ALL MY FAVORITE STUFFED ANIMALS.
SO YOU'RE OBLIGATED TO LET US LIVE HERE.
OR ARE YOU GOING TO COMPENSATE US FOR IT ALL?
GUH...

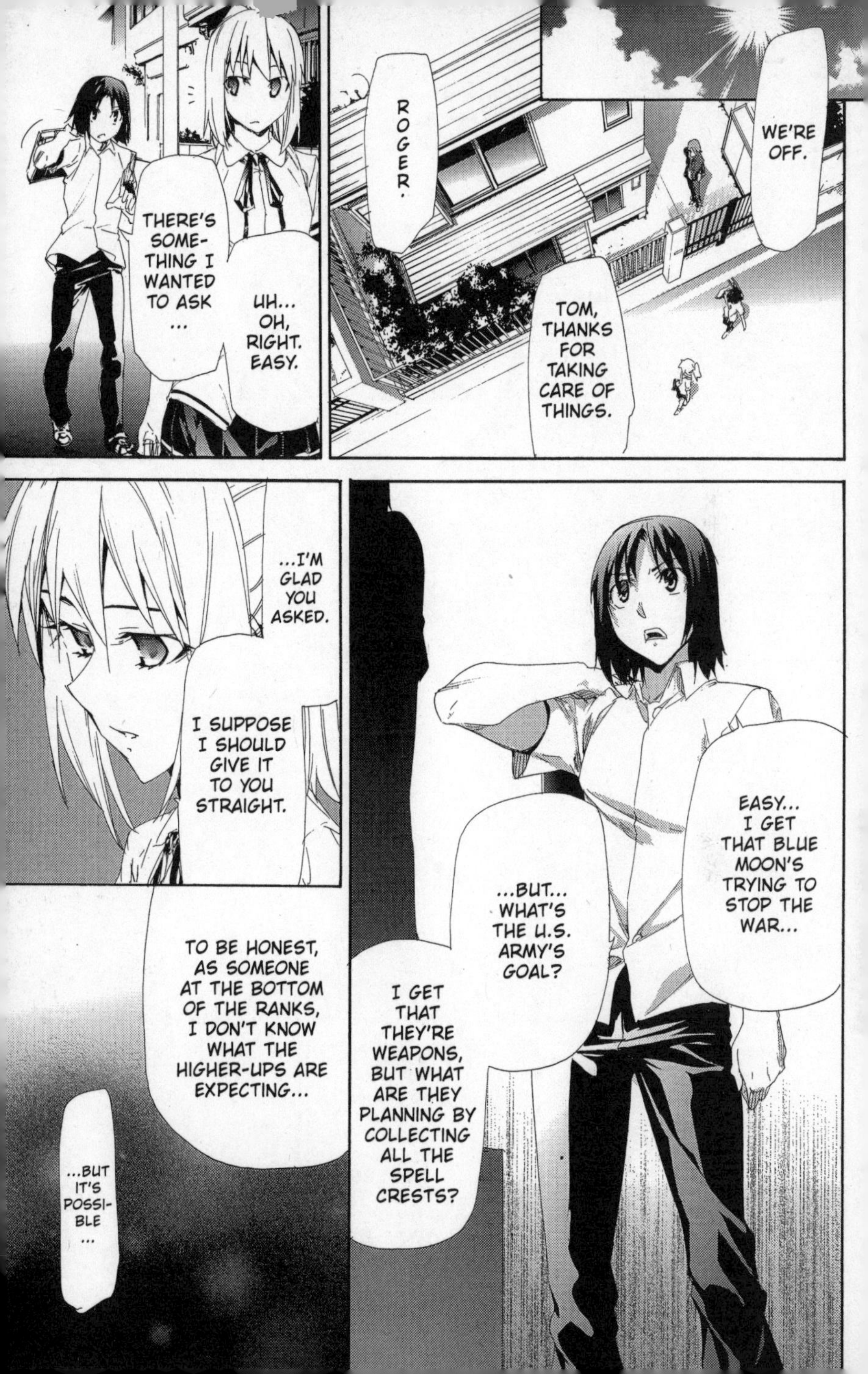
WE'RE OFF.
ROGER.
TOM, THANKS FOR TAKING CARE OF THINGS.
THERE'S SOMETHING I WANTED TO ASK...
UH... OH, RIGHT. EASY.
EASY... I GET THAT BLUE MOON'S TRYING TO STOP THE WAR...
...BUT... WHAT'S THE U.S. ARMY'S GOAL?
I GET THAT THEY'RE WEAPONS, BUT WHAT ARE THEY PLANNING BY COLLECTING ALL THE SPELL CRESTS?
...I'M GLAD YOU ASKED.
I SUPPOSE I SHOULD GIVE IT TO YOU STRAIGHT.
TO BE HONEST, AS SOMEONE AT THE BOTTOM OF THE RANKS, I DON'T KNOW WHAT THE HIGHER-UPS ARE EXPECTING...
...BUT IT'S POSSIBLE...

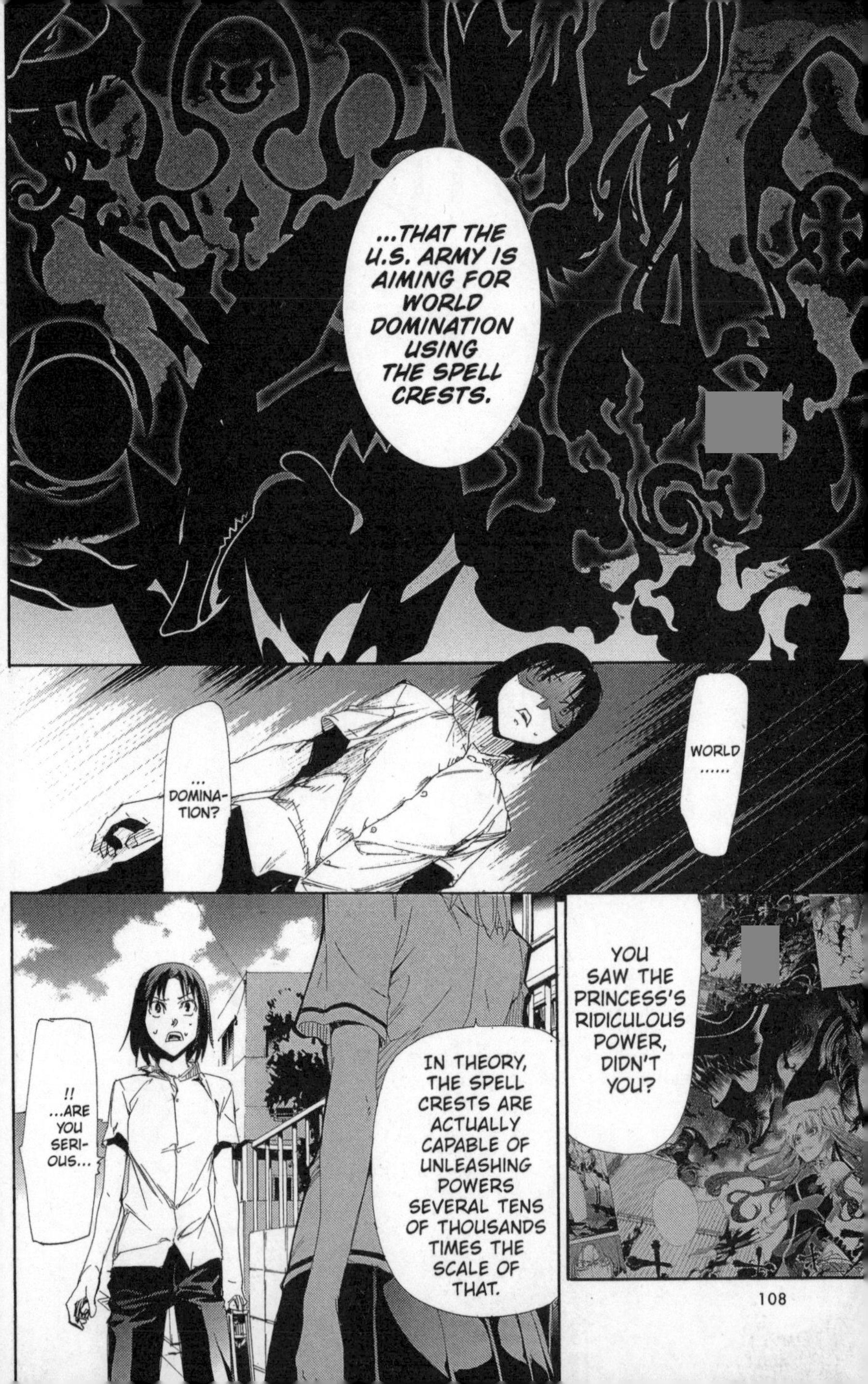
...THAT THE U.S. ARMY IS AIMING FOR WORLD DOMINATION USING THE SPELL CRESTS.
WORLD ......
... DOMINATION?
YOU SAW THE PRINCESS'S RIDICULOUS POWER, DIDN'T YOU?
IN THEORY, THE SPELL CRESTS ARE ACTUALLY CAPABLE OF UNLEASHING POWERS SEVERAL TENS OF THOUSANDS TIMES THE SCALE OF THAT.
!! ...ARE YOU SERIOUS...

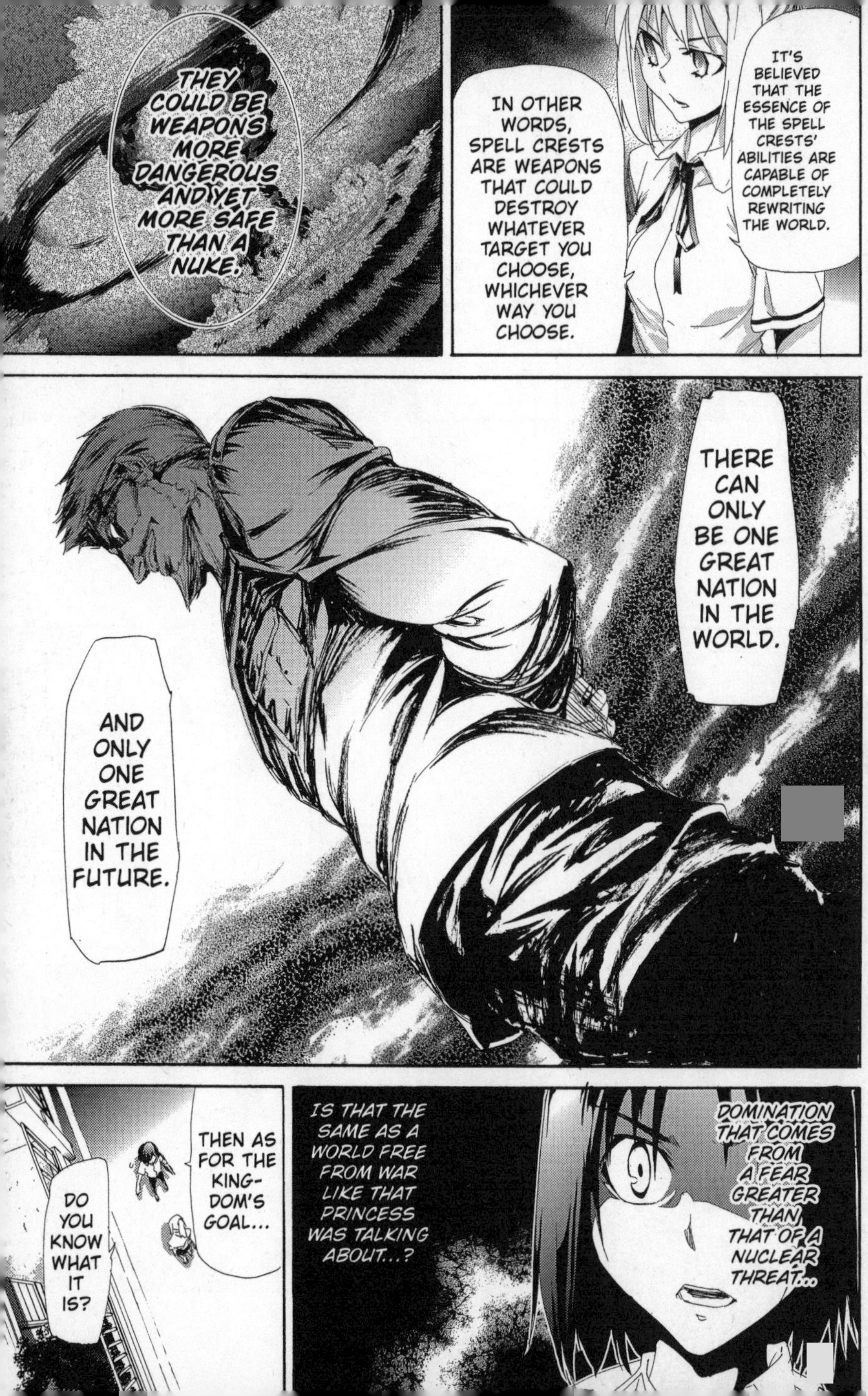
IT'S BELIEVED THAT THE ESSENCE OF THE SPELL CRESTS' ABILITIES ARE CAPABLE OF COMPLETELY REWRITING THE WORLD.
IN OTHER WORDS, SPELL CRESTS ARE WEAPONS THAT COULD DESTROY WHATEVER TARGET YOU CHOOSE, WHICHEVER WAY YOU CHOOSE.
THEY COULD BE WEAPONS MORE DANGEROUS AND YET MORE SAFE THAN A NUKE.
THERE CAN ONLY BE ONE GREAT NATION IN THE WORLD.
AND ONLY ONE GREAT NATION IN THE FUTURE.
DOMINATION THAT COMES FROM A FEAR GREATER THAN THAT OF A NUCLEAR THREAT...
IS THAT THE SAME AS A WORLD FREE FROM WAR LIKE THAT PRINCESS WAS TALKING ABOUT...?
THEN AS FOR THE KING-DOM'S GOAL...
DO YOU KNOW WHAT IT IS?

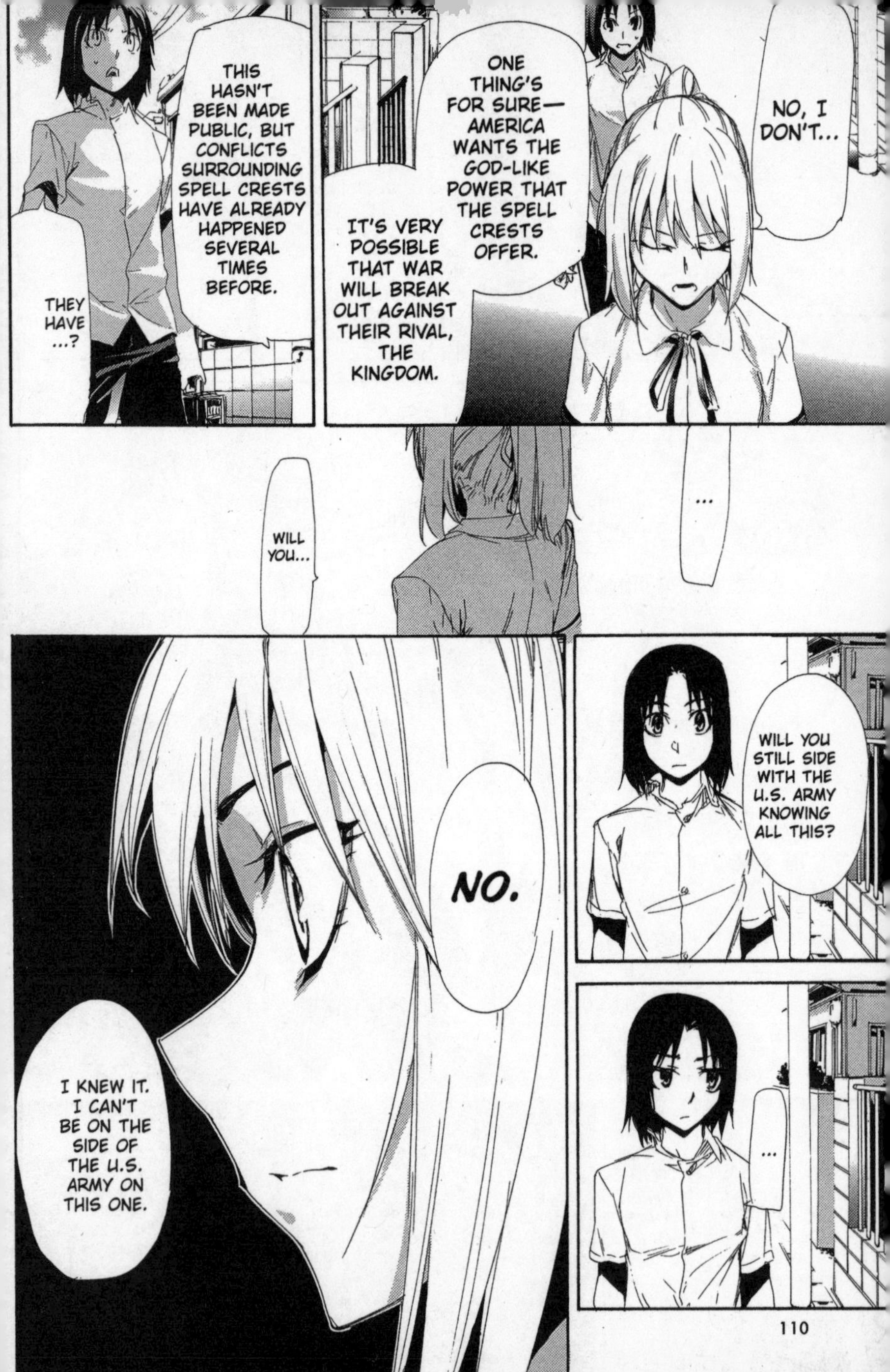
NO, I DON'T...
ONE THING'S FOR SURE— AMERICA WANTS THE GOD-LIKE POWER THAT THE SPELL CRESTS OFFER.
IT'S VERY POSSIBLE THAT WAR WILL BREAK OUT AGAINST THEIR RIVAL, THE KINGDOM.
THIS HASN'T BEEN MADE PUBLIC, BUT CONFLICTS SURROUNDING SPELL CRESTS HAVE ALREADY HAPPENED SEVERAL TIMES BEFORE.
THEY HAVE ...?
...
WILL YOU...
WILL YOU STILL SIDE WITH THE U.S. ARMY KNOWING ALL THIS?
...
NO.
I KNEW IT. I CAN'T BE ON THE SIDE OF THE U.S. ARMY ON THIS ONE.

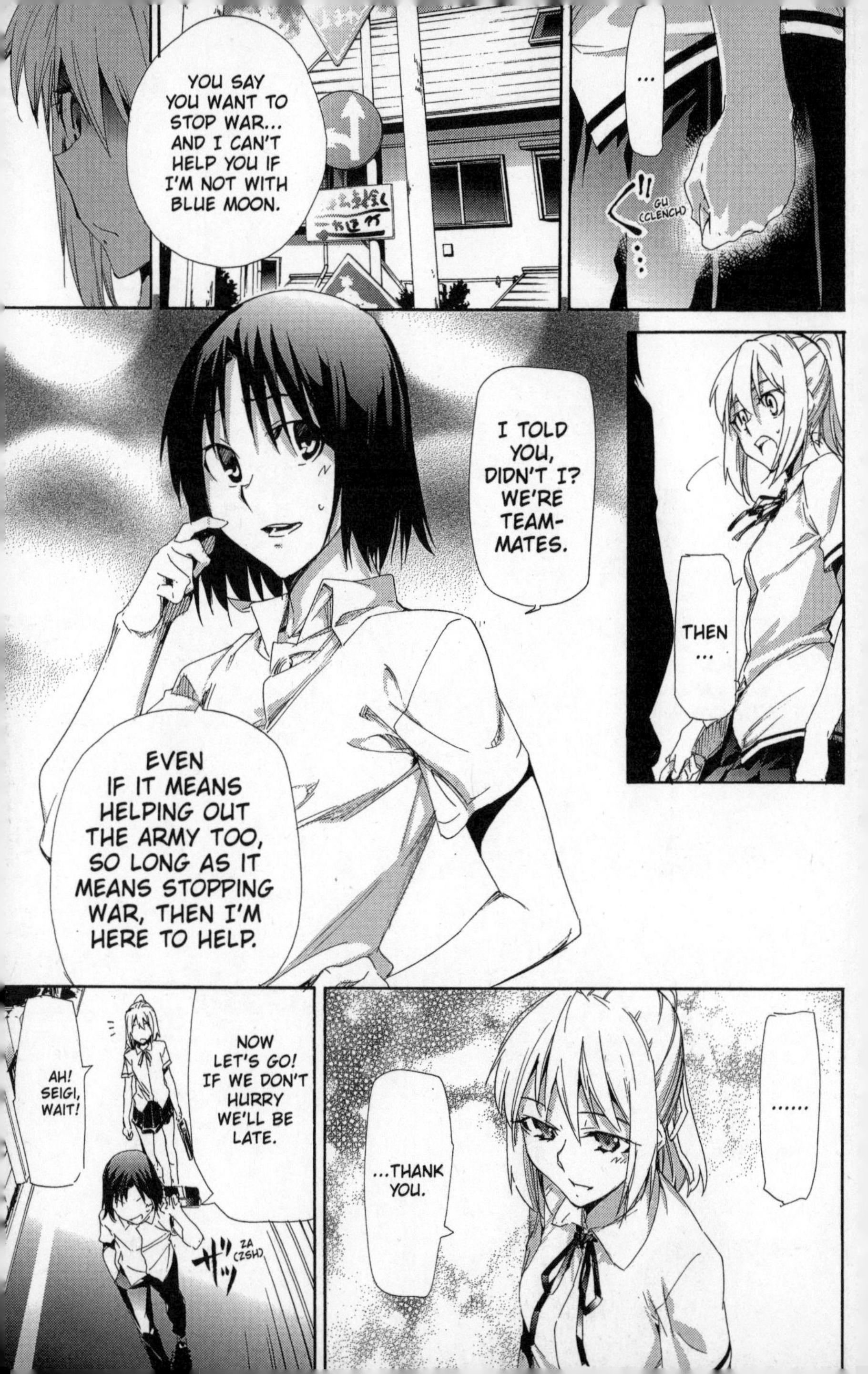
...
GU (CLENCH)
...
YOU SAY YOU WANT TO STOP WAR... AND I CAN'T HELP YOU IF I'M NOT WITH BLUE MOON.
THEN...
I TOLD YOU, DIDN'T I? WE'RE TEAM-MATES.
EVEN IF IT MEANS HELPING OUT THE ARMY TOO, SO LONG AS IT MEANS STOPPING WAR, THEN I'M HERE TO HELP.
......
...THANK YOU.
NOW LET'S GO! IF WE DON'T HURRY WE'LL BE LATE.
AH! SEIGI, WAIT!
ZA (ZSH)

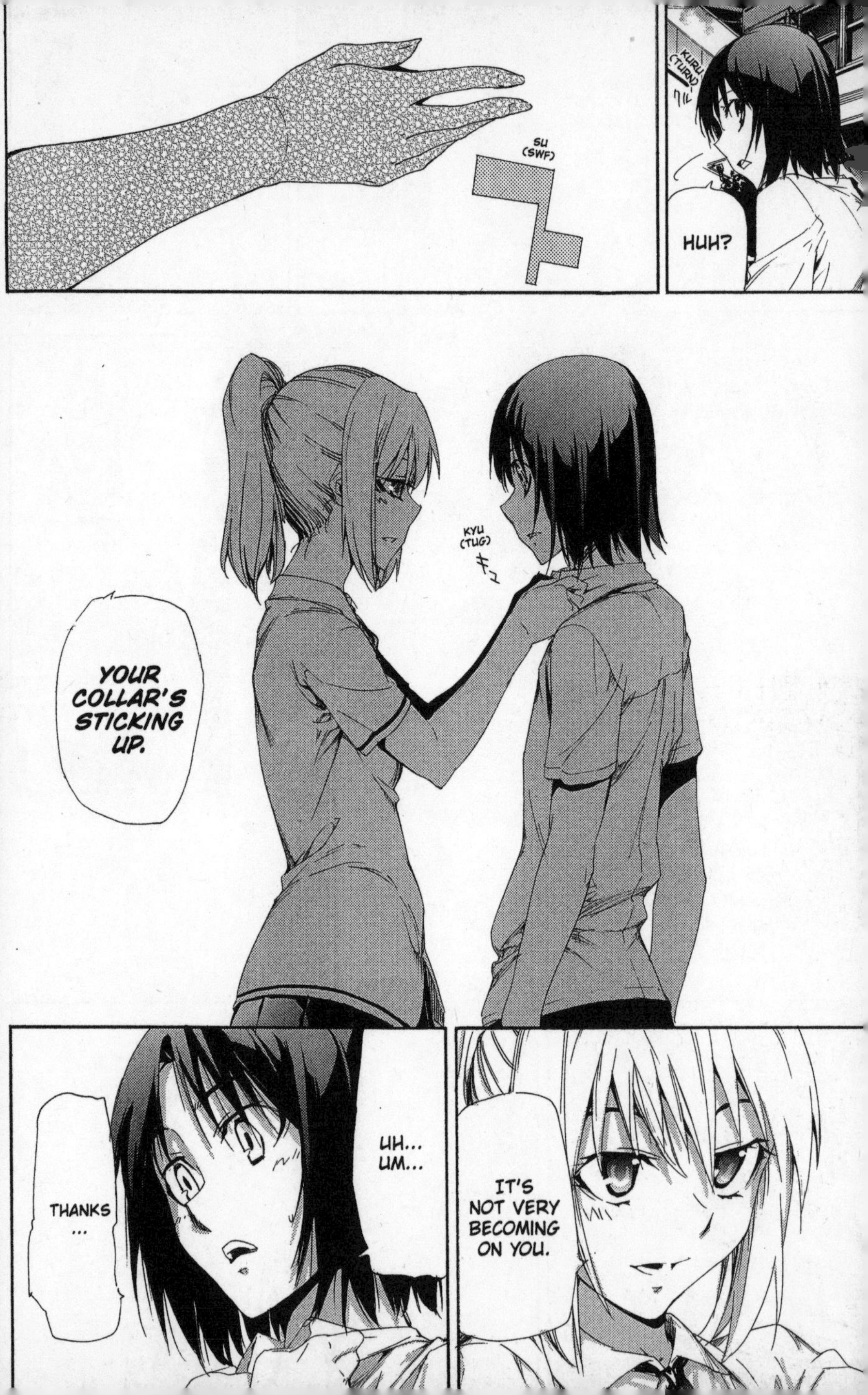
KURU (TURN)
クル
HUH?
SU (SWF)
KYU (TUG)
キュ
YOUR COLLAR'S STICKING UP.
IT'S NOT VERY BECOMING ON YOU.
UH... UM...
THANKS...

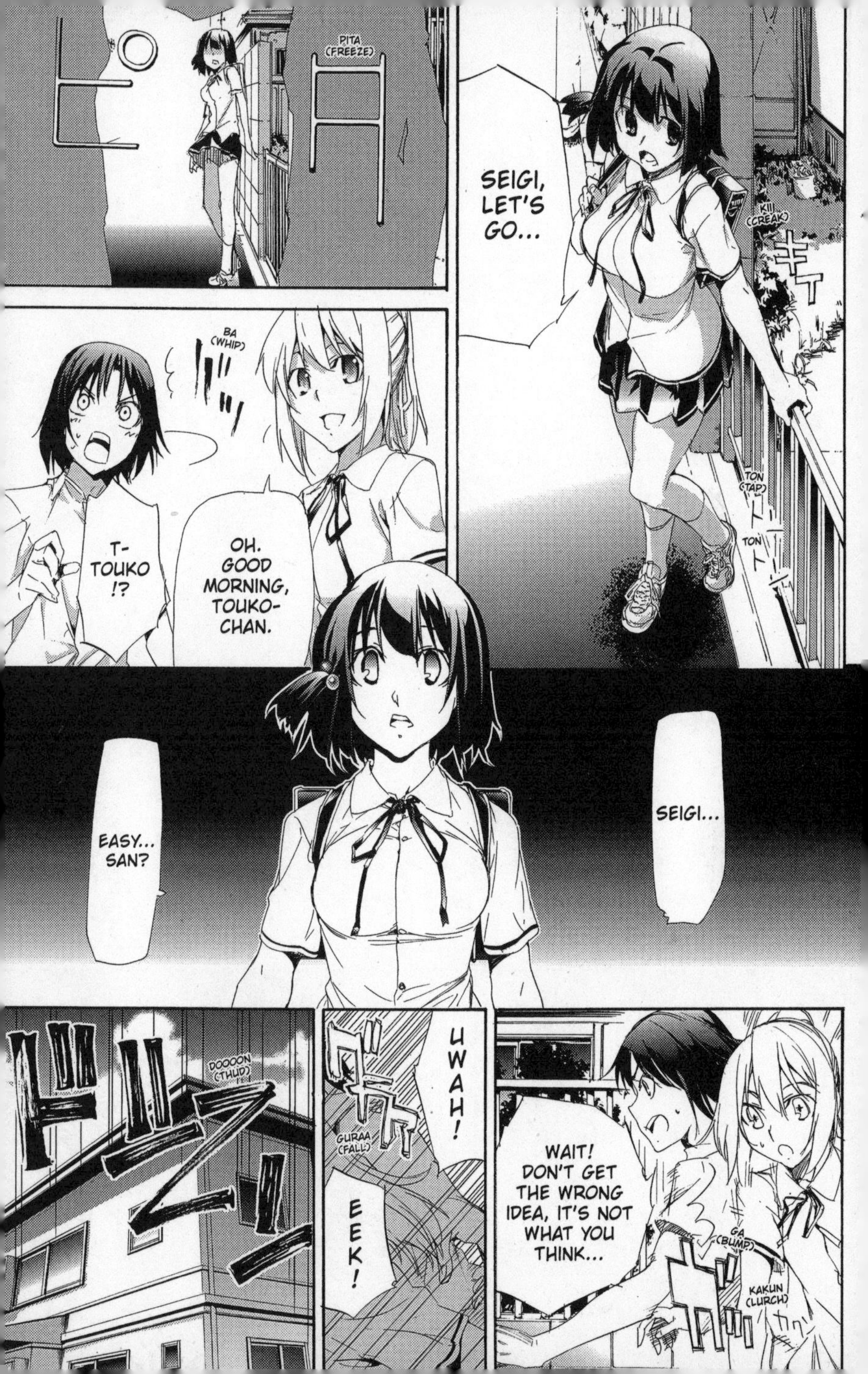

SEIGI, LET'S GO...
KII (CREAK)
TON (TAP)
TON
PITA (FREEZE)
BA (WHIP)
OH. GOOD MORNING, TOUKO-CHAN.
T-TOUKO!?
SEIGI...
EASY... SAN?
WAIT! DON'T GET THE WRONG IDEA, IT'S NOT WHAT YOU THINK...
GA (BUMP)
KAKUN (LURCH)
UWAH!
GURAA (FALL)
EEK!
DOOOON (THUD)

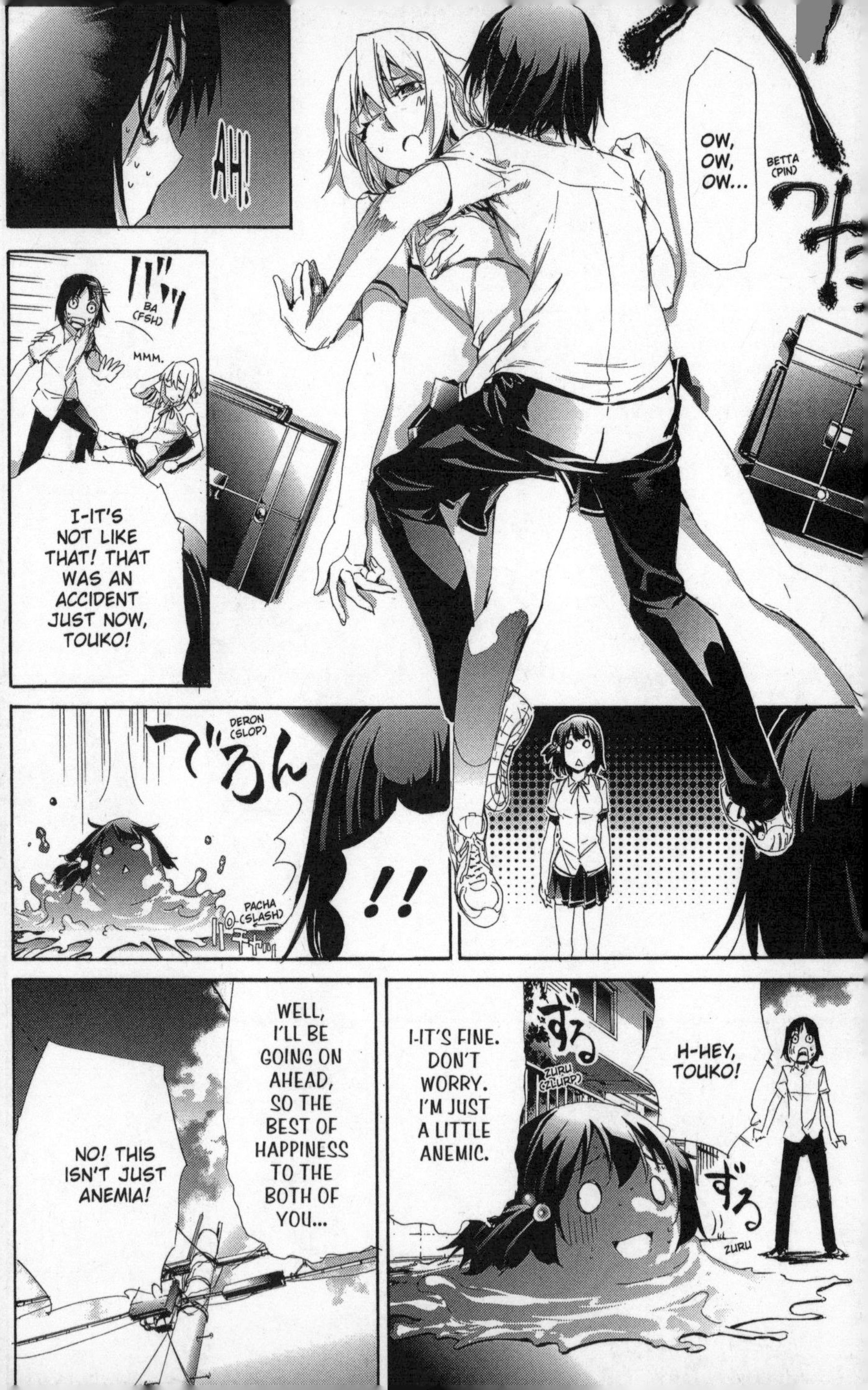
OW, OW, OW...
BETTA (PIN)
AH!
BA (FSH)
MMM.
I-IT'S NOT LIKE THAT! THAT WAS AN ACCIDENT JUST NOW, TOUKO!
!!
でろん
DERON (SLOP)
PACHA (SLASH)
H-HEY, TOUKO!
ずる
ZURU
ずる
ZURU (ZLURP)
I-IT'S FINE. DON'T WORRY. I'M JUST A LITTLE ANEMIC.
WELL, I'LL BE GOING ON AHEAD, SO THE BEST OF HAPPINESS TO THE BOTH OF YOU...
NO! THIS ISN'T JUST ANEMIA!

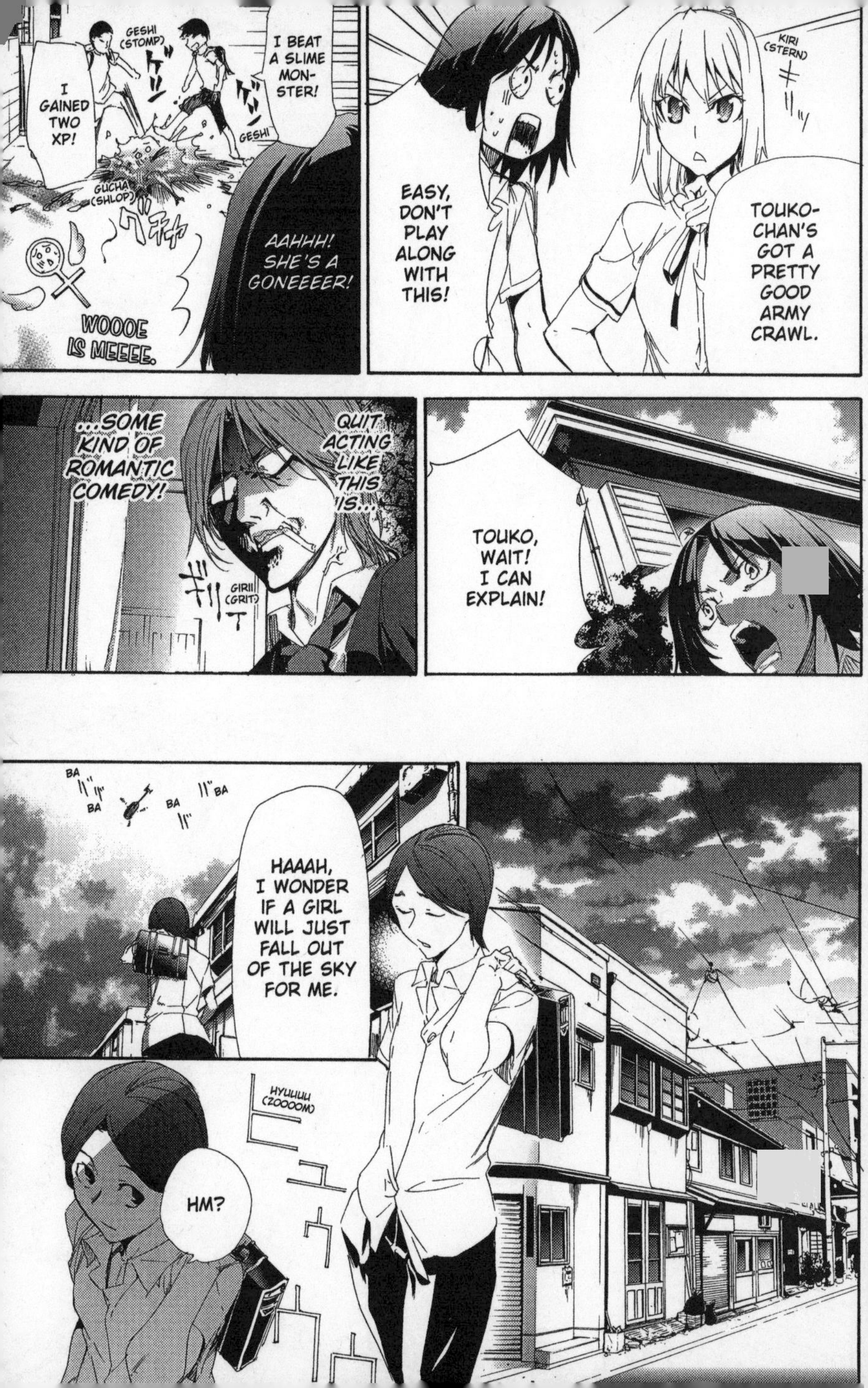
KIRI (STERN)
TOUKO-CHAN'S GOT A PRETTY GOOD ARMY CRAWL.
EASY, DON'T PLAY ALONG WITH THIS!
AAHHH! SHE'S A GONEEEER!
I BEAT A SLIME MONSTER!
GESHI (STOMP)
GESHI
I GAINED TWO XP!
GUCHA (SHLOP)
WOOOE IS MEEEEE.
TOUKO, WAIT! I CAN EXPLAIN!
QUIT ACTING LIKE THIS IS...
...SOME KIND OF ROMANTIC COMEDY!
GIRII (GRIT)
BA BA BA BA
HAAAH, I WONDER IF A GIRL WILL JUST FALL OUT OF THE SKY FOR ME.
HYUUUU (ZOOOOM)
HM?

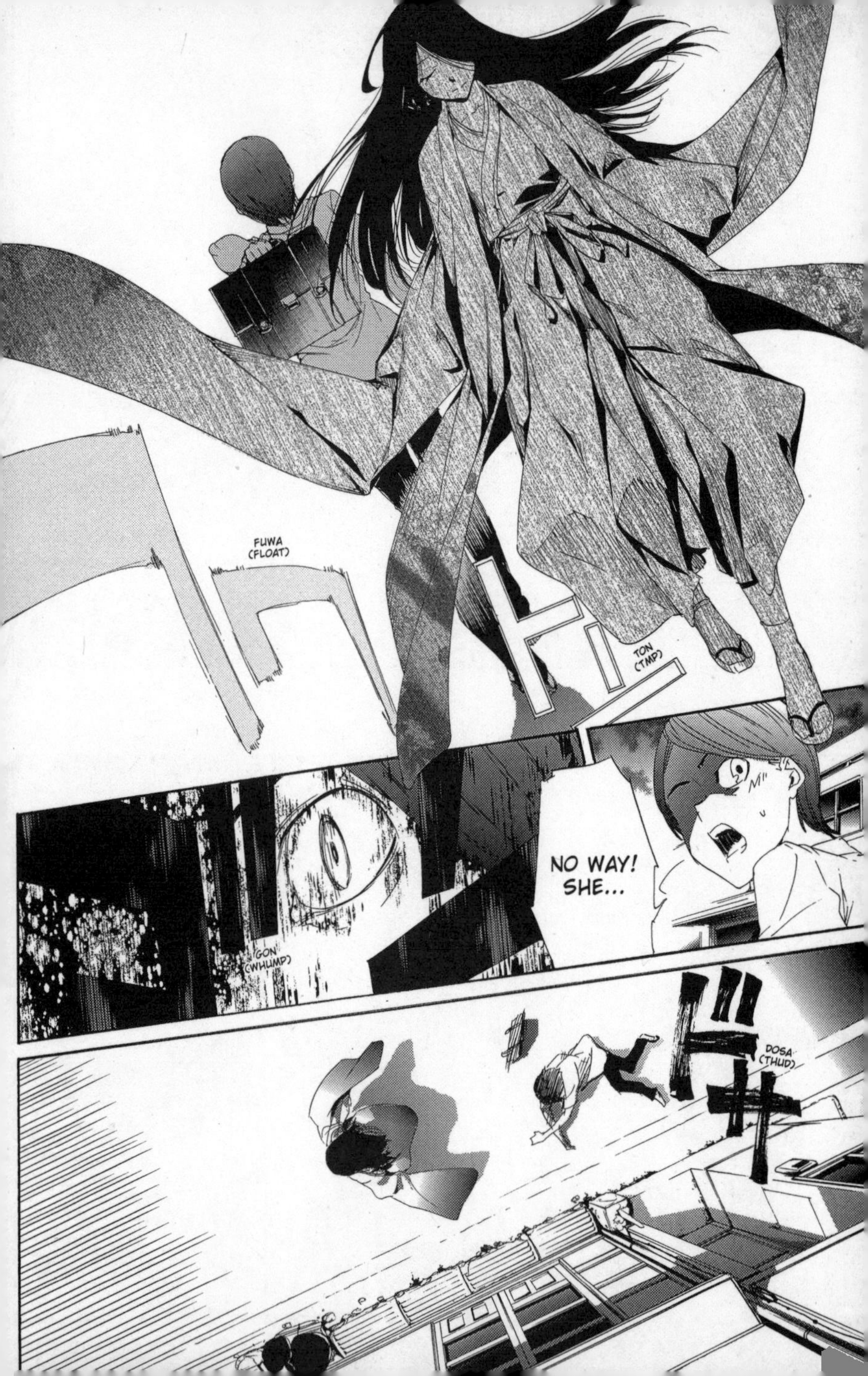
FUWA (FLOAT)
TON (TMP)
NO WAY! SHE...
GON (WHUMP)
DOSA (THUD)

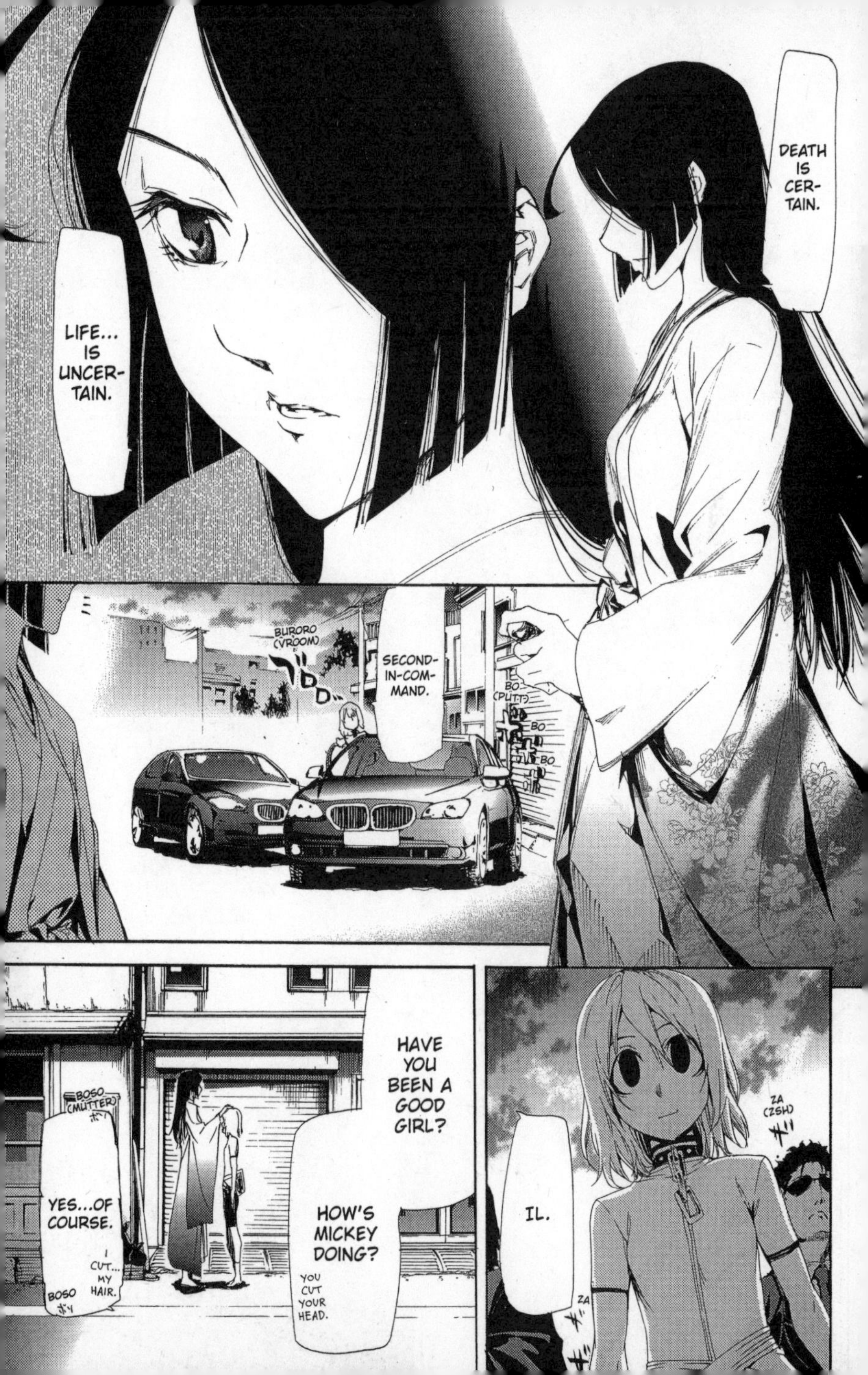
DEATH IS CER-TAIN.
LIFE... IS UNCER-TAIN.
BO (PUTT)
BO
BO
SECOND-IN-COM-MAND.
BURORO (VROOM)
ZA (ZSH)
IL.
ZA
HAVE YOU BEEN A GOOD GIRL?
HOW'S MICKEY DOING?
YOU CUT YOUR HEAD.
BOSO (MUTTER)
YES...OF COURSE.
I CUT... MY HAIR.
BOSO

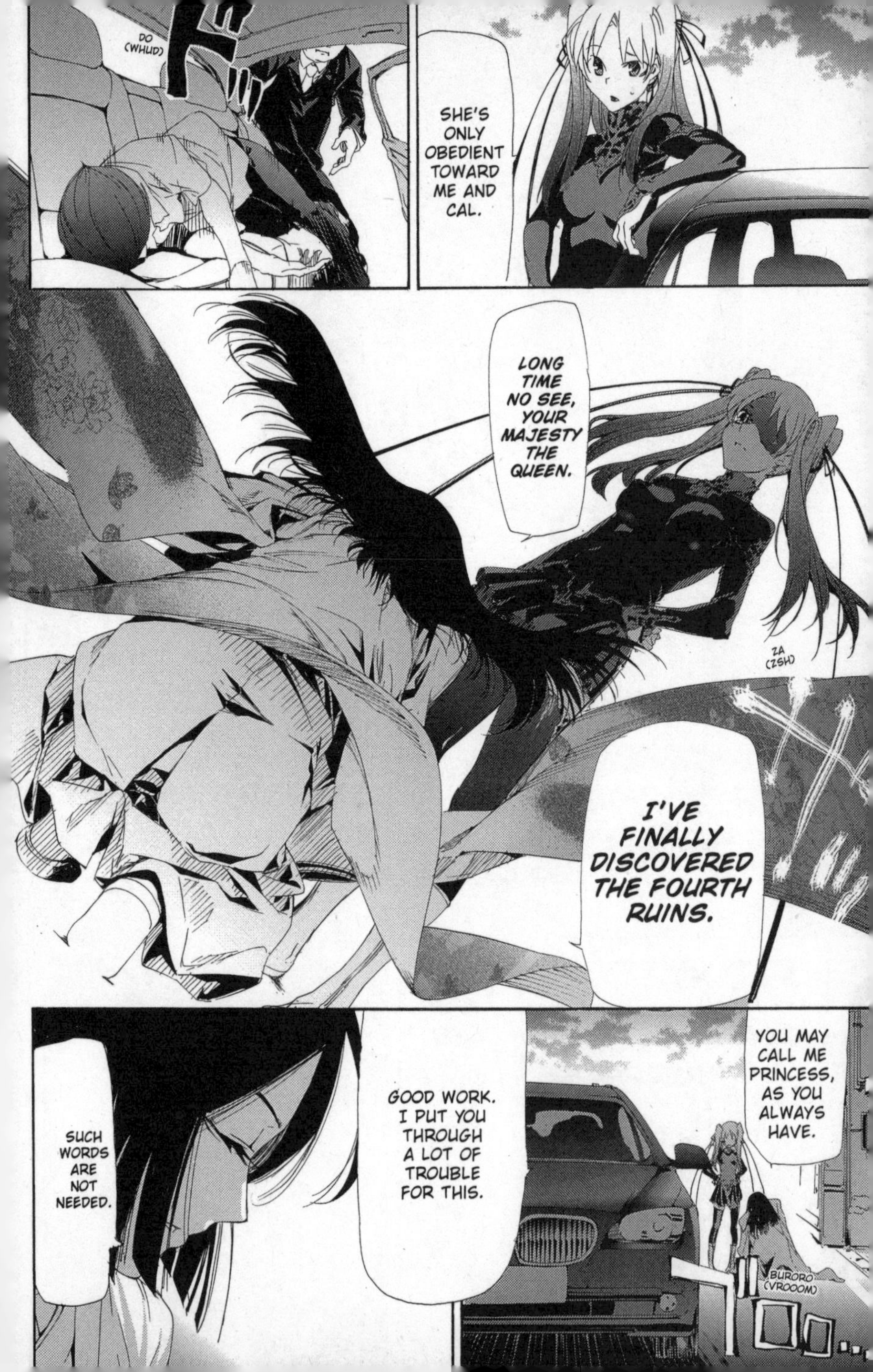
SHE'S ONLY OBEDIENT TOWARD ME AND CAL.
DO (WHUD)
LONG TIME NO SEE, YOUR MAJESTY THE QUEEN.
ZA (ZSH)
I'VE FINALLY DISCOVERED THE FOURTH RUINS.
YOU MAY CALL ME PRINCESS, AS YOU ALWAYS HAVE.
BURORO (VROOOM)
GOOD WORK. I PUT YOU THROUGH A LOT OF TROUBLE FOR THIS.
SUCH WORDS ARE NOT NEEDED.

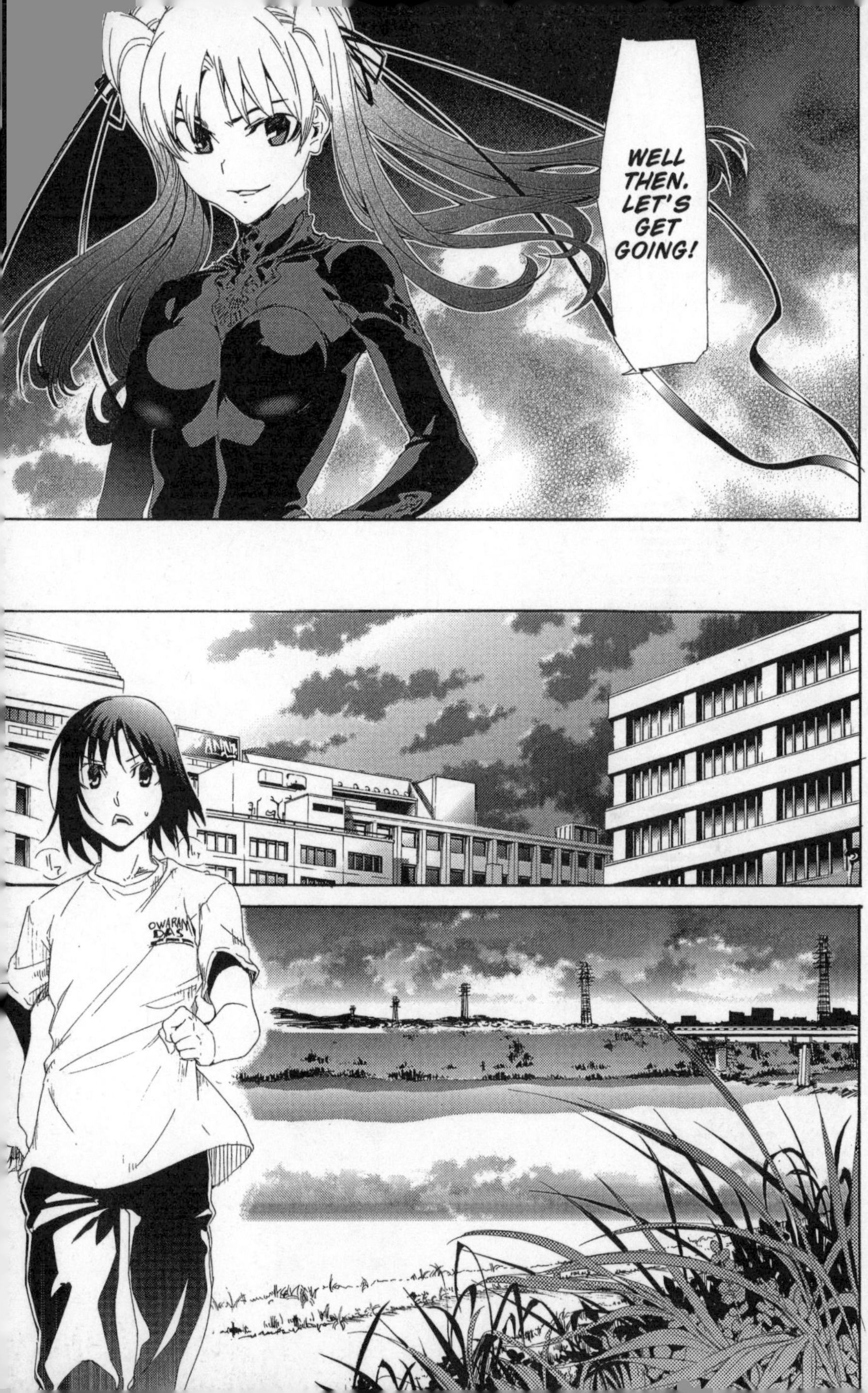
WELL THEN. LET'S GET GOING!

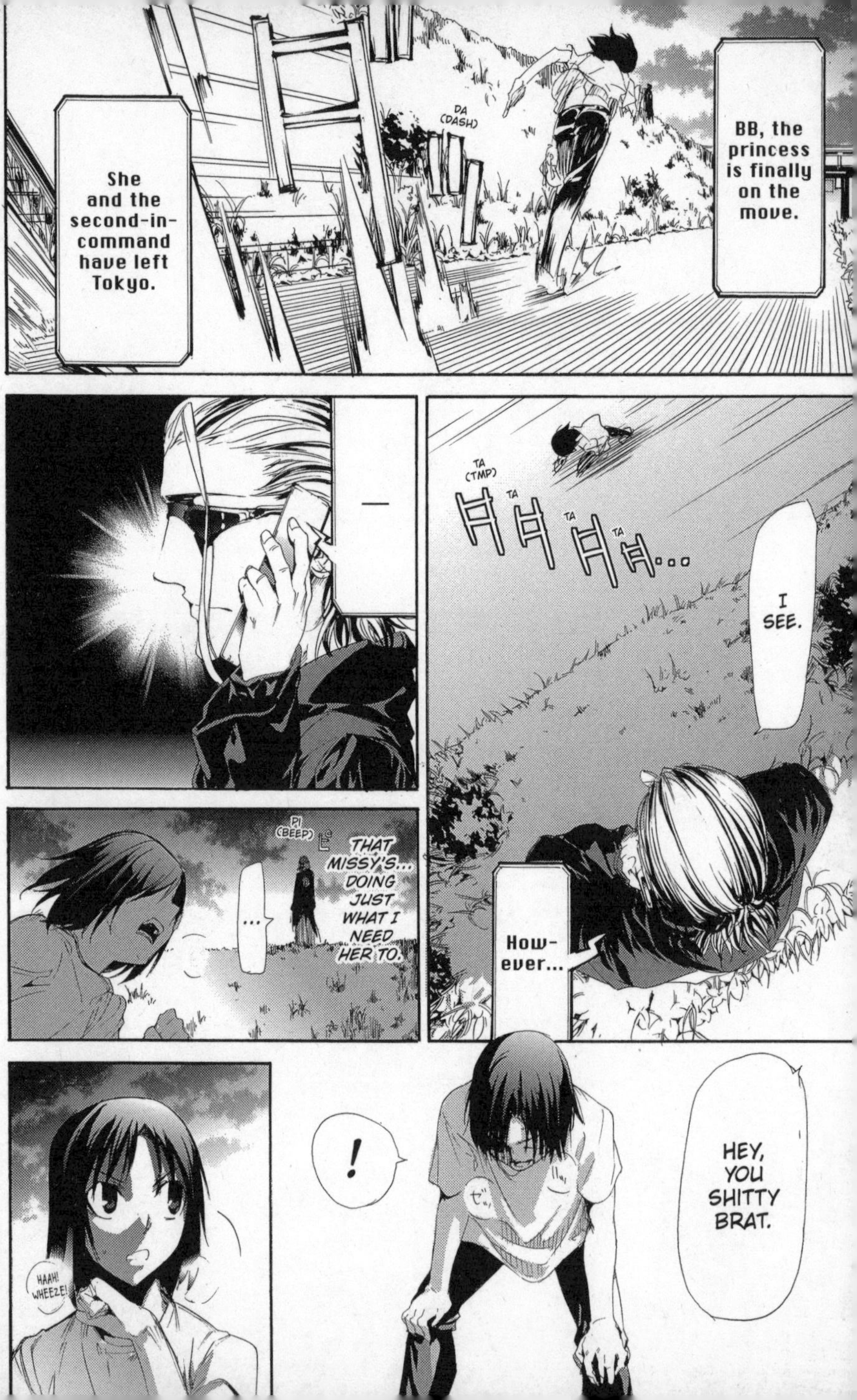
BB, the princess is finally on the move.
DA (DASH)
She and the second-in-command have left Tokyo.
TA (TMP)
TA
TA
TA...
I SEE.
However...
—
PI (BEEP)
THAT MISSY'S... DOING JUST WHAT I NEED HER TO.
...
HEY, YOU SHITTY BRAT.
!
HAAH! WHEEZE!

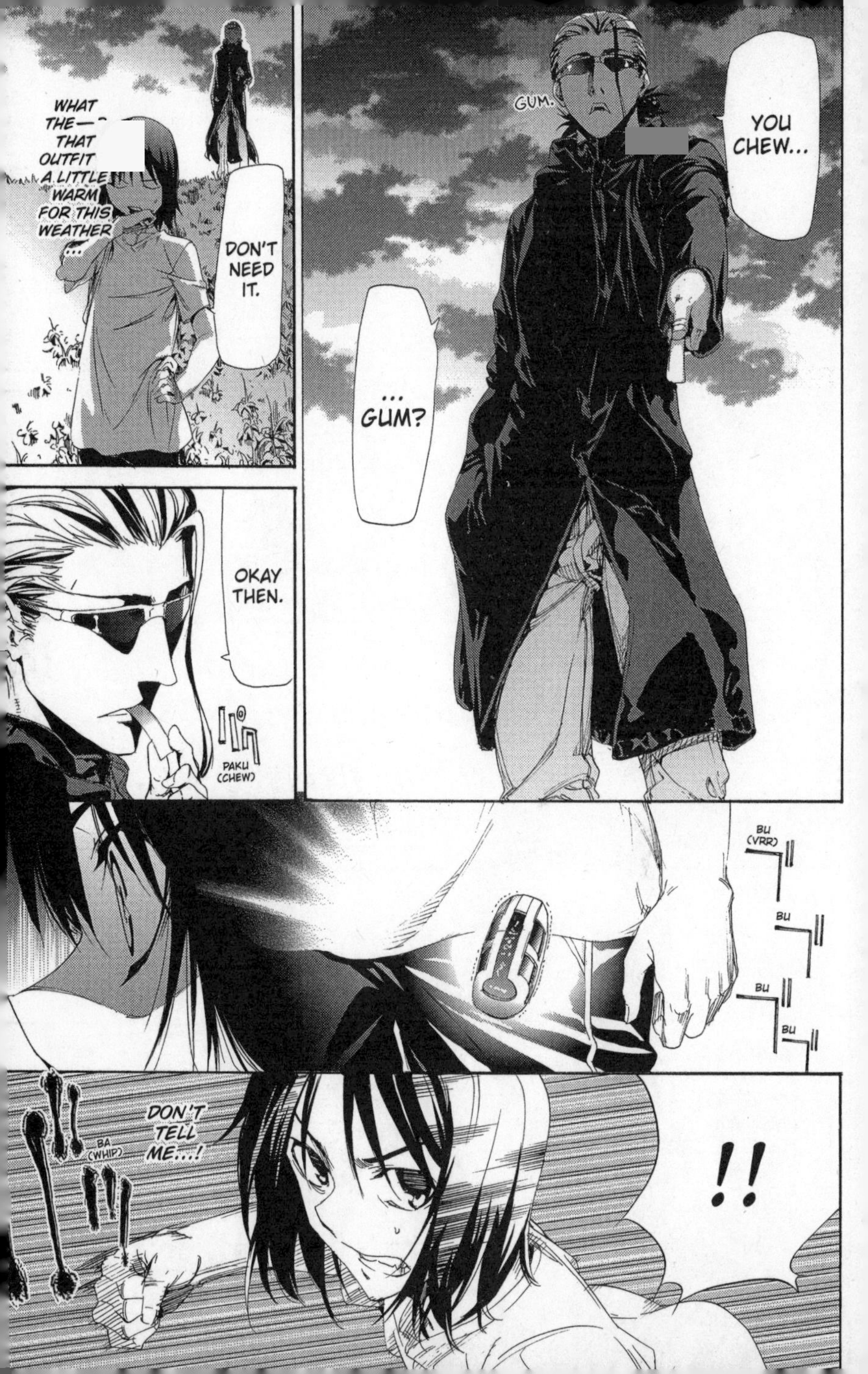
YOU CHEW...
GUM.
... GUM?
WHAT THE—? THAT OUTFIT A LITTLE WARM FOR THIS WEATHER...
DON'T NEED IT.
OKAY THEN.
PAKU (CHEW)
BU (VRR)
BU
BU
BU
!!
DON'T TELL ME...!
BA (WHIP)

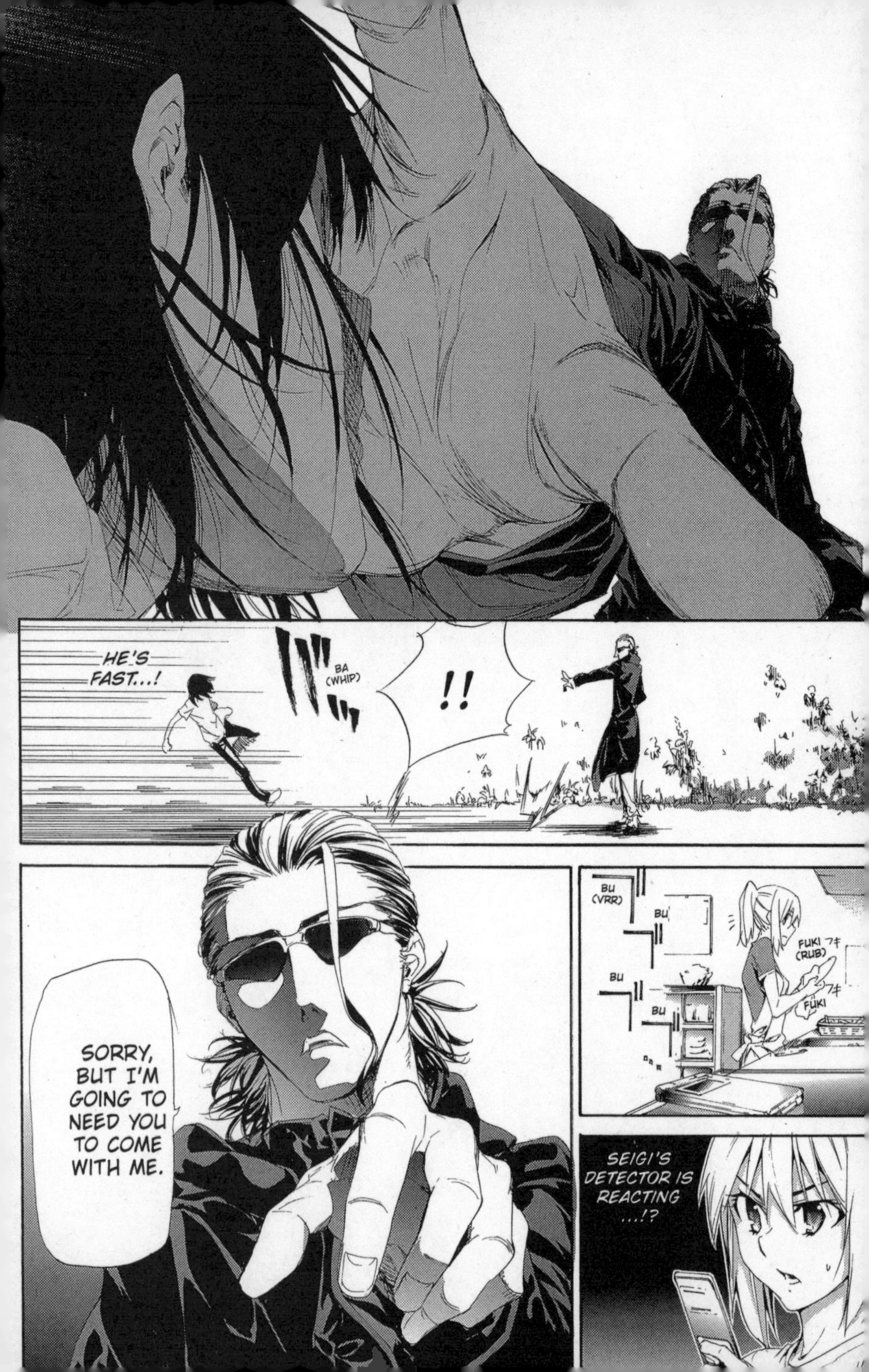
!!
BA (WHIP)
HE'S FAST...!
FUKI フキ (RUB)
フキ FUKI
BU (VRR)
BU
BU
BU
SEIGI'S DETECTOR IS REACTING ...!?
SORRY, BUT I'M GOING TO NEED YOU TO COME WITH ME.

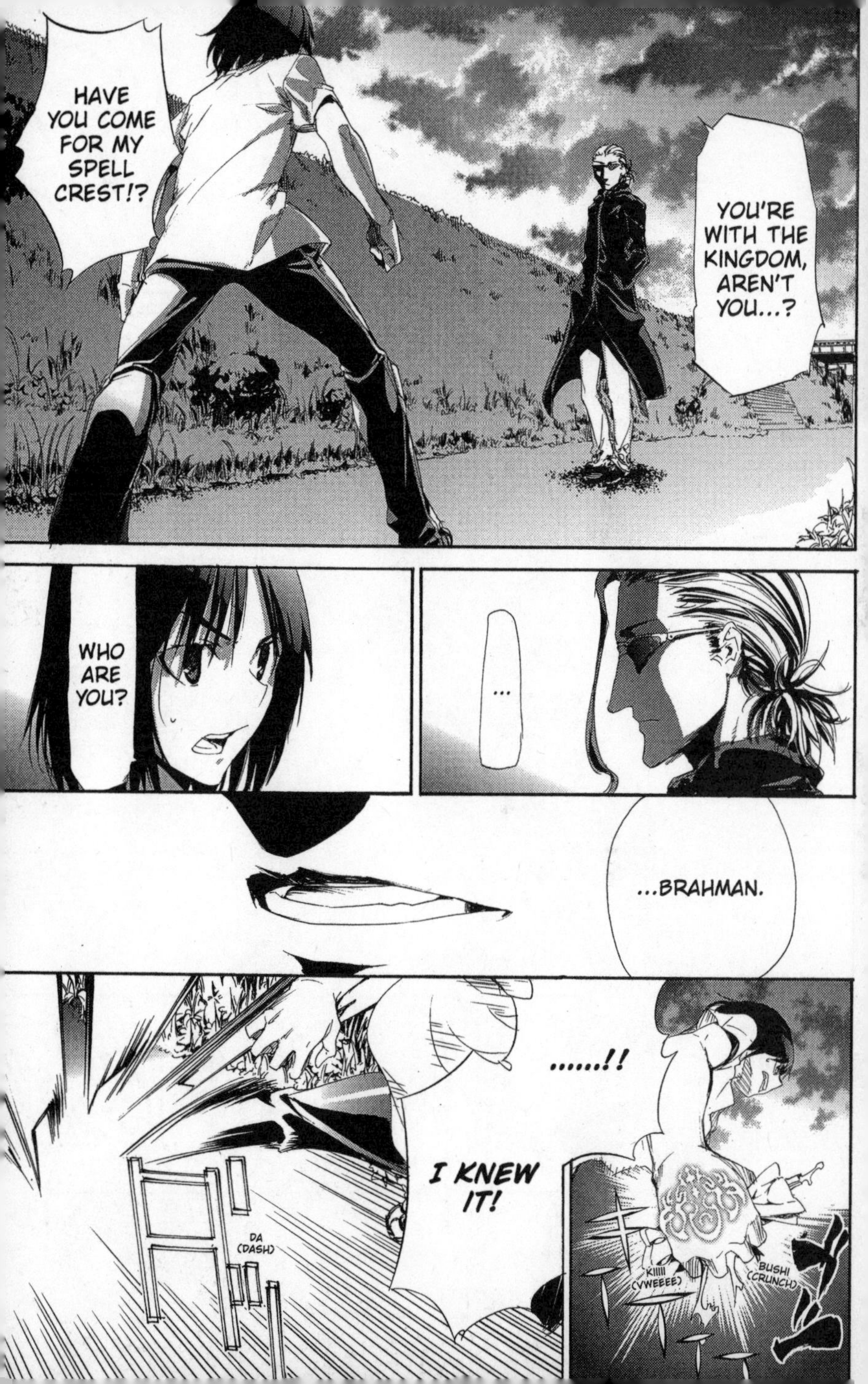

YOU'RE WITH THE KINGDOM, AREN'T YOU...?
HAVE YOU COME FOR MY SPELL CREST!?
...
WHO ARE YOU?
...BRAHMAN.
......!!
I KNEW IT!
BUSHI (CRUNCH)
KIIIII (VWEEEE)
DA (DASH)

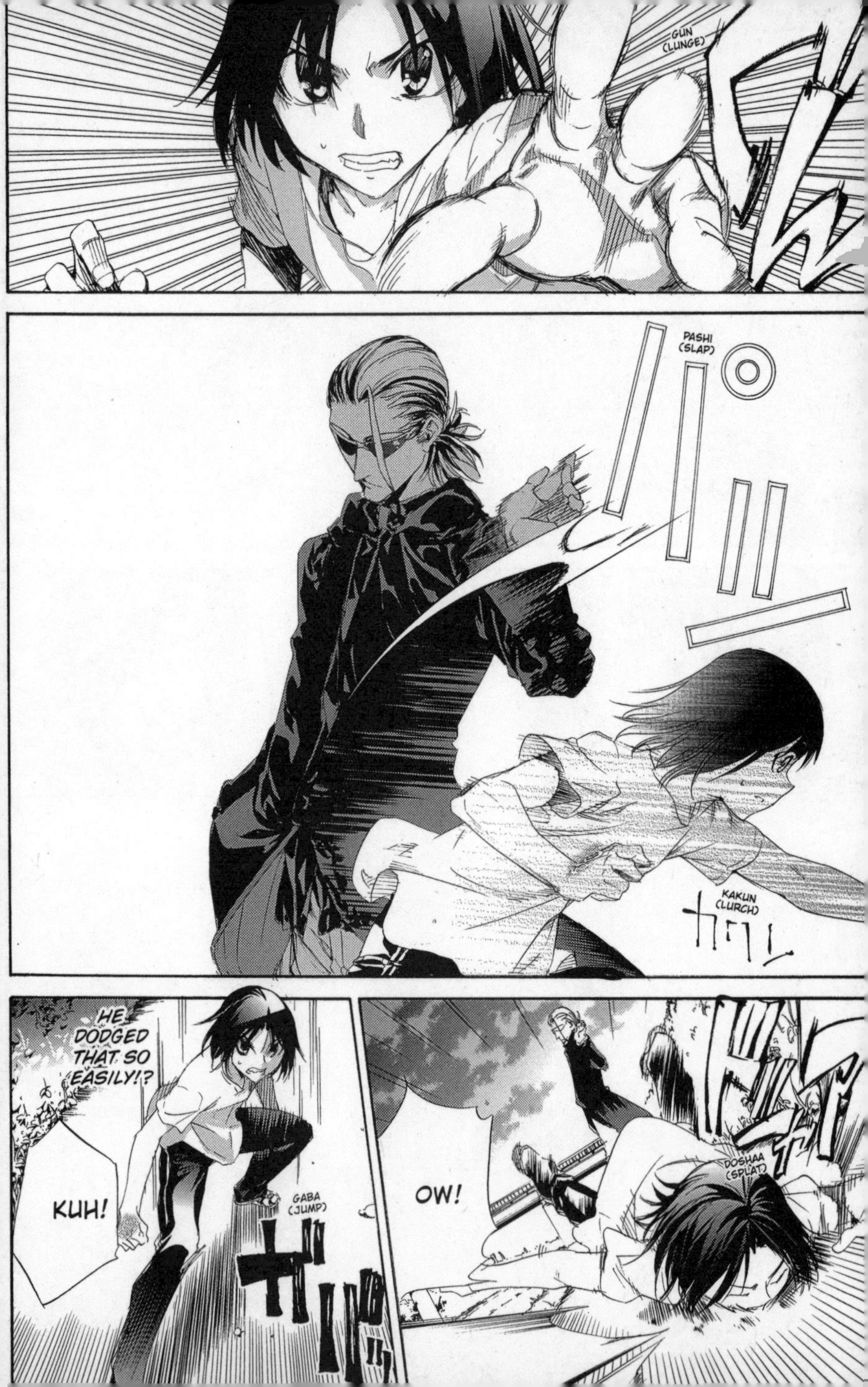
GUN (LUNGE)
PASHI (SLAP)
KAKUN (LURCH)
DOSHAA (SPLAT)
OW!
HE DODGED THAT SO EASILY!?
GABA (JUMP)
KUH!

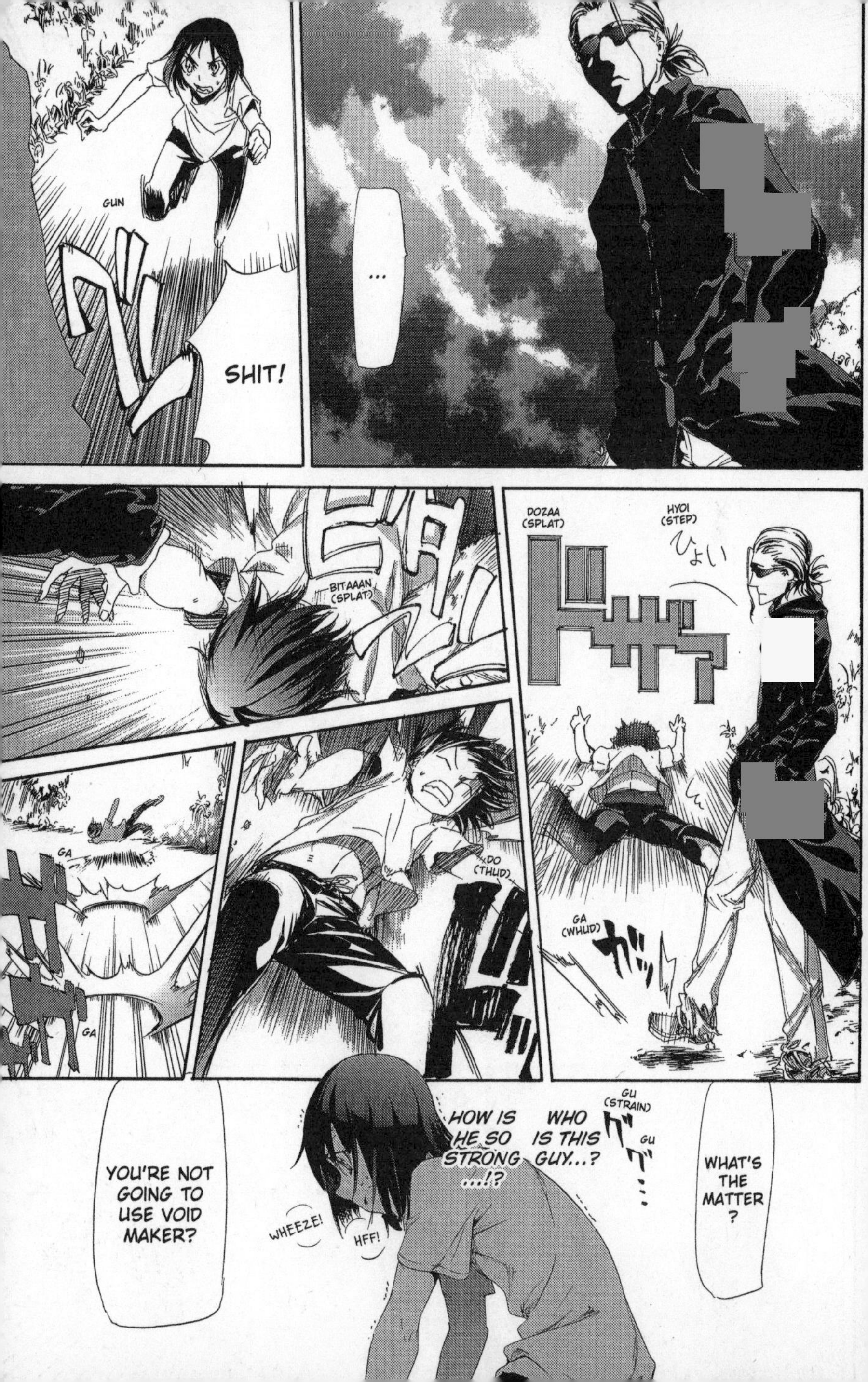
...
GUN
SHIT!
DOZAA (SPLAT)
HYOI (STEP)
ひょい
GA (WHUD)
BITAAAN (SPLAT)
DO (THUD)
GA
GA
WHAT'S THE MATTER?
GU (STRAIN)
GU
WHO IS THIS GUY...?
HOW IS HE SO STRONG ...!?
WHEEZE!
HFF!
YOU'RE NOT GOING TO USE VOID MAKER?

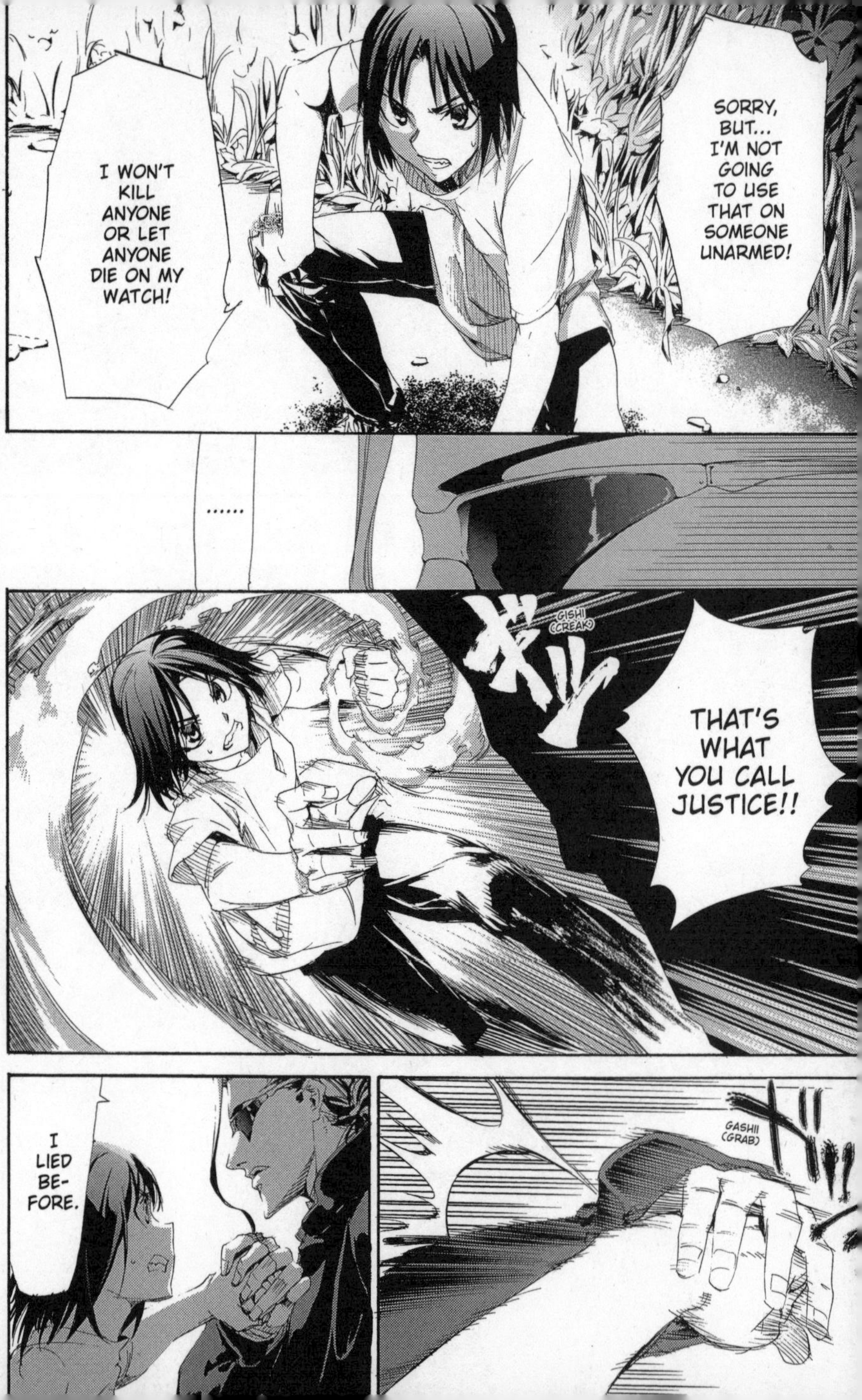
SORRY, BUT... I'M NOT GOING TO USE THAT ON SOMEONE UNARMED!
I WON'T KILL ANYONE OR LET ANYONE DIE ON MY WATCH!
......
GISHI (CREAK)
THAT'S WHAT YOU CALL JUSTICE!!
GASHII (GRAB)
I LIED BE-FORE.

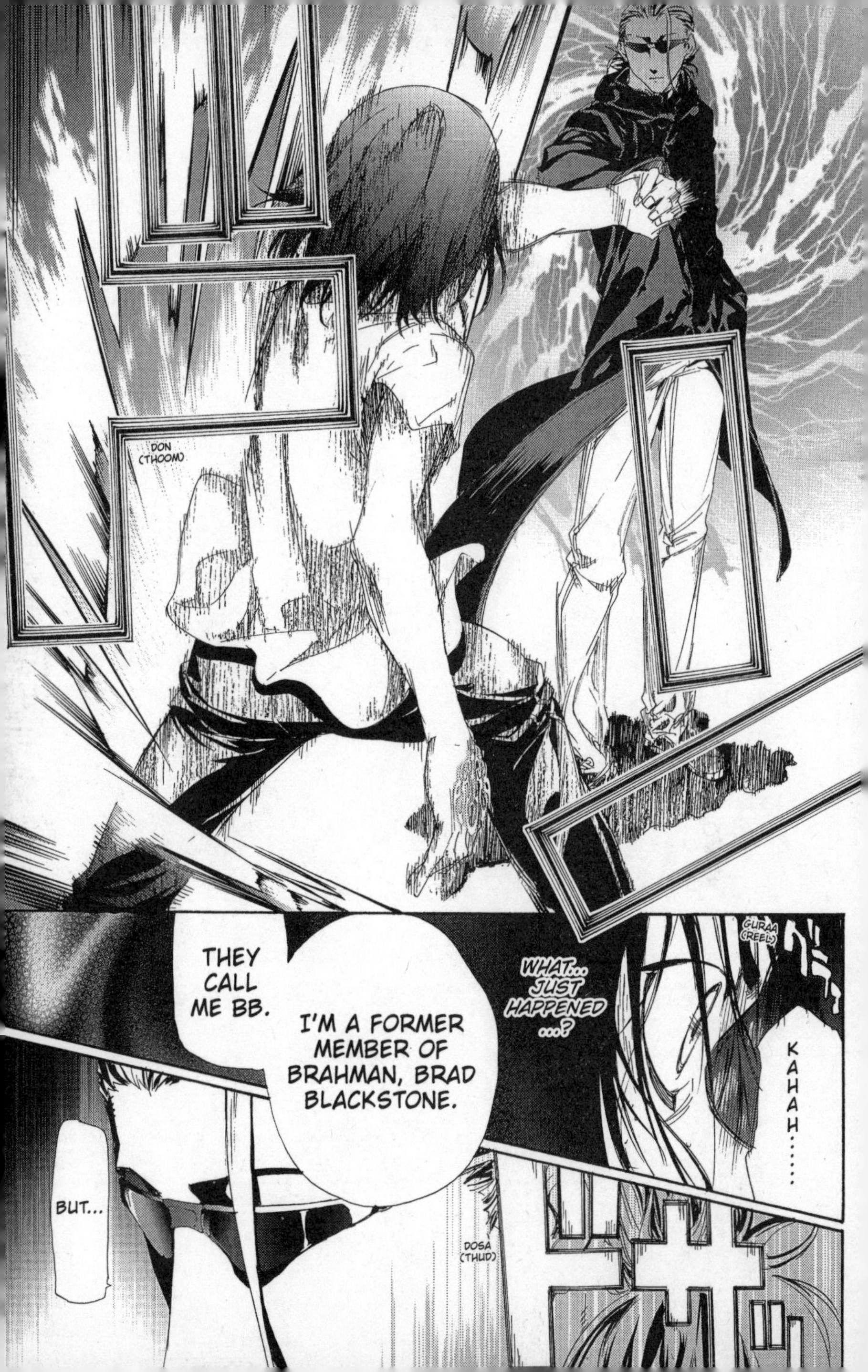
DON (THOOM)
GURAA (REEL)
WHAT... JUST HAPPENED ...?
KAHAH......
THEY CALL ME BB.
I'M A FORMER MEMBER OF BRAHMAN, BRAD BLACKSTONE.
DOSA (THUD)
BUT...

...IF THE KINGDOM'S PRINCESS IS THE FIRST PERSON, YOU'RE THE THIRD PERSON.

AND I'M...

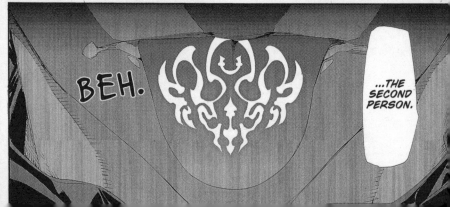

BEH.

...THE SECOND PERSON.

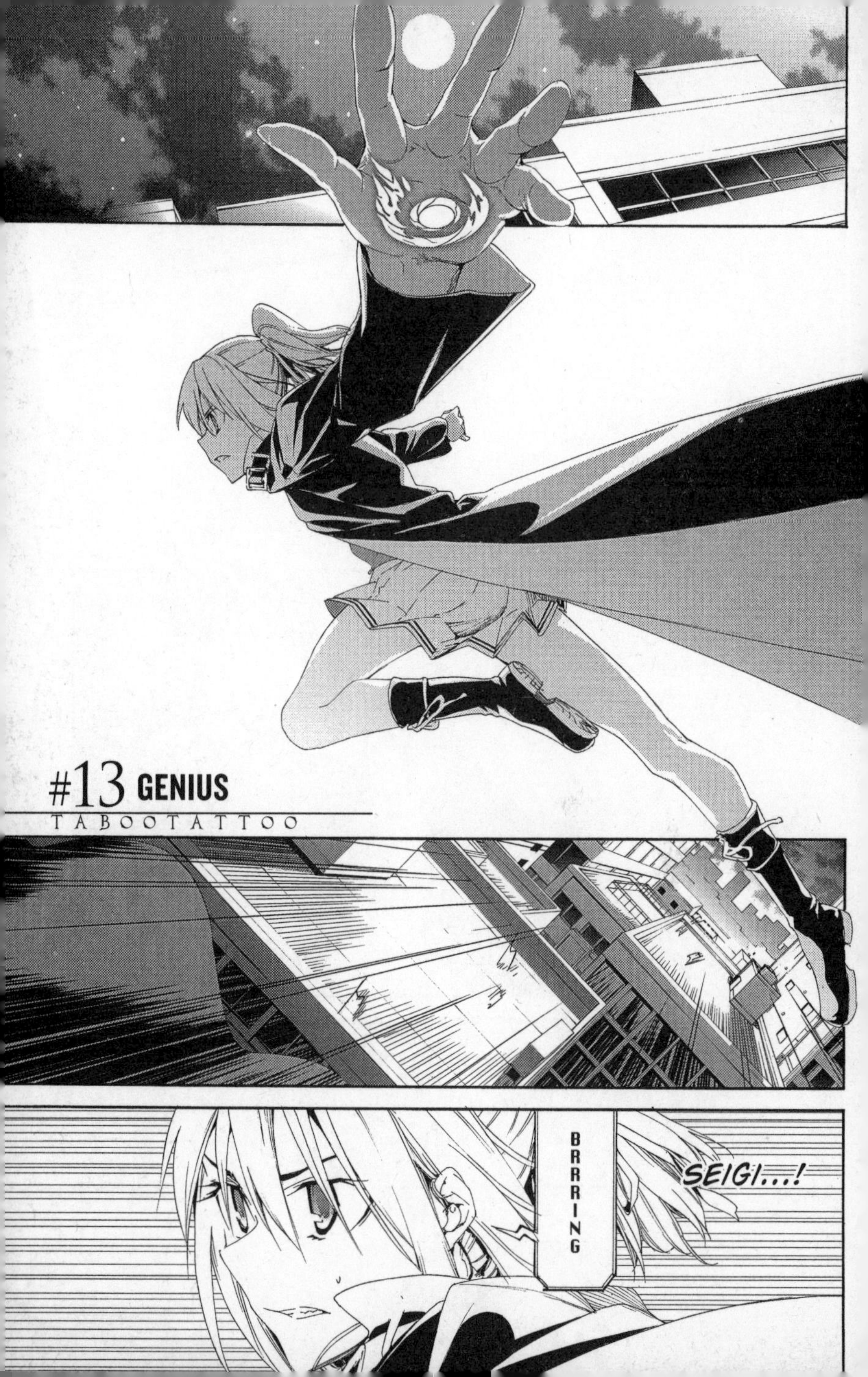
#13 GENIUS
TABOOTATTOO
SEIGI...!
BRRRING

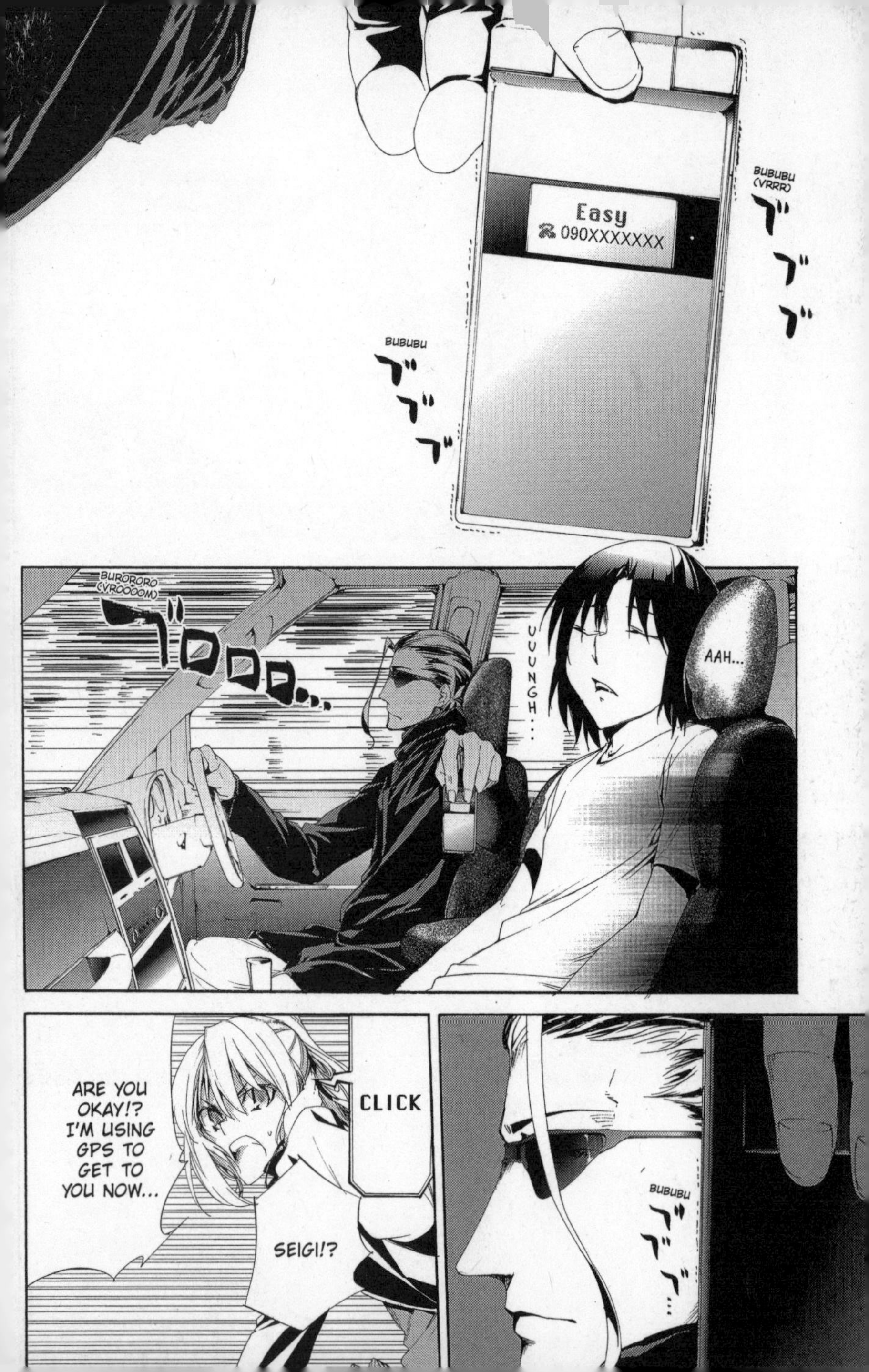
Easy
☎ 090XXXXXXX
BUBUBU (VRRR)
ブブブ
BUBUBU
ブブブ
BURORORO (VROOOOM)
ブロロロ...
AAH...
UUUNGH...
BUBUBU
ブブブ...
CLICK
ARE YOU OKAY!? I'M USING GPS TO GET TO YOU NOW...
SEIGI!?

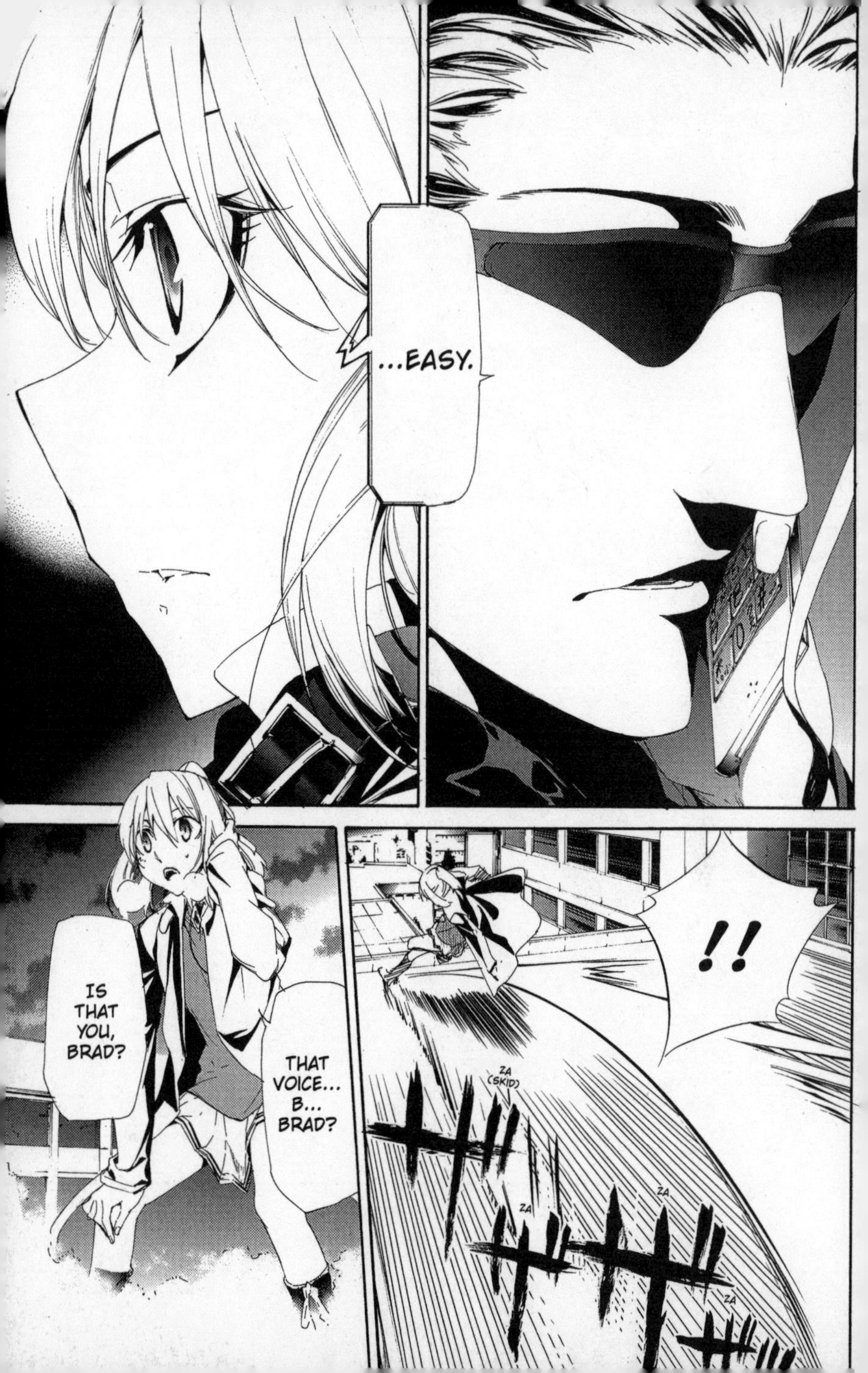
...EASY.
!!
ZA (SKID)
ZA
ZA
ZA
THAT VOICE... B... BRAD?
IS THAT YOU, BRAD?

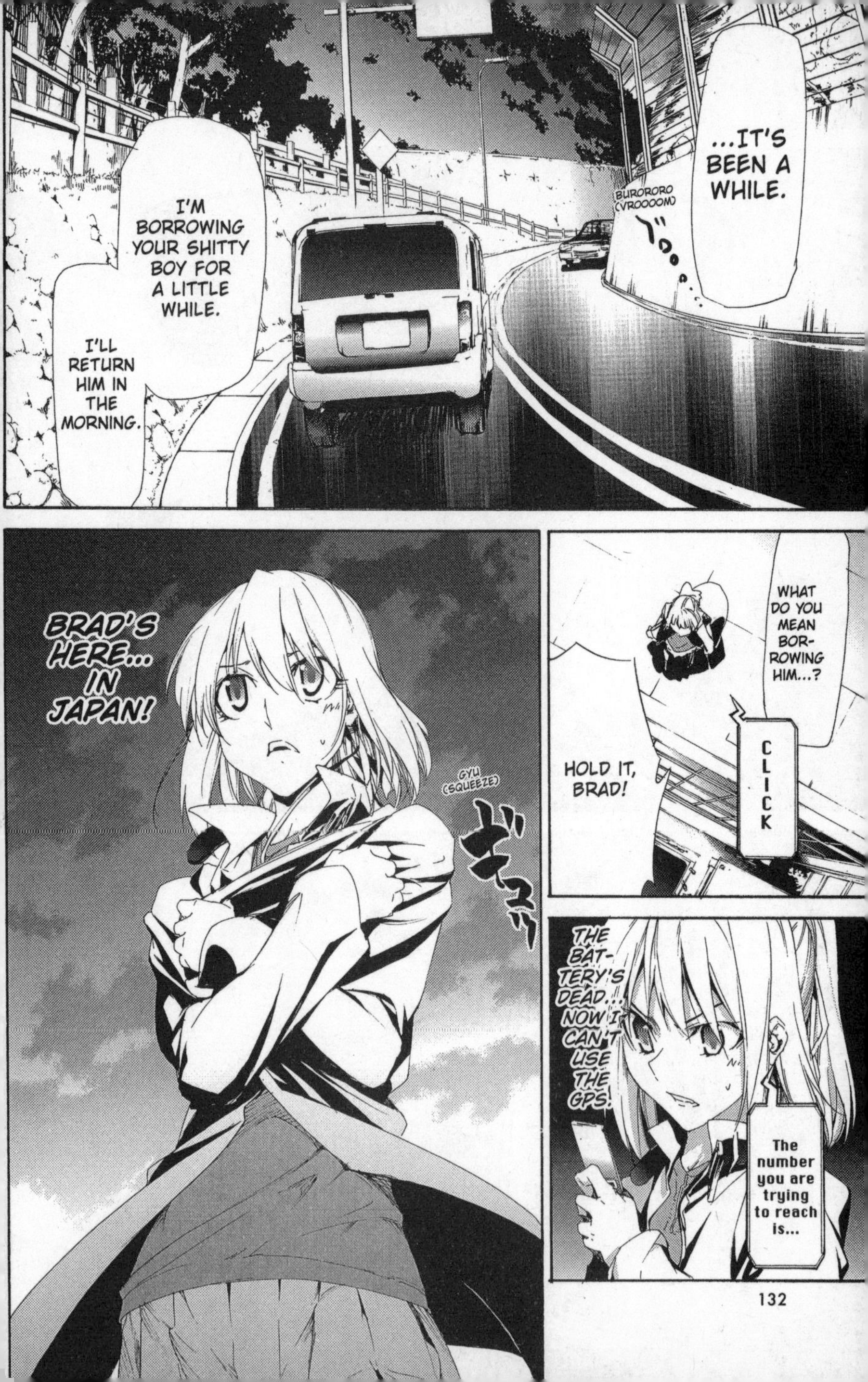
...IT'S BEEN A WHILE.
BURORORO (VROOOOM)
I'M BORROWING YOUR SHITTY BOY FOR A LITTLE WHILE.
I'LL RETURN HIM IN THE MORNING.
WHAT DO YOU MEAN BOR-ROWING HIM...?
CLICK
HOLD IT, BRAD!
THE BAT-TERY'S DEAD... NOW I CAN'T USE THE GPS!
The number you are trying to reach is...
BRAD'S HERE... IN JAPAN!
GYU (SQUEEZE)

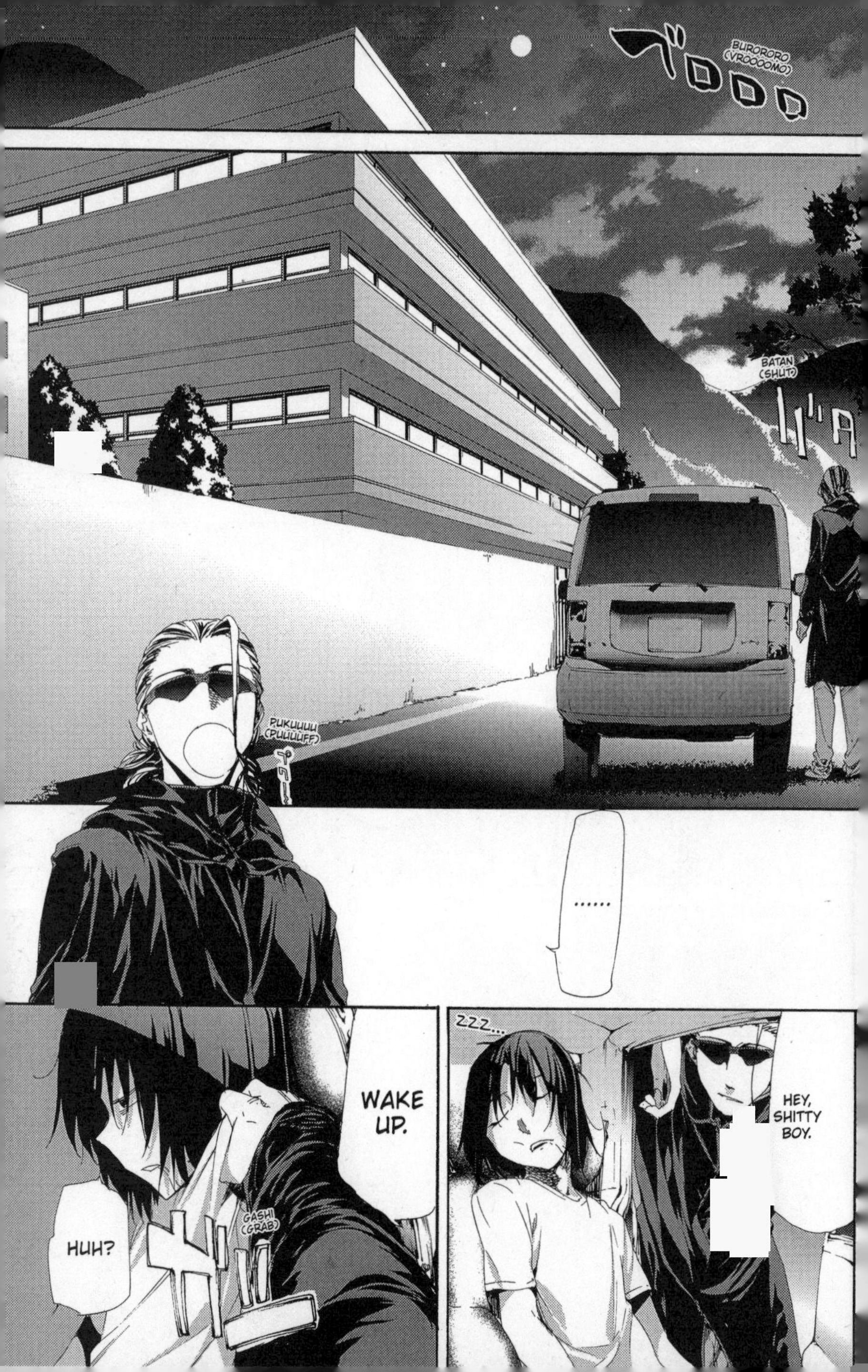
BURORORO (VROOOOOM)
BATAN (SHUT)
PUKUUUU (PUUUUFF)
......
ZZZ...
HEY, SHITTY BOY.
WAKE UP.
GASHI (GRAB)
HUH?

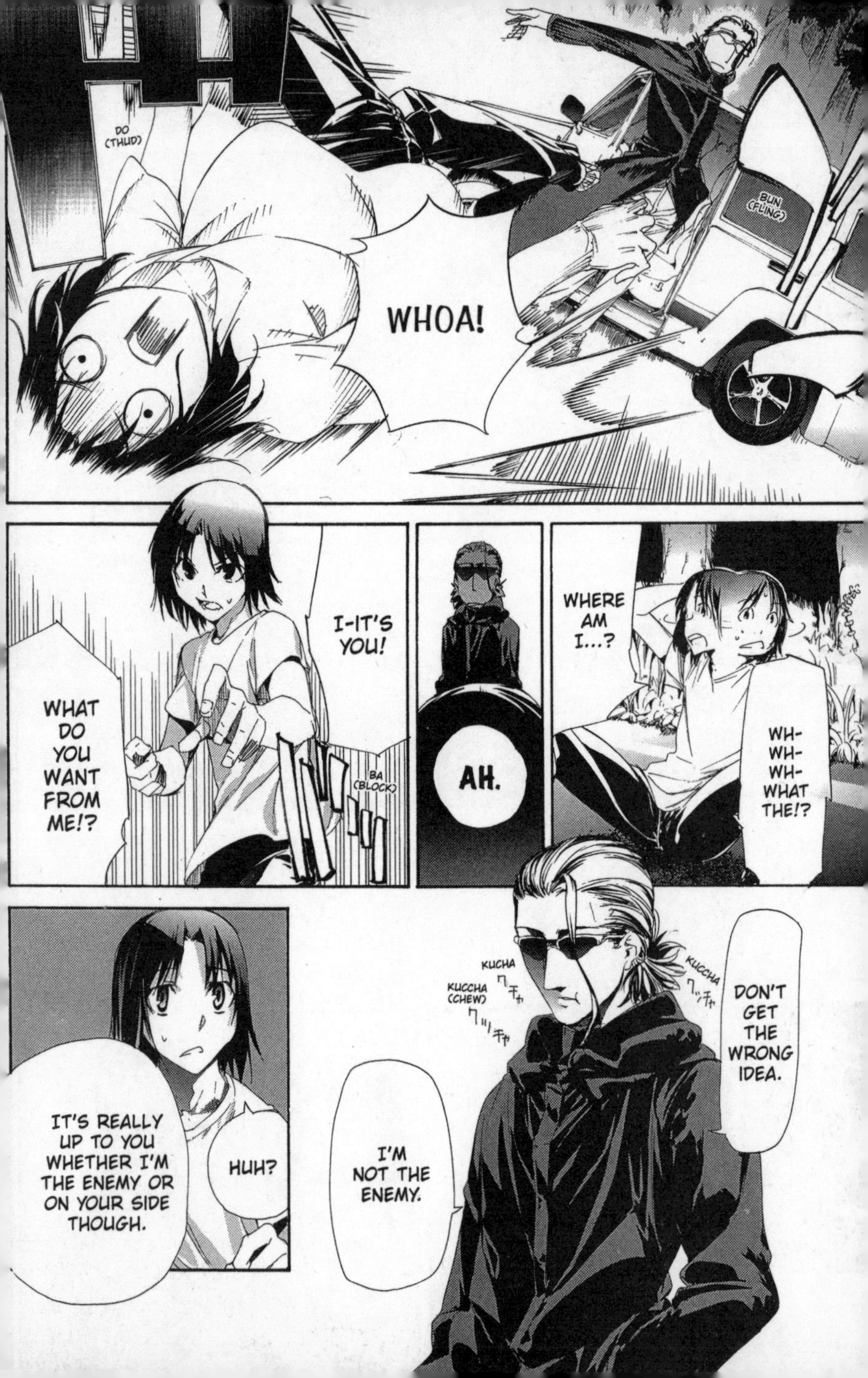
BUN (FLING)
DO (THUD)
WHOA!
WHERE AM I...?
WH-WH-WH-WHAT THE!?
AH.
I-IT'S YOU!
WHAT DO YOU WANT FROM ME!?
BA (BLOCK)
KUCCHA
KUCHA
KUCCHA (CHEW)
DON'T GET THE WRONG IDEA.
I'M NOT THE ENEMY.
HUH?
IT'S REALLY UP TO YOU WHETHER I'M THE ENEMY OR ON YOUR SIDE THOUGH.

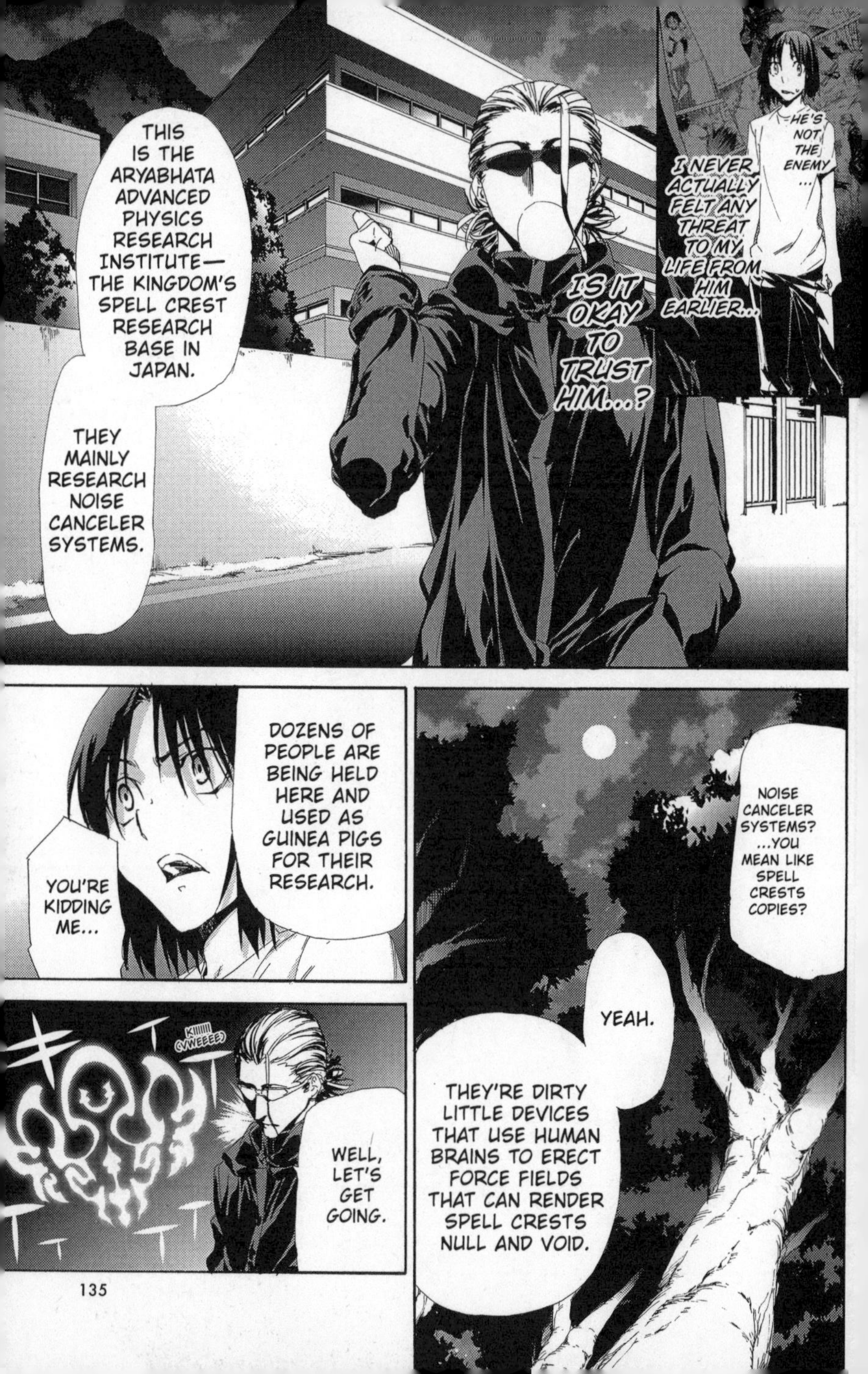
HE'S NOT THE ENEMY...
I NEVER ACTUALLY FELT ANY THREAT TO MY LIFE FROM HIM EARLIER...
IS IT OKAY TO TRUST HIM...?
THIS IS THE ARYABHATA ADVANCED PHYSICS RESEARCH INSTITUTE—THE KINGDOM'S SPELL CREST RESEARCH BASE IN JAPAN.
THEY MAINLY RESEARCH NOISE CANCELER SYSTEMS.
NOISE CANCELER SYSTEMS? ...YOU MEAN LIKE SPELL CRESTS COPIES?
YEAH.
THEY'RE DIRTY LITTLE DEVICES THAT USE HUMAN BRAINS TO ERECT FORCE FIELDS THAT CAN RENDER SPELL CRESTS NULL AND VOID.
DOZENS OF PEOPLE ARE BEING HELD HERE AND USED AS GUINEA PIGS FOR THEIR RESEARCH.
YOU'RE KIDDING ME...
KIIIIII (VWEEEE)
WELL, LET'S GET GOING.

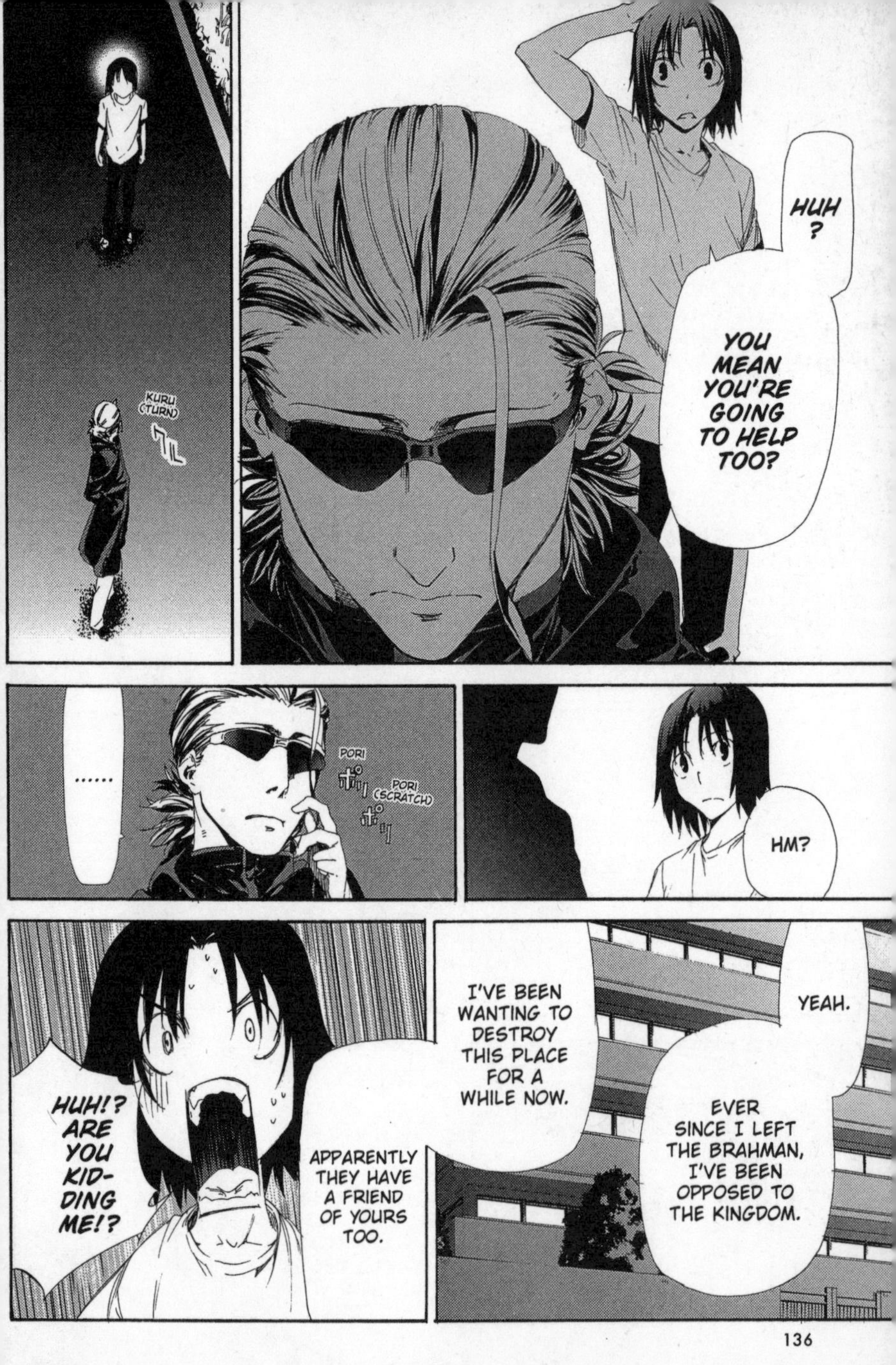
HUH?
YOU MEAN YOU'RE GOING TO HELP TOO?
KURU (TURN)
HM?
......
PORI PORI (SCRATCH)
YEAH.
EVER SINCE I LEFT THE BRAHMAN, I'VE BEEN OPPOSED TO THE KINGDOM.
I'VE BEEN WANTING TO DESTROY THIS PLACE FOR A WHILE NOW.
APPARENTLY THEY HAVE A FRIEND OF YOURS TOO.
HUH!? ARE YOU KID-DING ME!?

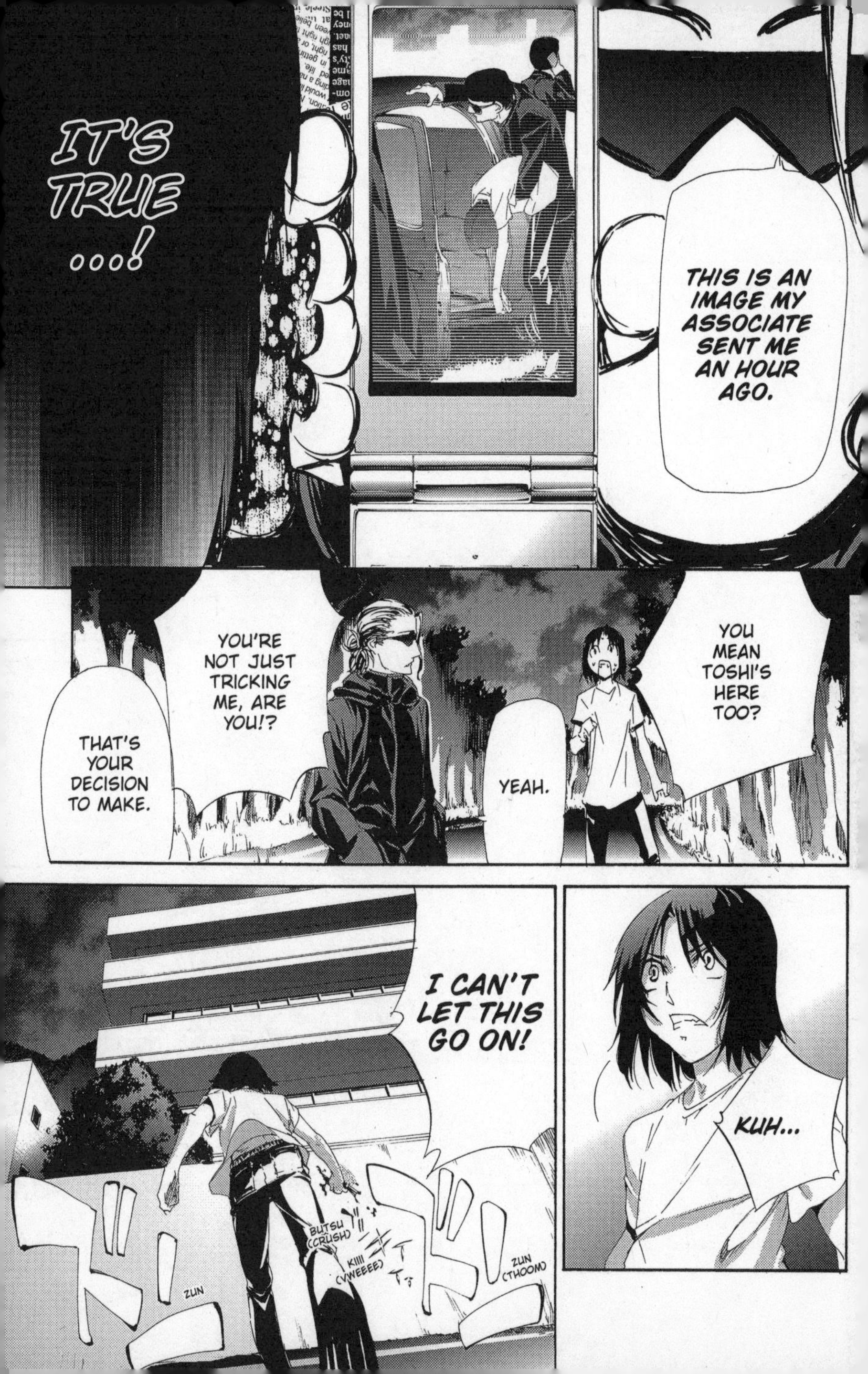
THIS IS AN IMAGE MY ASSOCIATE SENT ME AN HOUR AGO.
IT'S TRUE ....!
YOU MEAN TOSHI'S HERE TOO?
YEAH.
YOU'RE NOT JUST TRICKING ME, ARE YOU!?
THAT'S YOUR DECISION TO MAKE.
KUH...
I CAN'T LET THIS GO ON!
ZUN (THOOM)
BUTSU (CRUSH)
KIIII (VWEEEE)
ZUN

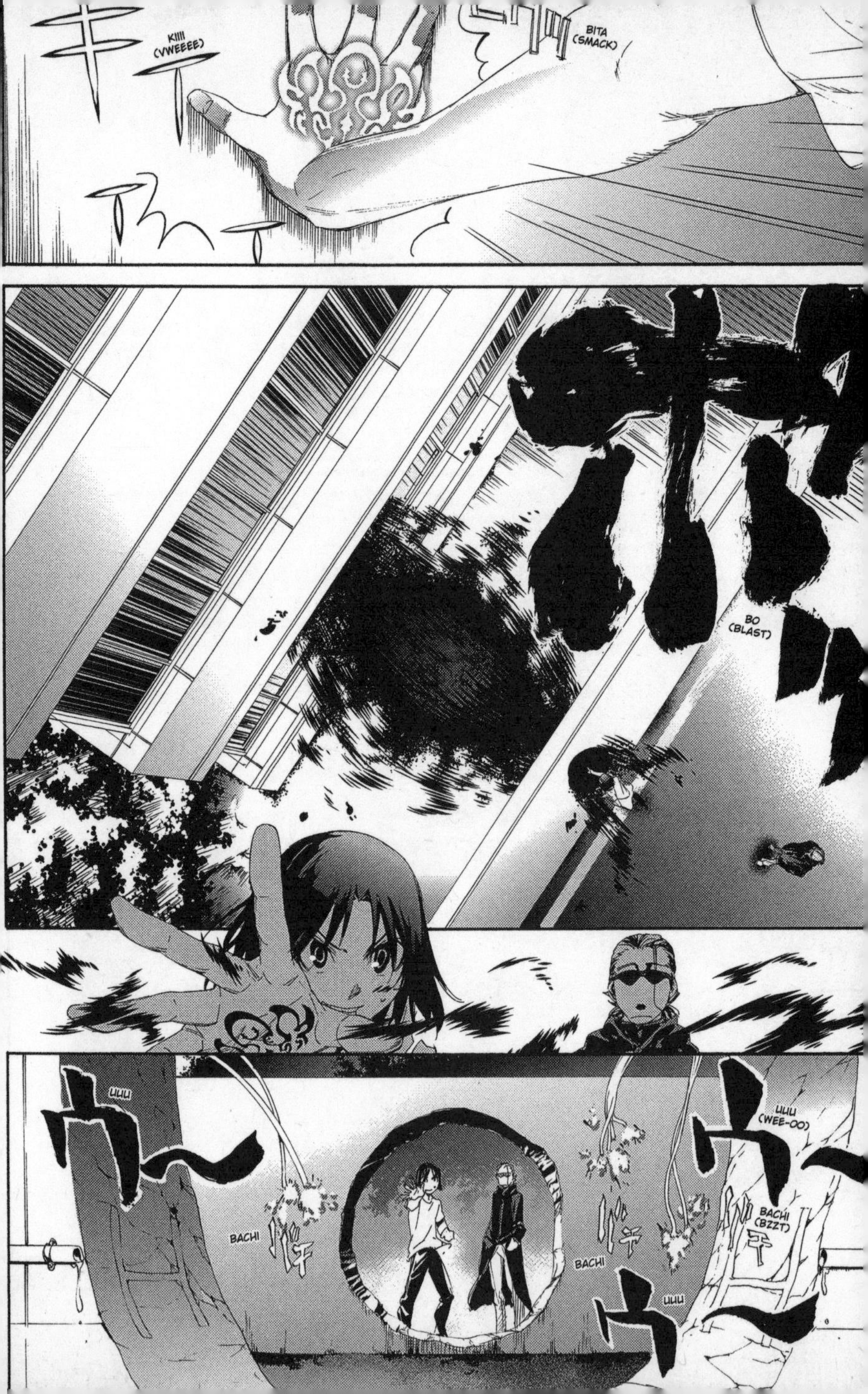
BITA
(SMACK)
KIIII
(VWEEEE)
BO
(BLAST)
UUU
(WEE-OO)
BACHI
(BZZT)
BACHI
UUU
UUU
BACHI

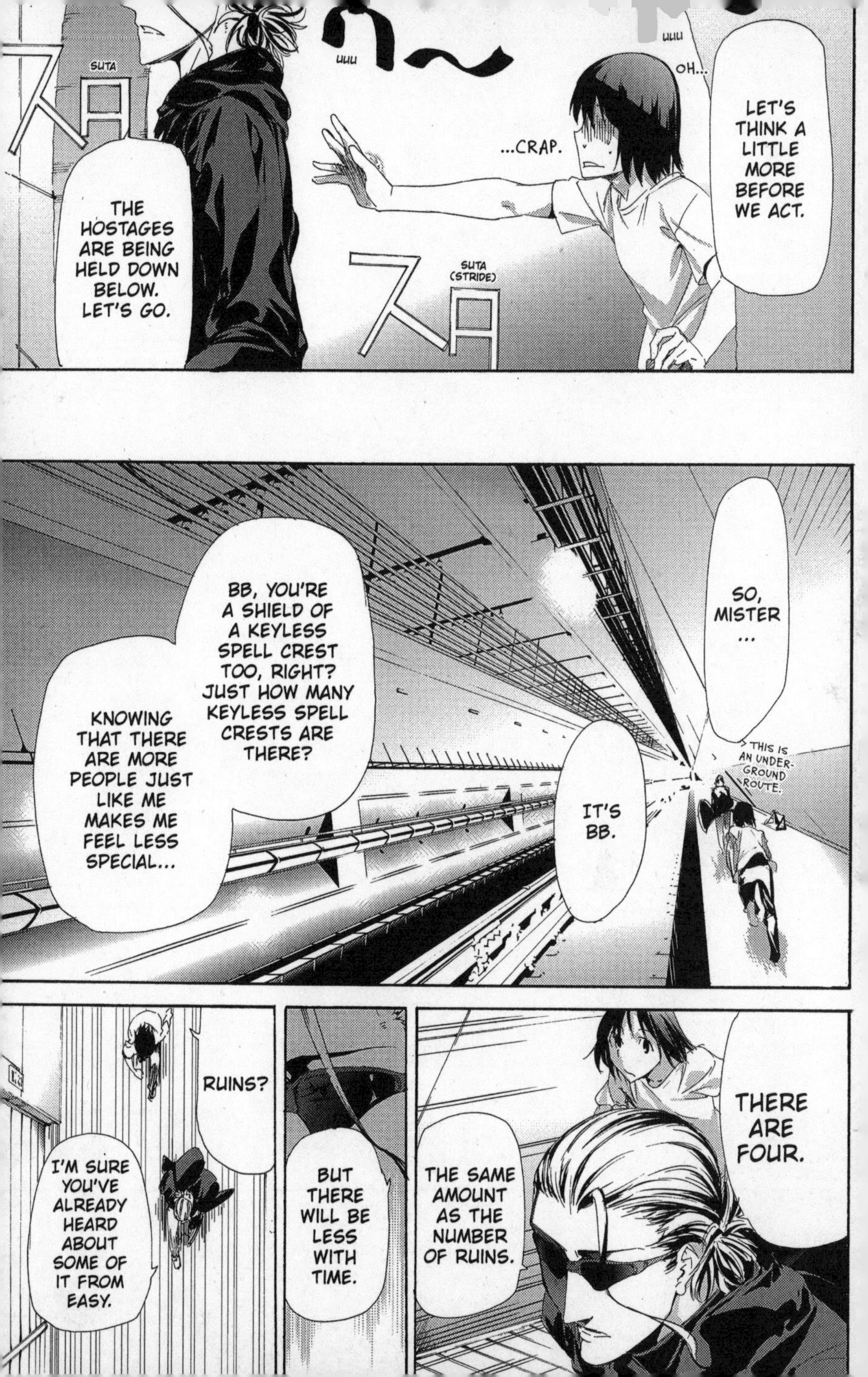
UUU
OH...
LET'S THINK A LITTLE MORE BEFORE WE ACT.
UUU
...CRAP.
SUTA
SUTA (STRIDE)
THE HOSTAGES ARE BEING HELD DOWN BELOW. LET'S GO.
SO, MISTER ...
THIS IS AN UNDERGROUND ROUTE.
IT'S BB.
BB, YOU'RE A SHIELD OF A KEYLESS SPELL CREST TOO, RIGHT? JUST HOW MANY KEYLESS SPELL CRESTS ARE THERE?
KNOWING THAT THERE ARE MORE PEOPLE JUST LIKE ME MAKES ME FEEL LESS SPECIAL...
THERE ARE FOUR.
THE SAME AMOUNT AS THE NUMBER OF RUINS.
BUT THERE WILL BE LESS WITH TIME.
RUINS?
I'M SURE YOU'VE ALREADY HEARD ABOUT SOME OF IT FROM EASY.

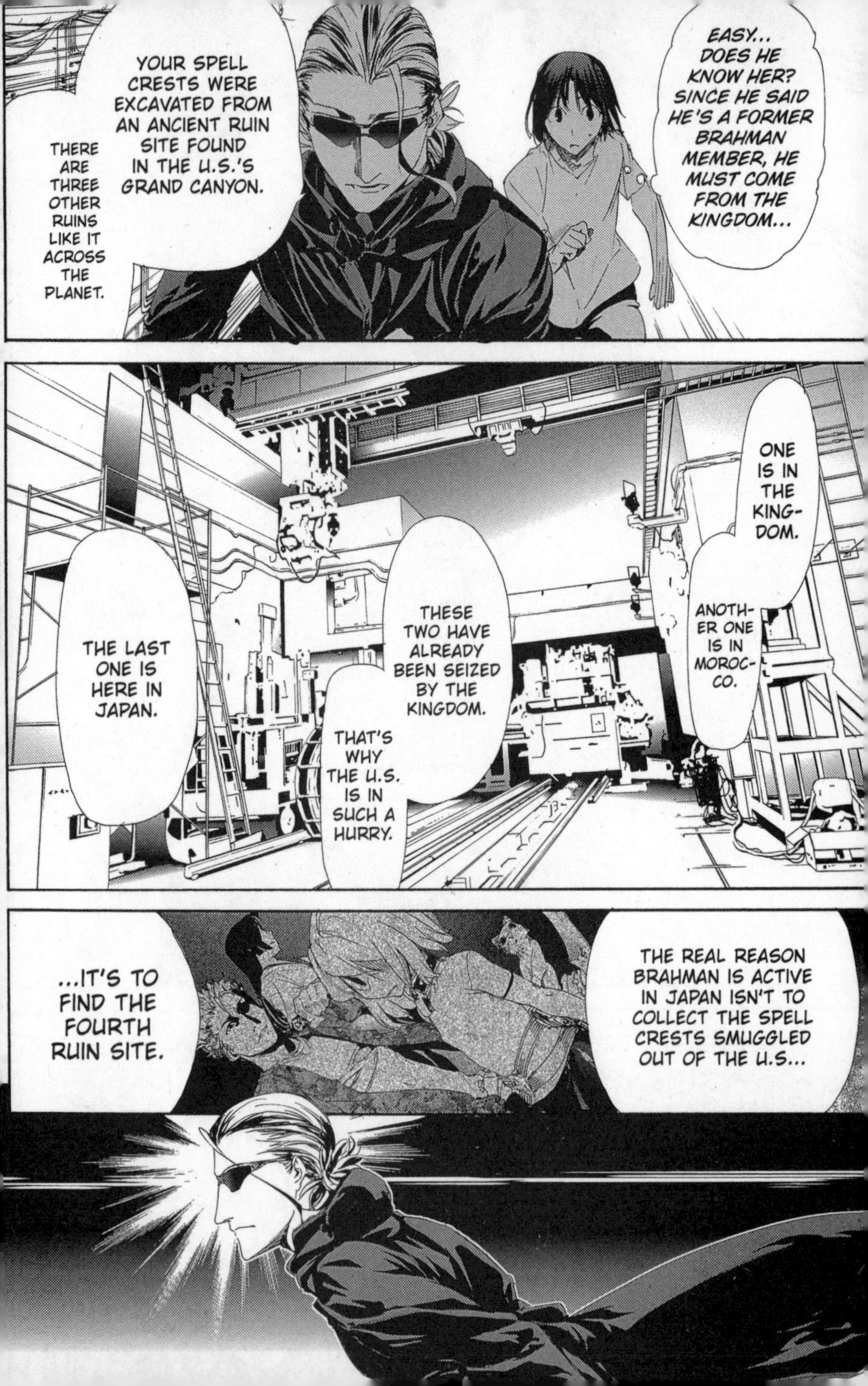
EASY... DOES HE KNOW HER? SINCE HE SAID HE'S A FORMER BRAHMAN MEMBER, HE MUST COME FROM THE KINGDOM...
YOUR SPELL CRESTS WERE EXCAVATED FROM AN ANCIENT RUIN SITE FOUND IN THE U.S.'S GRAND CANYON.
THERE ARE THREE OTHER RUINS LIKE IT ACROSS THE PLANET.
ONE IS IN THE KING-DOM.
ANOTH-ER ONE IS IN MOROC-CO.
THESE TWO HAVE ALREADY BEEN SEIZED BY THE KINGDOM.
THAT'S WHY THE U.S. IS IN SUCH A HURRY.
THE LAST ONE IS HERE IN JAPAN.
THE REAL REASON BRAHMAN IS ACTIVE IN JAPAN ISN'T TO COLLECT THE SPELL CRESTS SMUGGLED OUT OF THE U.S...
...IT'S TO FIND THE FOURTH RUIN SITE.

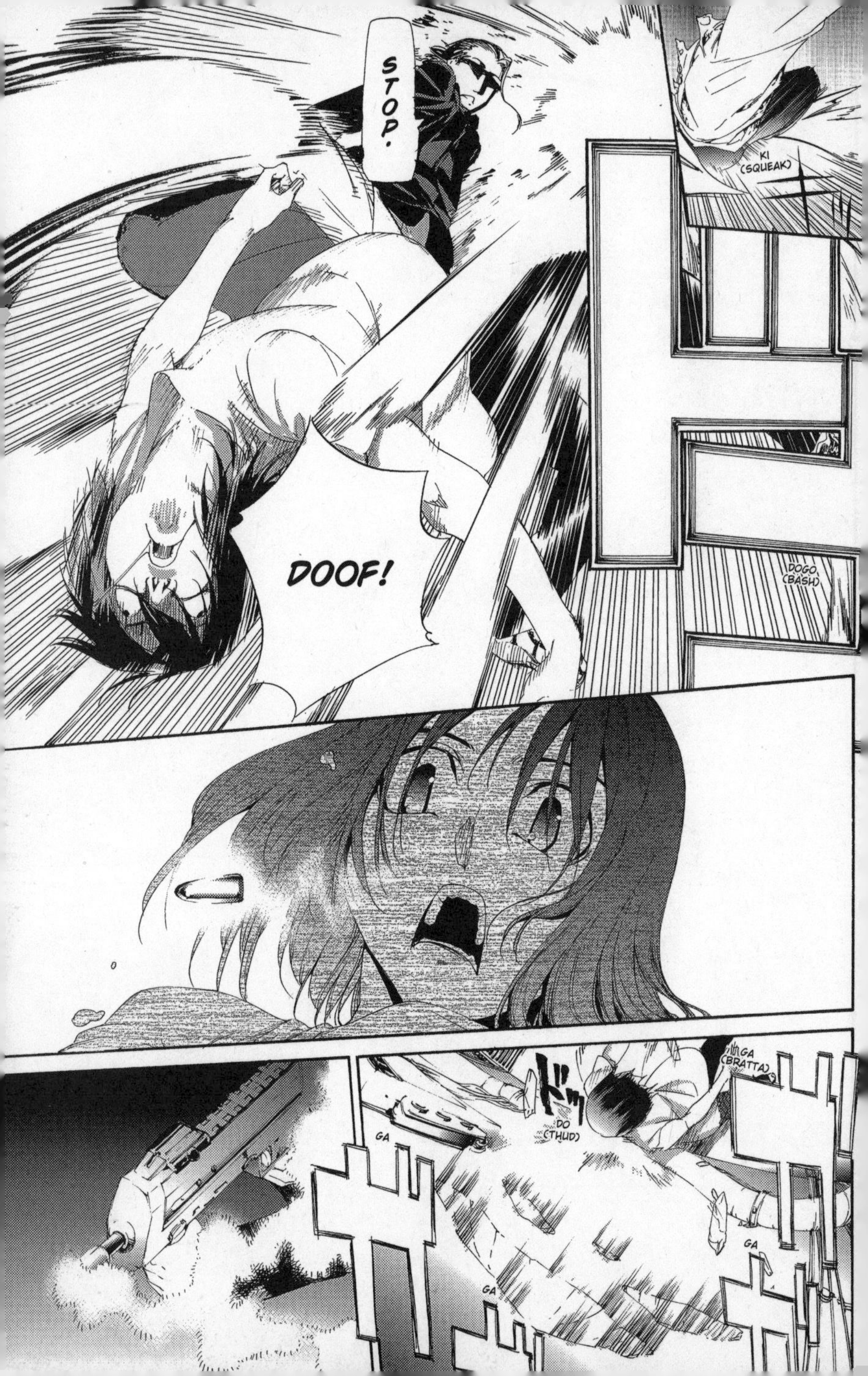
KI (SQUEAK)
STOP.
DOGO (BASH)
DOOF!
GA (BRATTA)
DO (THUD)
GA
GA
GA

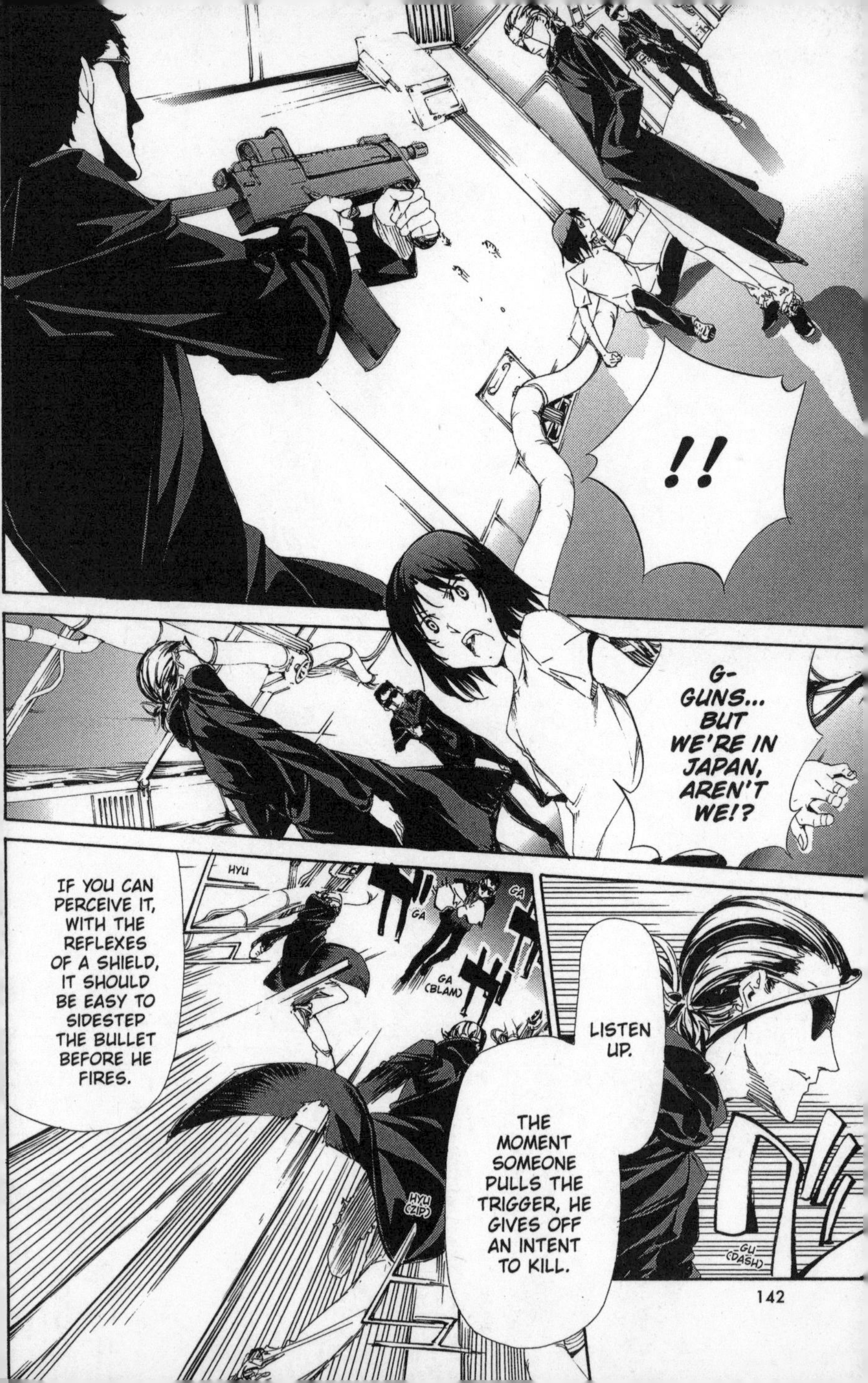
!!
G-GUNS... BUT WE'RE IN JAPAN, AREN'T WE!?
LISTEN UP.
THE MOMENT SOMEONE PULLS THE TRIGGER, HE GIVES OFF AN INTENT TO KILL.
GU (DASH)
GA
HYU
GA
GA (BLAM)
HYU (ZIP)
IF YOU CAN PERCEIVE IT, WITH THE REFLEXES OF A SHIELD, IT SHOULD BE EASY TO SIDESTEP THE BULLET BEFORE HE FIRES.

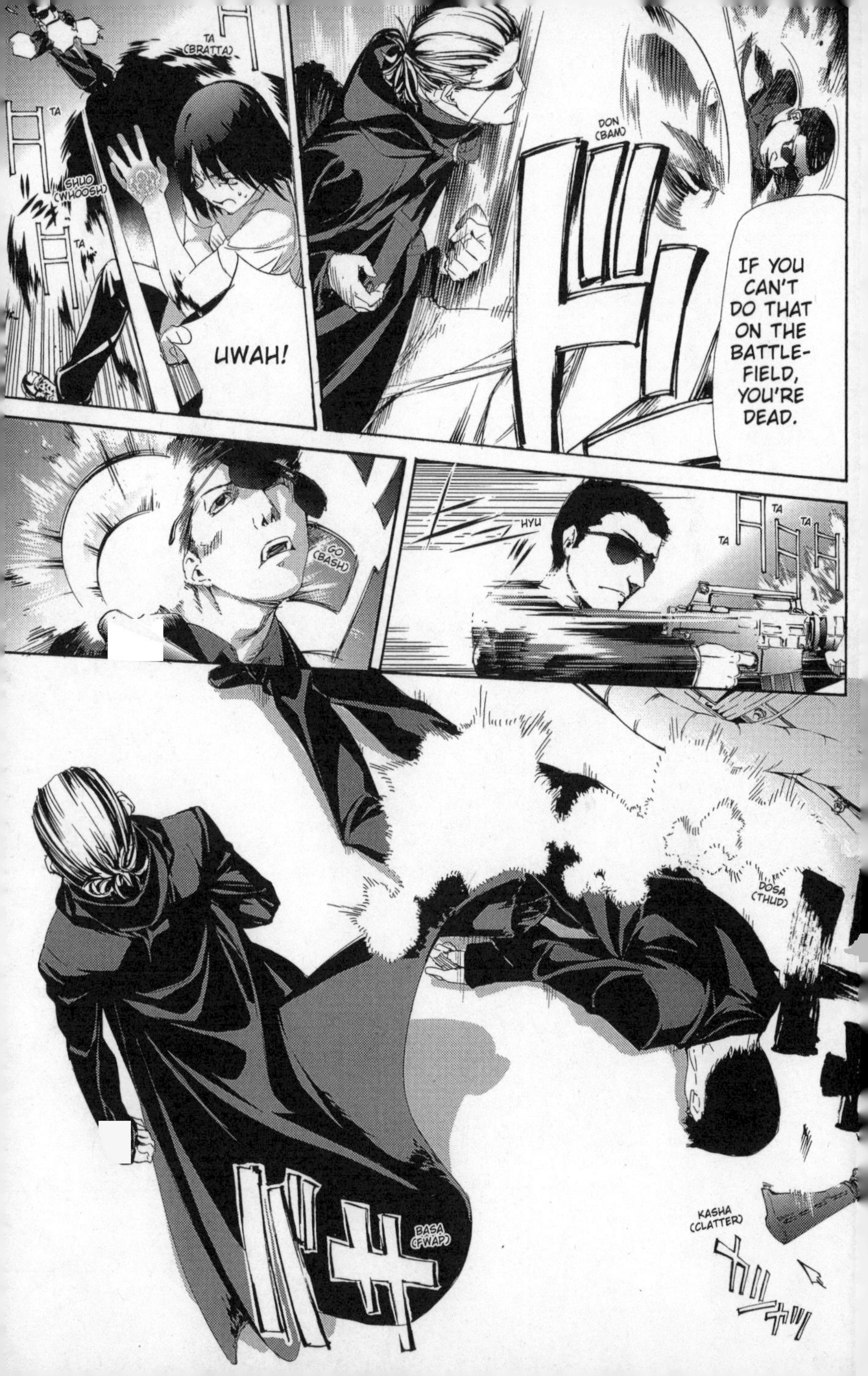
DON
(BAM)
IF YOU CAN'T DO THAT ON THE BATTLE-FIELD, YOU'RE DEAD.
TA
(BRATTA)
TA
SHUO
(WHOOSH)
TA
UWAH!
TA
TA
TA
HYU
GO
(BASH)
DOSA
(THUD)
KASHA
(CLATTER)
BASA
(FWAP)

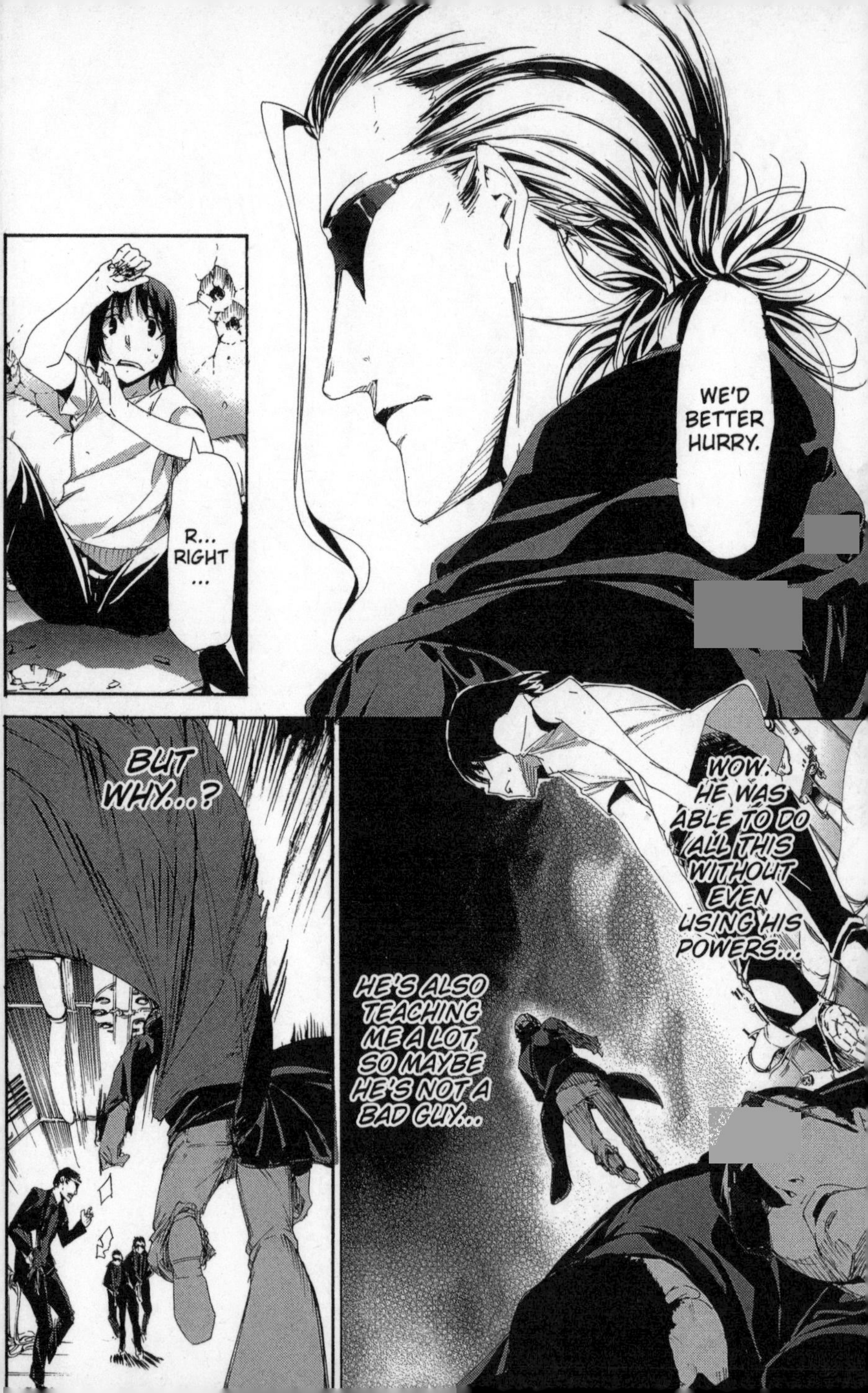
WE'D BETTER HURRY.
R... RIGHT ...
WOW. HE WAS ABLE TO DO ALL THIS WITHOUT EVEN USING HIS POWERS...
HE'S ALSO TEACHING ME A LOT, SO MAYBE HE'S NOT A BAD GUY...
BUT WHY...?

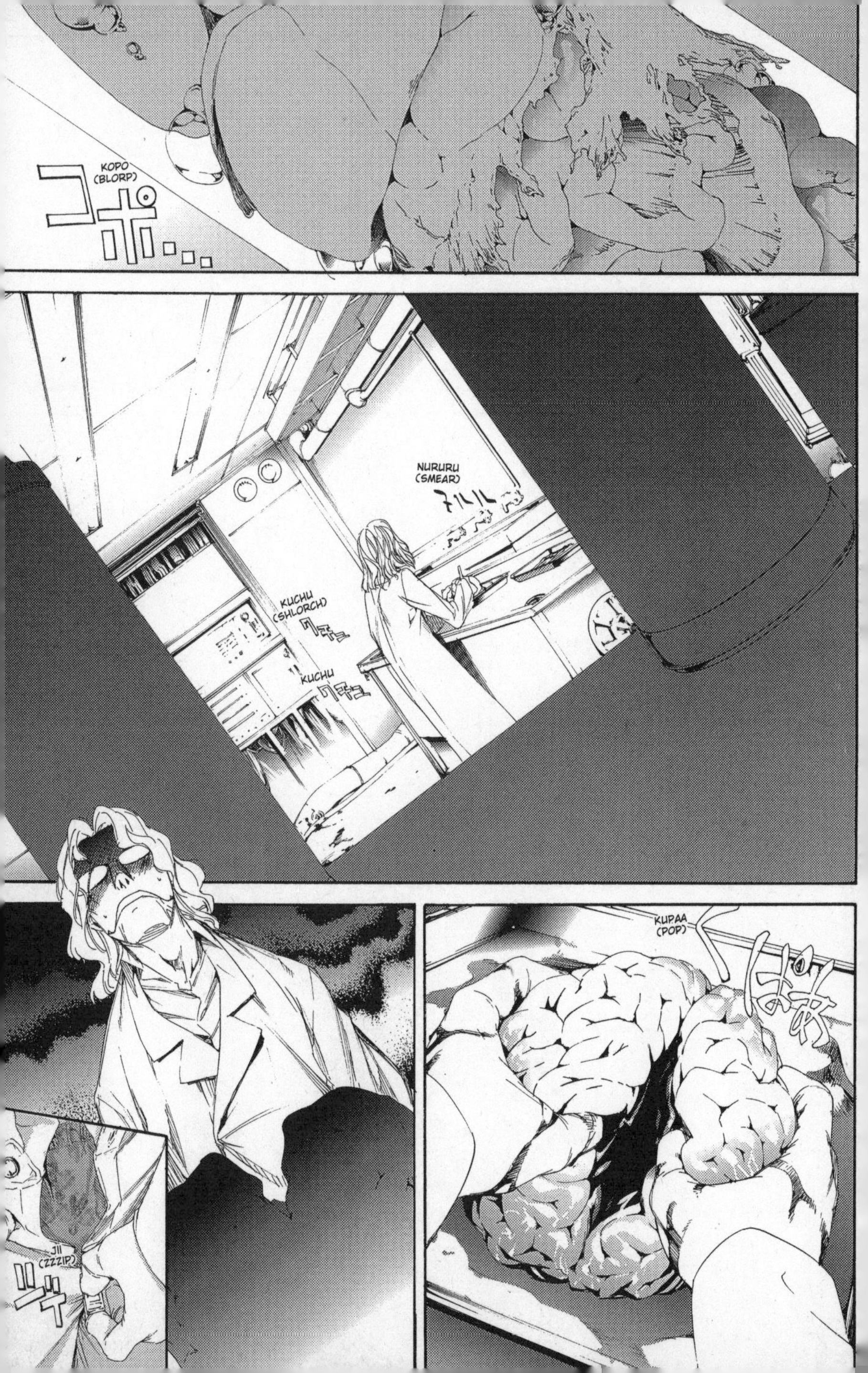
KOPO (BLORP)
NURURU (SMEAR)
KUCHU (SHLORCH)
KUCHU
KUPAA (POP)
JII (ZZZIP)

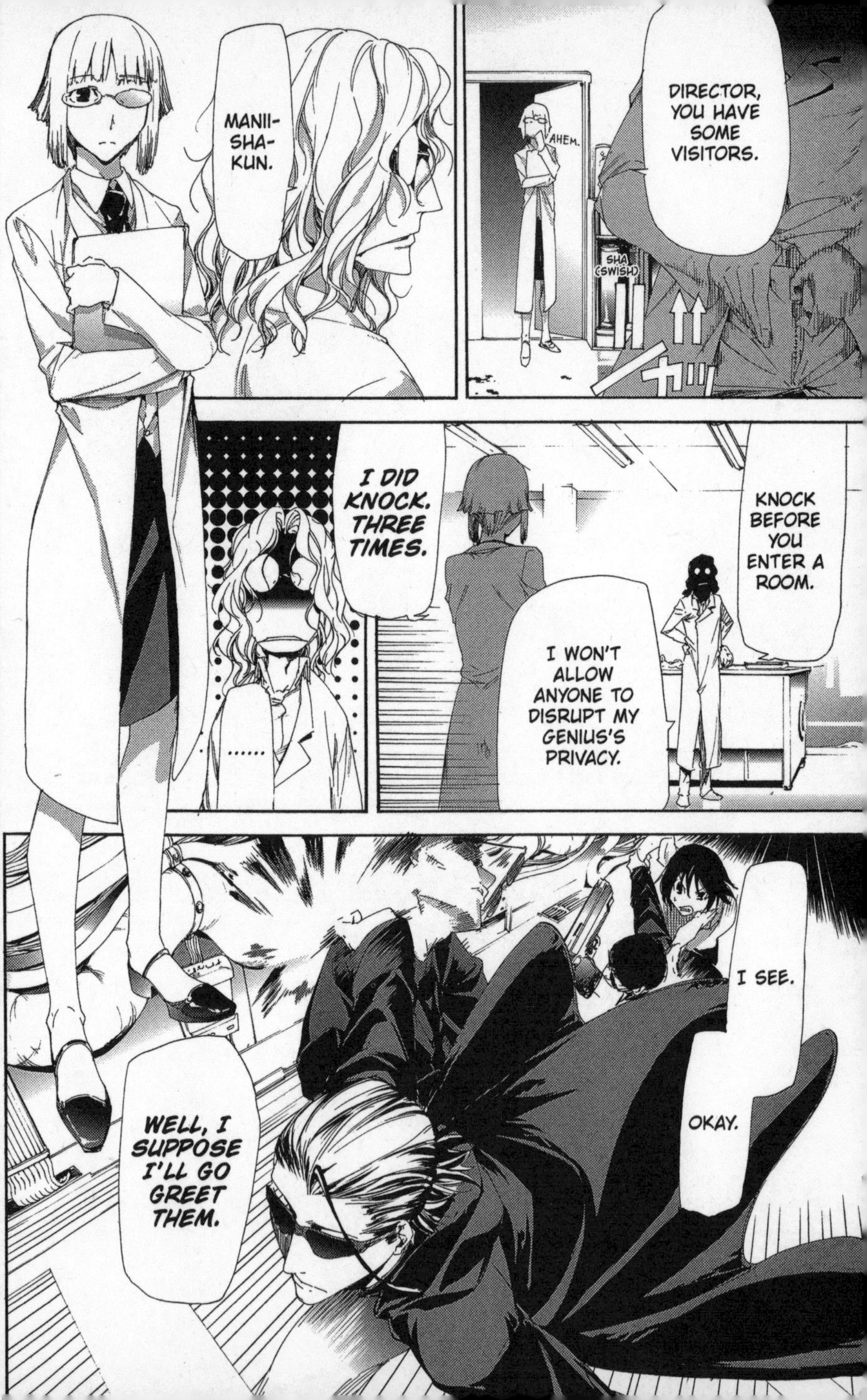
DIRECTOR, YOU HAVE SOME VISITORS.
AHEM.
SHA (SWISH)
カッ
MANII-SHA-KUN.
KNOCK BEFORE YOU ENTER A ROOM.
I WON'T ALLOW ANYONE TO DISRUPT MY GENIUS'S PRIVACY.
I DID KNOCK. THREE TIMES.
......
I SEE.
OKAY.
WELL, I SUPPOSE I'LL GO GREET THEM.

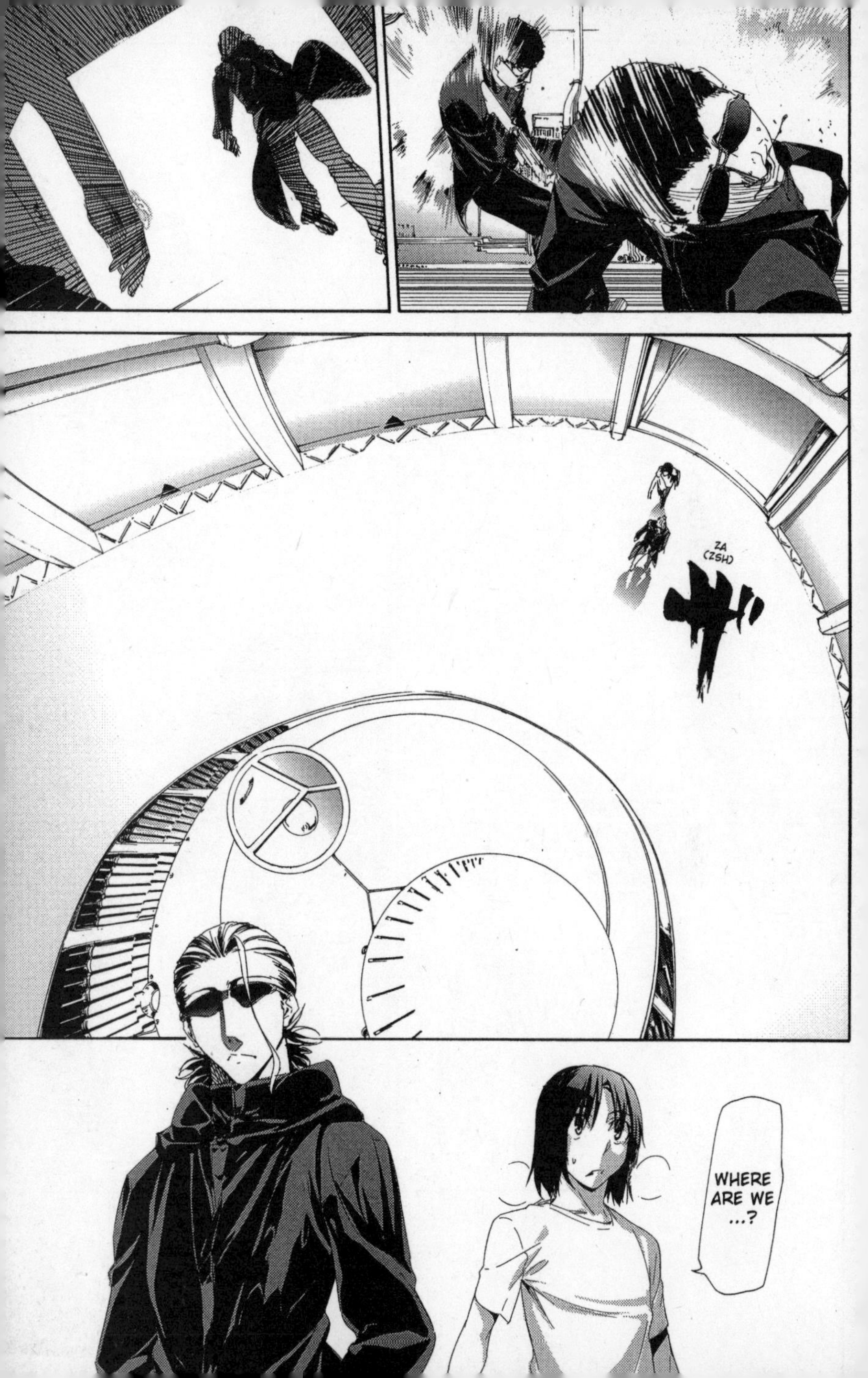
ザ
ZA (ZSH)
WHERE ARE WE ...?

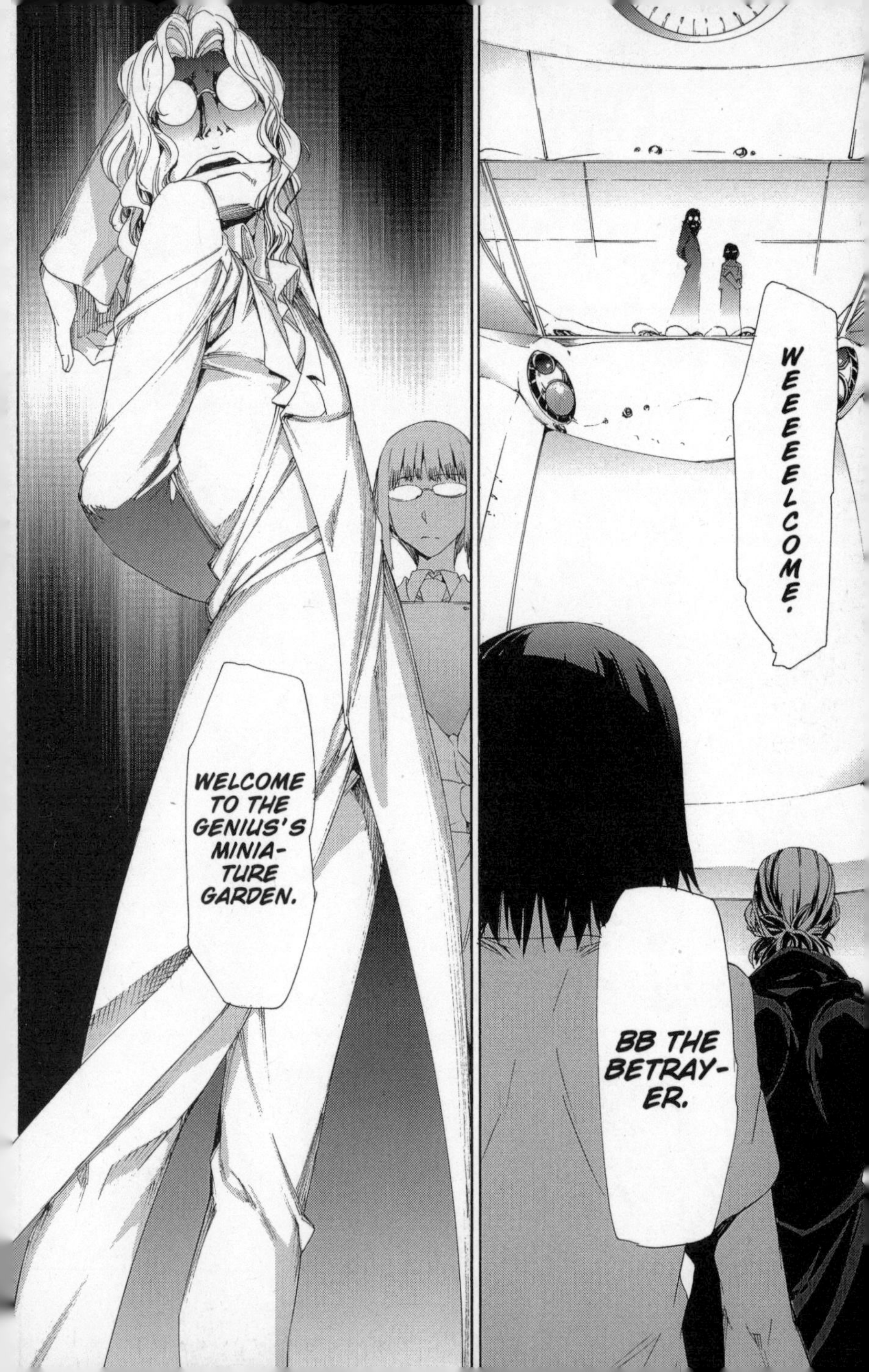
WEEEEELCOME.
BB THE BETRAY-ER.
WELCOME TO THE GENIUS'S MINIA-TURE GARDEN.

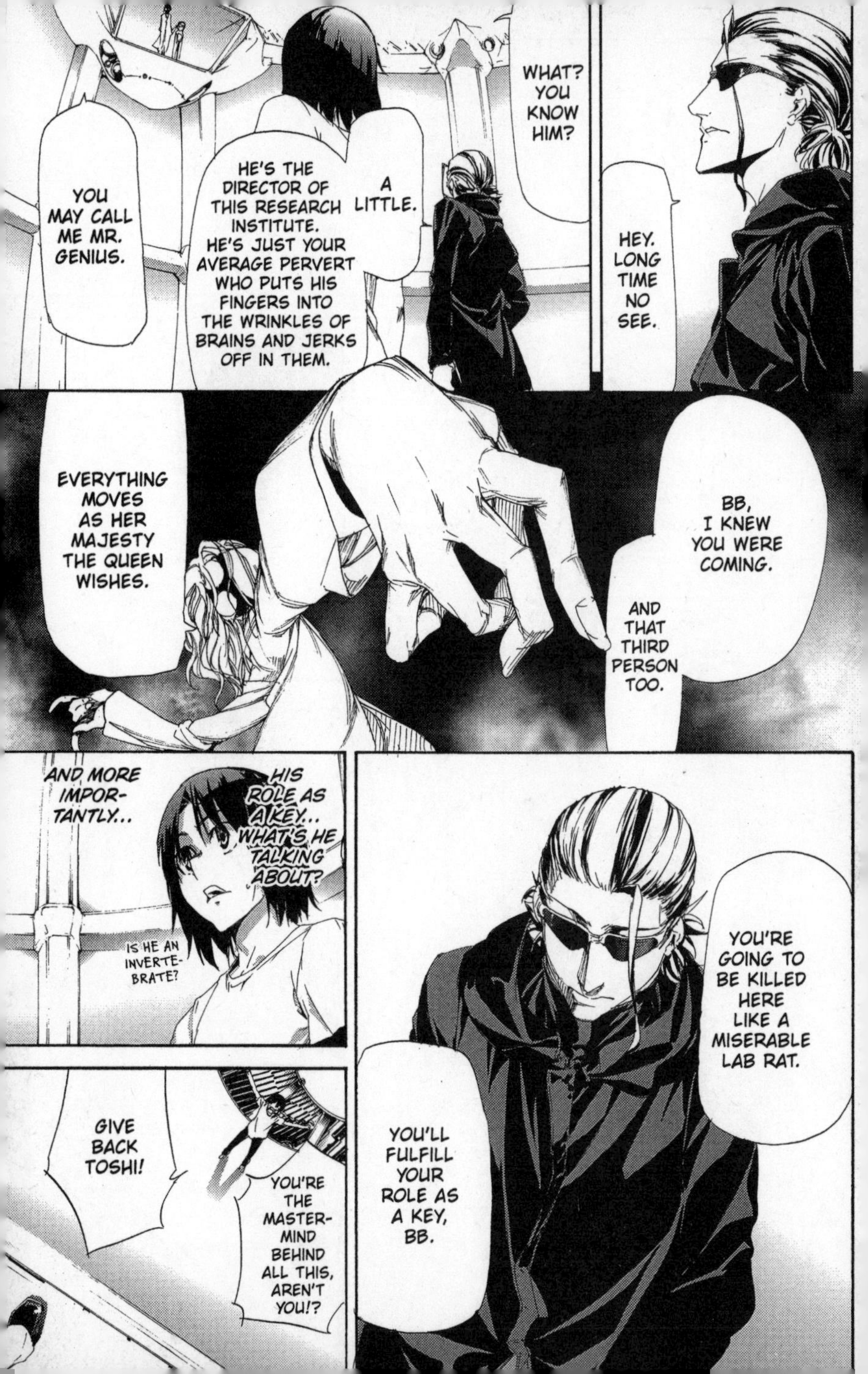
HEY. LONG TIME NO SEE.
WHAT? YOU KNOW HIM?
A LITTLE.
HE'S THE DIRECTOR OF THIS RESEARCH INSTITUTE. HE'S JUST YOUR AVERAGE PERVERT WHO PUTS HIS FINGERS INTO THE WRINKLES OF BRAINS AND JERKS OFF IN THEM.
YOU MAY CALL ME MR. GENIUS.
BB, I KNEW YOU WERE COMING.
AND THAT THIRD PERSON TOO.
EVERYTHING MOVES AS HER MAJESTY THE QUEEN WISHES.
YOU'RE GOING TO BE KILLED HERE LIKE A MISERABLE LAB RAT.
YOU'LL FULFILL YOUR ROLE AS A KEY, BB.
HIS ROLE AS A KEY... WHAT'S HE TALKING ABOUT?
AND MORE IMPOR-TANTLY...
IS HE AN INVERTE-BRATE?
YOU'RE THE MASTER-MIND BEHIND ALL THIS, AREN'T YOU!?
GIVE BACK TOSHI!

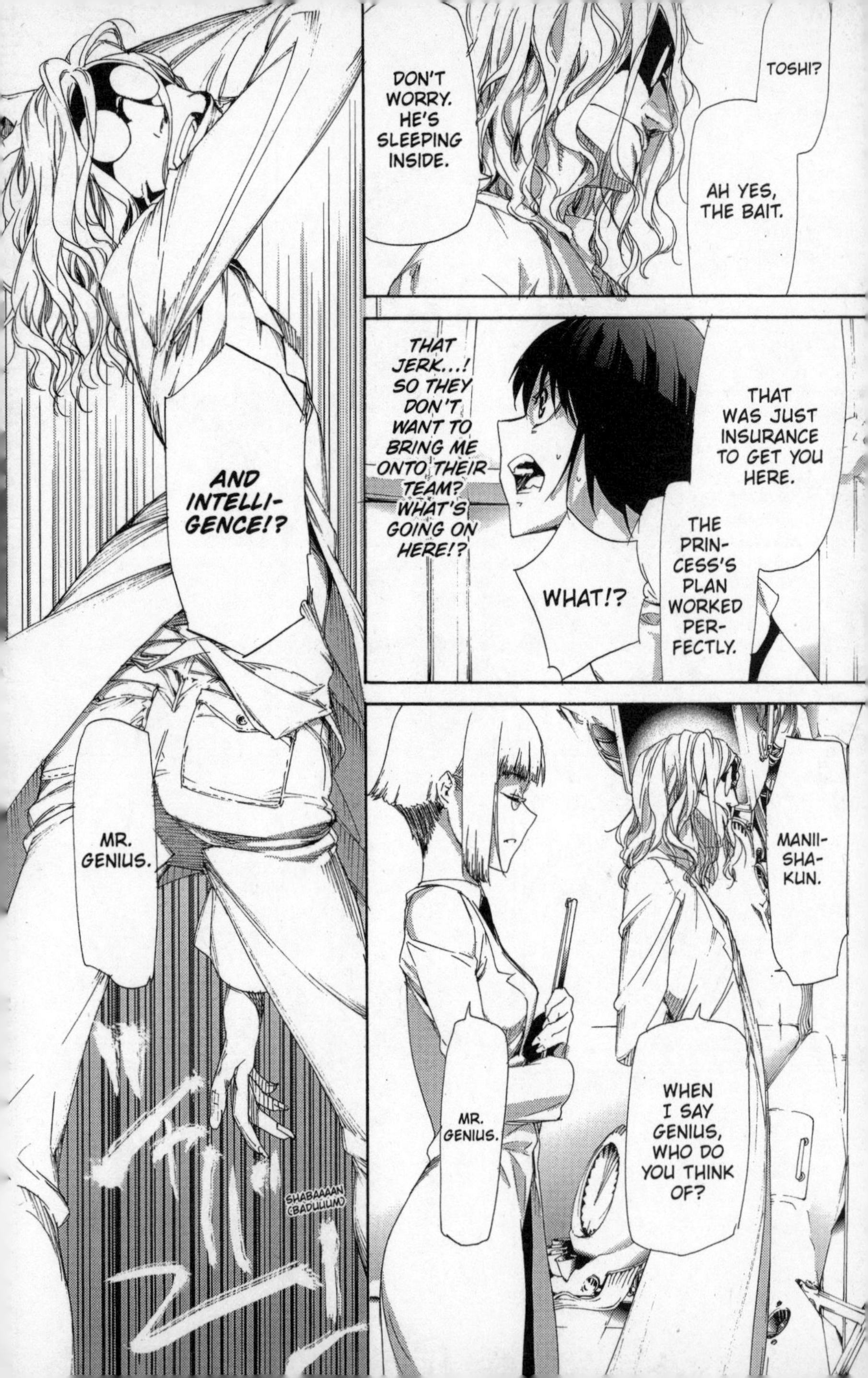
TOSHI?
AH YES, THE BAIT.
DON'T WORRY. HE'S SLEEPING INSIDE.
THAT WAS JUST INSURANCE TO GET YOU HERE.
THE PRINCESS'S PLAN WORKED PERFECTLY.
WHAT!?
THAT JERK...! SO THEY DON'T WANT TO BRING ME ONTO THEIR TEAM? WHAT'S GOING ON HERE!?
MANII-SHAKUN.
WHEN I SAY GENIUS, WHO DO YOU THINK OF?
MR. GENIUS.
AND INTELLIGENCE!?
MR. GENIUS.
SHABAAAAN (BADUUUM)

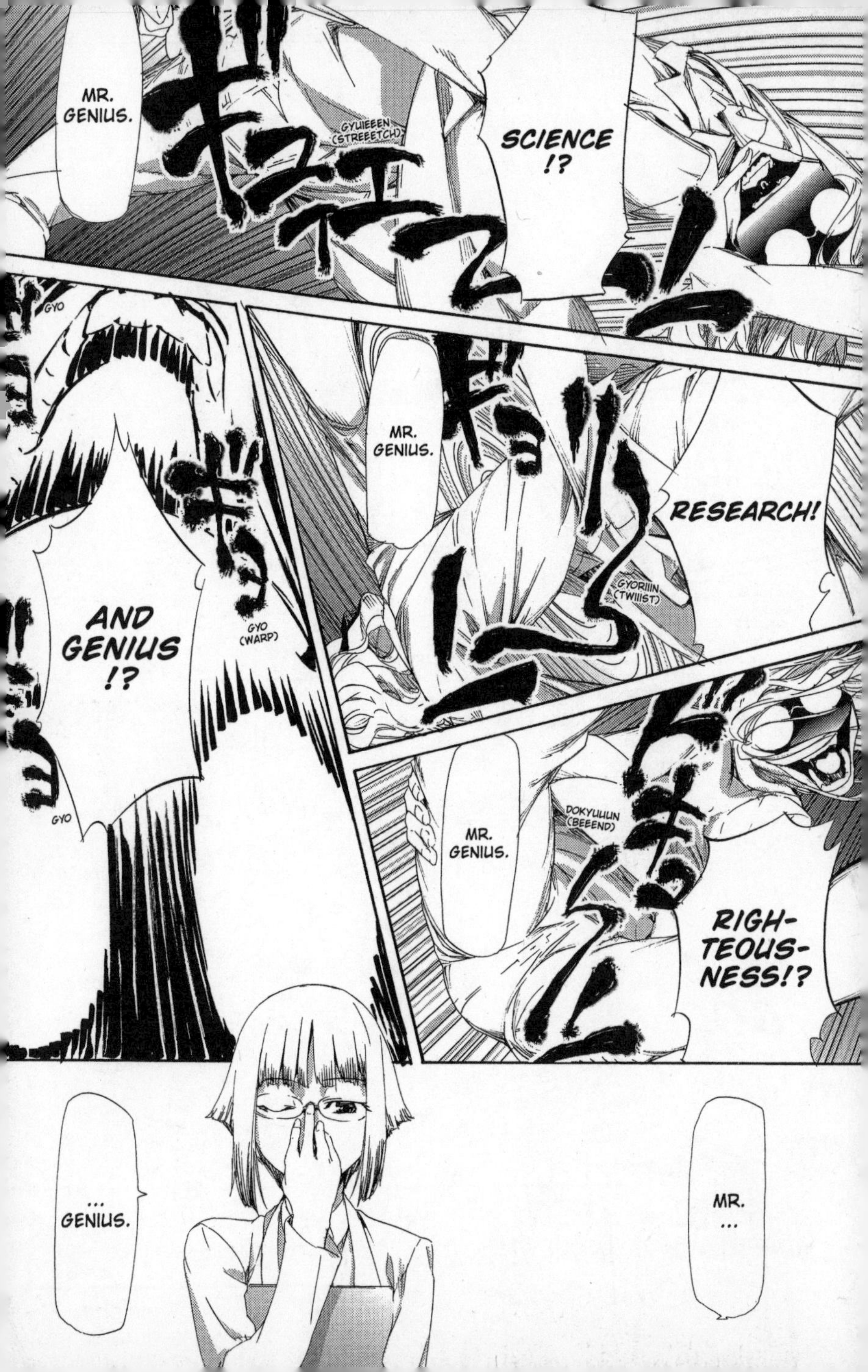
SCIENCE !?
GYUIEEEN (STREEETCH)
MR. GENIUS.
RESEARCH!
GYORIIIN (TWIIIST)
MR. GENIUS.
RIGHTEOUSNESS!?
DOKYUUUN (BEEEND)
MR. GENIUS.
AND GENIUS !?
GYO
GYO (WARP)
GYO
MR. ...
... GENIUS.

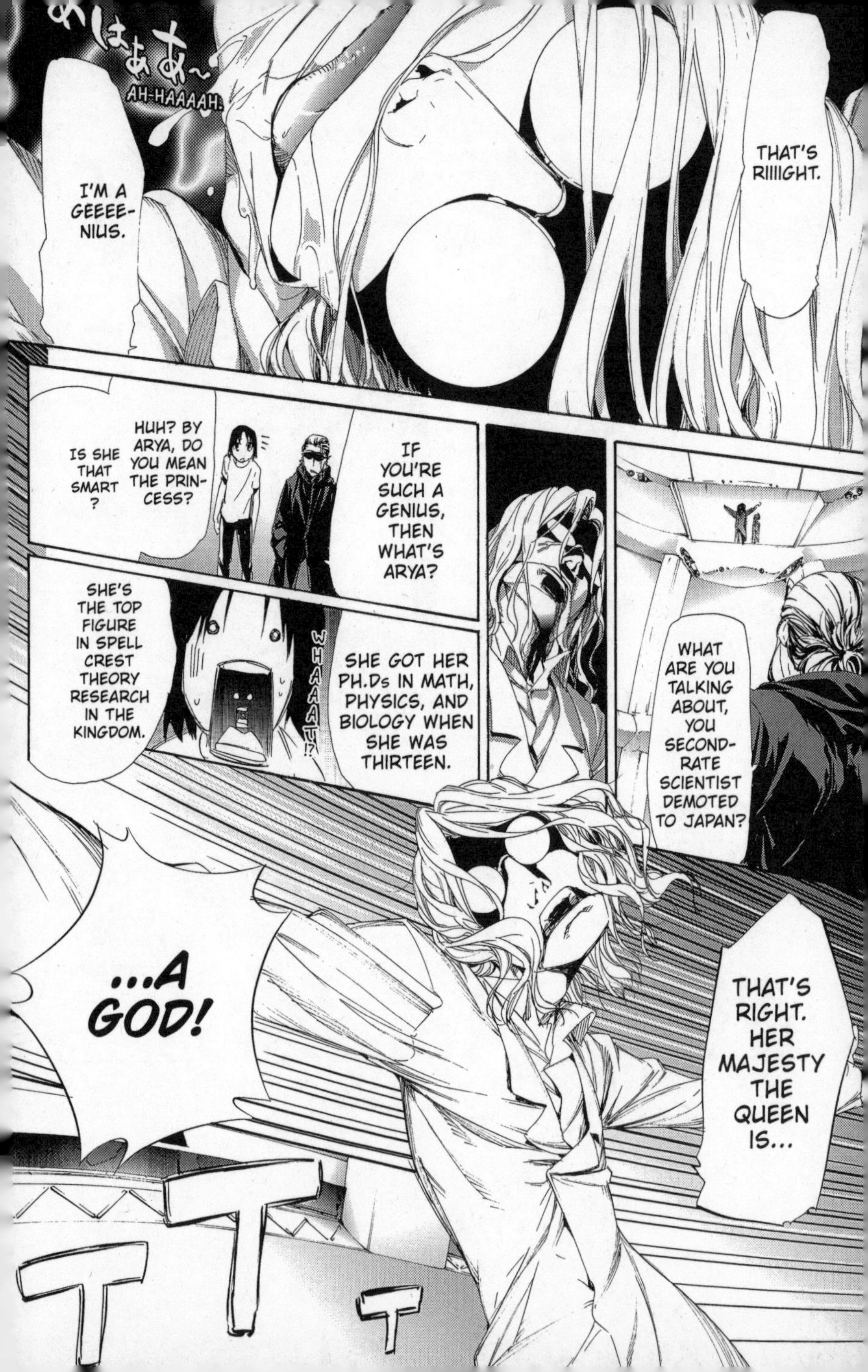
ぬはぁぁ~
AH-HAAAAH.
I'M A GEEEE-NIUS.
THAT'S RIIIIGHT.
IF YOU'RE SUCH A GENIUS, THEN WHAT'S ARYA?
HUH? BY ARYA, DO YOU MEAN THE PRINCESS?
IS SHE THAT SMART?
SHE GOT HER PH.Ds IN MATH, PHYSICS, AND BIOLOGY WHEN SHE WAS THIRTEEN.
WHAAAAAT!?
SHE'S THE TOP FIGURE IN SPELL CREST THEORY RESEARCH IN THE KINGDOM.
WHAT ARE YOU TALKING ABOUT, YOU SECOND-RATE SCIENTIST DEMOTED TO JAPAN?
THAT'S RIGHT. HER MAJESTY THE QUEEN IS...
...A GOD!

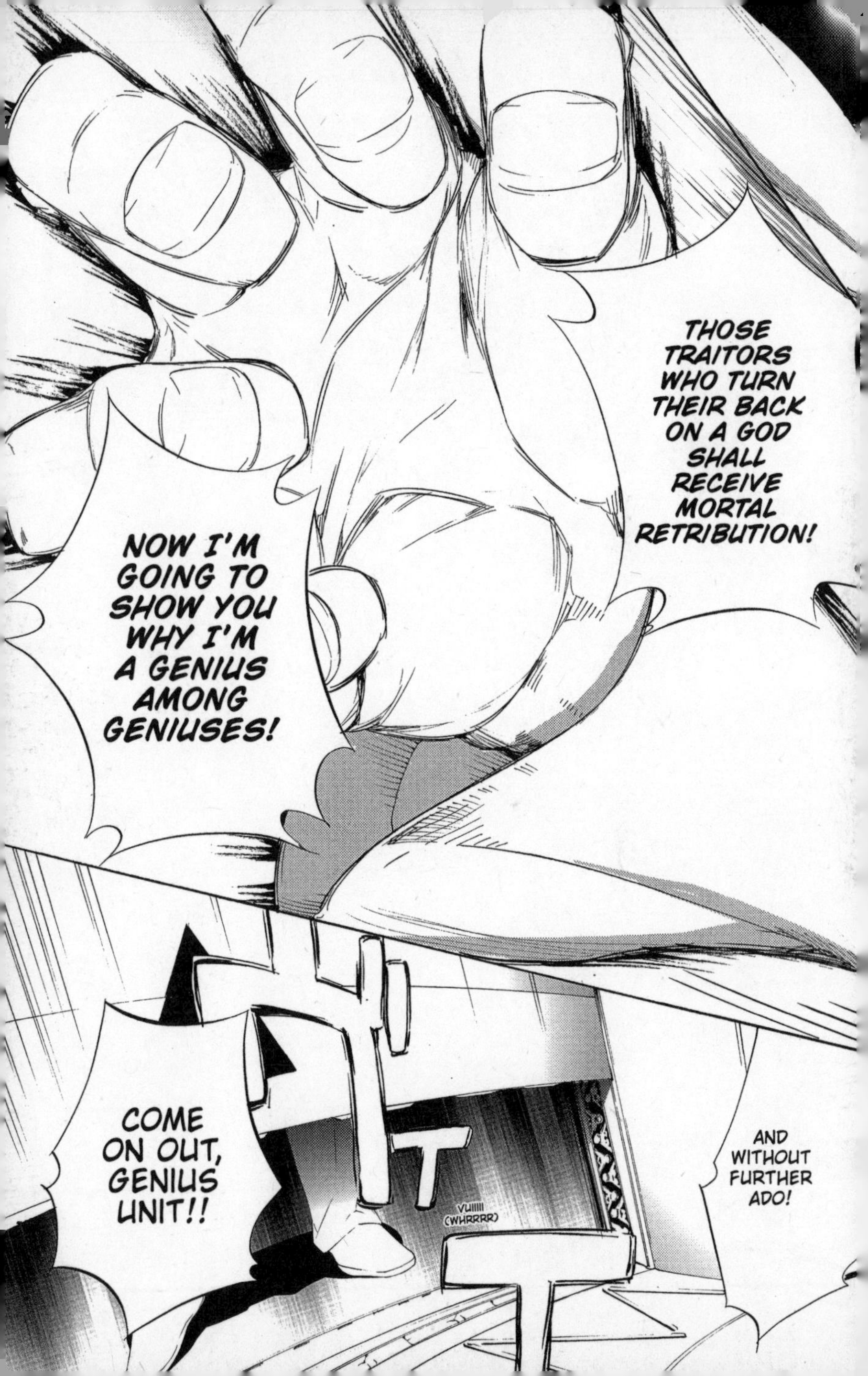
THOSE TRAITORS WHO TURN THEIR BACK ON A GOD SHALL RECEIVE MORTAL RETRIBUTION!
NOW I'M GOING TO SHOW YOU WHY I'M A GENIUS AMONG GENIUSES!
AND WITHOUT FURTHER ADO!
VUIIIIII (WHRRRR)
COME ON OUT, GENIUS UNIT!!

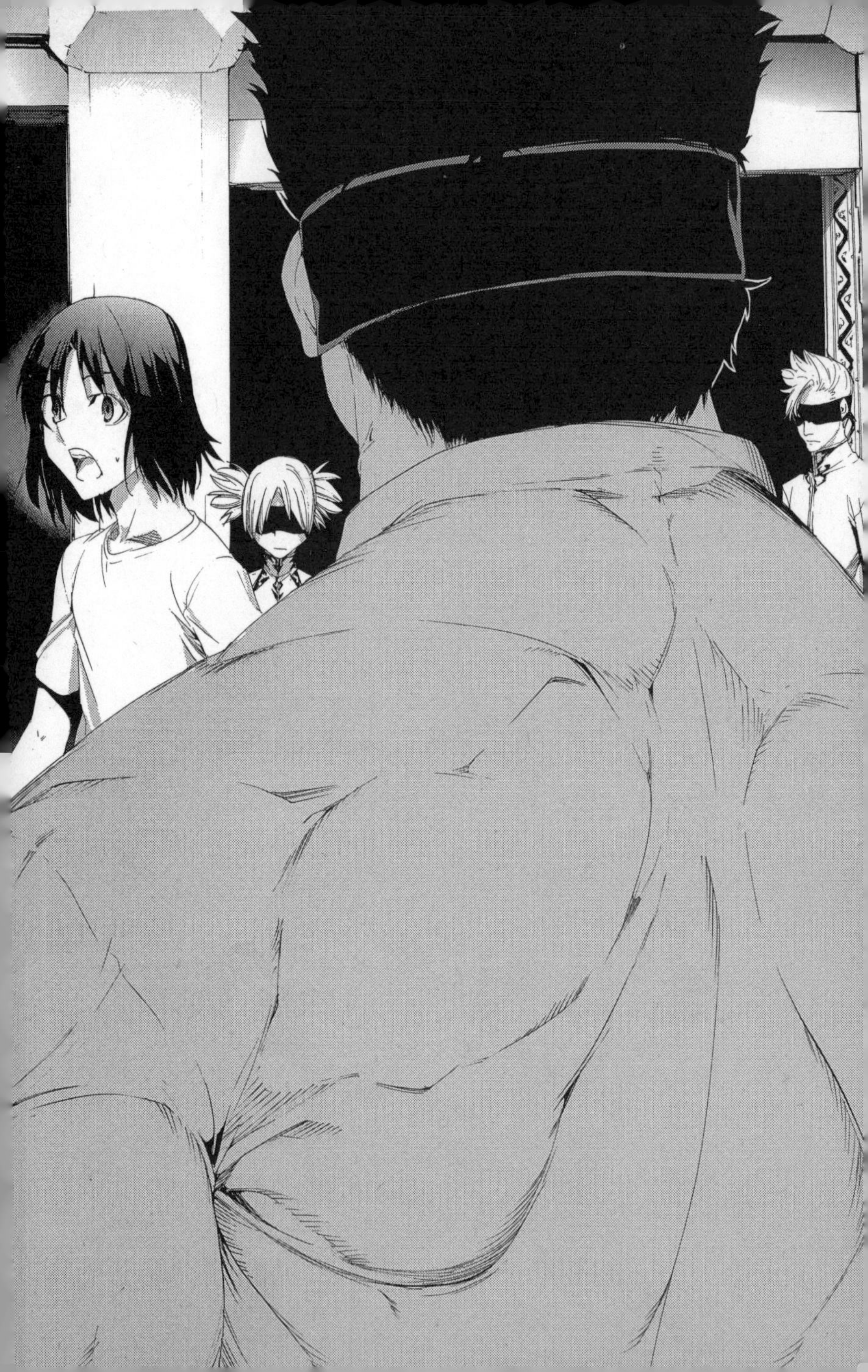

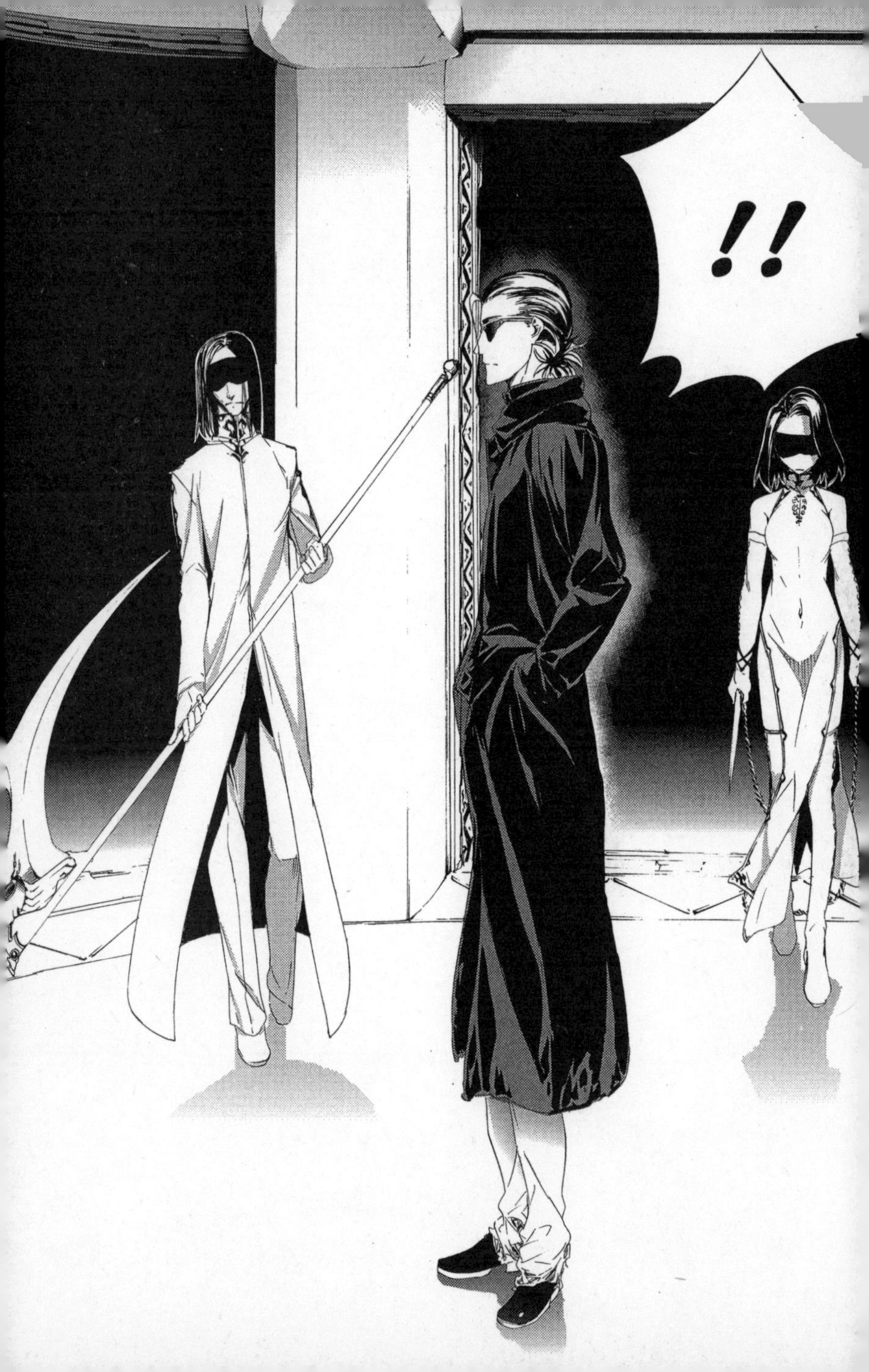
!!

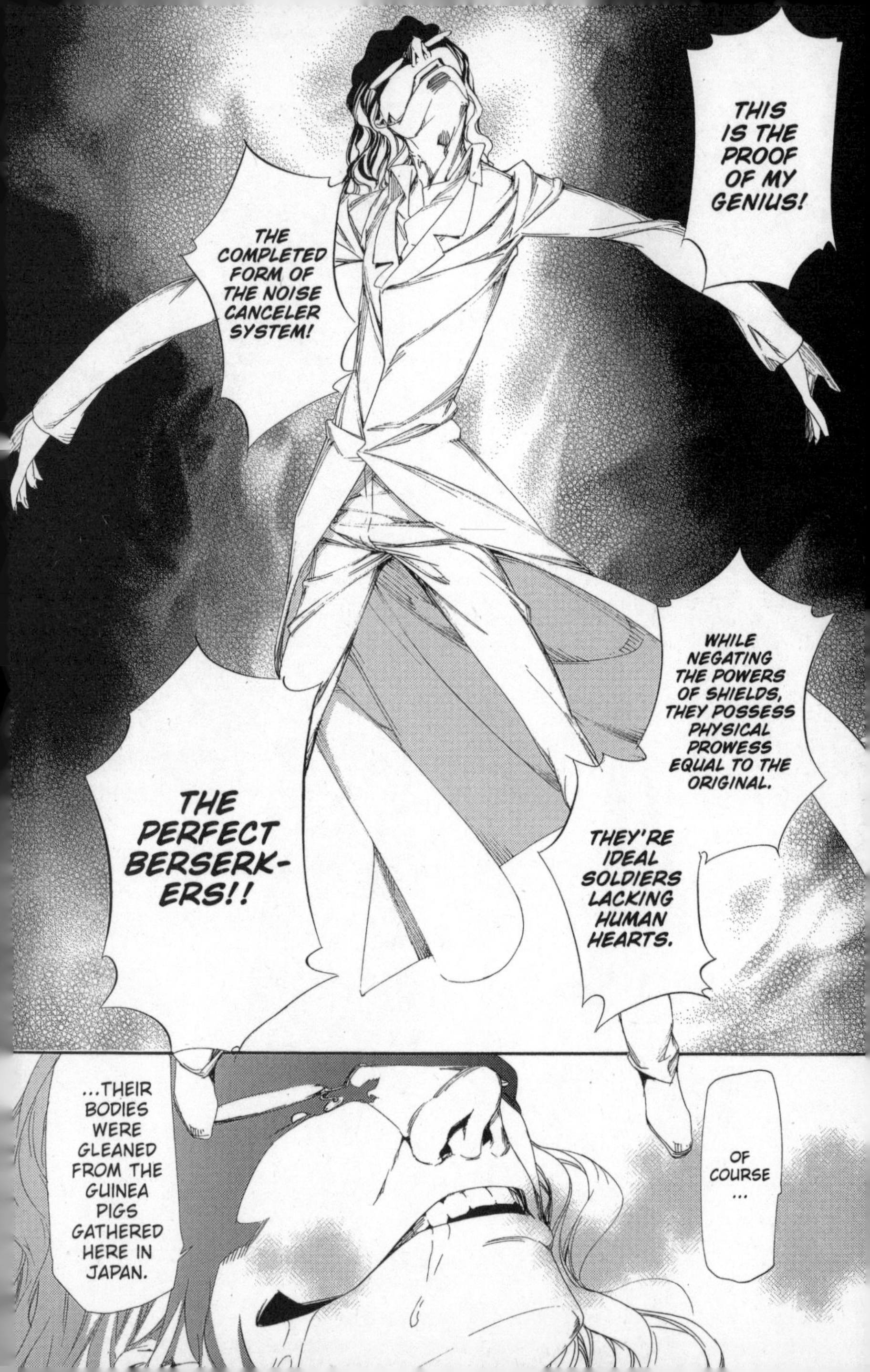
THIS IS THE PROOF OF MY GENIUS!
THE COMPLETED FORM OF THE NOISE CANCELER SYSTEM!
WHILE NEGATING THE POWERS OF SHIELDS, THEY POSSESS PHYSICAL PROWESS EQUAL TO THE ORIGINAL.
THEY'RE IDEAL SOLDIERS LACKING HUMAN HEARTS.
THE PERFECT BERSERK-ERS!!
OF COURSE ...
...THEIR BODIES WERE GLEANED FROM THE GUINEA PIGS GATHERED HERE IN JAPAN.

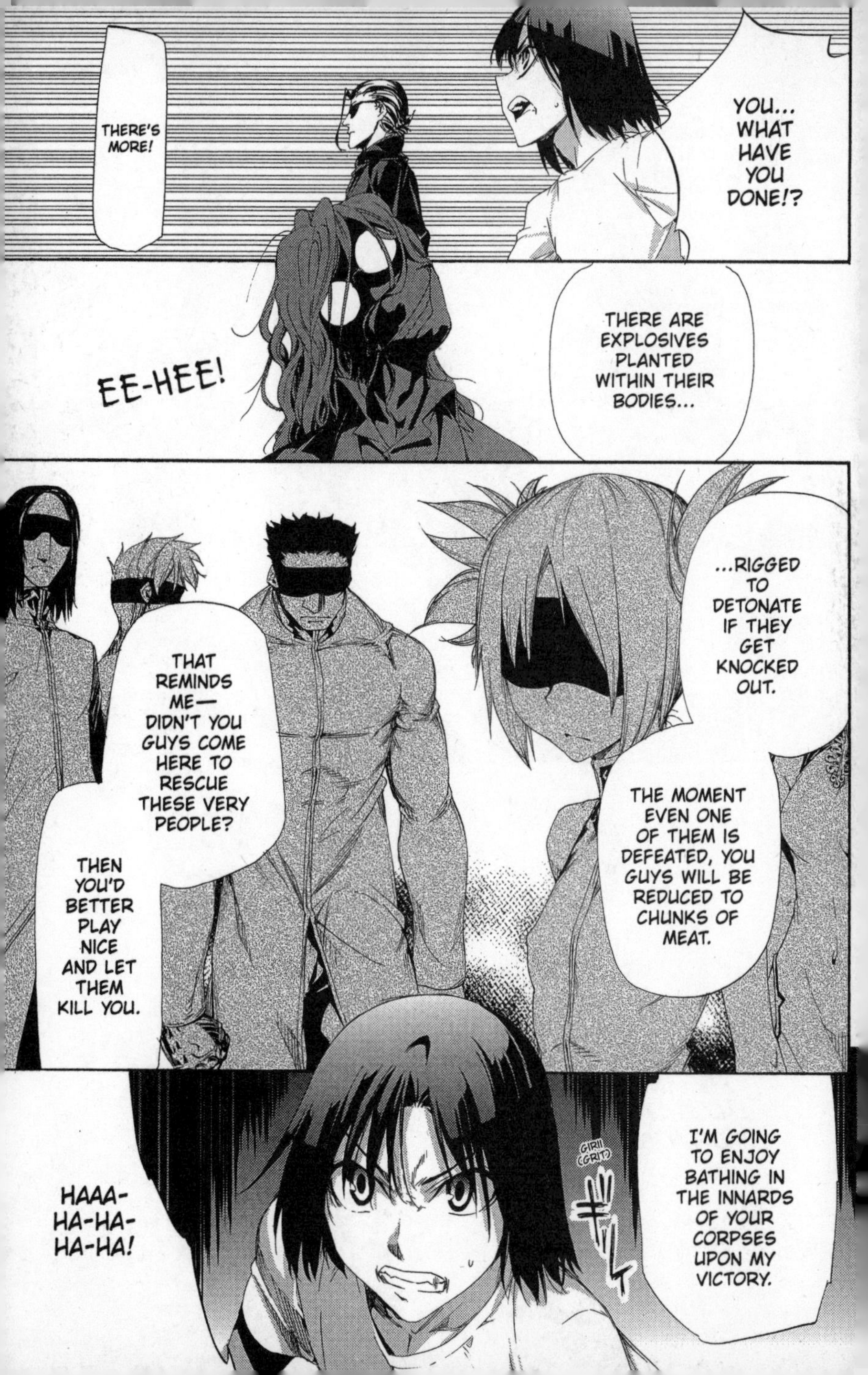
YOU... WHAT HAVE YOU DONE!?
THERE'S MORE!
THERE ARE EXPLOSIVES PLANTED WITHIN THEIR BODIES...
EE-HEE!
...RIGGED TO DETONATE IF THEY GET KNOCKED OUT.
THE MOMENT EVEN ONE OF THEM IS DEFEATED, YOU GUYS WILL BE REDUCED TO CHUNKS OF MEAT.
THAT REMINDS ME—DIDN'T YOU GUYS COME HERE TO RESCUE THESE VERY PEOPLE?
THEN YOU'D BETTER PLAY NICE AND LET THEM KILL YOU.
I'M GOING TO ENJOY BATHING IN THE INNARDS OF YOUR CORPSES UPON MY VICTORY.
GIRII (GRIT)
HAAAA-HA-HA-HA-HA!

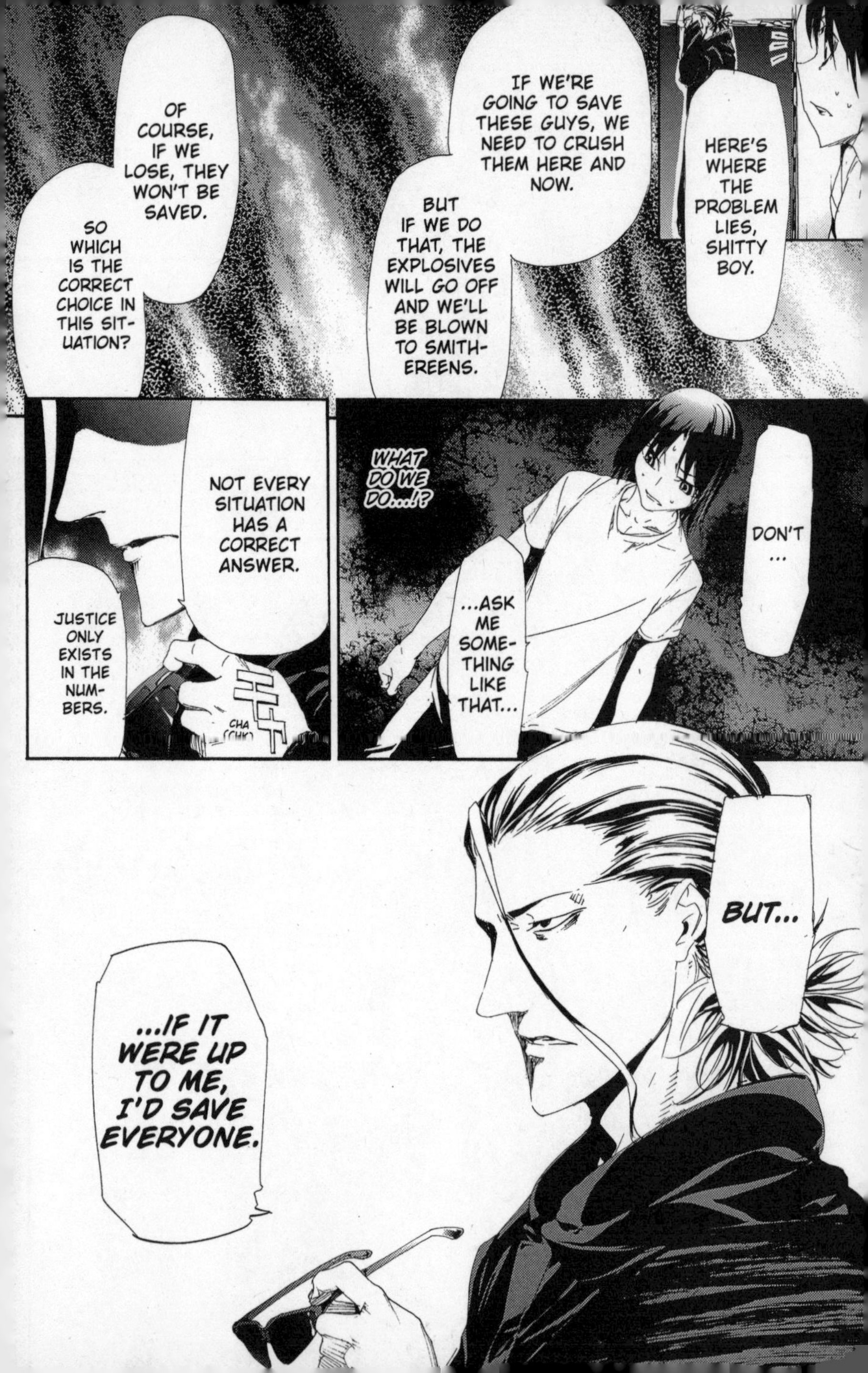
HERE'S WHERE THE PROBLEM LIES, SHITTY BOY.
IF WE'RE GOING TO SAVE THESE GUYS, WE NEED TO CRUSH THEM HERE AND NOW.
BUT IF WE DO THAT, THE EXPLOSIVES WILL GO OFF AND WE'LL BE BLOWN TO SMITH-EREENS.
OF COURSE, IF WE LOSE, THEY WON'T BE SAVED.
SO WHICH IS THE CORRECT CHOICE IN THIS SIT-UATION?
DON'T ...
...ASK ME SOME-THING LIKE THAT...
WHAT DO WE DO...!?
NOT EVERY SITUATION HAS A CORRECT ANSWER.
JUSTICE ONLY EXISTS IN THE NUM-BERS.
CHA CHK
BUT...
...IF IT WERE UP TO ME, I'D SAVE EVERYONE.

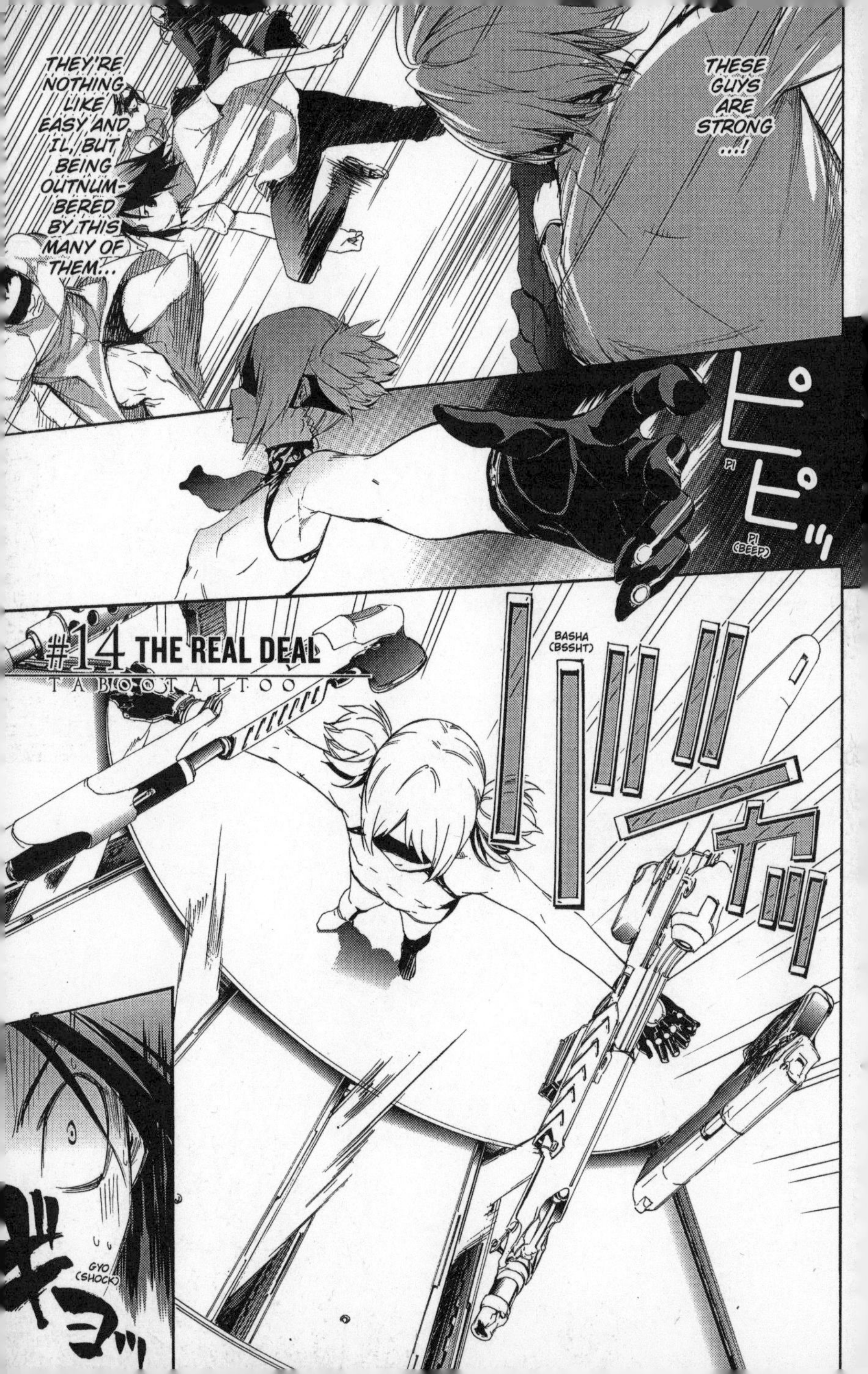
THESE GUYS ARE STRONG ...!
THEY'RE NOTHING LIKE EASY AND IL, BUT BEING OUTNUMBERED BY THIS MANY OF THEM...
PI
PI (BEEP)
BASHA (BSSHT)
#14 THE REAL DEAL
TABOO TATTOO
GYO (SHOCK)

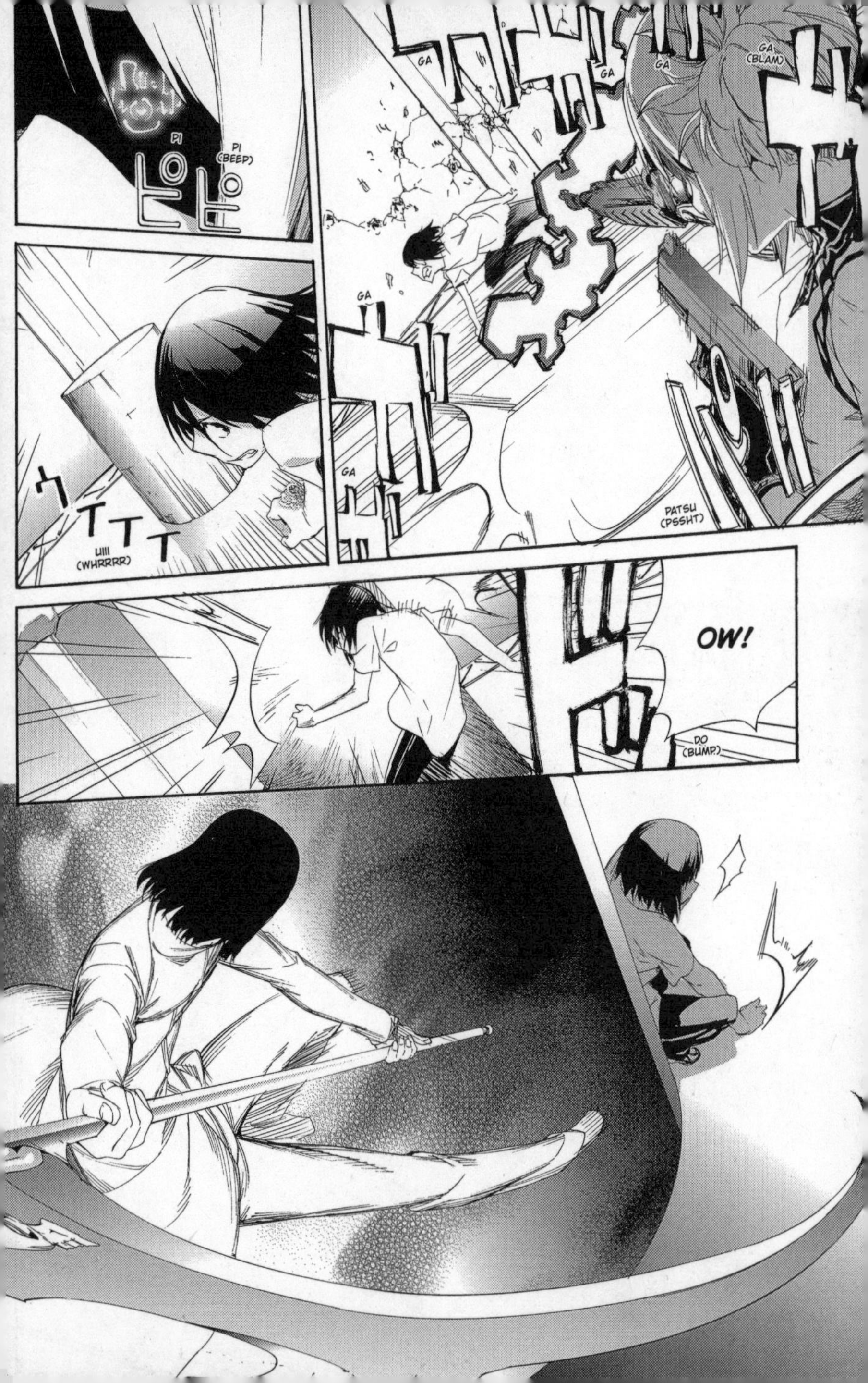

GA
(BLAM)
GA
GA
GA
GA
GA
PATSU
(PSSHT)
PI
PI
(BEEP)
UIII
(WHRRRR)
OW!
DO
(BUMP.)

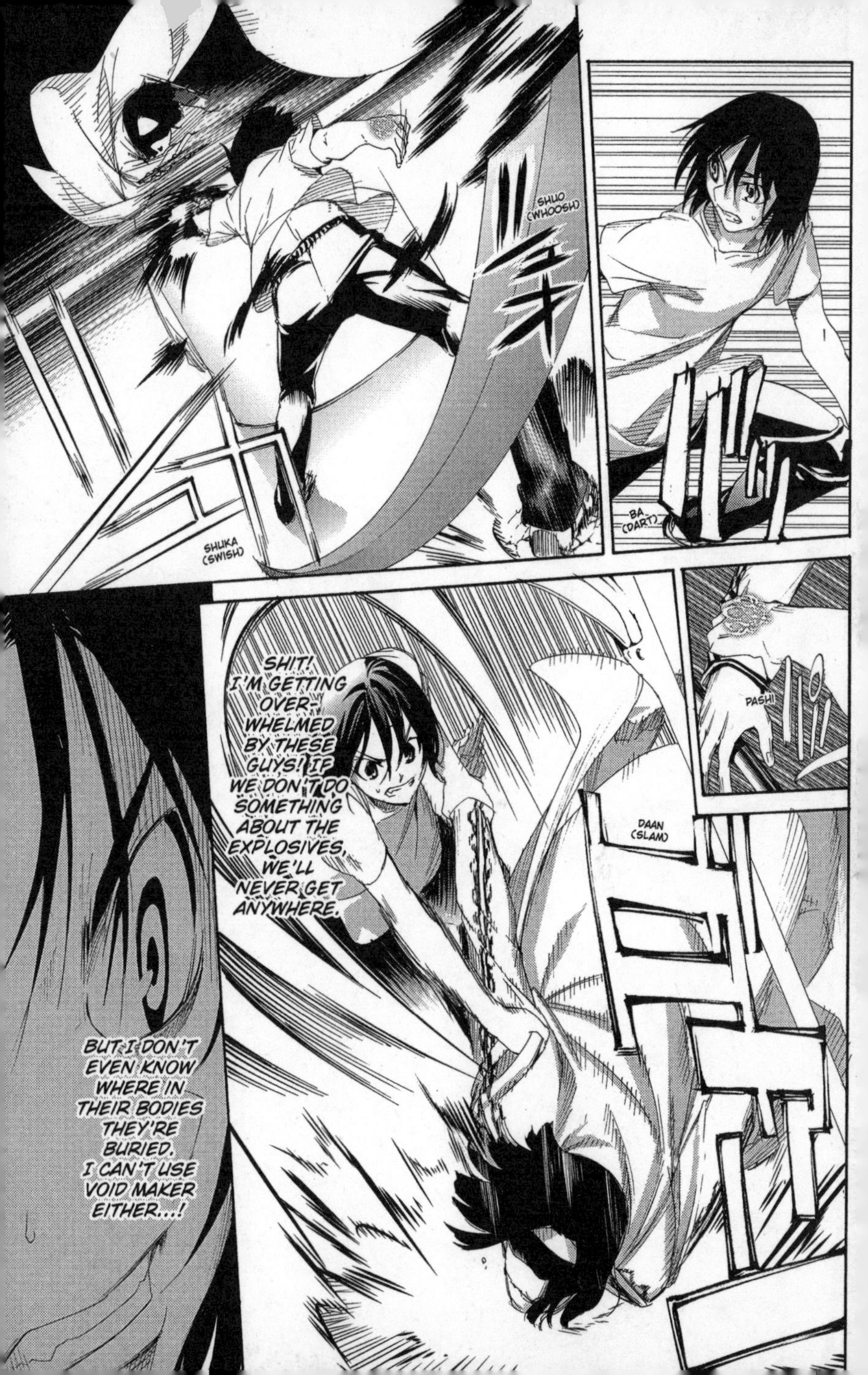
SHUO (WHOOSH)
BA (DART)
SHUKA (SWISH)
PASHI
SHIT! I'M GETTING OVER-WHELMED BY THESE GUYS! IF WE DON'T DO SOMETHING ABOUT THE EXPLOSIVES, WE'LL NEVER GET ANYWHERE.
DAAN (SLAM)
BUT I DON'T EVEN KNOW WHERE IN THEIR BODIES THEY'RE BURIED. I CAN'T USE VOID MAKER EITHER...!

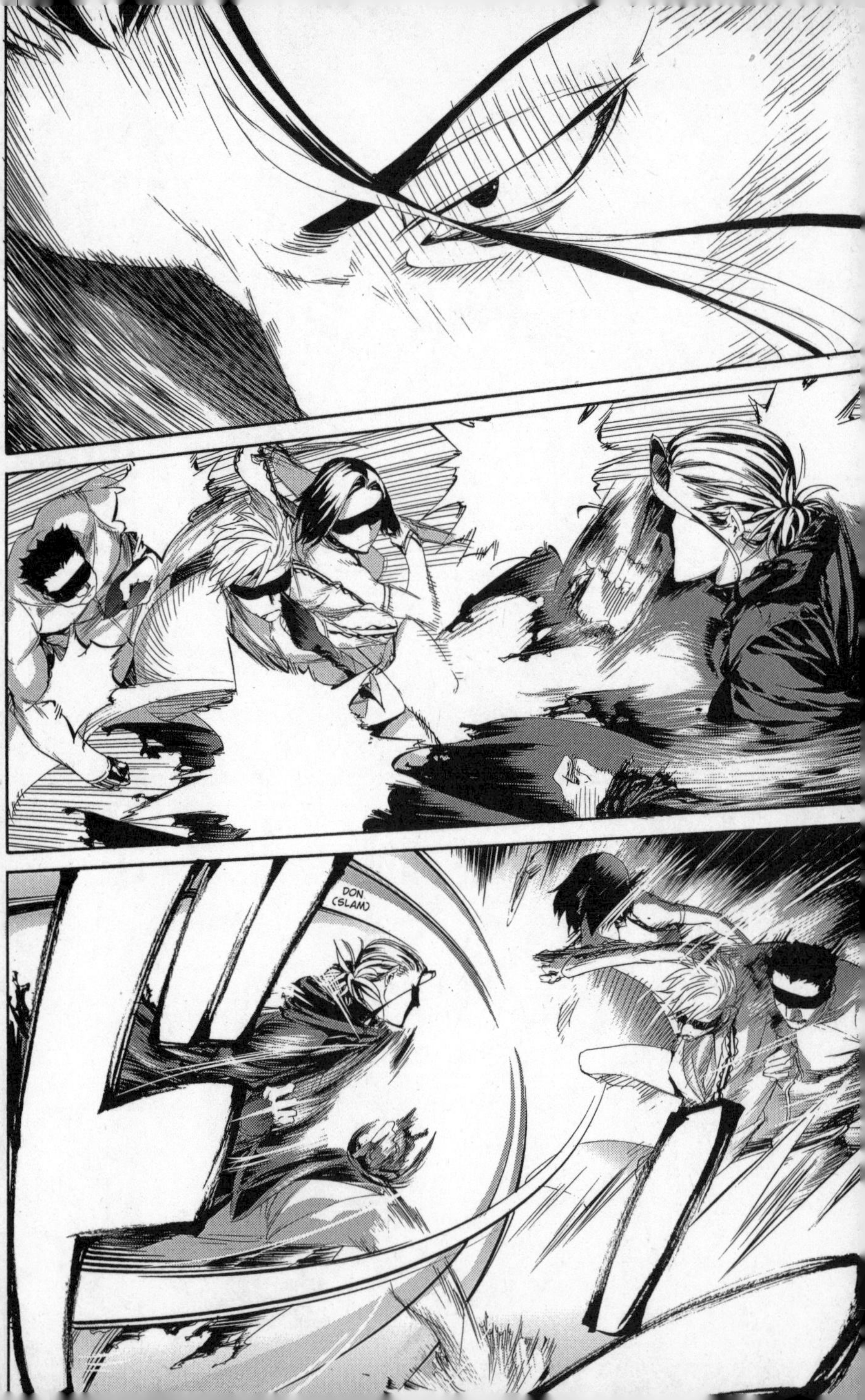
DON
(SLAM)

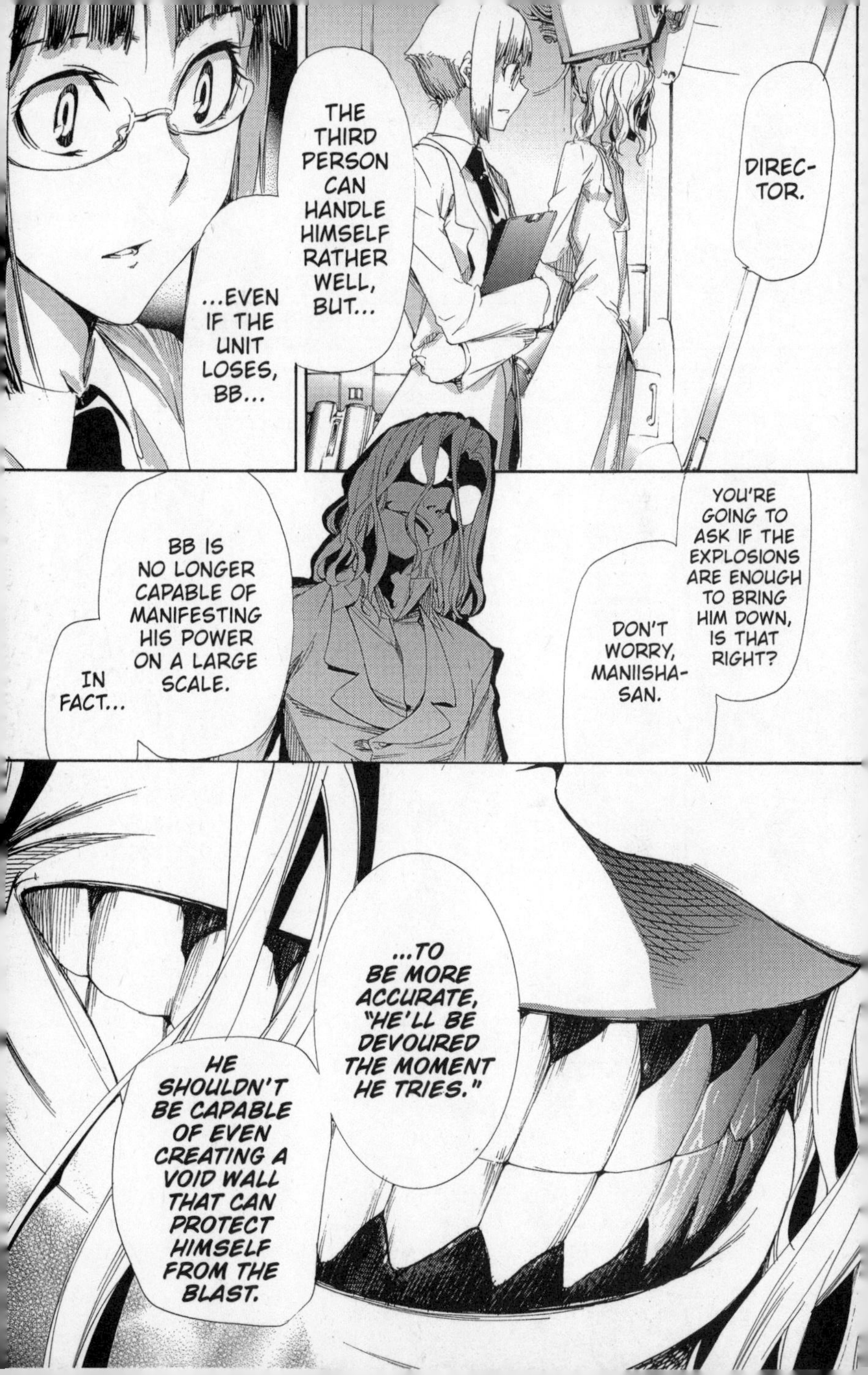
DIREC-TOR.
THE THIRD PERSON CAN HANDLE HIMSELF RATHER WELL, BUT...
...EVEN IF THE UNIT LOSES, BB...
YOU'RE GOING TO ASK IF THE EXPLOSIONS ARE ENOUGH TO BRING HIM DOWN, IS THAT RIGHT?
DON'T WORRY, MANIISHA-SAN.
BB IS NO LONGER CAPABLE OF MANIFESTING HIS POWER ON A LARGE SCALE.
IN FACT...
...TO BE MORE ACCURATE, "HE'LL BE DEVOURED THE MOMENT HE TRIES."
HE SHOULDN'T BE CAPABLE OF EVEN CREATING A VOID WALL THAT CAN PROTECT HIMSELF FROM THE BLAST.

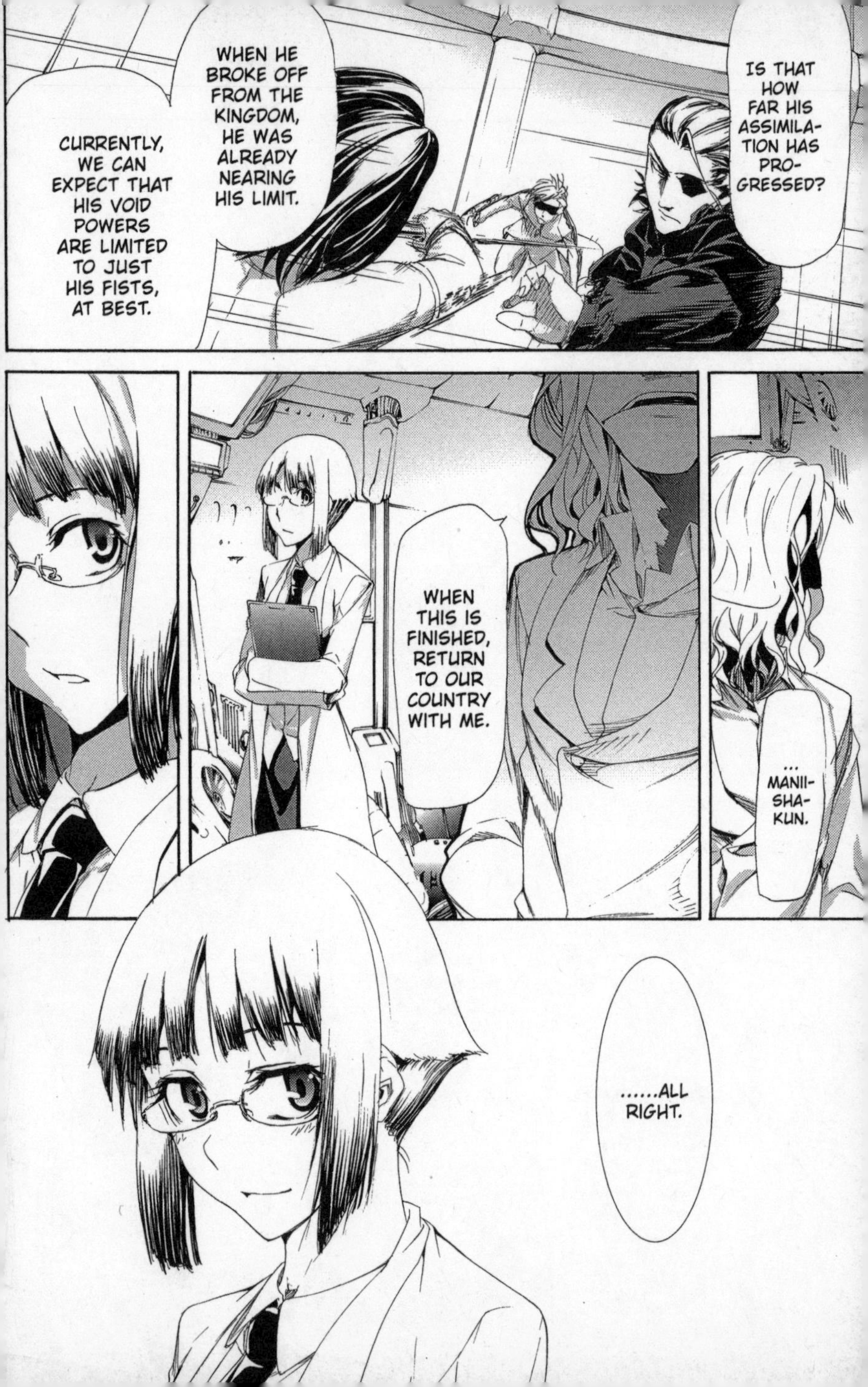
IS THAT HOW FAR HIS ASSIMILATION HAS PROGRESSED?
WHEN HE BROKE OFF FROM THE KINGDOM, HE WAS ALREADY NEARING HIS LIMIT.
CURRENTLY, WE CAN EXPECT THAT HIS VOID POWERS ARE LIMITED TO JUST HIS FISTS, AT BEST.
... MANII-SHA-KUN.
WHEN THIS IS FINISHED, RETURN TO OUR COUNTRY WITH ME.
......ALL RIGHT.

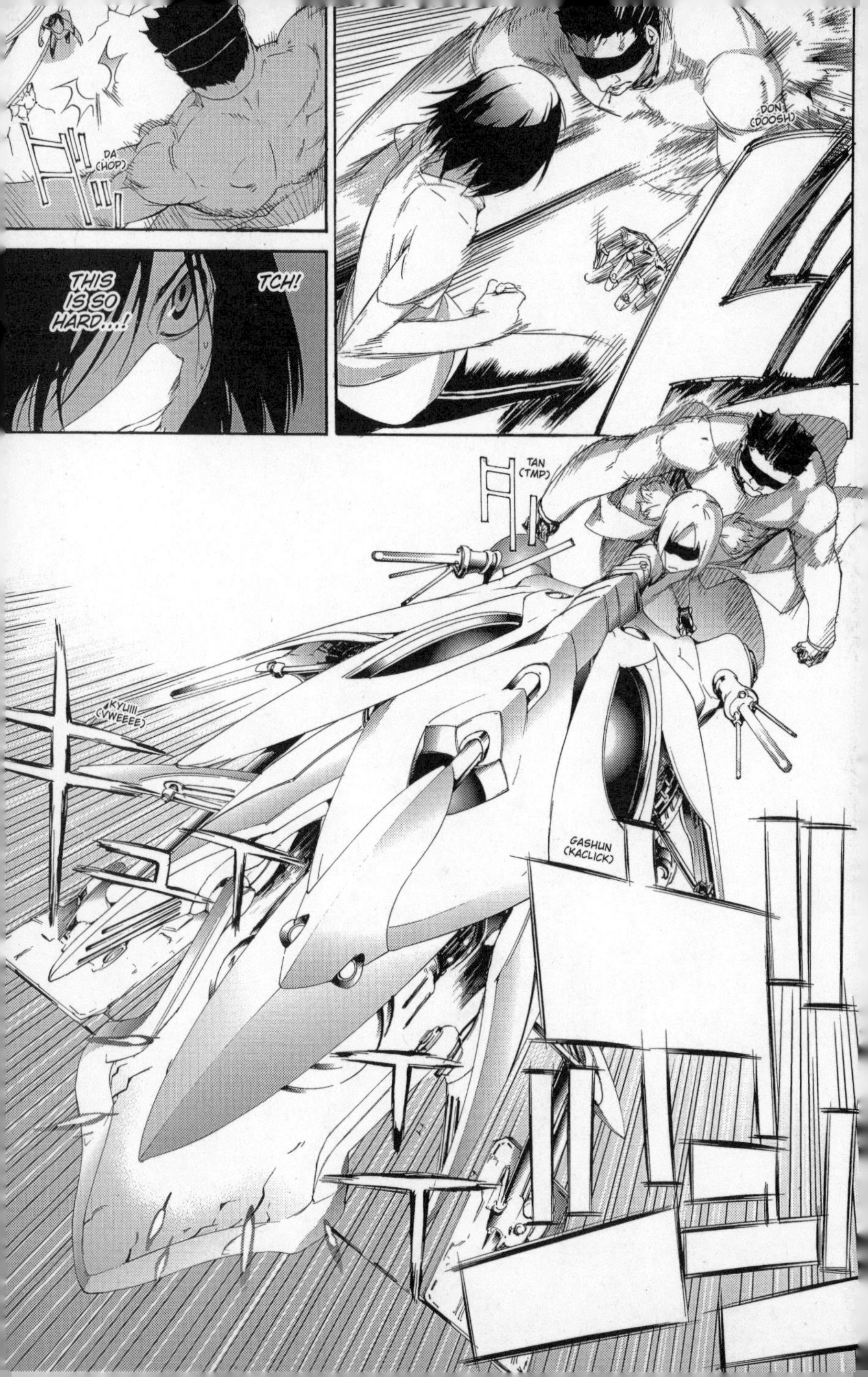
DON (DOOSH)
DA (HOP)
TCH!
THIS IS SO HARD...!
TAN (TMP)
KYUIII (VWEEEE)
GASHUN (KACLICK)

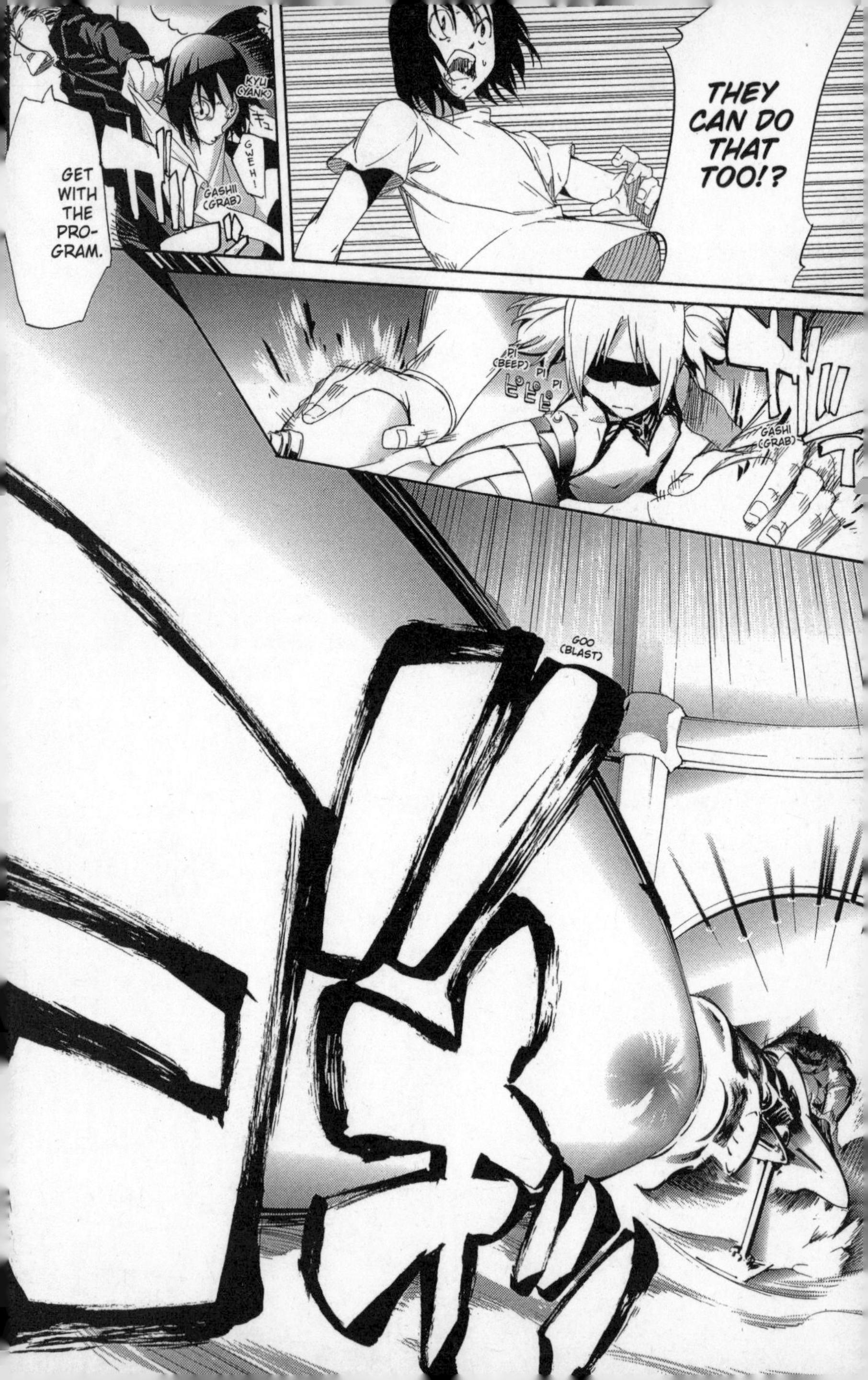
THEY CAN DO THAT TOO!?
KYU (YANK)
キュ
GWEH!
GASHII (GRAB)
GET WITH THE PRO-GRAM.
GASHI (GRAB)
PI (BEEP) PI PI
ピピピ
GOO (BLAST)

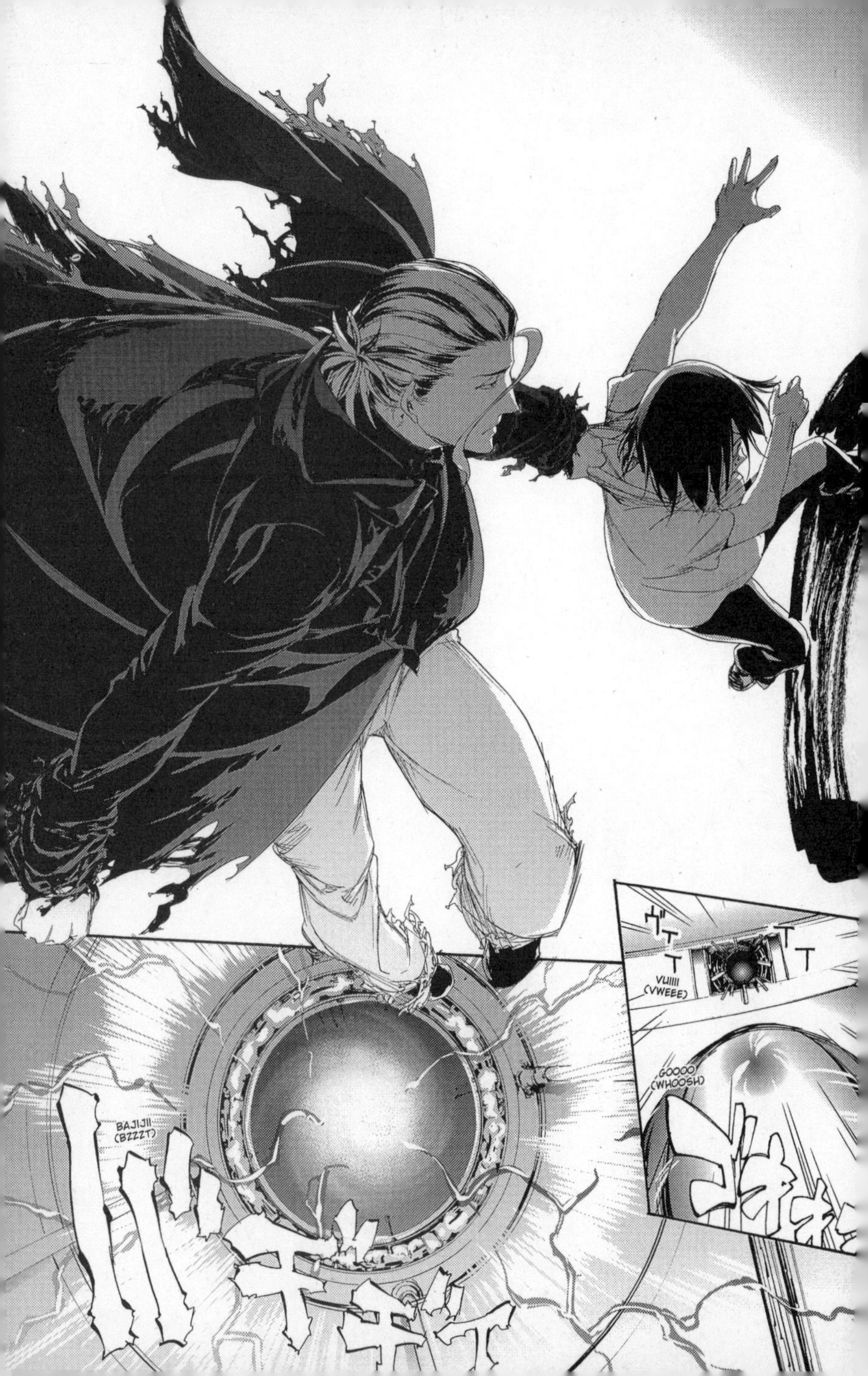
BAJIJII
(BZZZT)
VUIIII
(VWEEE)
GOOOO
(WHOOSH)

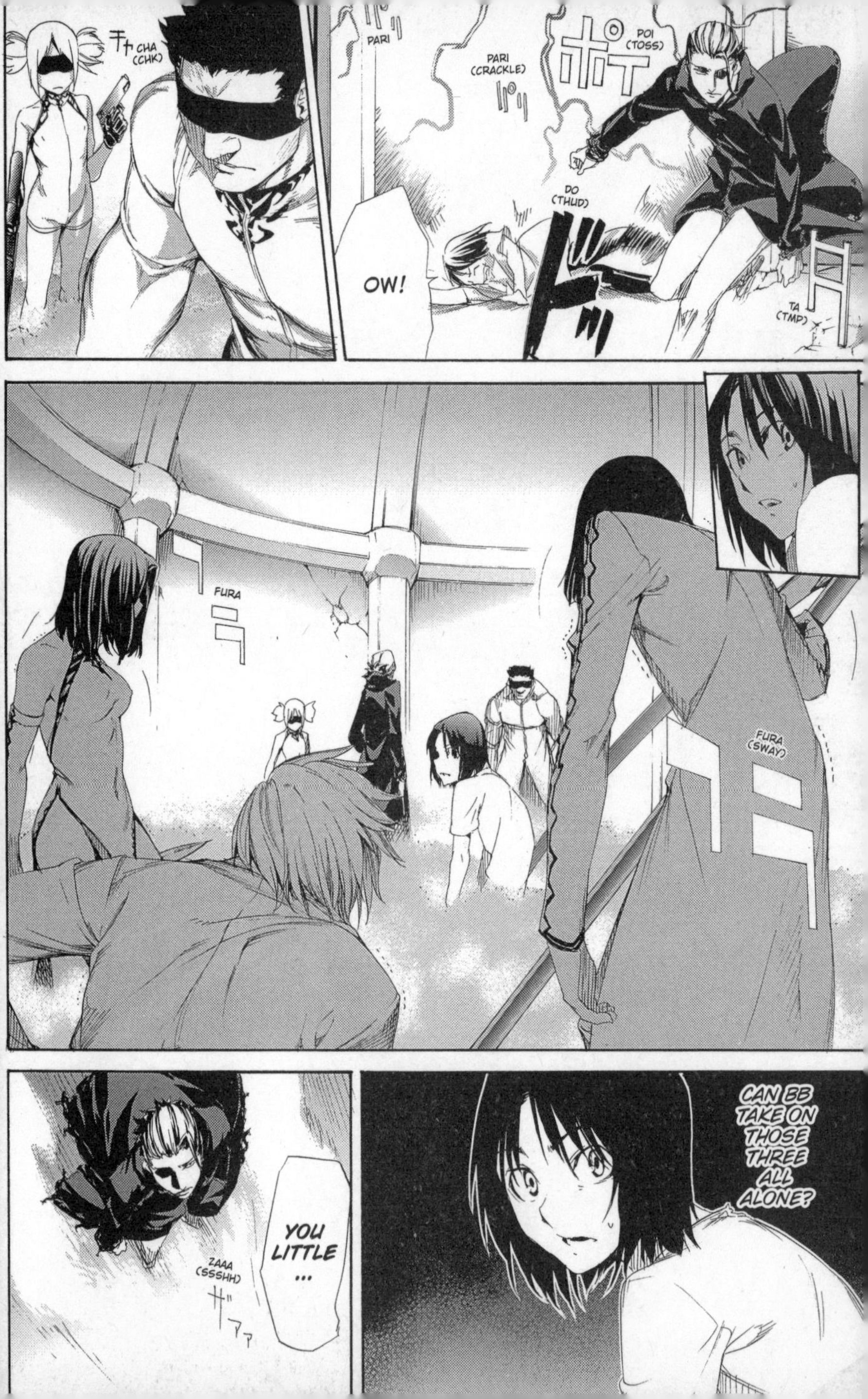
POI (TOSS)
PARI
PARI (CRACKLE)
DO (THUD)
OW!
TA (TMP)
CHA (CHK)
FURA (SWAY)
FURA
CAN BB TAKE ON THOSE THREE ALL ALONE?
YOU LITTLE ...
ZAAA (SSSHH)

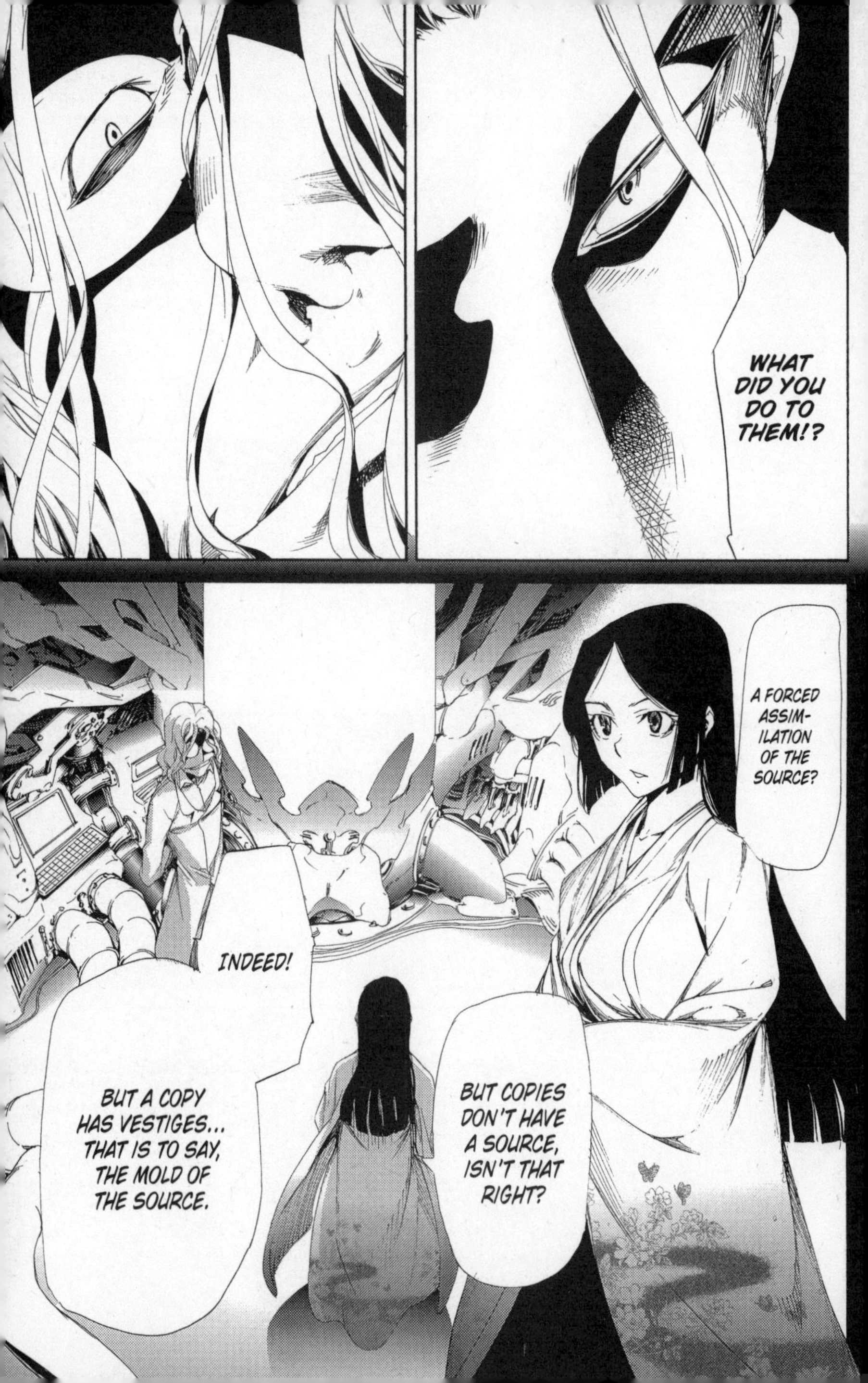
WHAT DID YOU DO TO THEM!?
A FORCED ASSIM-ILATION OF THE SOURCE?
BUT COPIES DON'T HAVE A SOURCE, ISN'T THAT RIGHT?
INDEED!
BUT A COPY HAS VESTIGES... THAT IS TO SAY, THE MOLD OF THE SOURCE.

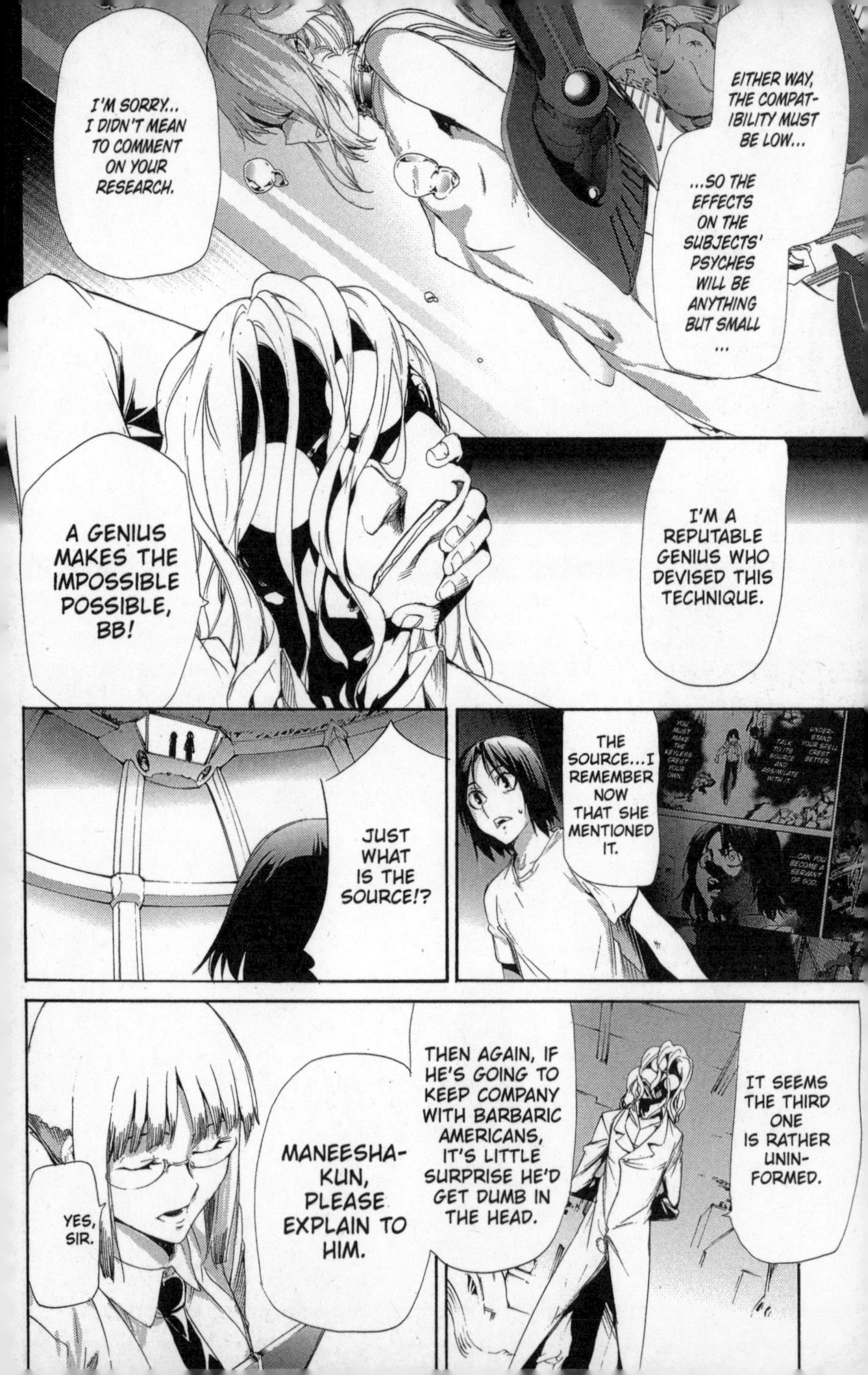
EITHER WAY, THE COMPATIBILITY MUST BE LOW...
...SO THE EFFECTS ON THE SUBJECTS' PSYCHES WILL BE ANYTHING BUT SMALL...
I'M SORRY... I DIDN'T MEAN TO COMMENT ON YOUR RESEARCH.
I'M A REPUTABLE GENIUS WHO DEVISED THIS TECHNIQUE.
A GENIUS MAKES THE IMPOSSIBLE POSSIBLE, BB!
UNDERSTAND YOUR SPELL CREST BETTER.
TALK TO ITS SOURCE AND ASSIMILATE WITH IT.
YOU MUST MAKE THE KEYLESS CREST YOUR OWN.
...CAN YOU BECOME A SERVANT OF GOD.
THE SOURCE...I REMEMBER NOW THAT SHE MENTIONED IT.
JUST WHAT IS THE SOURCE!?
IT SEEMS THE THIRD ONE IS RATHER UNINFORMED.
THEN AGAIN, IF HE'S GOING TO KEEP COMPANY WITH BARBARIC AMERICANS, IT'S LITTLE SURPRISE HE'D GET DUMB IN THE HEAD.
MANEESHA-KUN, PLEASE EXPLAIN TO HIM.
YES, SIR.

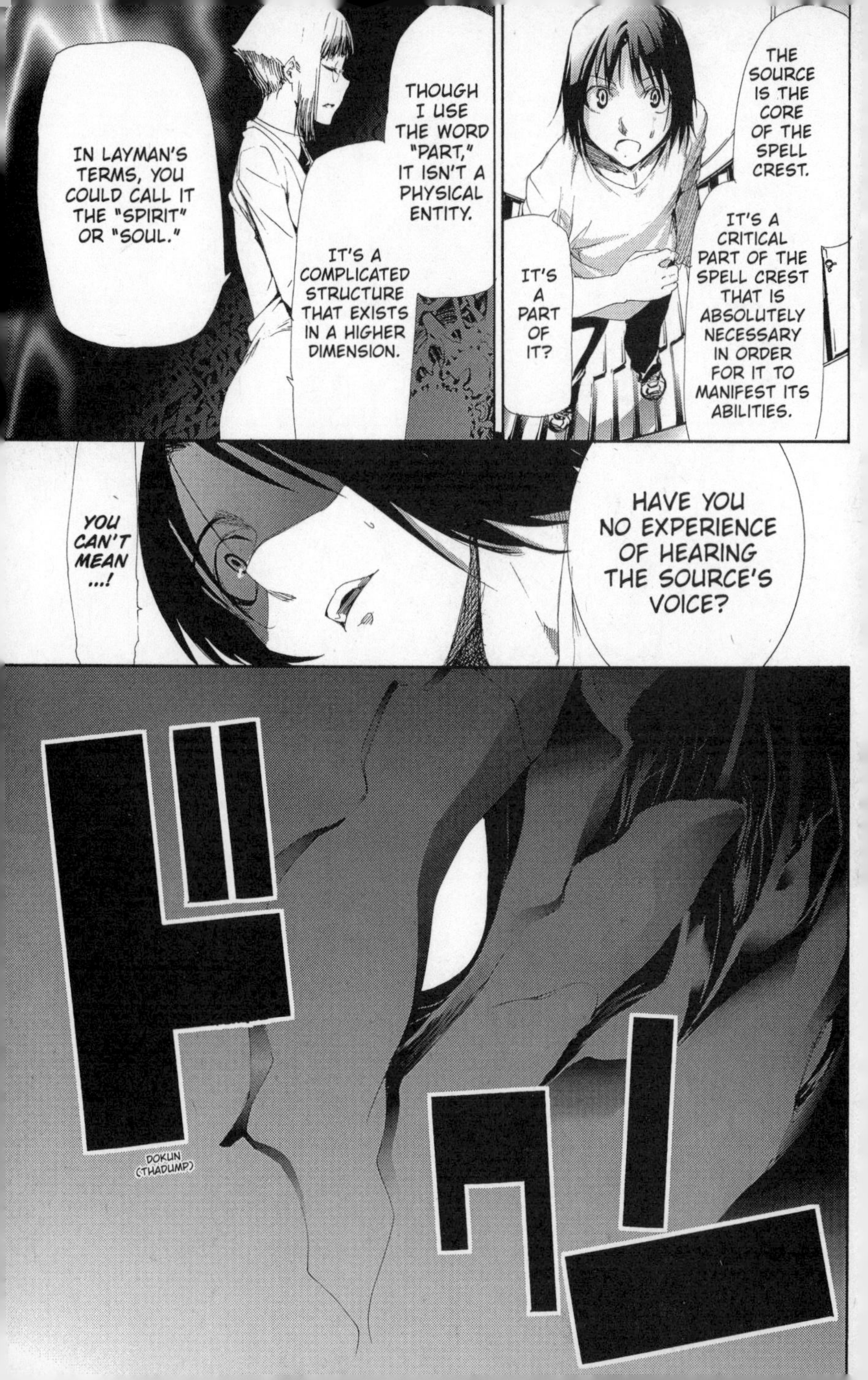
THE SOURCE IS THE CORE OF THE SPELL CREST.
IT'S A CRITICAL PART OF THE SPELL CREST THAT IS ABSOLUTELY NECESSARY IN ORDER FOR IT TO MANIFEST ITS ABILITIES.
IT'S A PART OF IT?
THOUGH I USE THE WORD "PART," IT ISN'T A PHYSICAL ENTITY.
IT'S A COMPLICATED STRUCTURE THAT EXISTS IN A HIGHER DIMENSION.
IN LAYMAN'S TERMS, YOU COULD CALL IT THE "SPIRIT" OR "SOUL."
HAVE YOU NO EXPERIENCE OF HEARING THE SOURCE'S VOICE?
YOU CAN'T MEAN ...!
DOKUN (THADUMP)

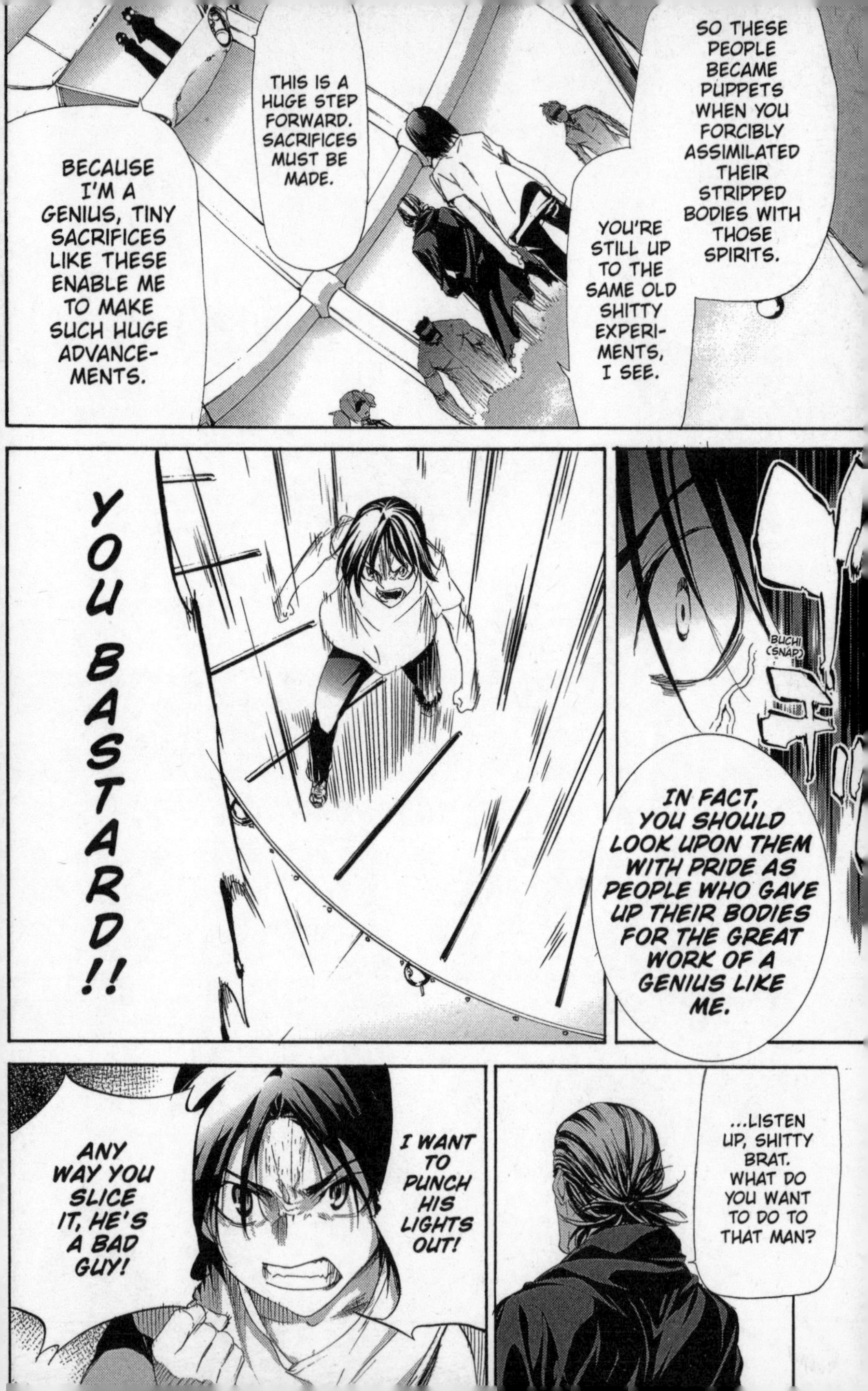
SO THESE PEOPLE BECAME PUPPETS WHEN YOU FORCIBLY ASSIMILATED THEIR STRIPPED BODIES WITH THOSE SPIRITS.
YOU'RE STILL UP TO THE SAME OLD SHITTY EXPERI-MENTS, I SEE.
THIS IS A HUGE STEP FORWARD. SACRIFICES MUST BE MADE.
BECAUSE I'M A GENIUS, TINY SACRIFICES LIKE THESE ENABLE ME TO MAKE SUCH HUGE ADVANCE-MENTS.
BUCHI (SNAP)
IN FACT, YOU SHOULD LOOK UPON THEM WITH PRIDE AS PEOPLE WHO GAVE UP THEIR BODIES FOR THE GREAT WORK OF A GENIUS LIKE ME.
YOU BASTARD!!
...LISTEN UP, SHITTY BRAT. WHAT DO YOU WANT TO DO TO THAT MAN?
I WANT TO PUNCH HIS LIGHTS OUT!
ANY WAY YOU SLICE IT, HE'S A BAD GUY!

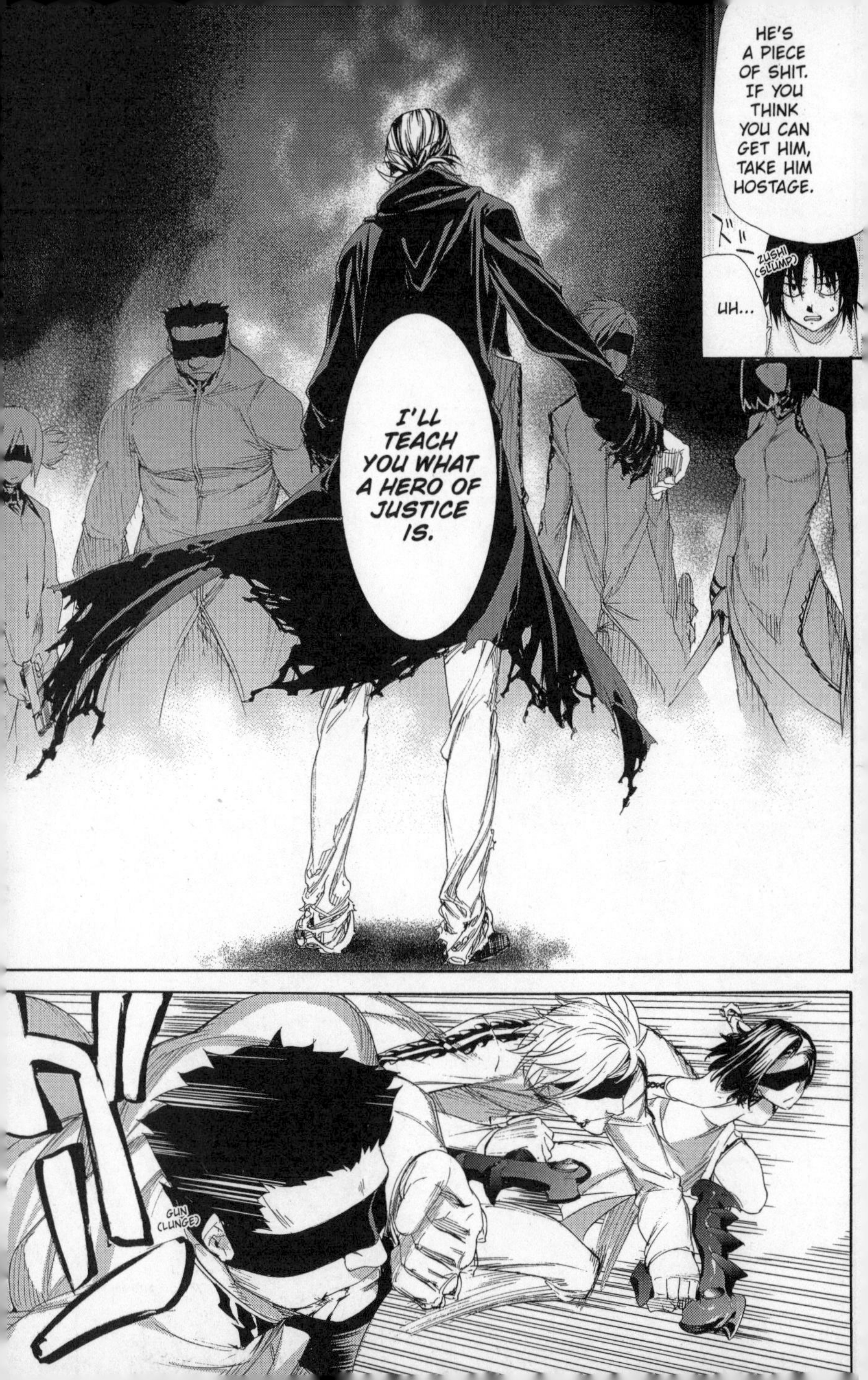
HE'S A PIECE OF SHIT. IF YOU THINK YOU CAN GET HIM, TAKE HIM HOSTAGE.
ZUSHI (SLUMP)
UH...
I'LL TEACH YOU WHAT A HERO OF JUSTICE IS.
GUN (LUNGE)

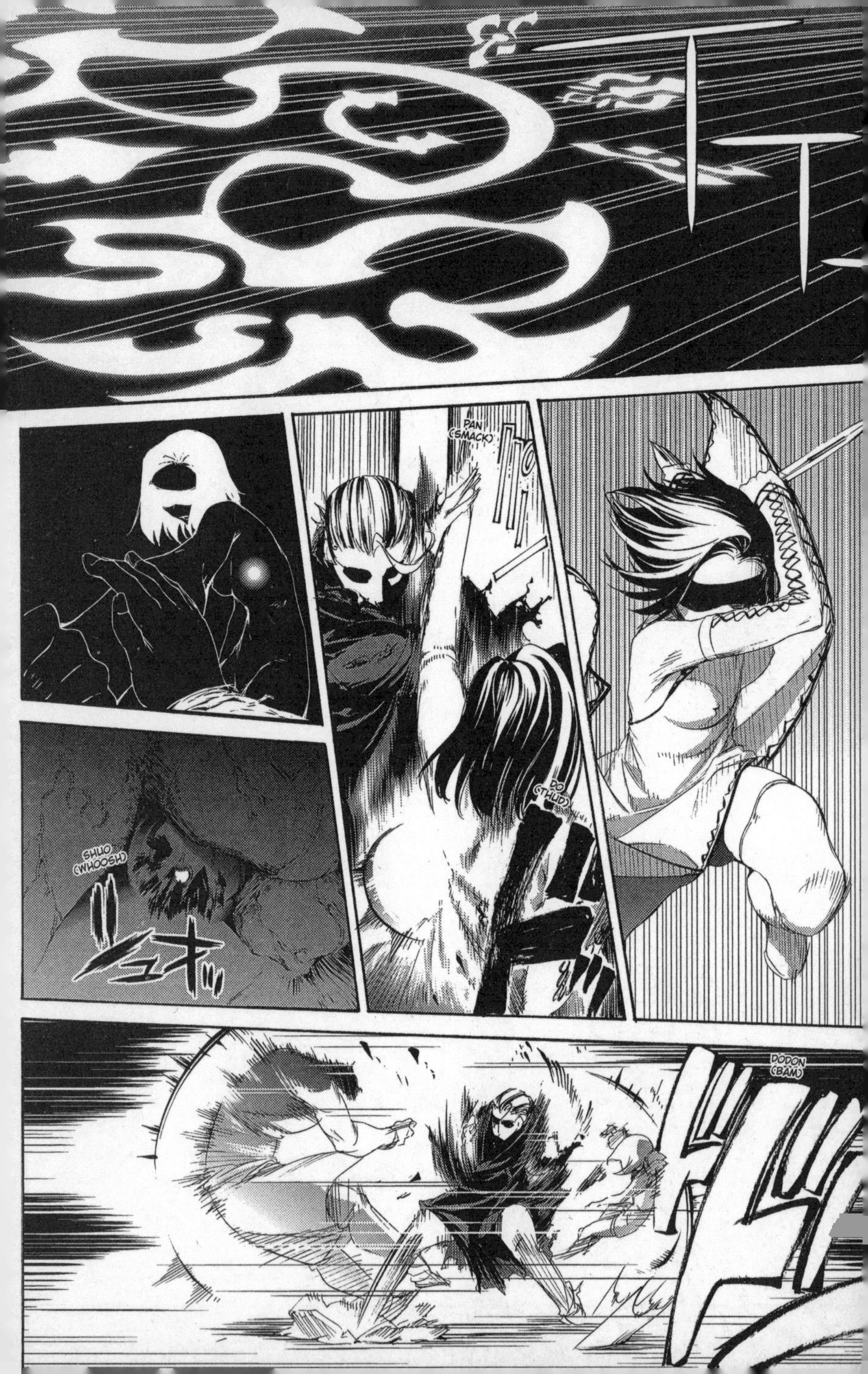
PAN (SMACK)
DO (THUD)
SHUO (WHOOSH)
DODON (BAM)

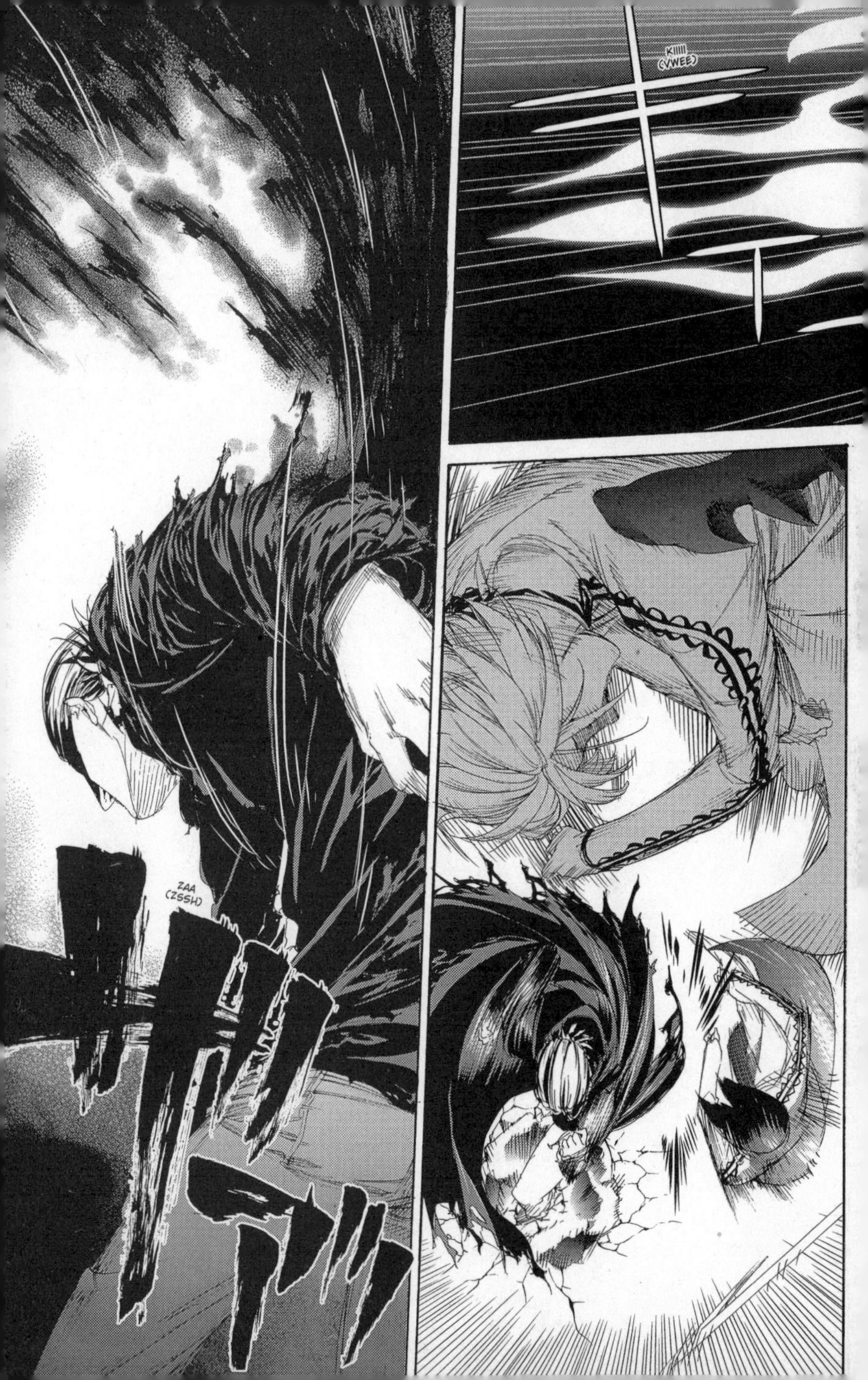
KIIIII
(VWEE)
ZAA
(ZSSH)

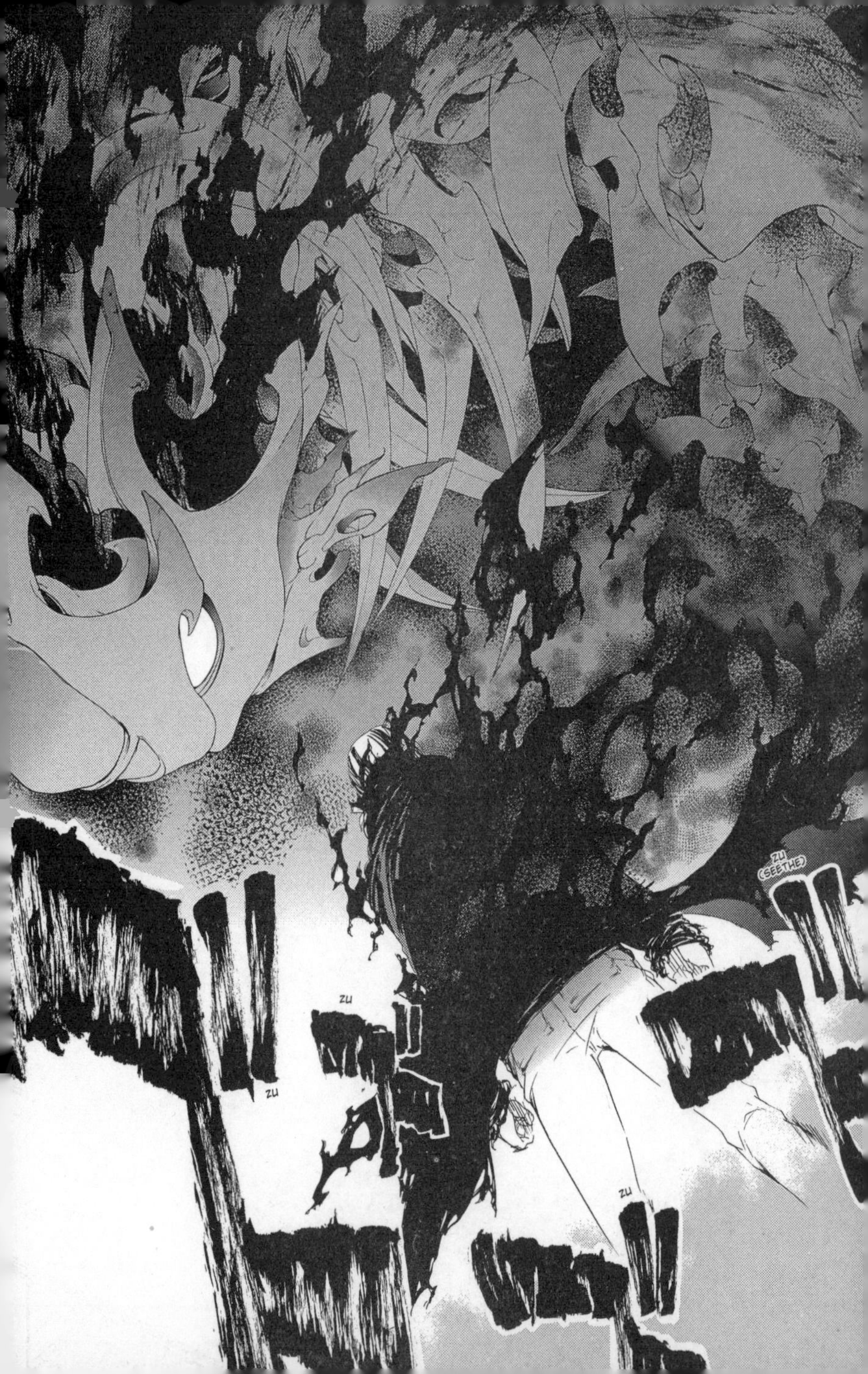
ZU
(SEETHE)
ZU
ZU
ZU

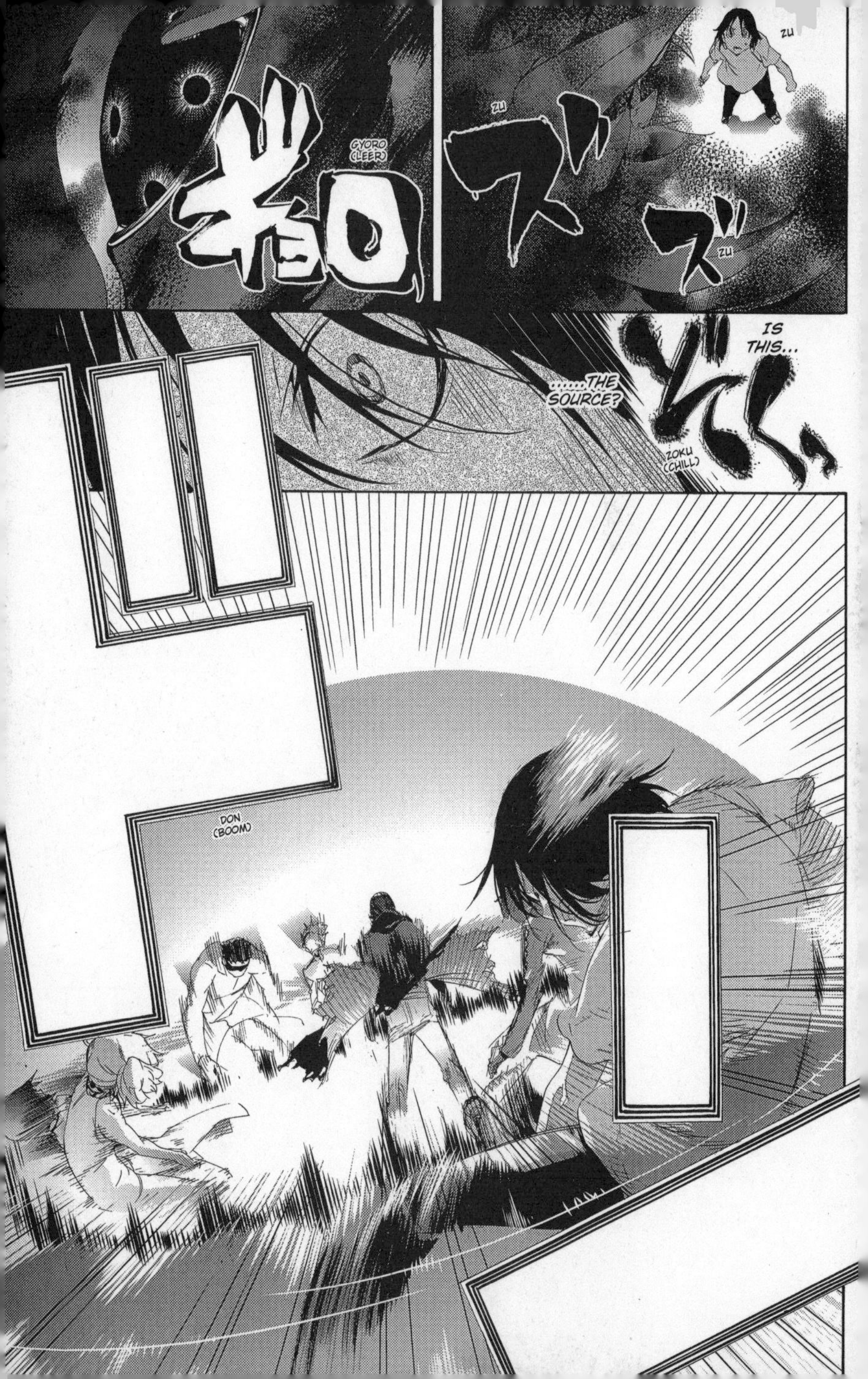
ZU
ZU
ZU
GYORO (LEER)
IS THIS...
......THE SOURCE?
ZOKU (CHILL)
DON (BOOM)

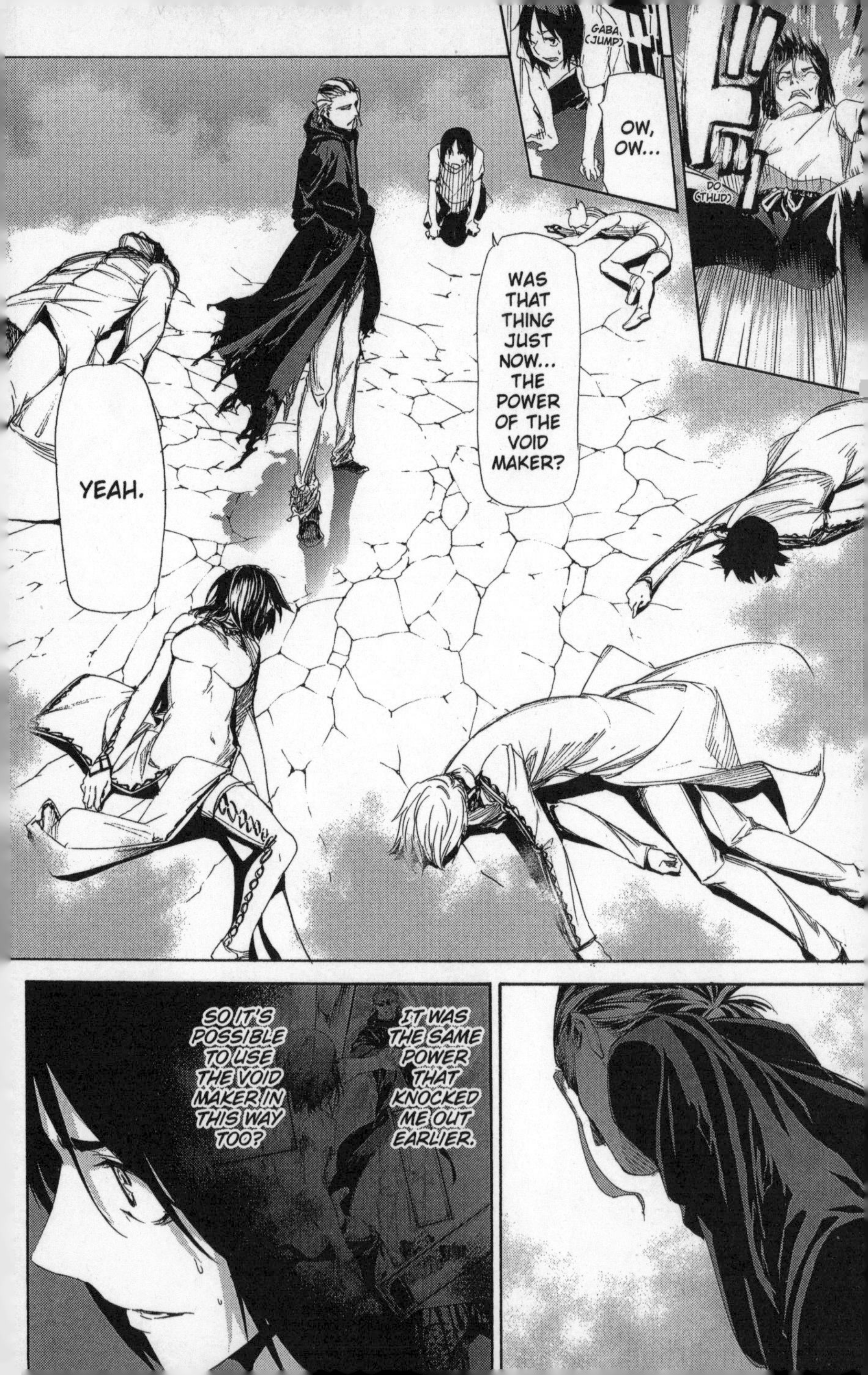
DO (THUD)
GABA (JUMP)
OW, OW...
WAS THAT THING JUST NOW... THE POWER OF THE VOID MAKER?
YEAH.
IT WAS THE SAME POWER THAT KNOCKED ME OUT EARLIER.
SO IT'S POSSIBLE TO USE THE VOID MAKER IN THIS WAY TOO?

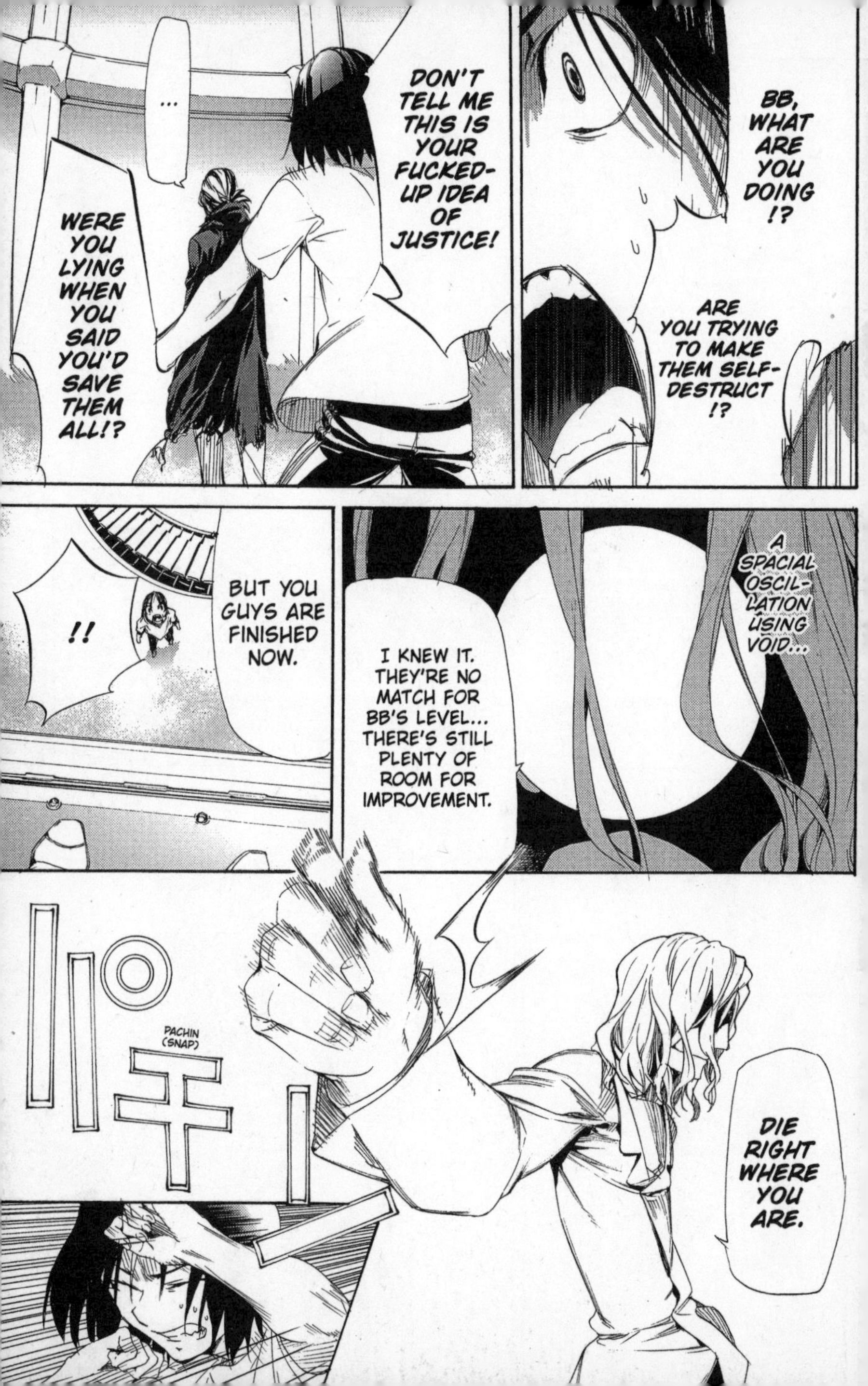
BB, WHAT ARE YOU DOING!?
ARE YOU TRYING TO MAKE THEM SELF-DESTRUCT!?
DON'T TELL ME THIS IS YOUR FUCKED-UP IDEA OF JUSTICE!
...
WERE YOU LYING WHEN YOU SAID YOU'D SAVE THEM ALL!?
A SPACIAL OSCIL-LATION USING VOID...
I KNEW IT. THEY'RE NO MATCH FOR BB'S LEVEL... THERE'S STILL PLENTY OF ROOM FOR IMPROVEMENT.
BUT YOU GUYS ARE FINISHED NOW.
!!
DIE RIGHT WHERE YOU ARE.
パチン
PACHIN (SNAP)

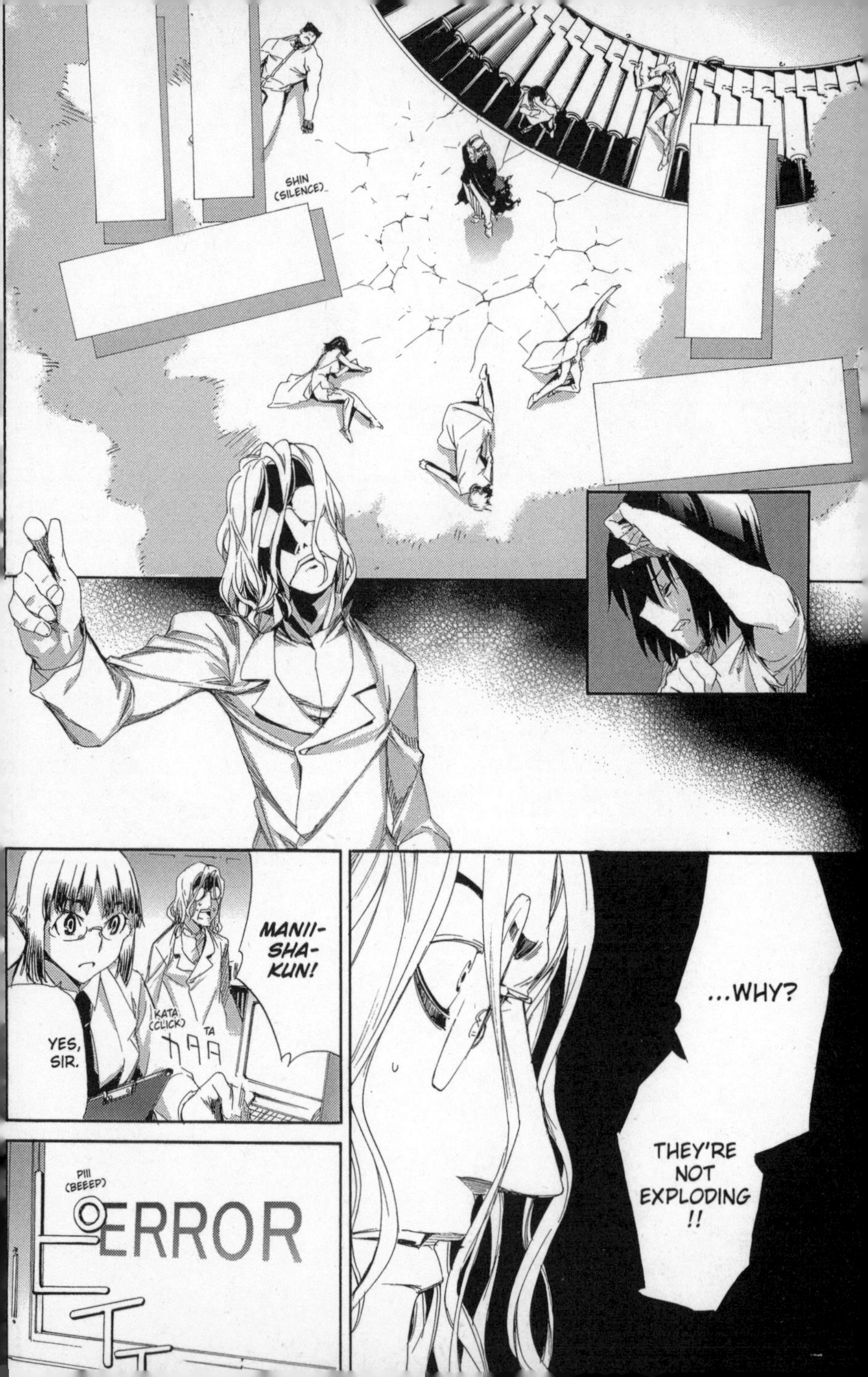
SHIN (SILENCE)
...WHY?
THEY'RE NOT EXPLODING !!
MANII-SHA-KUN!
TA
KATA (CLICK)
YES, SIR.
PIII (BEEEP)
ERROR

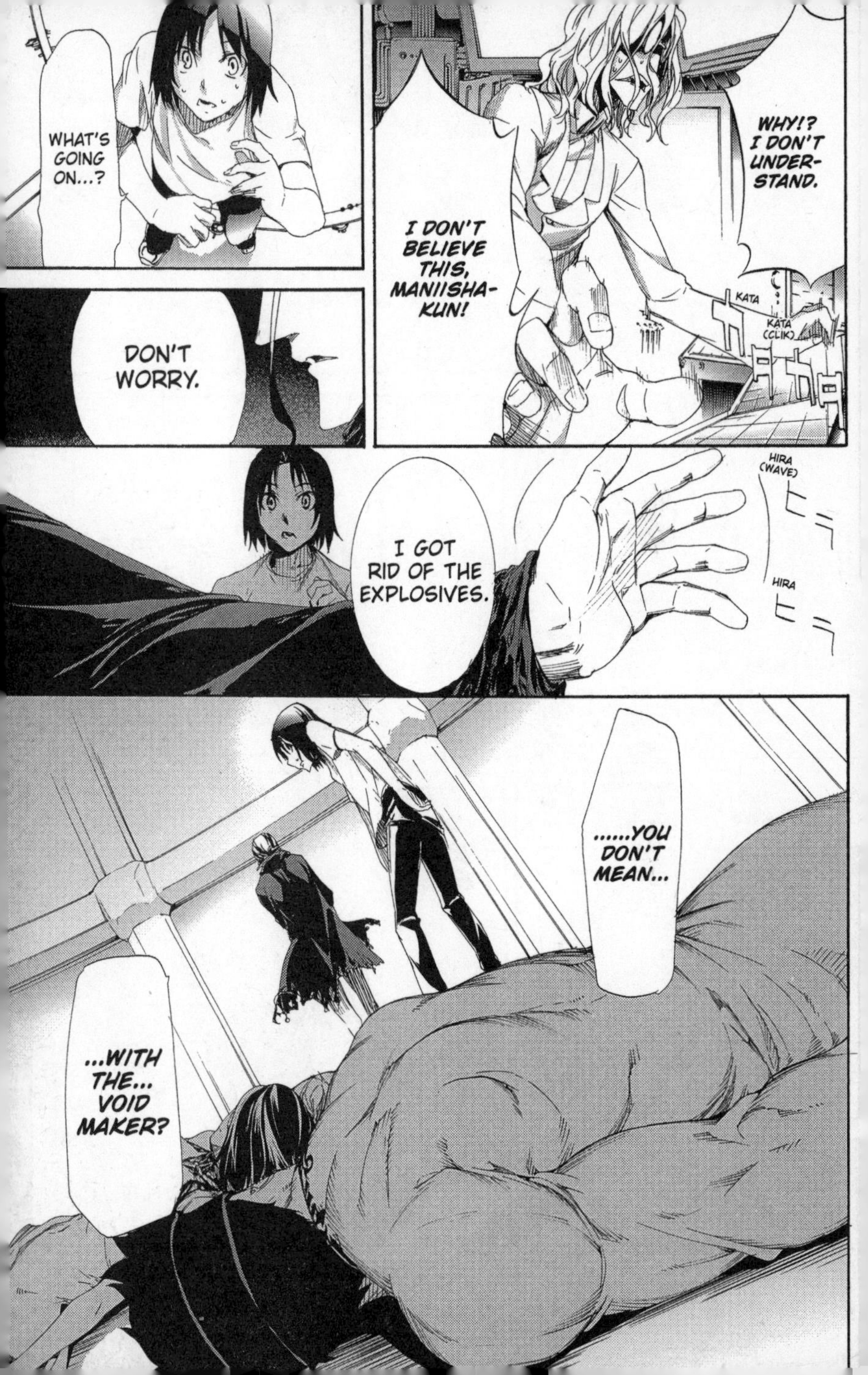
WHY!? I DON'T UNDER-STAND.
I DON'T BELIEVE THIS, MANIISHA-KUN!
KATA
KATA (CLIK)
WHAT'S GOING ON...?
DON'T WORRY.
HIRA (WAVE)
HIRA
I GOT RID OF THE EXPLOSIVES.
......YOU DON'T MEAN...
...WITH THE... VOID MAKER?

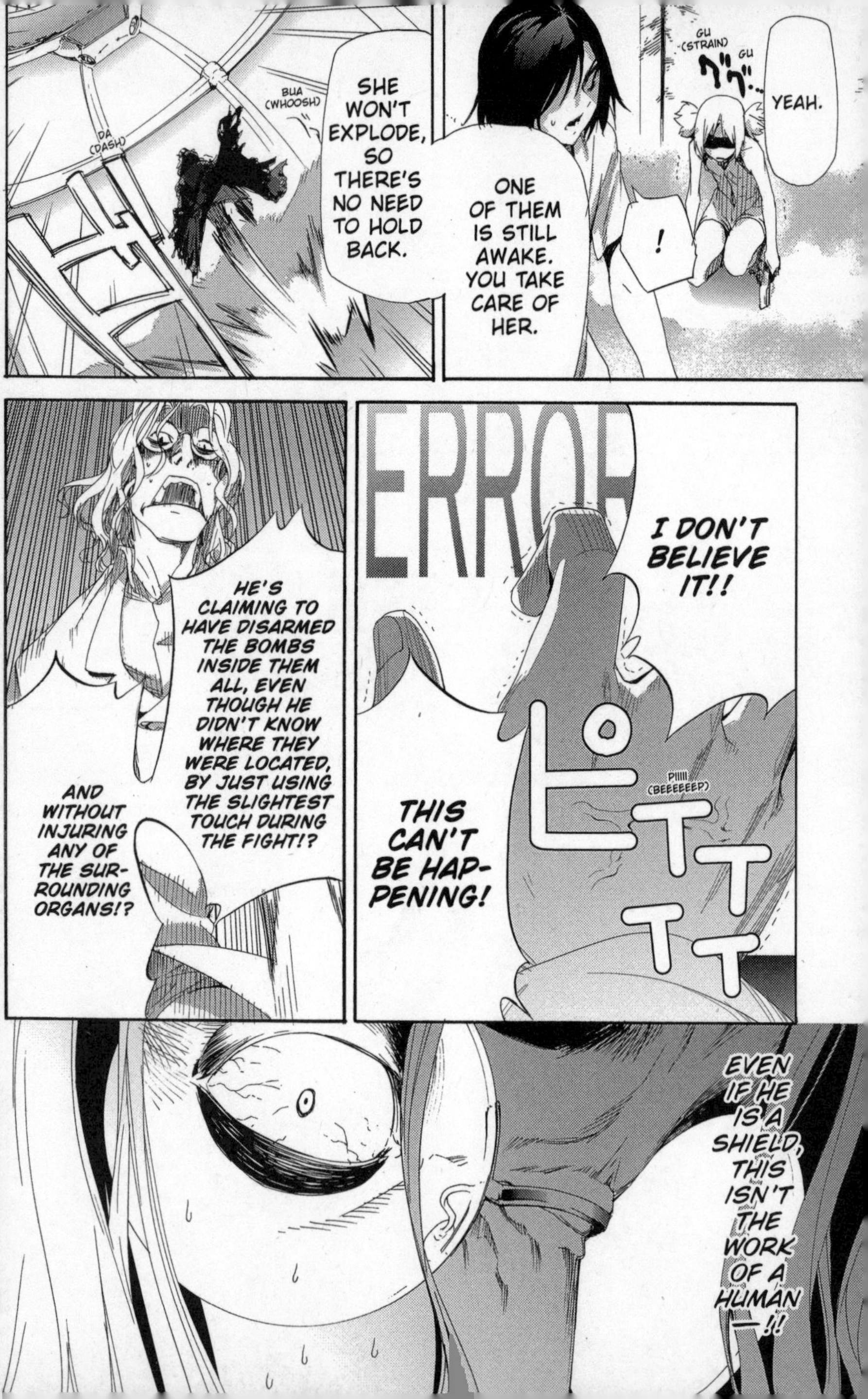
GU (STRAIN) GU
YEAH.
ONE OF THEM IS STILL AWAKE. YOU TAKE CARE OF HER.
!
SHE WON'T EXPLODE, SO THERE'S NO NEED TO HOLD BACK.
BUA (WHOOSH)
DA (DASH)
ERROR
I DON'T BELIEVE IT!!
PIIII (BEEEEEEP)
THIS CAN'T BE HAP-PENING!
HE'S CLAIMING TO HAVE DISARMED THE BOMBS INSIDE THEM ALL, EVEN THOUGH HE DIDN'T KNOW WHERE THEY WERE LOCATED, BY JUST USING THE SLIGHTEST TOUCH DURING THE FIGHT!?
AND WITHOUT INJURING ANY OF THE SUR-ROUNDING ORGANS!?
EVEN IF HE IS A SHIELD, THIS ISN'T THE WORK OF A HUMAN—!!

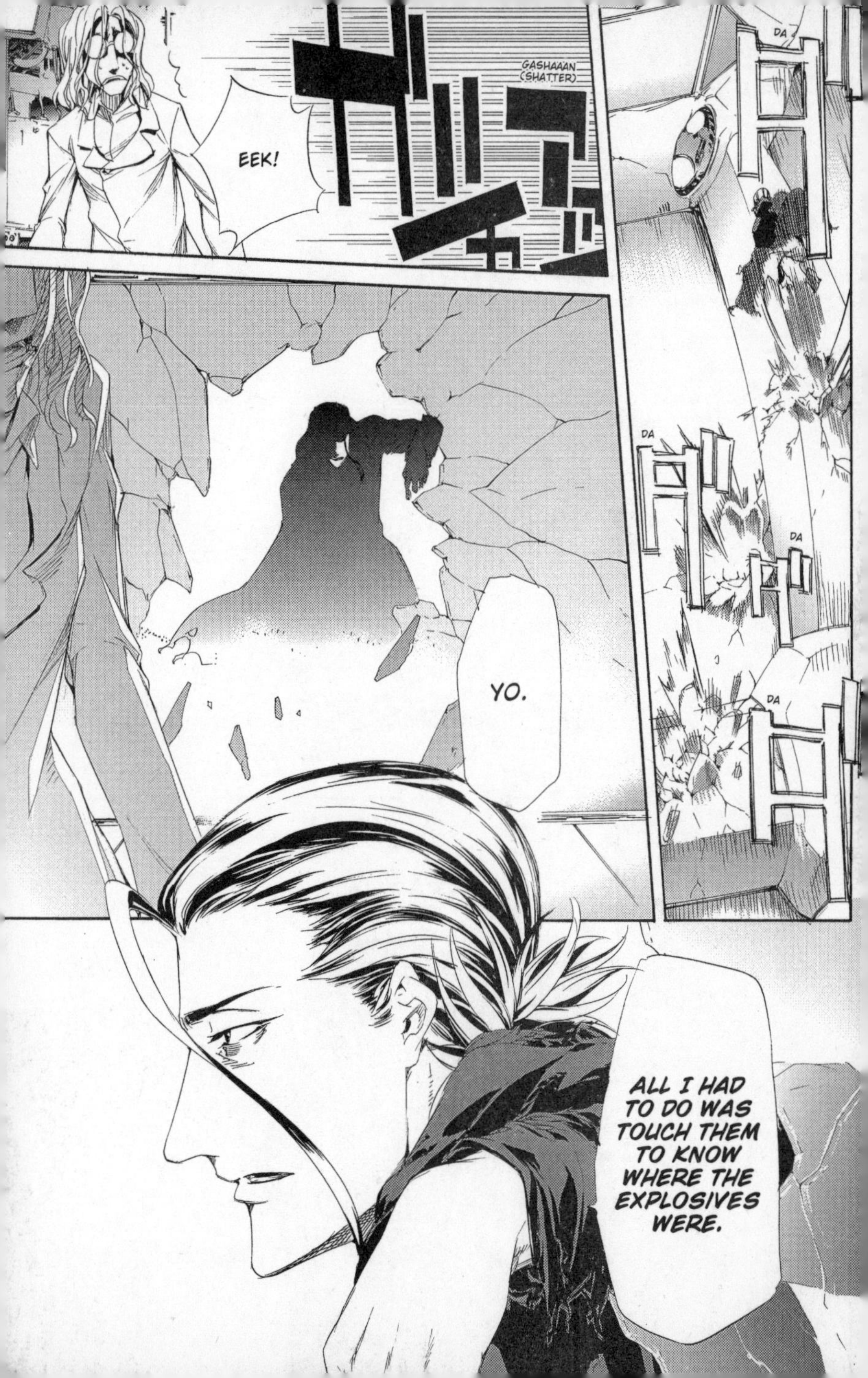
DA
DA
DA
DA
GASHAÄÄN (SHATTER)
EEK!
YO.
ALL I HAD TO DO WAS TOUCH THEM TO KNOW WHERE THE EXPLOSIVES WERE.

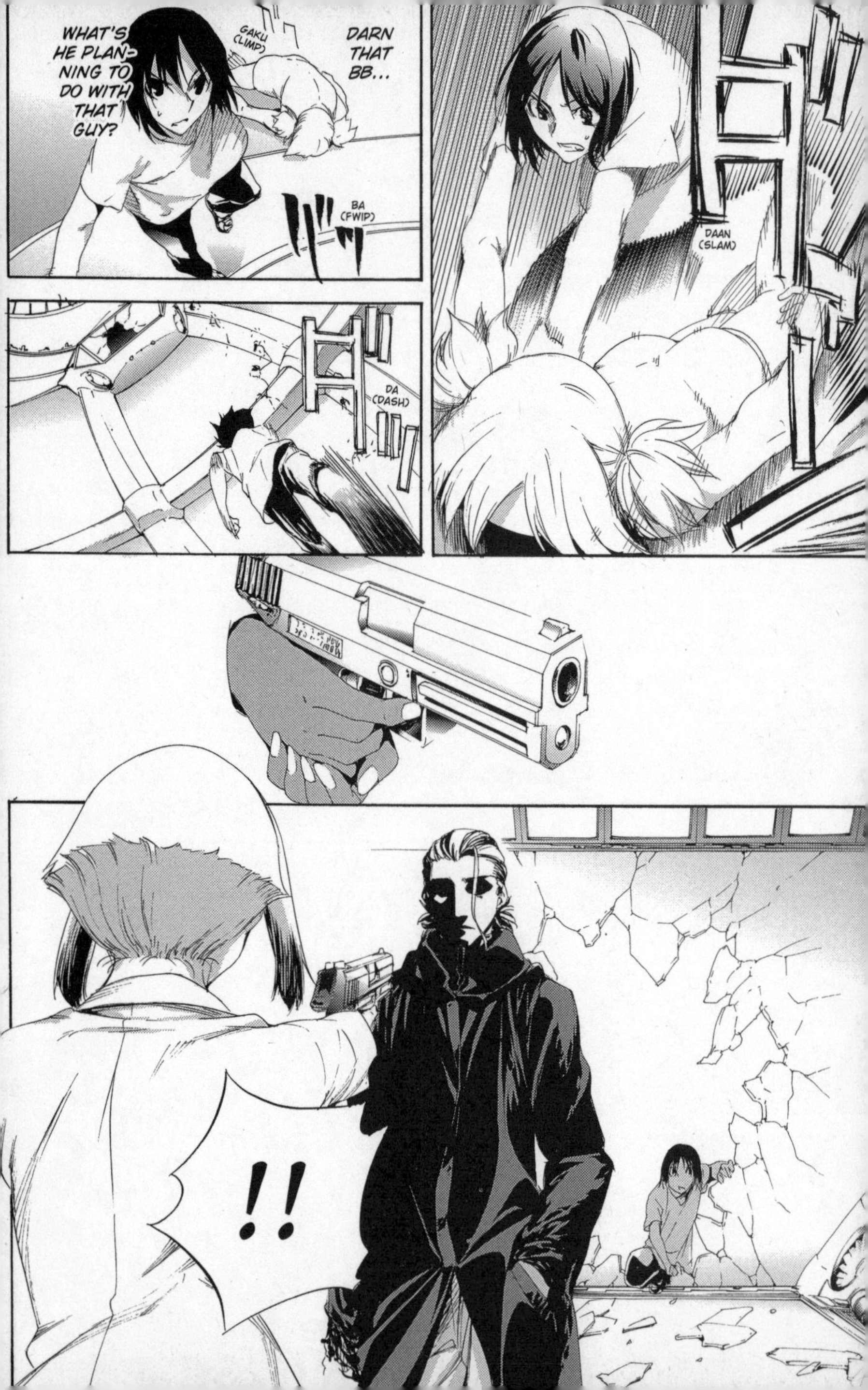
DAAN (SLAM)
DARN THAT BB...
GAKU (LIMP)
WHAT'S HE PLAN-NING TO DO WITH THAT GUY?
BA (FWIP)
DA (DASH)
!!

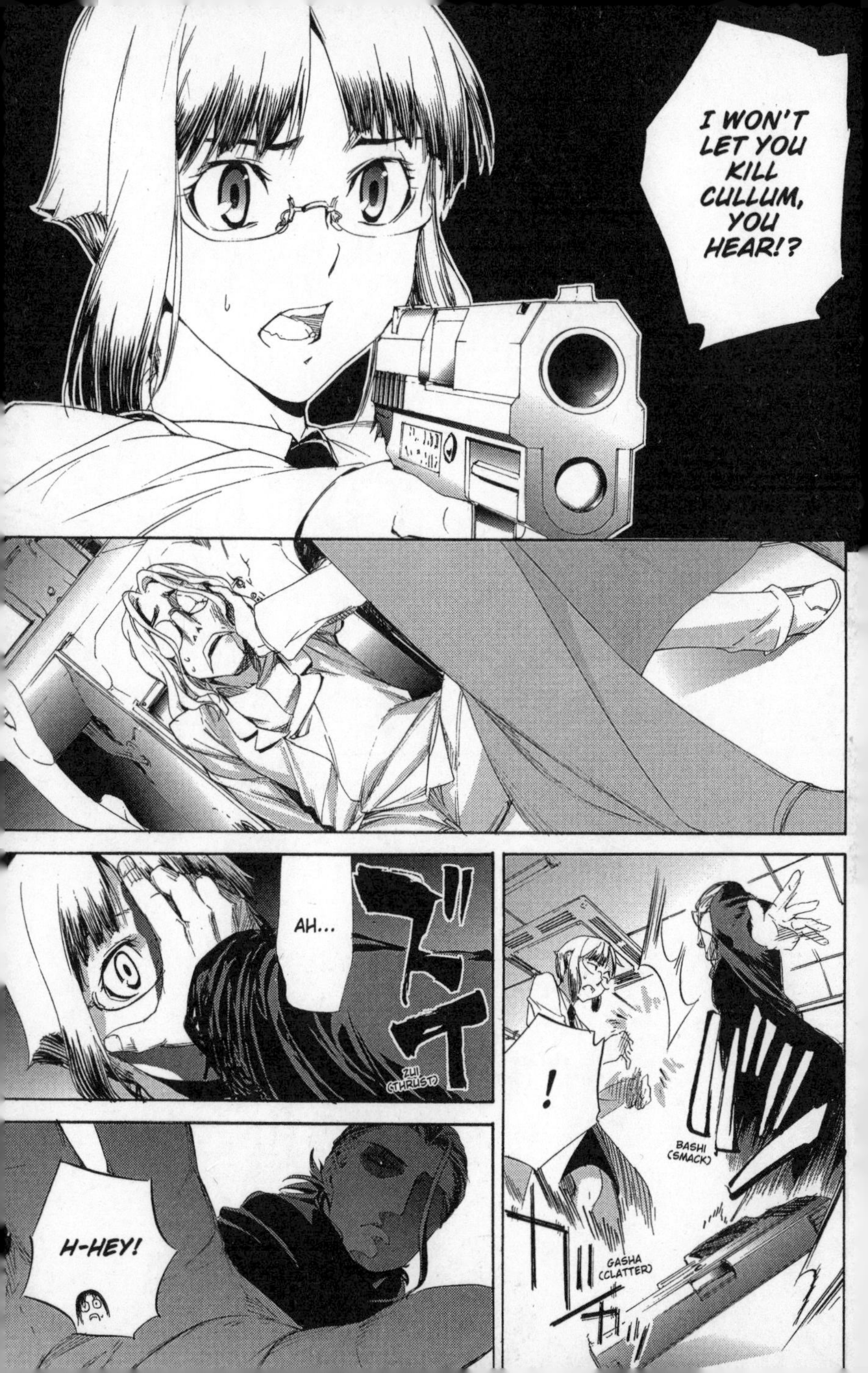
I WON'T LET YOU KILL CULLUM, YOU HEAR!?
!
BASHI (SMACK)
GASHA (CLATTER)
AH...
ZUI (THRUST)
H-HEY!

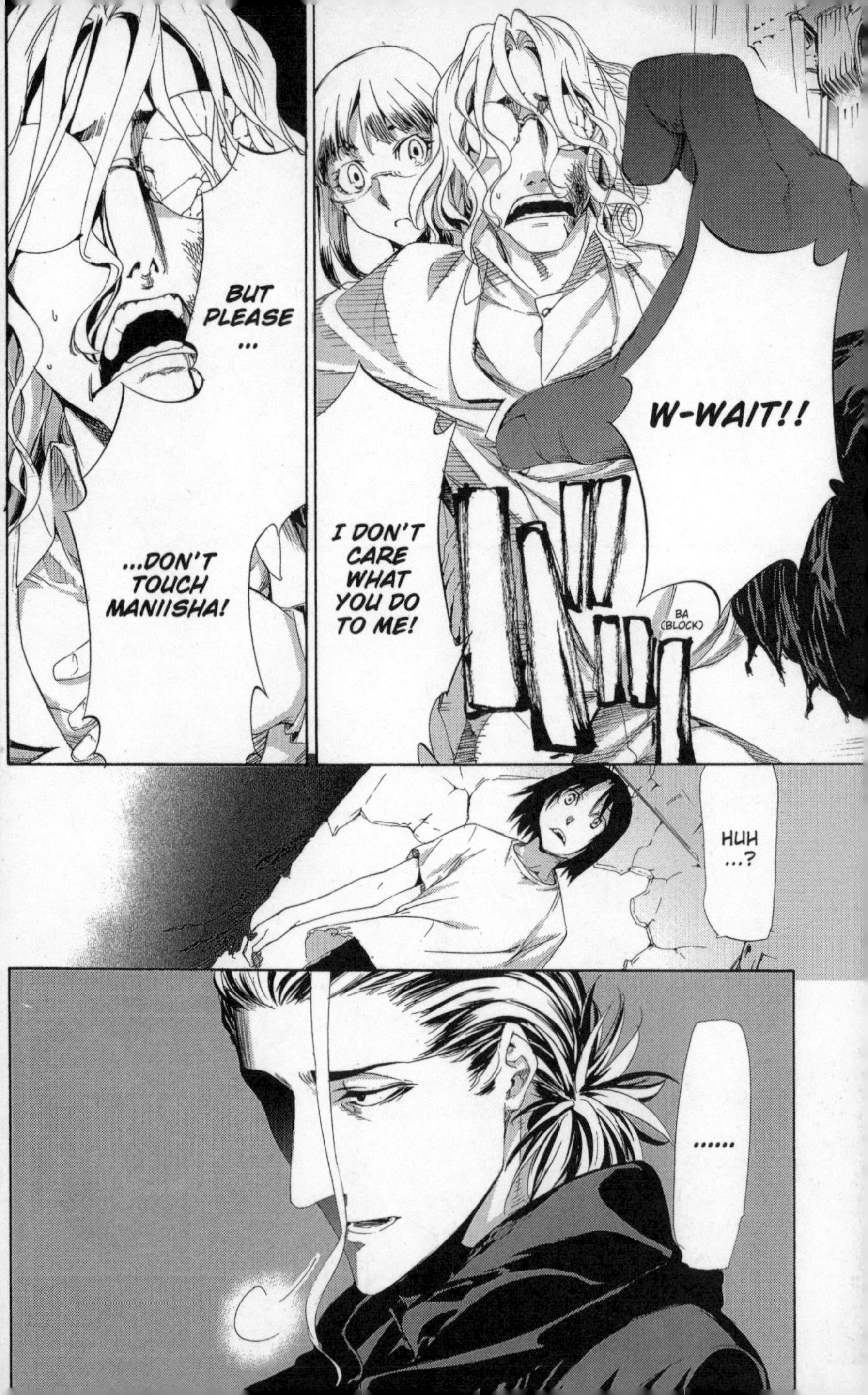
W-WAIT!!
I DON'T CARE WHAT YOU DO TO ME!
BA (BLOCK)
BUT PLEASE ...
...DON'T TOUCH MANIISHA!
HUH ...?
......

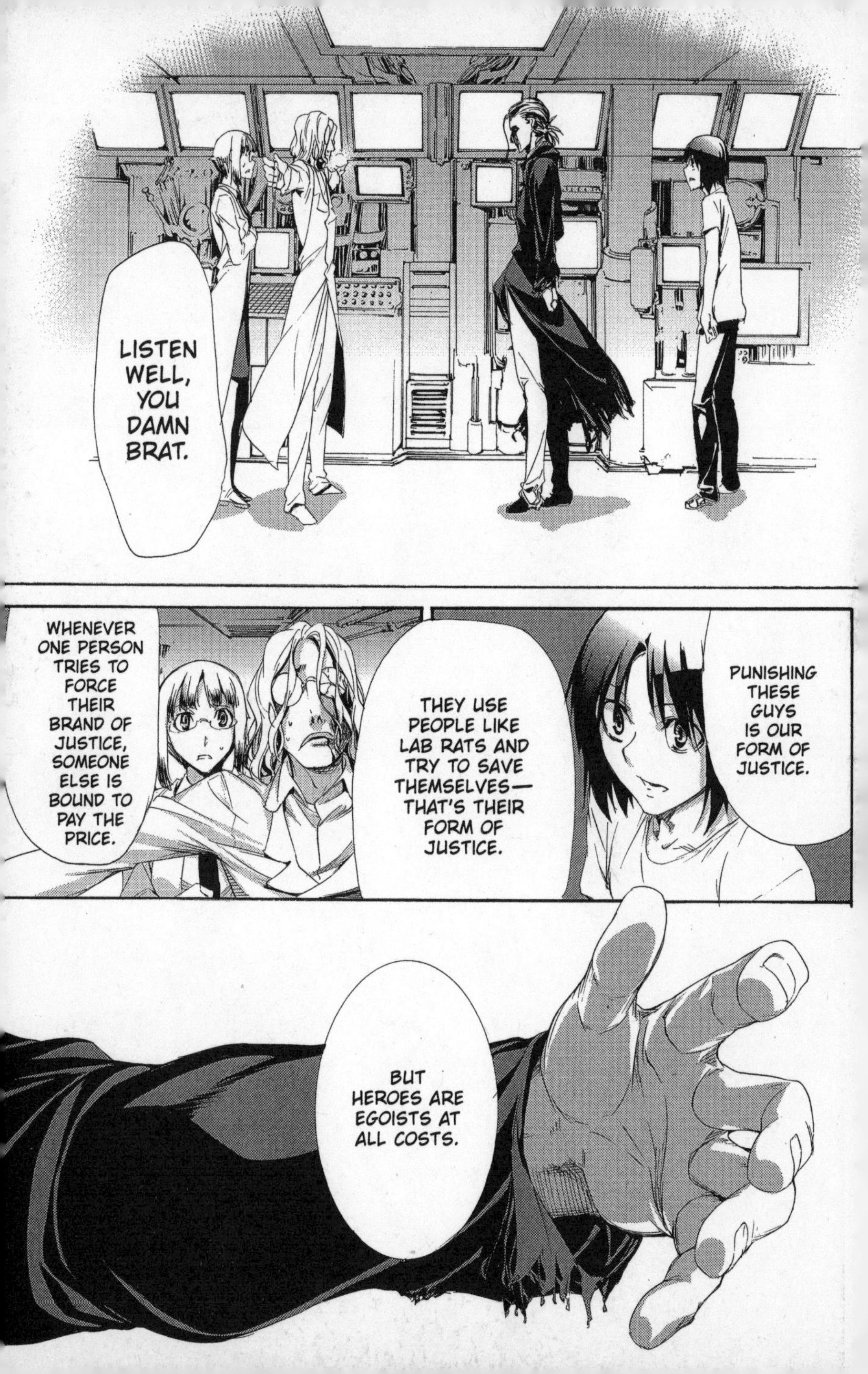
LISTEN WELL, YOU DAMN BRAT.
PUNISHING THESE GUYS IS OUR FORM OF JUSTICE.
THEY USE PEOPLE LIKE LAB RATS AND TRY TO SAVE THEMSELVES— THAT'S THEIR FORM OF JUSTICE.
WHENEVER ONE PERSON TRIES TO FORCE THEIR BRAND OF JUSTICE, SOMEONE ELSE IS BOUND TO PAY THE PRICE.
BUT HEROES ARE EGOISTS AT ALL COSTS.

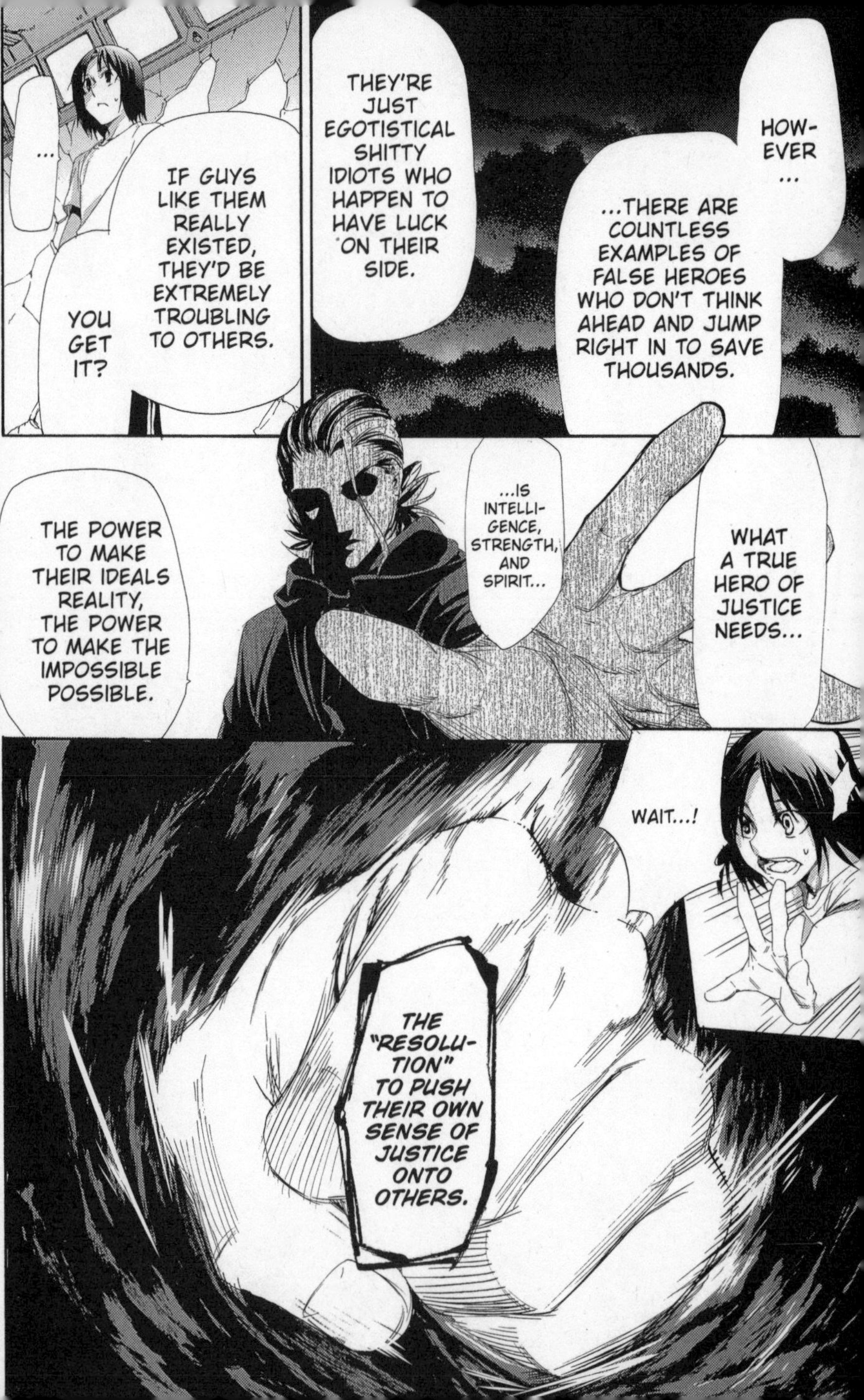
HOW-EVER...
...THERE ARE COUNTLESS EXAMPLES OF FALSE HEROES WHO DON'T THINK AHEAD AND JUMP RIGHT IN TO SAVE THOUSANDS.
THEY'RE JUST EGOTISTICAL SHITTY IDIOTS WHO HAPPEN TO HAVE LUCK ON THEIR SIDE.
IF GUYS LIKE THEM REALLY EXISTED, THEY'D BE EXTREMELY TROUBLING TO OTHERS.
YOU GET IT?
...
WHAT A TRUE HERO OF JUSTICE NEEDS...
...IS INTELLIGENCE, STRENGTH, AND SPIRIT...
THE POWER TO MAKE THEIR IDEALS REALITY, THE POWER TO MAKE THE IMPOSSIBLE POSSIBLE.
WAIT...!
THE "RESOLUTION" TO PUSH THEIR OWN SENSE OF JUSTICE ONTO OTHERS.

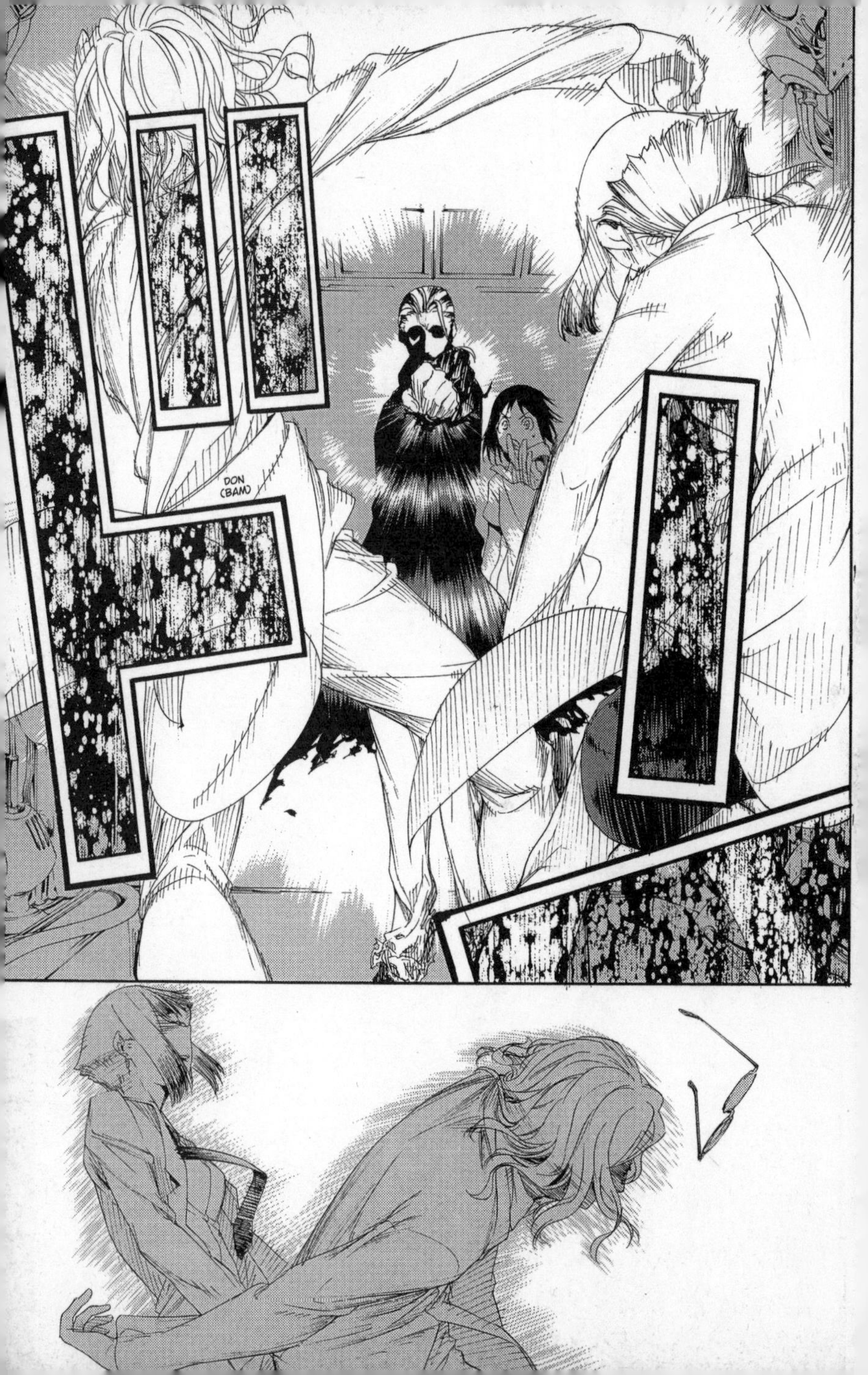
DON
(BAM)

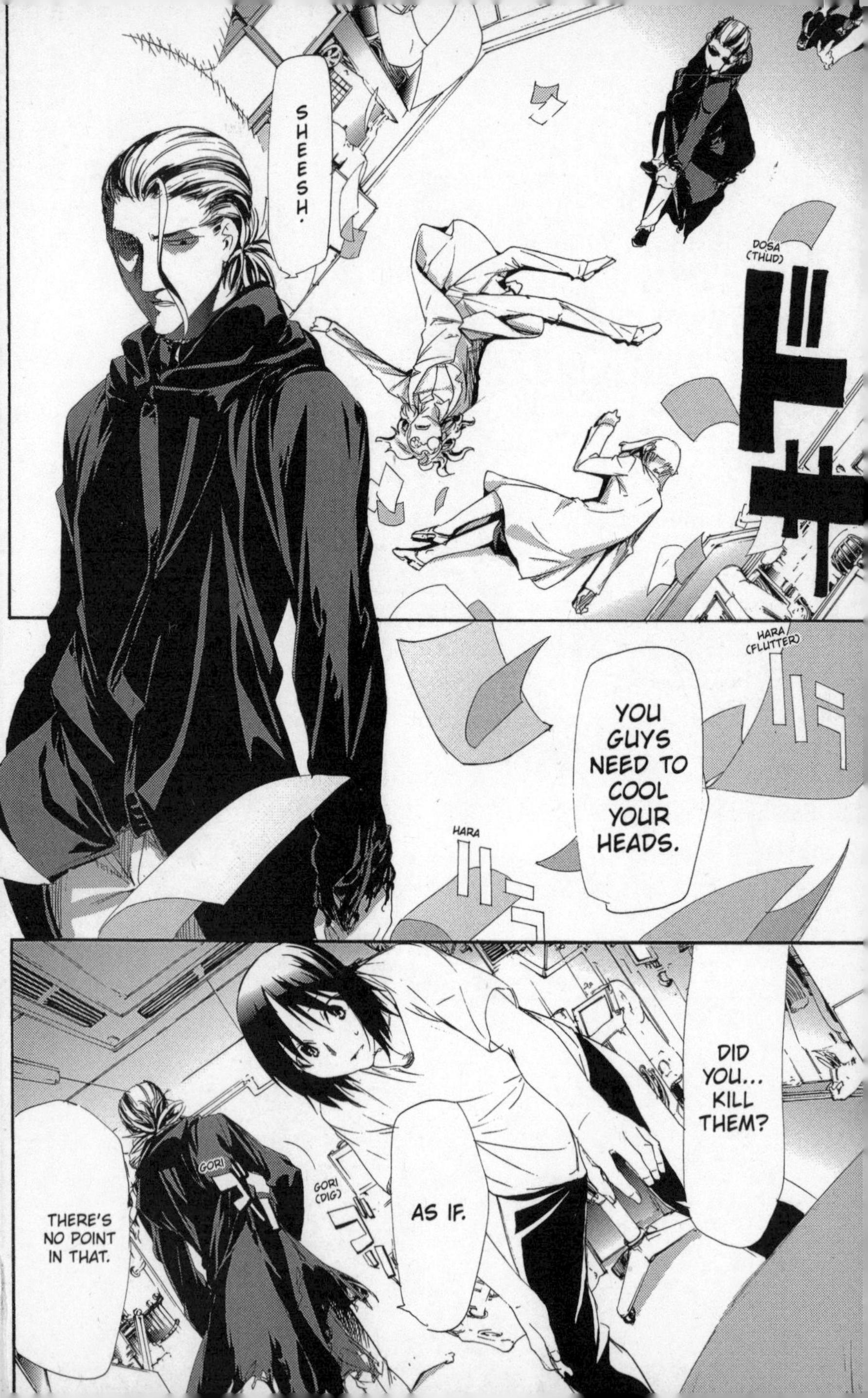
DOSA (THUD)
HARA (FLUTTER)
YOU GUYS NEED TO COOL YOUR HEADS.
HARA
SHEESH.
DID YOU... KILL THEM?
GORI (DIG)
AS IF.
GORI
THERE'S NO POINT IN THAT.

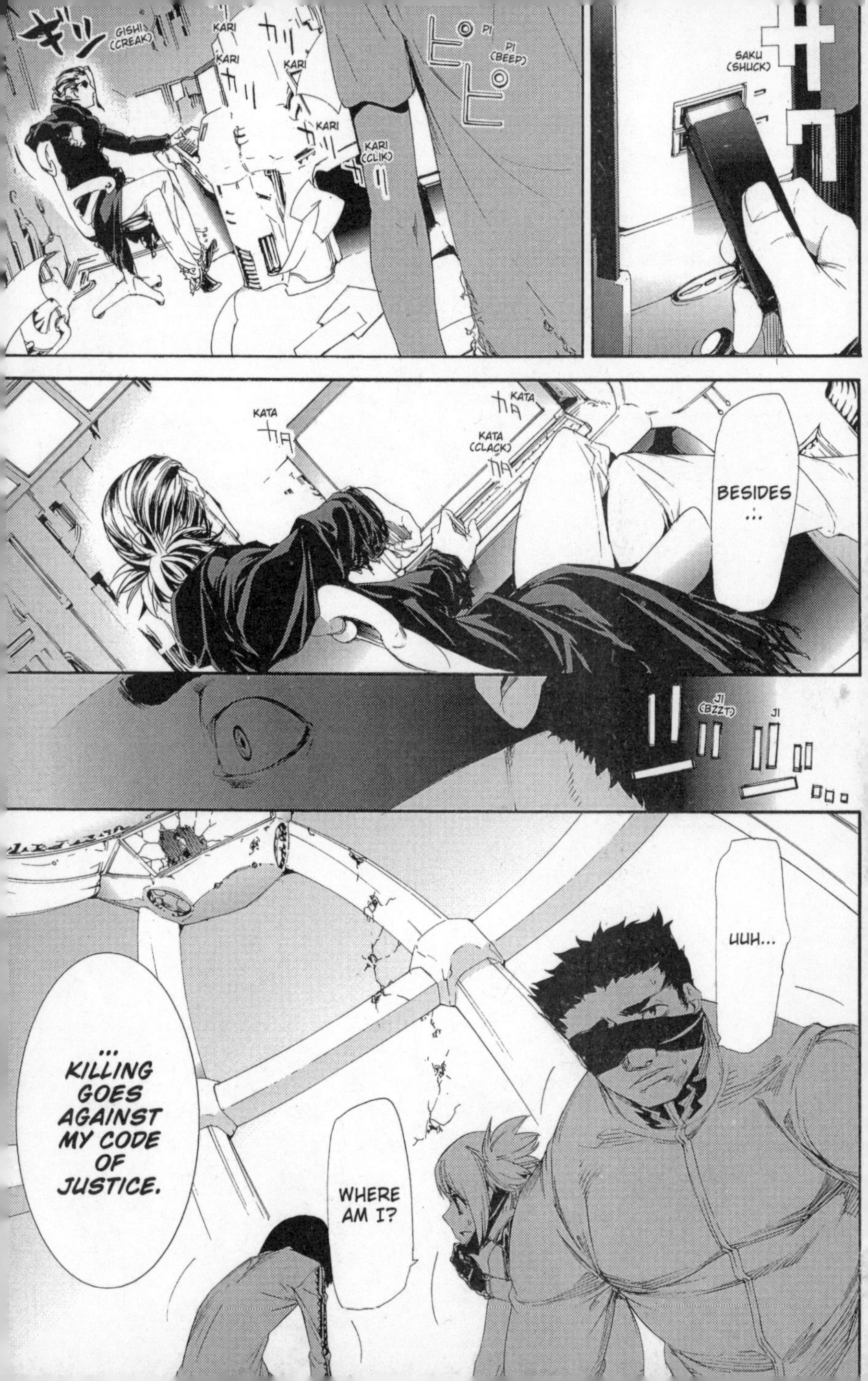
SAKU (SHUCK)
PI
PI (BEEP)
KARI (CLIK)
KARI
KARI
KARI
GISHI (CREAK)
KATA
KATA (CLACK)
KATA
BESIDES...
JI (BZZT)
JI
UUH...
... KILLING GOES AGAINST MY CODE OF JUSTICE.
WHERE AM I?

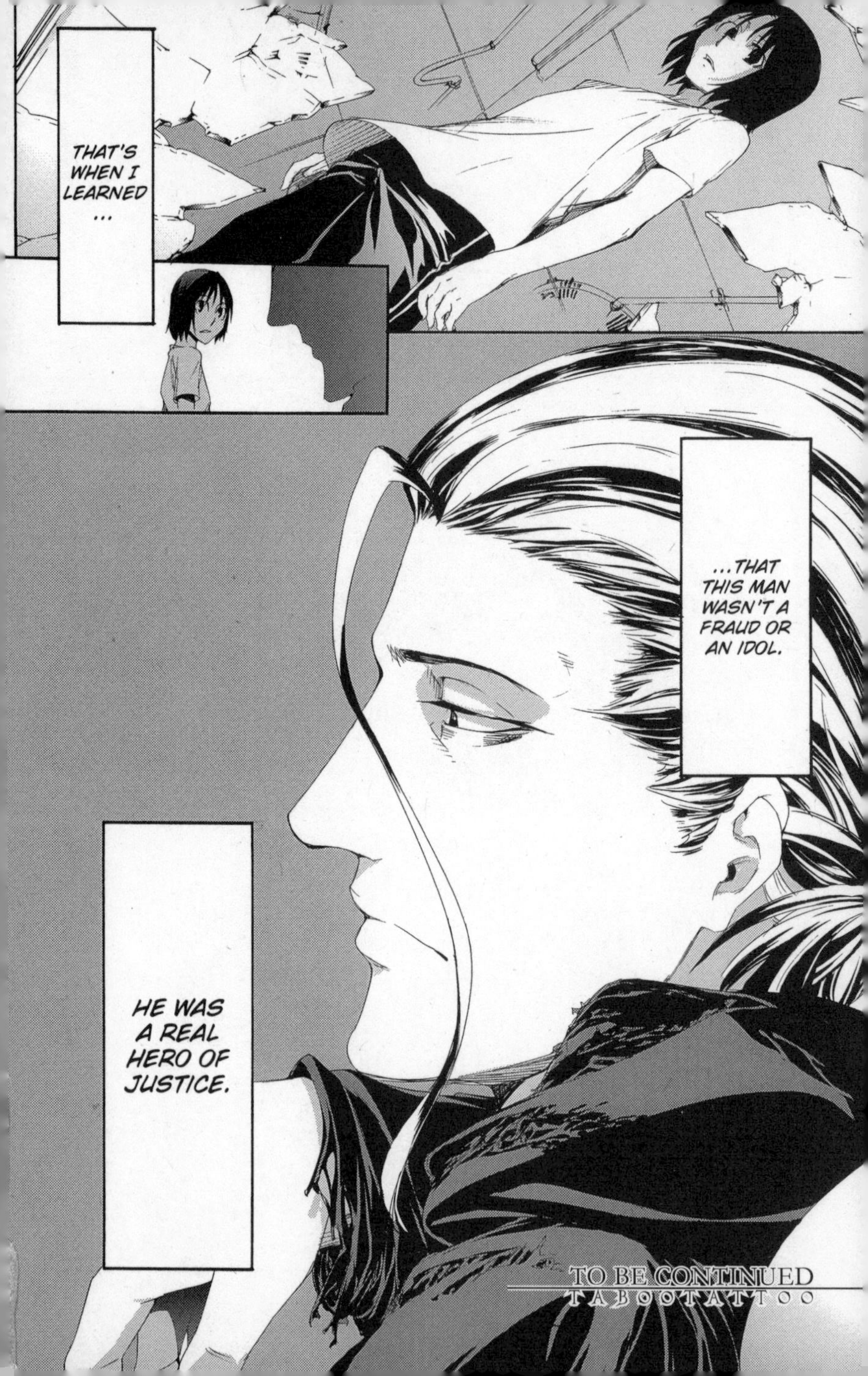
THAT'S WHEN I LEARNED ...
...THAT THIS MAN WASN'T A FRAUD OR AN IDOL.
HE WAS A REAL HERO OF JUSTICE.
TO BE CONTINUED
TABOO TATTOO

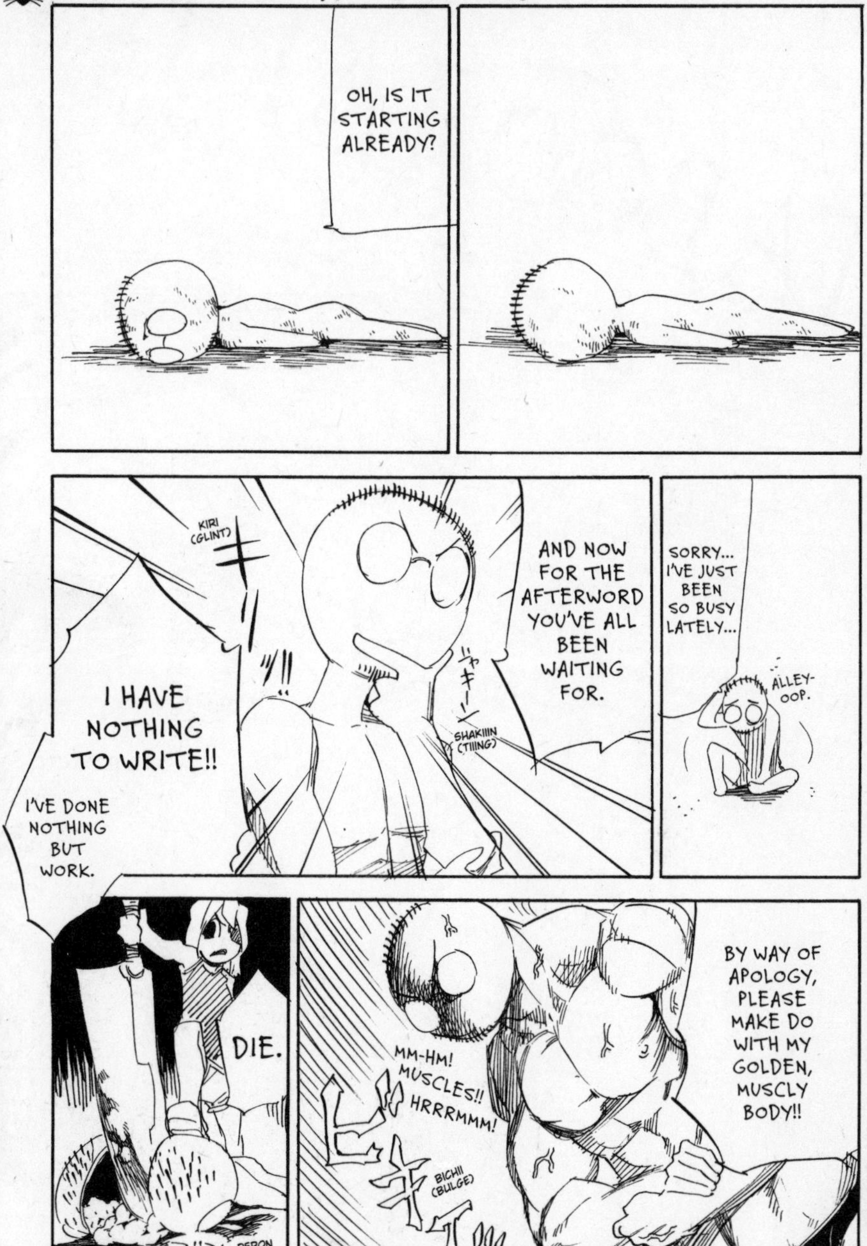
OH, IS IT STARTING ALREADY?
SORRY... I'VE JUST BEEN SO BUSY LATELY...
ALLEY-OOP.
AND NOW FOR THE AFTERWORD YOU'VE ALL BEEN WAITING FOR.
KIRI (GLINT)
SHAKIIIN (TIIING)
I HAVE NOTHING TO WRITE!!
I'VE DONE NOTHING BUT WORK.
BY WAY OF APOLOGY, PLEASE MAKE DO WITH MY GOLDEN, MUSCLY BODY!!
MM-HM! MUSCLES!! HRRRMMM!
BICHII (BULGE)
DIE.
DERON (ROLL)

☆Special Thanks: MARU NISHIKIYAMA

TABOO TATTOO

by **SHINJIRO**

Translation: Christine Dashiell • Lettering: Phil Christie

TABOO TATTOO
© Shinjiro 2011
Edited by MEDIA FACTORY
First published in Japan in 2011 by KADOKAWA CORPORATION.
English translation rights reserved by YEN PRESS, LLC under the license from KADOKAWA COPORATION, Tokyo through TUTTLE-MORI AGENCY, Inc., Tokyo.

English translation © 2016 by Yen Press, LLC

Yen Press
1290 Avenue of the Americas
New York, NY 10104

Visit us at yenpress.com
facebook.com/yenpress
twitter.com/yenpress
yenpress.tumblr.com

First Yen Press Edition: July 2016

Yen Press is an imprint of Yen Press, LLC.
The Yen Press name and logo are trademarks of Yen Press, LLC.

The publisher is not responsible for websites (or their content) that are not owned by the publisher.

Library of Congress Control Number: 2015952591

ISBNs: 978-0-316-31051-2 (paperback)
978-0-316-31053-6 (ebook)
978-0-316-31054-3 (app)

10 9 8 7 6 5 4 3 2 1

BVG

Printed in the United States of America